THE CREATION
OF AMERICAN LAW

ALSO BY JUDE M. PFISTER

*Charting an American Republic: The Origins
and Writing of the Federalist Papers*
(McFarland, 2016)

*America Writes Its History, 1650–1850:
The Formation of a National Narrative*
(McFarland, 2014)

THE CREATION OF AMERICAN LAW

John Jay, Oliver Ellsworth and the 1790s Supreme Court

Jude M. Pfister

McFarland & Company, Inc., Publishers

Jefferson, North Carolina

LIBRARY OF CONGRESS CATALOGUING-IN-PUBLICATION DATA

Names: Pfister, Jude M., author.
Title: The creation of American law : John Jay, Oliver Ellsworth and the 1790s Supreme Court / Jude M. Pfister.
Description: Jefferson, North Carolina : McFarland & Company, Inc., 2019. | Includes bibliographical references and index.
Identifiers: LCCN 2018047641 | ISBN 9781476669083 (softcover : acid free paper) ∞
Subjects: LCSH: United States. Supreme Court—History. | Constitutional history—United States.
Classification: LCC KF8742 .P36 2019 | DDC 347.73/2609033—dc23
LC record available at https://lccn.loc.gov/2018047641

BRITISH LIBRARY CATALOGUING DATA ARE AVAILABLE

ISBN (print) 978-1-4766-6908-3
ISBN (ebook) 978-1-4766-3355-8

Front cover images of John Jay (top) and Oliver Ellsworth and background images © 2019 iStock

Printed in the United States of America

McFarland & Company, Inc., Publishers
Box 611, Jefferson, North Carolina 28640
www.mcfarlandpub.com

To my wife, Miriam

Acknowledgments

Writing a book, far from being a solitary undertaking as often portrayed, is more the work of an author and a support team. And, as with any collaborative effort, it is difficult to know where to place the most emphasis when offering one's thanks. To begin, I would like to thank my colleagues Joni Rowe and Sarah Minegar. Both Joni and Sarah are inspirations through their hard work and dedication to cultural and historic preservation. The Morristown National Historical Park's magnificent Lloyd W. Smith archival and rare book collection was once again an invaluable source. I wish to thank Superintendent Tom Ross of Morristown NHP, and I want to acknowledge the Washington Association of New Jersey for its trailblazing efforts in historic preservation more than a century ago. I wish to thank the late E. Barrett Prettyman for his encouragement concerning the research of early Supreme Court history. I also wish to acknowledge the staff at the Supreme Court Historical Society and especially Kathy Shurtleff. Many thanks are due to Chris Anderson, Rick Mikulski, Johanna Edge, and Marc Boisclair at the Drew University Library.

A special thank you is due to Kevin Eckstrom at the Washington National Cathedral. Catherine Fitts, John Fields, and the staff in the office of the curator of the Supreme Court were generous with their time. Thanks are due as well to Sheldon Snook, office of the counselor to the chief justice. I wish to thank Michael von der Linn with The Lawbook Exchange, Ltd. Thanks are due as well to Lesley Schoenfeld at the Harvard Law School Library. Finally, I want to thank Charles Perdue and the staff at McFarland Publishing for their wise counsel and keen eye.

Finally, no matter how many people are part of the process, only one person decides what is ultimately written to form the narrative. As such, I take full responsibility for any errors within.

Table of Contents

Preface

The time period and focus of this book is primarily the development of American law from the writing of the Constitution (1787) until 1801, yet it is hard not to look at the most significant aspect in American law prior to the Constitution: the Revolution. While the arguments for independence played out on the battlefield and not the courtroom, it is enticing to wonder what the outcome of a court case would have been had American lawyers gone head-to-head with their British counterparts over the issues which led to war. There, in a courtroom, without the aid of the French, or Dutch, or Spanish, how would America have fared? This, of course, never occurred.[1] But what the fighting wrought—independence—necessarily brought with it a crossroads in law. What law would the colonies, now states, follow? Could the old colonial-era charters and constitutions provide the necessary legal framework for a new nation? Those early documents could govern a state with some adjustments, but not a country. In conjunction with the national law, however, every state had to draft or amend a new constitution to reflect the new realities after 1783. Although some simply recycled and relied on their colonial charters to guide them, it is clear enough to say, "as a logical consequence of the Revolution, responsibility for American law passed into American hands."[2]

Legal Thinking for an Empire

By the American Revolution, Britain had consolidated its powers over the colonies, ruling them as a unit rather than individually. This was a process that began under Charles II after the Restoration (1660) and continued through to 1776. In fact, by 1765, a revived policy was put forth by "Sir Thomas Osborne ... [concerning] the idea of a uniform course of colonial government predicated on Crown ascendency."[3] As the decades passed through the eighteenth century, it became clear that England wanted colonial laws that did not run counter to English laws.[4]

Clear examples of this process are seen in the various acts that Parliament passed before the Revolution, starting with the Stamp Act in 1765. Such a policy could never have occurred had the colonies not already been seen as a whole, rather than as individual entities by the British. Although individually was exactly how many of the colonists saw themselves prior to the First Continental Congress.

To be fair, England in the seventeenth century did not present the best role model for the system of law in use at the time, the common law. The colonists could easily be forgiven for wondering about possible lectures coming out of Parliament. Mid–seventeenth century colonists saw the breakdown of English common law in civil war and regicide in the death of Charles I as not the most encouraging promotion for the rule of law. In fact, throughout the latter half of the seventeenth century, England could not be seen as providing much guidance to anyone concerning the rule of law. England suffered through eight different leaders throughout the century, nearly one per decade. Besides the civil war and the death of Charles I, there was the Restoration and the Glorious Revolution. Both events, however, produced their share of thinkers who in one form or another provided some ideas for the future American Founders. Especially notable among this group from the period was John Locke, often seen as having had a great influence on Thomas Jefferson, among others. It was thus a busy time in England and it produced little continuity—the most important ingredient in law.

Throughout the turmoil in England, other nations vied for influence on the North American continent, and with that effort came their unique set of laws as well: the French in Louisiana; Spanish in Florida; Dutch in New Amsterdam (New York); the Swedes in the Mid-Atlantic. Yet, in the end, it was England that proved victorious over other nations bringing the North American continent (eastern seaboard) under their control, although that control was not total. "Uniform government in the colonies was never completely achieved."[5] Still, by 1701, "the government of the colonies was already well on the path to maturity."[6] While the Crown would acquire control of most colonial founding charters by the mid-eighteenth century, and thus institute a more "modern" eighteenth-century approach to governing, Rhode Island and Connecticut still maintained control in their royal charters and with it a seventeenth-century outlook in governance and law.

By no means should the rest of the colonies (beyond Rhode Island and Connecticut) be seen as completely compliant with English directives. Given the relatively lax oversight during the seventeenth century, a legal tradition evolved which saw the combination of the best of the British common law while factoring in the local characteristics found throughout the individual colonies.

The individual quality of colony-centered law seems to beg the question whether Britain had total legal control of its possessions in America. In fact, the great lawyer and philosopher Adam Smith made this very point in 1776, the year Americans declared independence. Smith wrote that the government of Britain "[has] for more than a century past, amused the people with the imagination that they possessed a great empire on the west side of the Atlantic. This empire, however, has hitherto existed in imagination only. It has hitherto been not an empire but the project of an empire."[7]

Anthony Pagden concluded, "As Smith had seen, the de facto situation in the colonies, where every individual settlement enjoyed its own peculiar rights, laws were made at a local level, and separate constitutions ... might be established, could hardly be an 'empire' as the term was currently employed."[8] Across the decades of transition, thousands of immigrants arrived and among them were those who had varying degrees of learning and understanding of law. These people no doubt were well received, despite some prejudice against lawyers. This was especially true when those with legal ability sought to profit from that knowledge, usually to the detriment of their neighbors. Law was thus something original and genetically modified while a central foundation provided support. In an essay on regionalism in early American law, historian David Thomas Konig has written:

> It is worth emphasizing the legal precocity of the colonies and the particularities of their legal forms in order to underscore how deeply the process of legal change advanced ideological goals and to justify the claim that what appears to be inexpert rustic degeneracy in the law actually represents a more sophisticated eclecticism.[9]

This is a rather esoteric way to say that law is malleable, dependent on the societal twists and turns of how people live their lives and view their place in the larger world. "Legal rules thus reflect at least in some measure the picture of what men of a particular time regard as the ideal of relations among men, thereby further illumining from another standpoint our understanding of a particular society."[10]

It was this transient nature of regional law that the Founders had to deal with by the 1780s. And it was symptomatic of American law at this time. Paul Samuel Reinsch has written that American law up to 1789 was an "unconscious development of custom, reversal to simpler forms, adaptation and modification of technical systems brought from abroad, conscious reform, and, finally, the effort to cast all legal relations into a simple and lucid system."[11] The separation from Britain, in the eyes of America's leaders, had to have some foundation in law; the last thing they wanted was a revolution founded on whim and fancy. This could produce nothing lasting, as the basis of the dispute would have been meaningless. The disputes with Britain, had no legitimate legal basis been found, would have rested on the personal ambitions, or damaged egos, of America's leaders. This is a vital point which leads directly to the creation of the Supreme Court under Article III of the Constitution and takes in the question previously asked: Had the American dispute with Britain played out in a courtroom rather than the battlefield, what would the outcome have been? This is a prospect few of the Founders wanted to contemplate. It is a topic that is rarely debated, even in the world of legal history. In fact, Article III of the Constitution was the revolutionary part of the document: "The Supreme Court of the United States has come to be regarded as the unique feature of the American governmental system. It is a feature which distinguishes the American government from practically all modern political systems."[12]

This book is a book for readers, specifically, readers of serious narrative who appreciate a challenge. It is not designed as a primer on being a lawyer—it is a book of history. It is not designed to descend into the depths of legal practice that is often termed "being a lawyer." The author is not a lawyer; he is an historian, and as such he will approach law in a way that may leave those learned in the sophisms of legal pleading wanting more. The technical fine points are not at issue here. As James Madison wrote to Spencer Roane in 1821, concerning technical legal aspects that Roane had asked Madison's opinion on, "I am particularly aware moreover that they [certain court decisions] are made to rest not a little on technical points of law, which are as foreign to my studies as they are familiar to yours."[13] The author therefore will follow the lead of Madison and forego the "technical points of law." Rather, this book is framed around being a thinker, thinking that takes legal history as its starting point. To clarify further, legal history as history, not legal history as legal precedent that lawyers rely on to argue cases. In other words, this book does not expect to find itself referenced in a court of law as a basis for or against some particular point of debate pending a legal action with a plaintiff and a defendant. Legal historians who work as historians and legal historians who work as lawyers are two different breeds with two different (perhaps at times complimentary) outcomes expected from their work. This book is by a legal historian who works as an historian. One final comment about the purpose of the book: it is about national law, not colony or state law. As such, references to law will always mean a national legal system unless otherwise stated. Sections pertaining to state, regional or local law will be identified as such.

A brief note concerning the construction of some of the chapters is in order. While every chapter is infused with the observations and writings of people of the past who participated in the events covered, concluding sections of two chapters, those dealing with the Judiciary Act of 1789 and the Jay Court, will be devoted exclusively (with commentary) to an overview of the surviving literature of the period. Spanning diaries, letters, and newspaper essays, these writings are powerful reflections on the issues involving the creation and development of a system of American jurisprudence. The Judiciary Act and the Jay Court represent the two earliest attempts at American law.

Also, styles and punctuation of eighteenth-century writing have been modernized at no dilution of the meaning or intent of the original author. For this book, it is more important what was said as opposed to how it was said.

Introduction

On a cold January night in 1801 (as John Marshall recalled it a quarter century later in an 1827 letter to Justice Joseph Story), President John Adams, preparing to leave office after one term, was casting about for a new chief justice of the United States Supreme Court.[1] His first choice was former chief justice John Jay, who declined the appointment. Now in retirement in New York, Jay wrote a letter to President Adams giving his reasons for declining the nomination (see Appendix D). Adams, still despondent over his election defeat the previous November, looked around his office in a moment of sighing frustration, and fixed his eyes on Secretary of State John Marshall. According to the oft-told story, Adams abruptly offered the post of chief justice to Marshall on the spot. The rest, as the saying goes, is history. Marshall went on to serve for thirty-four years and has dominated early Supreme Court historical discussion. However, Marshall was actually the fourth chief justice to serve. So what has happened to the three previous chiefs in America's historical memory? More important, what has become of the other thirteen justices appointed by presidents Washington and Adams prior to 1801 when Marshall arrived?

Long a period of intense historical study, the 1790s (the early national period) provide scholars a look at the nascent aspects of American national development. President Washington naturally dominates discussion of the early national period; Congress, with James Madison and a host of worthies, is a close second. The third branch of the government, the judiciary, is, however, virtually overlooked. The titanic struggles for the course of the young country which played out between Thomas Jefferson and Alexander Hamilton are not as prevalent in the judiciary, especially the Supreme Court; at least until Thomas Jefferson was president and Alexander Hamilton was dead. It is notoriously difficult to parse the meaning of written legal decisions in a way the written executive and the legislative branch decisions are not.[2] Furthermore, similar to how President Washington overshadows the executive branch during this period in the historical imagination, Chief Justice John Marshall overshadows the Supreme Court. While he did not serve in a judicial capacity during the 1790s, Marshall's presence is nonetheless felt due to his nearly thirty-five-year service on the Court during the nineteenth century. Indeed, many cases decided or precedents established during the 1790s are today invariably contrasted with something John Marshall did as chief in an effort to further strengthen Marshall's dominance in early Court history.

This book will bring the first decade of the United States Supreme Court back into the national dialog with the other two branches of government where it belongs. The impact of numerous cases decided during the 1790s are with us to this day. Consider *Chisholm v. Georgia* which led directly to the passage of the Eleventh Amendment in 1794. Consider *Glass v. the Sloop Betsy* which forever forbade the establishment of foreign courts on American soil in 1794.

It will be abundantly clear that the 1790s Court established the bedrock foundations of American constitutional law. Over the next nine chapters the first decade of the United States Supreme Court will be chronicled through a narrative sequence that will help to elucidate the twisting plots associated with the formation of the American government beginning in 1789. This elucidation will include the justices of the Court, representative cases decided, the political climate, the understanding and meaning of law, and the all-too-human aspects of American national government. No attempt will be made to try and connect the dots over the last two centuries from the 1790s to today. This book is a work of history whose purpose is to be found in the decade of the 1790s.

George Washington took the oath of office as the first president of the United States on April 30, 1789. Under the new Constitution, Washington, as president, became the head of the executive branch of the government. In addition to the executive, a new legislative branch was also created, and both were voted on by those who qualified to cast ballots in late eighteenth-century America. The judiciary branch, however, had no such provision for election of its members. The justices of the Supreme Court were to be chosen by the president and confirmed by the Senate before they could take their seat. Thus, the third branch was in essence a creation of the other two branches, yet it held equal status as an independent member of the new American government.

For us in the twenty-first century, it seems quite natural that our government would have some supreme adjudicative body to act as a final arbiter of the instrument designed to articulate that government (the Constitution). Quite the opposite was the case in the late eighteenth century. The idea of a supreme court in post–Revolutionary America was just as radical as the concept of a written constitution. Under the Articles of Confederation (which nominally governed the colonies/states from 1777 to 1789), the country had no institution of government designed with sufficient authority to compel member states in the obligations of the Articles. Thus, many requirements of the Articles went unfulfilled. Naturally, the absence of a supreme judicature was not the only reason the states habitually ignored many aspects of the Articles. It is impossible to say though whether the presence of a supreme court in the Articles would have facilitated adherence from member states, although it seems unlikely.

How did a supreme court come to be a part of the new Constitution? With no real precedent, and no real guidance, how could an institution be created to ensure compliance with the new document which called for the court to exist? It was as though the Constitution spawned its own defensive network. The Supreme Court thus became the Constitution's "immune system."

Broadly speaking, while the court was a novel idea, the concept of law as a way to structure a society was not. Law, regardless of its foundation, provided the boundaries wherein human beings lived their lives. "Law is not divorced from life; it is an intimate part of it. Law is a subject which in every era forms an essential stratum in the structure of society."[3] Governments also found themselves bound by the requirements of law. More likely, though, it was the individual who felt the greatest burden imposed by law. Law could be an oppressive instrument designed to ensure the boundaries society functioned within were precisely the way those who created the law choose for society to live. At no point did a society (given the low number of voters) have a significant say in the laws under which they desired to live their lives. Over time, this came to be one of the most appealing aspects of the American Constitution which allowed for the expansion of the right to vote, even if it took an extended period and is still constantly under attack.

Law, as understood in this context, becomes a central force in the creation and sustainability of society. Perhaps not fully a cultural ingredient in the anthropological sense, it nonetheless becomes a binding force in ensuring a cohesive approach to life from citizens of varying cultural backgrounds.

Popular law has many problems, of course, vigilantism is just one of many. Without some systems to rely upon, other than each individual person's whim, society could not function. Law, codified, is an anecdote to the centrifugal force of lawlessness.

The United States Supreme Court is one of the most unique tribunals to have come into existence in the post–Mediaeval/Renaissance world.[4] The Supreme Court clearly had roots which can be traced back into the mists of English law prior to the writing of the first version of Magna Carta in 1215.[5] Over a period of roughly a millennium and a half, the varied shreds of English law slowly developed into a codified system of practice which could be relied upon to provide some structured order to everyday life and to larger issues of state. By the time this law attempted to manage a worldwide empire in the eighteenth century, it had become too featureless to respond in a meaningful way to prevent revolt.

The law we live by today would be both recognizable and unrecognizable to our American law-makers of two centuries ago. This is proper. We cannot expect to live completely in their world anymore than we could have expected them to look into the future to imagine ours. This book therefore, as history, will keep the focus and narrative within the time period as described in the title: the years from the writing of the Constitution in 1787 to 1800, approximately thirteen years. Legal history is fraught with nuance and is far from tidy. Is legal history properly about cases and trends in adjudicating legal conflict? Is legal history what lawyers rely on to provide them the precedent they usually need to build their cases? Can there be such a thing as legal history without some reference to contemporary situations? This book will argue that, yes indeed, there is such a thing as legal history which is not dependent on contemporary norms. As such, this book is not a "how to" manual for practicing (or aspiring) lawyers. "Lawyers are typically interested in the question: What is *the law* on a particular issue? This is always a local question and answers to it are bound to differ according to the specific jurisdiction in which they are asked. In contrast, philosophy of law is interested in the general question: What is Law?"[6] This book is a history of the world lawyers, politicians, and the public occupied every hour of every day during the 1790s.[7] Specifically, this book is a history of the creation of American Constitutional law in the Supreme Court during the first ten years of the Court's existence. It is written, as already stated, from the perspective of an historian, not a lawyer.

Law

Law is the central feature of the regime [society] and consists of the body of precepts and received ideals, and the techniques of using them, consciously established or implicitly recognized by politically organized society for the delimitation and securing of interests.[8]

As a topic, law has been written about since our literate ancestors first put pen to paper, stylus to clay or brush to papyrus. Much of the earliest writing to survive details the activities of law. Sumerian, Babylonian, Egyptian, Greek, Roman, and other ancient civilizations all left written records of their legal practices. What this shows us, in part, is a long-running attempt by humanity to find a way to create rules that all could live by. This enables us to know a great deal about how society functioned. For our purposes, however, these ancient times are too far outside the boundaries of this book. The earliest references in direct lineal ancestry from our Constitution will be the various versions of Magna Carta—while acknowledging this lineage, we also acknowledge profound differences between the two documents.

In 1897, the great American jurist Oliver Wendell Holmes, Jr., wrote in the *Harvard Law Review* an essay titled "The Path of the Law." He opined, "The prophecies of what the courts will do in fact, and nothing more pretentious, are what I mean by the law."[9] In essence, then, law was nothing more than what you can convince a judge and jury it is. Cynical, perhaps, but it no doubt has some truth to it. Thanks to television and social media, we today as a people enjoy access to the workings of the law in more depth than anyone in any period in history. This access to how "the sausage is made" can be troublesome to those inclined to view life as black and white rather than gray. This wide access we enjoy to lawmaking has also created the phenomena of the celebrity lawyer or judge. Celebrity lawyers and judges have always existed; Cicero in ancient Rome was certainly one, but not to the extent such celebrities are in our modern world. Law, whether in the courtroom or political space, has become theater. In that sense, Oliver Wendell Holmes, Jr., had a valid point with his conception of law. Thanks to modern access to the legal system, we almost come to expect law to be a fast-paced mix-and-match world where nothing is exactly as it seems. Law is essential for active, knowledgeable citizenship. Legal scholar Charles Warren wrote in 1925: "An American citizen will never understand the form of government under which he is living, unless he understands why we must have a Supreme Court. And he will never understand why we must have a Supreme Court, until he understands the form of government under which he is living."[10]

What we forget is that law can be both exciting and mundane. Within those two extremes lies the basis of most legal work. Of course, before any legal work can commence, the law had to be written and codified. For our purposes, that began in 1787 with the Constitutional Convention and the creation of an American jurisprudence, yet it all did not happen as fast as we imagine. Like most facets of American life, law was negatively impacted by the Revolution. "For a generation after the Revolution, law and lawyers suffered from the ill effects of this period of depression."[11] The creation of American law was stifled and put back a number of years in development as a result of the war years and the loss of political continuity. Even with this setback, historian Paul Samuel Reinsch wrote, "when American legal history comes to be studied, it will perhaps be found that no country presents, in the short space of three centuries such a variety of interesting phenomena."[12]

This is an often-overlooked point in American legal history. We are familiar with hearing about the military, political, economic, and social aspects of the war. Rarely is the disruption of the legal infrastructure mentioned. One who knew this intuitively was William Cushing, who would serve on the future Supreme Court for twenty years. In the early 1770s, however, he was a judge with the Massachusetts Superior Court and as such a royal appointee. His career, detailed more in Chapter 4, is a record of the ebbs and flows of transitioning from British to American legal systems. In the caldron of war, leaders like Cushing were asked "to work out from our inherited legal materials a general body of law for what was to be a politically and economically unified land."[13]

Law can be experienced both in a theoretical and a practical way. In most instances, the practical aspects of law are by far what constitute the interactions we tend to associate with law, whether firsthand or in the television and movie versions.

1

Colonial American Law

Colonial American law is not the same as colony specific law. Colonial American law was the big theoretical and practical framework under which Britain governed its empire. As part of that empire until 1776, the American colonies were governed from London just like any other part of Britain's global possessions. This meant that the colonies as a whole functioned under a system that saw them as part of a larger collection of territories rather than as individual units. The law that held this empire together, including the American colonies, was the work of a handful of eminent legal scholars who provided the intellectual foundation for all legal learning in the eighteenth-century British legal world of thought. The two names which stand above all others, Edward Coke and William Blackstone, were joined by a handful of lesser known English and European legal scholars who formed the core of any aspiring lawyer's training between 1675 and 1775, and beyond. According to the twentieth-century American legal scholar and Harvard Law School Dean Roscoe Pound, to the eighteenth-century student, even after the Revolution, "for practical purposes Coke's Second Institute and Blackstone [were] the repositories of the law."[1]

Sir Edward Coke

Edward Coke (pronounced "Cook" in his day) was born in Mileham, Norfolk, on February 1, 1552. He came from a highly-educated family, his father being a lawyer at Lincoln's Inn (one of the Inns of Court—more discussion on them later in this chapter) and his mother possessing an impressive formal education for the time period for a woman. In 1567, Coke entered Trinity College, Cambridge, and later enrolled in 1571 at Clifford's Inn (a preparatory legal school), transferring to Inner Temple a year later. After being called to the bar in 1578, he experienced one of the most storied careers in English legal history.

Coke was more than a great lawyer; he was a great thinker. He was some-one who sought to find the working mechanisms of civil society. The main ingredient in a civil society was, according to Coke, law. He was involved with seminal cases throughout the late sixteenth and early seventeenth centuries which became standard reading material for future law students, including those in America over a century later.

Coke would hold high-level positions during the reigns of both Queen Elizabeth I and King James I. His list of judicial appointments under James I was just as impressive as under Elizabeth I. He was a recorder, solicitor general, and attorney general. He also served as speaker of the House of Commons in 1593 and was a member of Parliament at varying points throughout his career. During the last decade of Queen Elizabeth's life (1593–1603) Coke was involved with a multitude of treason cases which he prosecuted. His work was so thorough in fact, that he was knighted by King James I in 1603. He was also involved with prosecuting the most sensational plot of the early seventeenth century: the infamous Gunpowder Plot.[2] Coke's most famous case as a judge, and one that he is most remembered for, is *Bonham's Case,* in 1610. This case "laid down the foundations for judicial review of legislation, allowing judges to strike down statutes."[3] This case was the first English acknowledgment where the doctrine of declaring a law as unconstitutional was put in a written form which judges and lawyers could look to as precedent, an all-important concept in the legal community.

Coke saw law as an integral, seminal, construction of civil society. So ingrained did Coke come to see law and society that it led him at times into direct conflict with James I over a myriad of topics impacting what James saw as his divine right as king and what Coke saw as the divine right of society. Coke "traced the source of law to custom and judicial wisdom rather than to royal command. He gave mythic dimensions to the common law by tracing legal doctrines into dim antiquity."[4]

As the reign of James I gave way to Charles I, Coke began to play a more confrontational role in Parliament towards the crown in the beginning of the long slide to civil war and the death of Charles I in 1649. One hundred and thirty years later, Coke's arguments against royal prerogative found a new voice when they were brought to bear in another conflict between a king and the American colonies. In particular, during the crisis under Charles I, Coke "provided an ideology that closely associated liberty and property," much like the thinking of America's Founders.[5]

Coke retired from active life in 1628. For the next six years, until his death in 1634, he worked on his great study of English law, known as the *Institutes of the Laws of England.* The first volume, known as *Coke on Littleton,* was the most famous and the volume most studied by American legal students throughout the eighteenth and well into the nineteenth century. It "is a perpetual commentary upon a short treatise written by Sir Thomas Lit-tleton,"[6] (1407–1481), a highly respected fifteenth-century legal scholar whom Coke took upon himself to follow in preparing an expansive legal narrative. Littleton's book, generally considered to have appeared around 1481, would have been one of the earliest books to appear in printed form in England. Littleton's estimation in the legal community was such that, "Although Lit-tleton almost never adduces any authority in support of his opinions, his credit has always been so high, that in the earliest times anything cited from him was no more considered open to dispute or question than a precedent solemnly adjudged by the courts."[7] By 1634, the year of Coke's death, over one hundred editions of Littleton's original work, including those expanded upon by Coke, had been published.[8] It is hard to overstate the debt Anglo-American law owes to Coke. English legal historian William Holdsworth wrote that "Coke's works have been to the common law what Shakespeare has been to literature, and the King James Bible to religion."[9]

Thomas Littleton and Edward Coke, from our twenty-first century van-tage point, seemed destined to have descended to posterity by their exten-sive individual scholarship. It was just as inescapable that the younger of the two (Coke) would edit and expand upon the work of the older (Littleton). Although they lived in different centuries but less than a hundred years apart, they may as well have been from different millennia. Littleton was firmly rooted in the Mediaeval world while Coke sprang from the Renaissance. "They were separated in point of time by less than a century, yet Littleton stands at the end of the ancient period of English law and Coke at the begin-ning of the modern period."[10] Yet, in terms of their views on law and society they were remarkably similar given their respective world perspectives during the times in which they lived.

Edward Coke first "met" Thomas Littleton while a student at the Inns of Court. Coke, along with all his fellow classmates, studied Littleton as dili-gently as future generations of students would study *Coke on Littleton*. In fact, even before students in the American colonies ever got hold of Coke he was procured in 1647 as part of a reference library for use of the General Court of the Massachusetts Bay Colony.[11] Coke was quoted often during the Revolution by Adams (John and Samuel), Thomas Jefferson, James Otis, and many more.[12] As a young law student of George Wythe in 1762, Thomas Jef-ferson, writing to his friend John Page on Christmas day, lamented that he was struggling to get through with his reading of Coke. Jefferson wrote: "For God knows I have not seen him [Coke] since I packed him up in my trunk in Williamsburg [where Jefferson was a student]. Well, Page, I do wish the Devil had old Coke, for I am sure I never was so tired of an old dull scoundrel in my life."[13] It goes without saying that Coke is woefully antiquated to us today. Still, there are nuggets here and there that have stood the test of time, just like Magna Carta. However, for the Colonial American student like Thomas Jefferson, Alexander Hamilton, John Dickinson, and many others, Coke was viewed as a contemporary in his thinking and highly esteemed, no matter how much of an "old dull scoundrel" he was. Late in life, writing to legal scholar Thomas Cooper, Jefferson would refer to Coke as "the father of our science [law]."[14]

In 1812, the first American edition of *Coke on Littleton* was published. Based on the sixteenth European edition, it consisted of three volumes. Ten years later, a new American publication, the *North American Review*, published an overview of the three-volume set.[15] The *Review* article began by lamenting the fact that there were "no detailed accounts of most of the great luminaries of the science [law], in a form accessible to ordinary readers."[16] The *Review* thought accessible editions of all the great writers of legal works should be available to "ordinary readers." In fact, the *North American Review* saw it as a duty to their readers "to add our mite to the department of legal biography, by laying before our readers some account of the life and writings of the distinguished commentator [Coke]."[17] Coke had become by the early nineteenth century not just a drudgery for law students but a proper topic of interest for the educated reader. In fact, not long after the *North American Review* article, Coke made an appearance in Sir Walter Scott's novel *The Antiquary*, published in 1816, so familiar had Coke become by that point.[18]

The *North American Review*, in 1812, summed up Coke's achievements to legal scholarship as: "The Reports and Institutes cover the whole ground of the common law, from the prerogatives of the king and the privileges of parliament down to the lowest copyhold-tenure and the rights of villenage [a feudal tenant arrangement] itself."[19] Surprisingly, only volume one of *Coke's Institutes* was published in full during his lifetime. This was owing in part to the strained relations Coke had with King Charles I. In fact, as Coke lay dying in 1634, Charles I had Coke's papers confiscated. They were not returned to the family until several years later. Coke's earlier writings, titled the *Reports*, were published during his lifetime but did not have the later impact of the *Institutes*.

Inns of Court

American legal education was less than organized in the period 1750–1800 (in part because America was not organized). The first members of the Supreme Court studied law between 1755 and 1770. As such, their studies were strictly British in content and focus. This meant that their studies were dictated by procedures set down over a century or more before they commenced their studies. These procedures were founded upon a course of study

[handwritten inscription]

3272

LE
QVART PART
DES REPORTES DEL

EDWARD COKE *Chiualier*, Lattorney general le Roy : De diuers Refolutions & Iudgements *dónes fur folemnes arguments, & auec graund delibera-*tion & conference des Trefreuçrend Iudges & fages de la Ley de cafes difficult, en queux font graund diuerfities des Opinions, et queux ne fueront vnques refolues, ou adiudges, & reporte par deuant : Et les raifons & caufes des dits refolutions et Iudgements ; publies en le primier An (le printempts de tout heureufitè) de trefheureux regiment de trefhault et trefilluftre I A Q_v E s Roy Dengleterre, Fraunce, & Ireland, & de Efcoce le 37. Le foun-taine de tout pietie & Iuftice, & la vie dela Ley.

Abominabiles Regi qui agunt impiè, quoniam Iuftitia firmat folium. PROVERB. 16. 12.

Voluntas Regis labia iufta, qui recta loquitur diligetur. PROVERB. 16. 13.

Cuftodi innocentiam, & vide æquitatem, quoniam funt reliquiæ homini pacifico. PSAL. 36. 37.

LONDINI
In ædibus Thomæ VVight. 1604.

Cum Priuilegio.

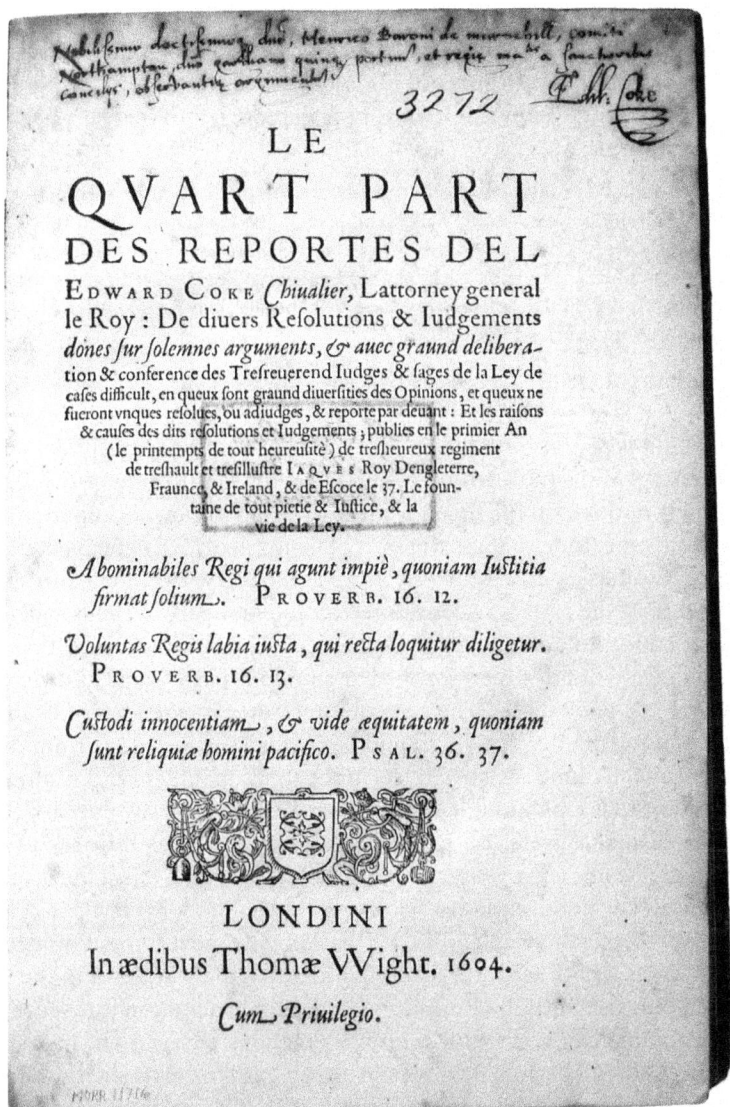

Edward Coke, fourth part of *The Reports*. Signed and with an inscription by Edward Coke, 1604 (Morristown National Historical Park).

established primarily through the English Inns of Court system (Middle Temple, Lincoln's Inn, Gray's Inn, and Inner Temple). The Inns of Court began over the course of centuries after Magna Carta in 1215 identified the need for a profession trained in the law—a nationwide law. The main English universities, Oxford and Cambridge, resisted the call to establish law schools to compete with the dominate religious education provided at those institutions. Through permutations of time, those wishing to study and practice law began to gather near the royal courts (the monarchs' courts) in organized groups which eventually developed into inns near the court, thus formally becoming the Inns of Court:

> ... it was not a boarding house or dormitory existence. The members of each Inn—its students, or apprentices, and its barristers, readers, and benchers—lived together and argued together in a companionship of legal study. There were daily discussions of live, although technical, problems in the developing law of England, with eager debates in the moots [mock trials], lectures by leaders of the Bar, and regular attendance upon the neighboring courts at Westminster.[20]

The Inns of Court were so infused with English character, and vice versa, by 1600, that it is widely understood that Shakespeare himself acted in at least two of his plays presented at Gray's Inn.[21] For a time, much like Oxford or Cambridge, England's young male elite were sent to one of the Inns to refine their outlook on life. Even if the law, or any serious occupation, were not the outcome, time spent at the Inns of Court provided valuable networking opportunities essential for England's aristocracy. "Residence for a year or so at one of the Inns was considered an integral part of the normal gentlemanly education, and it seems to have been widely accepted that even those who were not destined for the bar should acquire some knowledge of the law during their stay."[22] The pattern established by the Inns of Court did not transfer to America (and it should be remembered that a fair number of Founders attended the Inns of Court) in the sense that there came into being one location that embodied legal learning. Part of that was due to geography—the distances were too great; part of the issue was how society was structured. The immense geographical distances worked against the evolution of American law and indeed led to "a veritable cult of local law."[23] Colonials instinctively looked to England as the "nationwide" government model. The colonies, each with a separate sovereign identity, did not develop the sense of shared purpose until the Revolution and did not act upon this sense until after independence. Without a central indigenous government in America during the colonial period, it would have been hard to create such a school(s) of study. One aspect that did transfer nicely to American legal education was the practice of common placing, or note taking in a commonplace book. There are endless references to such practices during and after the colonial period. Some of these commonplace books even are found today as collectables in antiquarian book shops.

The Inns of Court, while prestigious, had their problems. While many sons of American wealth spent time at one of the Inns, it was still very much a matter of the student being responsible for obtaining the most he could out of the experience. One graduate of the Inns, an Englishman named Roger

North, wrote around 1730, that the study of common law was very much neglected by the faculty. According to North:

> There are societies which have the outward show or pretense of Collegiate Institutions, yet in reality nothing of that sort is now to be formed in them; and whereas in more ancient times there were exercises used in the Hall, they were more for probation than institution; now even those are shrunk into mere form, and that preserved only for conformity to rules, that gentlemen by tale of appearances in exercises rather than by any sort of performances might be entitled to be called to the bar.[24]

There was probably some level of embellishment here, but North's was not the only criticism of legal education in England. Still, the number of Americans who attended indicates that there was value in being schooled at the Inns of Court. In addition to potential valuable future contacts, many American students returned home with precious lists of law books to acquire, if not already with the books in tow with them. Once some of these books were finally obtained, many left just as quickly during the Revolution as many prominent lawyers fled the American War with their precious libraries.

William Blackstone

As influential as Edward Coke was, he became eclipsed by an even brighter star, Sir William Blackstone (1723–1780). Blackstone, who no doubt during his early career had studied Coke, rose to even greater status than Coke with his *Commentaries on the Laws of England*. Blackstone's work arrived on the American scene fully by 1770 and as such was a bit late for the older Founders who studied law before Blackstone's books arrived, but right on time for the generation coming of age in the rapidly evolving crisis between the colonies and Britain. Although Blackstone (pronounced "Bluxton" in his day) was no fan of the American Revolutionaries, his depiction of Anglo-American law was eagerly studied by American students for decades, well into the nineteenth century.[25]

William Blackstone was born in the Cheapside section of London on July 10, 1723. An orphan by age twelve, he showed an early inclination to scholarly work and entered Pembroke College at Oxford University in 1738 at age fifteen. In 1741, he was admitted to Middle Temple. He practiced law privately for seven years but found it unrewarding. Thus, in 1753, he accepted a teaching position at Oxford University and prepared to teach courses on the laws of England. In short order, he was appointed professor of Civil Law and by 1758 occupied the chair of law at Oxford and began a series of lectures which ultimately became his masterpiece *Commentaries on the Laws of England*.[26] It was not just Blackstone's *Commentaries* that were so revolutionary in the matter of legal education. What was also ground breaking was the method of teaching the law that Blackstone embarked upon at Oxford: the lecture format. Blackstone's reliance on an ancient teaching method slowly formalized and professionalized the study of law by students. In fact, when Blackstone gave his early lectures on English law, "no one had ever dared to deliver such lectures at Oxford."[27] It was not that teaching law did not occur at Oxford over the centuries, it did; what did not occur was lecturing about English law as opposed to the archaic Roman, or European, law.

William Blackstone was held in high regard during much of the latter eighteenth century and well in to the nineteenth century. It has been written, "Before American law schools developed a full course of law study, the youth who wished to become a lawyer apprenticed himself to some practitioner who immediately gave him Blackstone's *Commentaries* to read in between his duties as messenger boy and copyist. If you read Blackstone, you read the law."[28] Rather than reading law in a law office with an established lawyer, the Blackstone example was to find adherents in the new United States when George Wyeth of Williamsburg, Virginia, was appointed professor of law at William and Mary College in 1779, making Wyeth the first professor of law in the United States, much like Blackstone was the first in England.

The first of Blackstone's four volumes was published in England in 1765. Copies began arriving in America a year later. Many of the early Founders (or their fathers) were subscribers when Blackstone first arrived in the colonies. Volume two appeared in 1766, three in 1768, and four in 1769. By 1770, all four volumes were available in the colonies. In total, over one thousand sets of the English edition appeared in the colonies.[29] Given the stature of both Coke and Blackstone, it might be easy to forget that neither man was without his detractors.

It should also not be thought that Coke and Blackstone form the only two foundations around which American law was created, this is far from accurate. While Coke and Blackstone are two of the best known, other English and European names which influenced American law included Baron de Montesquieu, Samuel von Puffendorf, Hugo Grotius, Adam Smith, John Locke, Matthew Hale, and others. Furthermore, America would produce its own widely read scholars of legal thought who would begin to appear in the nineteenth century after the foundation of American nationhood was secure. Late in life, Thomas Jefferson looked at Anglo-American law as a "road of a traveler, divided into distinct stages, or resting places, at each of which a review is taken of the road passed over so far. The 1st of these was Bracton's *De Legibus Angliae*; the 2nd Coke's *Institutes*; the 3rd the *Abridgment of the Law* by Matthew Bacon, and the 4th Blackstone's *Commentaries*."[30] The topic of law books in the American colonies is an interesting study in and of itself. The *Colonial Laws of Massachusetts* was the first American law book of any significance. Historian Daniel Boorstin, writing in the 1940s, looked at the prevalence of law books in private libraries in the early decades of colonization and wrote that:

In the 17th century, law books made up the biggest single group: not only in the large libraries of people like Robert Carter (whose library contained three hundred titles, of which one hundred were on law), but even in small libraries. Col. Southey Littleton, a

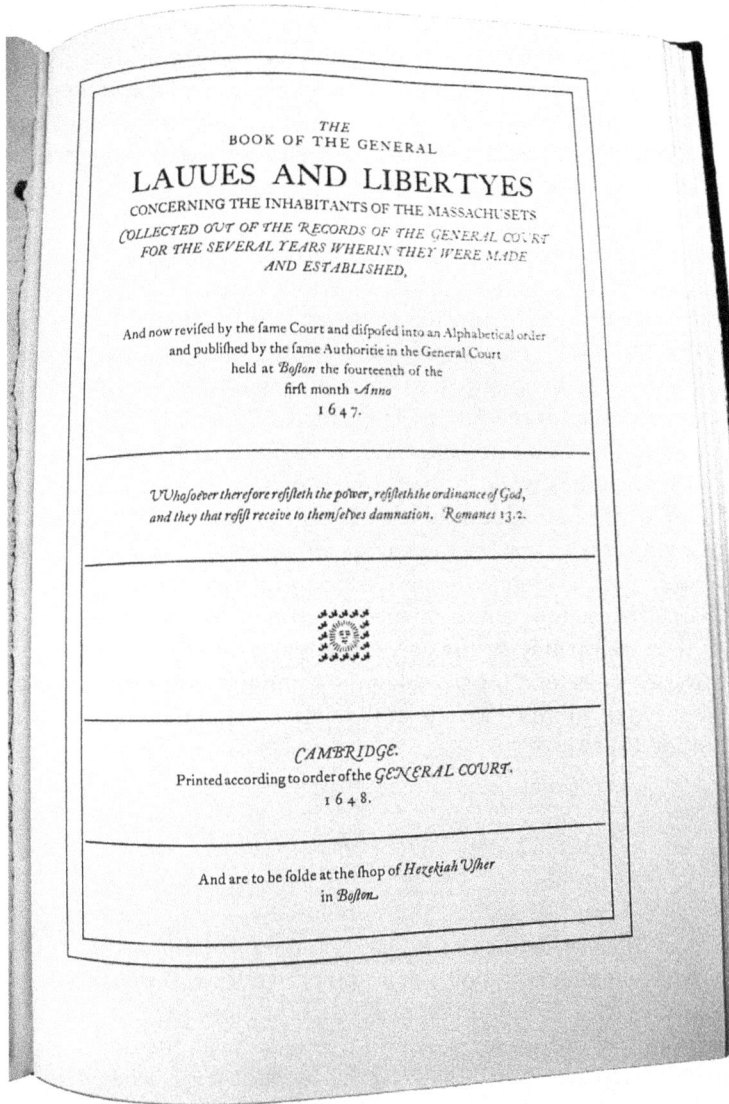

THE
BOOK OF THE GENERAL

LAUUES AND LIBERTYES

CONCERNING THE INHABITANTS OF THE MASSACHUSETS
*COLLECTED OUT OF THE RECORDS OF THE GENERAL COURT
FOR THE SEVERAL YEARS WHERIN THEY WERE MADE
AND ESTABLISHED.*

And now revised by the same Court and disposed into an Alphabetical order
and published by the same Authoritie in the General Court
held at *Boston* the fourteenth of the
first month *Anno*
1 6 4 7.

*VVhosoever therefore resisteth the power, resisteth the ordinance of God,
and they that resist receive to themselves damnation. Romanes 13.2.*

CAMBRIDGE.
Printed according to order of the *GENERAL COURT.*
1 6 4 8.

And are to be solde at the shop of *Hezekiah Usher*
in *Boston.*

Facsimile of the first law book printed in the colonies, the *Laws and Liberties of Massachusetts*, 1648 (Morristown National Historical Park).

leading planter of Accomac County, on his death in 1680 left seventeen books, of which four were on law; Capt. Christopher Cocke of Princess Anne County in 1716 left a library of twenty-four titles, nine on law. The proportion of law books seems to have increased during the 18th century; not alone among lawyers, but also among physicians, clergymen, and especially among the large planters.[31]

The first American editions of Blackstone printed in the colonies appeared on the eve of the Revolution, 1773. In fact, the publication of Blackstone's *Commentaries* was promoted as a patriotic gesture; it was argued that publishing in the colonies would boost American manufacturing and commerce.[32] The first American edition was sold by subscription, as was common at the time and was printed by Robert Bell in Philadelphia. It was also the first multi-volume set to be published in America. The first American edition of 1773 was taken from the fourth London edition of 1770.[33] Some of the original subscribers included nearly all the colonial governors, and individuals such as John Adams, John Jay, James Wilson, St. George Tucker, and Isaac Roosevelt (ancestor of Franklin Delano Roosevelt). Sixteen subscribers to the first American edition were members of the Continental Congress.[34] Booksellers also purchased sets in anticipation of high demand. "In all, 1,400 sets were ordered in advance" of the American-printed edition.[35]

Over two hundred years later, it is difficult to understand the role the arrival of Blackstone's work in the colonies played. At a significant point in the development of an American identity leading to the Revolution, Blackstone's *Commentaries* arrived to provide an argument for the strength of a concentrated, formal system of law. Historian Charles Warren wrote: "It was the advent of Blackstone which opened the eyes of American scholars to the broader field of learning in the law. He taught them, for the first time, the continuity, the unity, and the reason of the Common Law—and just at a time when the need of a unified system both in law and politics was beginning to be felt in the Colonies."[36]

Blackstone and the Study of Law

When William Blackstone was appointed to the position of Vinerian Professor of English Law at Oxford University in 1758 (named after Charles Viner who donated the funding), he began his tenure with what was, and still is, common for the new appointee: a speech. Blackstone gave a highly modern and in many ways adaptive speech on the need for proper legal education which, with some variation, is as prescient today as it was when delivered. If one could imagine what it must have been like in 1758 at All Souls College where Blackstone spoke. Blackstone, already a celebrated author and lecturer at the time, would have been viewed as an authority and much anticipated.

COMMENTARIES

ON THE

L A W S

OF

E N G L A N D.

IN FOUR BOOKS.

B Y

Sɪʀ WILLIAM BLACKSTONE, Kɴᴛ.

ONE OF HIS MAJESTY's JUDGES OF THE COURT OF COMMON PLEAS.

RE-PRINTED ꜰʀᴏᴍ ᴛʜᴇ BRITISH COPY,
PAGE ꜰᴏʀ PAGE ᴡɪᴛʜ ᴛʜᴇ LAST EDITION.

A M E R I C A:

PRINTED ꜰᴏʀ ᴛʜᴇ SUBSCRIBERS,

By R O B E R T B E L L, at the late Uɴɪᴏɴ Lɪʙʀᴀʀʏ, in *Third-street,*

PHILADELPHIA. M DCC LXXI.

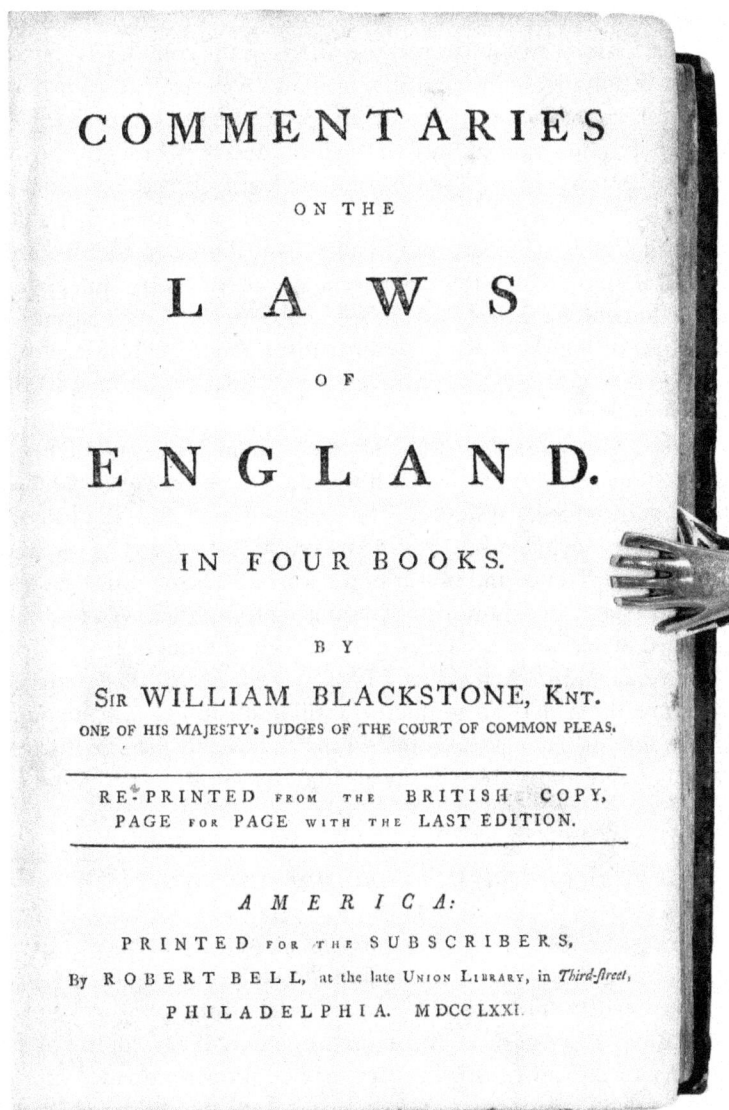

Title page of first American edition of William Blackstone's *Commentaries on the Laws of England*, 1771 (The Lawbook Exchange, Clark, New Jersey).

This professorship was the first attempt to establish a chair of English law anywhere in England except for the Inns of Court, which operated differently. Blackstone would have faced an audience of the most seasoned and respected legal minds in England. The anticipation would have been great for Blackstone's arrival and for the new position.

The establishment of the Law professorship was a seminal moment in English legal history, and it had reverberations in the colonies as well. It has been pointed out already numerous times that American sons, if possible, would attend one of the Inns of Court to study law. Several members of the Founding generation were alumni of the Inns, and they brought the understanding and practice of the English common law back to the colonies when they returned. There is no doubt of an argument to be made that a greater understanding of English law and history contributed to the overarching philosophical approach to the determination of American independence. Thomas Jefferson and James Wilson, while not Inns of Court alumni, were two examples of Founders who wrote treatises about English legal history and its role in the American controversy with Britain—although Wilson's was published later.

During the debate of the Judiciary Act in 1789, senators often quoted from Blackstone's *Commentaries*, such was the power his work held over the world of organized legal systems.[37] The comparisons to the English system in America were inevitable; but the reliance on Blackstone was merely another example of the influence and power of his work. Blackstone was such a recognized and established authority that quoting from him, even on the floor of the United States Senate, was not given a second thought.

However, in 1758, when William Blackstone faced the assembled guests for his lecture, the American conflict was still in the future. For the moment, Blackstone and his listeners celebrated English law and the role it played in maintaining a safe and stable society around the world.

The Beginnings of Colonial American Law

As early as 1829, there was an awareness of multiple periods of legal history in America. From the arrival at Jamestown in 1607 until 1829 covered two hundred and twenty-two years. In an article from the *North American Review* entitled "The American Jurist," in the January 1829 issue, it was stated: "The history of the law in this country may be properly divided into three several epochs. The first, from the settlement until the charter of 1692. The second, from that period to the time of the Revolution, and third, from the year 1780 to the present time [1829]."[38]

The 1692 charter referenced allowed the royal governor to veto numerous law-related undertakings in British colonies. The charter itself was issued in response to the capture of Edmund Andros, Governor of the Dominion of New England. This was a short lived organizational collection of northeastern colonies governed out of Boston. With the fall of King James II in 1689 as a casualty of the Glorious Revolution, the fate of the British colonies in North

Statue of William Blackstone outside of the Elijah Barrett Prettyman Courthouse in Washington, D.C., present day (General Services Administration).

America were briefly tried. Governor Andros was made a prisoner by a mob in Boston. Once order was restored in England, a new charter firmly establishing judicial power with England was created. This charter, in part, mandated that "all laws made in the colonial assembly were to be sent to England for approval, and all civil causes, above three hundred pounds, were to be carried to England by appeal for adjudication."[39] Mild as these may seem, it was the first of many official actions designed to limit the power of the colonies in legal matters, thus necessitating lengthy actions requiring perilous journeys to England. Still, even though these edicts created an England-centered legal system, once America gained independence the legal system created by the Founders had a very familiar look and feel about it. As the *North American Review* article pointed out, "with all the various modifications and revolutions through which this country has passed since that period [1693], the general outline of a great judicial establishment ... has been in a great measure still preserved."[40]

Colonial American law is an enormous topic. Nominally, the colonies were under the British common law. While this was correct in as far as the pattern of law pursued, it was not the case with the actuality of the law as practiced. In fact, the common law, as a system of national law, was non-existent in the colonies. What existed was a set of thirteen concepts of the common law for each individual colony, which combined in most cases aspects of their colonial charters into the amalgam of law that guided each colony. This naturally makes attempting to summarize the pattern of colonial law on a general level somewhat perilous. As historian William Nelson wrote, "the American colonists ended up receiving only so much of the common law as was appropriate to their needs and circumstances."[41] Still, for the purposes of this study, an overview is important to set the stage for the evolving maturation of national law that led to the Supreme Court under the new Constitution during the 1790s. Another observation from William Nelson is that "the thirteen mainland colonies were founded by different groups—indeed, by different nations—for many different purposes. Insofar as law reflects the societal conditions under which it operates, tremendous differences had to exist among the legal systems of the early colonies."[42]

As with all aspects of history, trying to deconstruct events down to the actions of one person or idea is self-defeating. Every aspect in history was impacted by what came before and what came after. The easiest concept in history is the interconnectedness of events and actions, or, cause and effect. Similarly, the same holds true for law.

Looking at a map of Colonial America we see the two earliest English settlements in Virginia (1607) and Massachusetts (1619) are roughly equidistant when the entire eastern seaboard is considered. These two future colonies were destined to have an outsized influence on what would become the United

A N

ACCOUNT

OF THE

𝕷𝖆𝖙𝖊 𝕽𝖊𝖛𝖔𝖑𝖚𝖙𝖎𝖔𝖓

I N

NEW-ENGLAND.

Together with the

DECLARATION

OF THE

Gentlemen, Merchants, and Inhabitants of *BOSTON*, and the Country adjacent. *April* 18. 1689.

Written by Mʳ. *NATHANAEL BYFIELD*, a Merchant of *Briſtol* in *New-England*, to his Friends in *London*.

LICENSED, *June* 27. 1689. *J. Fraſer.*

LONDON:

Printed for **Ric. Chiſwell**, at the *Roſe* and *Crown* in St. *Paul's* Church-Yard. MDCLXXXIX.

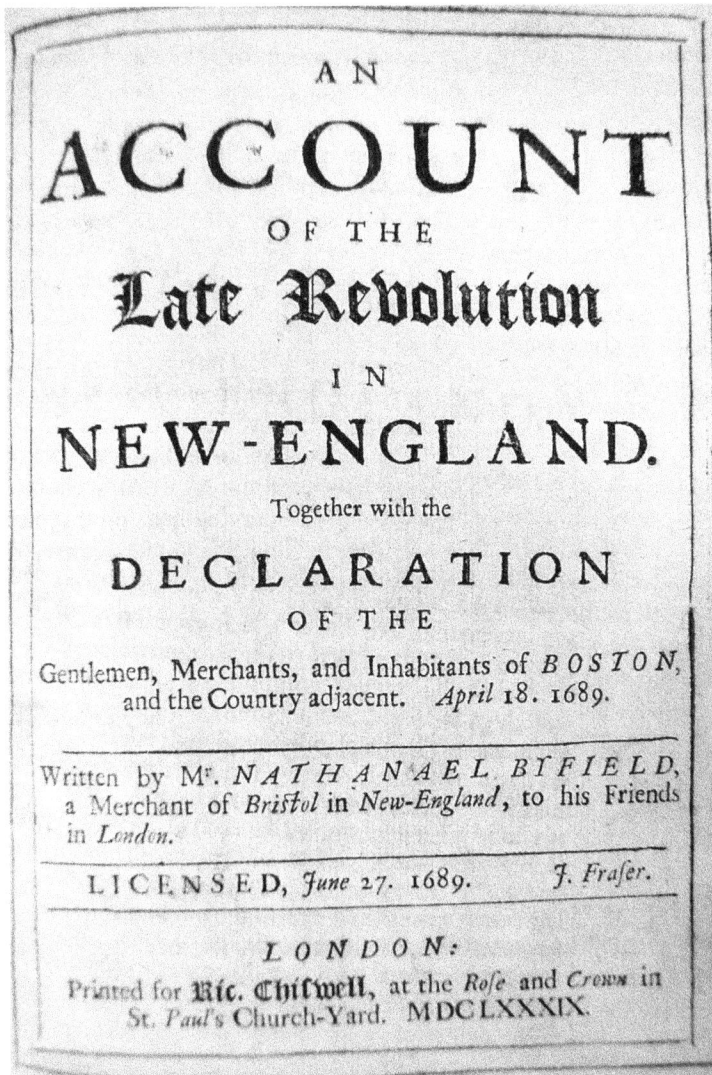

Title page of a pamphlet outlining the revolution in New England under Governor Andros, 1689 (Morristown National Historical Park).

States. In the early years however, their roles in the realm of law could not have been more different. In Massachusetts, founded as a religious haven, law tended to be guided by such thoughts and purposes. Virginia, founded as a commercial enterprise, tilted their law in that direction. These two approaches to legal development fanned out in roughly concentric circles anchored in their respective founding colony. While this is a broad-brush understanding to a highly complex creation (Colonial American law) it nonetheless offers a working perspective from which to explore the subtler nuances which sprang from those beginnings in the early seventeenth century. However, we must remember that the English common law was not the first law enacted in either settlement. While the common law certainly was what the immigrants knew when they arrived, it provided no real guidance towards the essence of the laws enacted at either settlement. In the early Massachusetts law, "there is absolutely no reference to the common law of England."[43] The essence of the law enacted at both outposts was designed for survival. Each colony needed to survive and prosper before the luxury of an extensive legal system such as the common law (which took centuries in England to evolve) could gain some foothold. At first, both settlements needed law of course; but it was basic, hard, law to ensure their survival. Yet, we need to acknowledge this antecedent to American law: "We cannot understand the history of our law, nor justly value the characteristic development of our jurisprudence, unless we know the actual attitude of the earliest colonists towards the common law, an attitude sometimes of apathy, of lack of understanding, sometimes of resistance or ignorance."[44] The lack of a formal adoption of English common law in the American colonies during the period 1620–1700, according to legal historian Charles Warren, was: "The colonists were making a common law for themselves; and their usages and customs, and the expedients to which they were forced, in order to adapt their rules of life to the surroundings and the time, gradually hardened into positive rules of law."[45] For Charles Warren, the reason there were so few lawyers, judges, or common law, in the colonies was truly the natural way the new world forced colonists to live. Without most of the elements of civil seventeenth-century life, colonists were left to their own wits and devices for survival. Not that they existed in some type of Biblical Eden in America, far from it. Nothing could have been more from the truth of their experience. Their experience was raw and unrefined, and did not lend itself to easy compartmentalizing to a code of law over a millennium in development. As Warren wrote:

> Prior to 1700, the law had been a layman's law, a popular equitable system, which worked well enough under the simple conditions of the times. As the practice of the law became more extended and disciplined however, and as contingencies unprovided for by statute constantly arose, judges grew more and more into the habit of borrowing from the provisions of the English common law.[46]

It should be remembered too that the seventeenth century in England was hardly a stable time for the blossoming of law. With a protracted civil war, a Restoration, a Glorious Revolution, and the continuing religious strife, it was not itself the best example for the colonies to emulate.

Another aspect, more practical, concerning the lack of lawyers in the colonies was simply a lack of books. Books for reference and study were not generally available widely. In fact, prior to the seventeenth century "hardly twenty-five law books had been printed" in England.[47] This may seem strange to our modern world where we can obtain a book from a library, bookstore, or digitally. For the seventeenth century student, it was a real struggle to find study material. Throughout the seventeenth and certainly in the eighteenth century, books were printed more broadly, were more affordable, and consequently were more readily available. This development went hand and hand with the increase in demand for greater clarity and nuance in legal dealings on both the personal and public level. Questions of law became more complex and less straight-forward. No longer were the edicts of a religious code two millennia old satisfactory for determining a burgeoning mercantile economy and lifestyle spanning an ocean.

As time moved on, and life got more sophisticated, law became a greater necessity to keep pace with societal changes. By 1625, it was recognized that the Virginia colony was governed by the common law, just like any other part of the British Empire.[48] In fact, the first royal governor (a traditional symbol of ordered government) arrived in 1625, the first royal governor arrived in Massachusetts in 1629. It is also during the 1620s that law courts in Virginia began to rule with an established legal system in place. "By 1640, the General Court of Virginia had committed the colony's legal order to governance under the rule of law, though the commitment remained fragile."[49]

Two jurisprudential principles had accompanied the migration of English common law to America, and those principles established the framework for common law decisions in the colonies. One principle was that of repugnancy; the other principle was that of divergence.[50] In other words, no Colonial American law should be contrary to English common law, yet American law could incorporate and recognize the unique circumstances which existed in the newly founded colonies. The migration of the common law was, and is, still a very active area of scholarship. As such, no definitive explanation can be offered:

> Common law pleading and procedure were exceptionally intricate. Colonial process never attained the heights, or depths, of the English common law. There were wide differences between colonies—between the loose, informal justice of early Massachusetts and the more conservative, more formal process in the Middle Atlantic and Southern colonies. But everywhere, the general, long run trend was the same: from simplicity and innovation to more complexity, and ever greater doses of secondhand English form.[51]

It has been pointed out that America's two earliest, and therefore significant, colonies were Massachusetts and Virginia. It has also been pointed out that the purpose of their creation had a lot to do with their relationships to the common law. Virginia, a commercial venture, quickly saw a need beyond the "frontier justice" that got the small settlement off to a strong start.

Massachusetts however was something completely different. As a utopian religious community their outlook on life was demonstrably different. A religious paradise on earth was more concerned with law that would be to the benefit of their beliefs, to the exclusion of all else. Individual rights were not important; the maintenance of the group was far more significant. "With a homogenous population holding the same general views on morals and polity, a true popular system of law could thus be produced, unrefined by juristic reasonings, untrammeled by technical precedents, satisfying, in general, the sense of right in the community."[52] Any intrusion by an "other" meant a threat to their societal norms. It seems absurd to us today, but people suffered under this imposed rigidity for decades.

What these laws were missing were of course the human component. There was no element of government, as Lincoln would say two hundred years later, of, by, and for the people. Specifically, as is probably well known, Puritan idealism guided the early Massachusetts settlers. For them, "Puritanism was both a theology and a political theory. Puritans strove to comprehend the relationship between divine sovereignty and human free will as well as to structure a government that balanced hierarchical authority with liberty."[53] One aspect that hindered the development of American law was the reliance on the clergy to form the foundation of life in the early colonies. As legal historian Charles Warren has written:

> It was to their clergymen that the colonists looked to guide their new governments, and in their clergymen, they believed, lay all that was necessary and proper for their lawful and righteous government. It followed, therefore, that the "word of God" played a greater part in the progress and practice of the law than the words of Bracton, Littleton, or Coke.[54]

There was no uniform American law during the eighteenth century (or seventeenth either) that Americans could look to for guidance or belonging. While this may have been a moot point to those for whom their colony or state was their country, for most this was not the case. For America to work as a concept and reality, law was needed to guide, however superficial that may have been. In fact, one of the first things the colonists did after any crisis with England was to call a congress to discuss a possible unified response and consider the legal ramifications of their actions and of those taken by the British. This approach looked at the colonies as a whole, not individually as separate countries, even though some certainly took that stance. Trying to fashion an overview today of Colonial American law is highly problematic prior to the Constitution in 1787 given the individual nature of the colonies/states. Coming together to oppose Britain was one thing, following the same legal system which was rebelled against, was quite another.

This review of Colonial American law is written from the perspective of the English tradition. While not expressly looking at other traditions, it should be remembered that America, and American law, were the results of input from a host of intermingled peoples, sources, and pasts. This includes, among them, Dutch, Swedish, French, German, Spanish, Native American, and perhaps even some African influences. If nothing else is known about Colonial American law, it can be summed up as unreliable, unwritten (for the most part), unresponsive, and something no one from the twenty-first century would want to experience.

The Idea of Law in Colonial and Revolutionary America

While the American Revolution is often seen as some spontaneous act, it was a long time germinating in the thoughts (direct and indirect) and actions (direct and indirect) of countless figures who combined brought about the activities we know today as the American Revolution.

The law that existed in Colonial America before the Revolution proved to be too weak to operate on a national scale. This was made abundantly clear during the Articles of Confederation period (ca. 1777–1789). The law as it existed prior to the new Constitution of 1787 was an amalgamation of over a century of lawmaking in the colonies and for the colonies. The crucial aspect to keep in mind is that until 1788, with the new Constitution, no government was making nationwide law in the United States except for the Continental Congress, which proved wholly inadequate.

The transition from colony to nation entailed more than just declaring, and achieving, independence; it also required determining which laws from England would work in America and which would not. It would fall as a task of the first decade of the Supreme Court (1790–1800) to start the process by which America began to answer that question. It is a question that can never be completely answered and is always in a continual state of interrogation and finessing.

As an example, take what is probably the most famous, or infamous, colonial-era trial known widely today: The Salem Witch Trials. These "trials," held in a sleepy backwater of Massachusetts Bay Colony, had no impact whatsoever on the law of Colonial America in the sense that they held any precedent-setting quality for the rest of the colonies overall. Indeed, the town of Salem found them an embarrassment and a stain on the rule of law, relying as they did on hearsay and unproven aspects more accurately found in a church and not a court of law. Still, these "trails" captured the later American consciousness and to this day do brisk business as a tourist attraction focused more on the gory aspects of late seventeenth century torture and killing than on any legal aspect which may have been present in 1692, regardless of how camouflaged actual legal principles were in Salem. Conducted in the court of Oyer and Terminer (to hear and to determine), the "trials" represented something of a high-water mark in the tacit admixture of law and theology. "It seems just to conclude that usually the administration of law was carried on not according to the technical rules of a developed system of jurisprudence but by a popular tribunal according to the general popular sense of right."[55] The law the colonists inherited during the later (post–1715) colonial period was the English common law. In an 1829 Supreme Court case (*Van Ness v. Pacard*), Justice Joseph Story wrote: "The common law of England is not to be taken in all aspects to be that of America. Our ancestors brought with them its general principles, and claimed it as their birthright; but they brought with them and adopted only the portion which was applicable to their condition."[56] Prior to roughly 1760, there was a wide variance in the approach to how the individual colonies accepted and adapted the common law. The "English common law, 1620–1709, was in force in New England only so far as it was specifically adopted by statute—or so far as the colonists, by custom, had assented to its binding force."[57] "With the growth of national feeling there comes also a growth of unification of legal principles, for which the English common law affords the ideal or criterion."[58] This movement could be seen as having been attempted during the Articles of Confederation period (ca. 1777–1789), but it was not truly recognized until the Constitutional Convention sat in 1787. This does not mean that the colonies were lawless. Each colony had a unique set of laws, in most cases written and codified, which usually harkened back to their establishment as a colony. Unlike England therefore, with its largely unwritten law code, Americans from an early point were familiar with and settled upon the idea of a written code of law.[59] This familiarity in part enabled the Founders to draft a written constitution for the new nation. A system of written law was already engrained in the American psyche: "A general trait of early colonial law is codification. It seems to have been universally considered necessary to state the essential elements of law for the guidance of the colonists who had taken up their abode in a wilderness without books or facilities for legal study."[60] Similarly, what was new, even radical, was adapting written law to a nationwide prominence under the Constitution. Similarly, instituting a tribunal (the Supreme Court) was just as radical a concept within the Constitution—Article III.

Another aspect which translated well for the Founders was the concept of the mutability of law. This concept, or actuality, was plain for everyone to see. It did not take someone trained in the law to know that not every aspect of the law is immutable. On the contrary, things change; life is, and must be, lived in the here and now. While certain elements no doubt never change, there can be significant variations in the tone and tenor of much else in a written legal system. This is hardly a foreign concept in law, any law, not just

American. It would be impossible for us to live by the Constitution as written in 1787. Historian Lawrence Friedman wrote, "Law constantly changes; and old law is basically useless, except to scholars. Only collectors and historians care much about the laws of Massachusetts of 1830. The laws of 1648 are even deader; they were already quaint and outdated when John Adams was alive."[61] This awareness permeated the colonial period and is reflected in the overarching philosophy of the Constitution: Article I, Section 8, Clause 18, gives Congress the power "to make all laws which shall be necessary and proper for carrying into execution the foregoing powers." Congress can, or cannot, act as they see fit to carry into existence law which they can, as its creator, alter too.

Even within some of the legal advances brought about in the colonies, certain aspects of the ancient common law were resurrected over the decades. Some instances included:

> Archaic ideas of the jury were given a new lease on life [a topic which would surface in the writings of the Anti-Federalists].
> The idea of tort liability for crimes was revived.
> The most important and interesting revival of older institutions is found in the popular courts composed of a comparatively large number of judges, recalling the twelve thanes of early English law, who declared law and custom in a simple, straightforward manner [a precursor to the multi-member supreme court].[62]

By the time of the American Revolution, the colonies had become Anglicized to such an extent that they were the most homogenous in terms of demographics than they had been in their entire history. This homogeneity allowed for the consolidated response to perceived British aggressions following the French and Indian War which so infuriated the Americans. This continuity of the social, political, and economic ties between the colonies also promoted the approach to a colony-wide, later nationwide, development of law.

Learning

The world of American law during the 1790s was naturally different than what we experience today. Whether this was expectation of law, delivery of law, understanding of law, or studying law with a view towards a legal career. It is well known that would-be lawyers in the United States had few options for learning the law and trade of being a lawyer. There were only a handful of colleges where law was taught by 1790—William and Mary, University of Pennsylvania, Columbia—and they were fairly exclusive.[63] Traveling to England or Europe was another option, but very expensive and time consuming. For a vast majority of legal aspirants, reading law with an established lawyer was the only option. And, depending on the ability of the lawyer-mentor, a student could have been greatly restricted in his exposure to meaningful legal study.

The first recorded person to practice law in the colonies was Thomas Morton (ca. 1620).[64] The first lawyer educated as such in the colonies was Thomas Lechford.[65] Benjamin Lynde was the first recorded colonist to specifically study law in England, at the Inns of Court. He graduated from Harvard College in 1686.[66]

Three important dates in the development of legal education in the United States were:

> The Harvard Law School, the first colligate school of law now in existence, was founded in Massachusetts in 1817. The first private school of law, the Litchfield Law School, was opened in Connecticut thirty-three years earlier, in 1784. The first American professorship of law was established at the College of William and Mary in Virginia in 1779.[67]

Early American lawyers (seventeenth century) "were few in number, lacking in education, and weak in influence."[68]

One student who left a short memoir about his days as a law student was James Kent. Kent was destined to become a giant in the legal landscape of the United States during the first quarter of the nineteenth century. During his life (1763–1847) Kent held positions as judge of the Supreme Court of New York, chief justice of the Supreme Court of New York, and chancellor of New York. Responding to a letter from attorney Thomas Washington of Nashville, Tennessee, in 1828, Kent recounted his beginnings in the legal profession. Kent began "as to the rest of your letter concerning my life and studies, I hardly know what to say, or to do."[69] Kent led a rather abstemious life as a young man: "I had never danced, or played cards, or sported with a gun, or drank anything but water."[70] This lack of social engagement allowed for plenty of time studying law. Like so many others at this time (1779), Kent suffered at the hands of the invading British army; ironically, he immediately found redemption in the reading of a British author. Kent was a student at Yale studying the requisite courses when British forces closed the college. Kent removed from New Haven to a small village where he stayed with a farm family: "I retired to a country village and finding Blackstone's Commentary I read the 4th volume, parts of the work struck my taste, and the work inspired me at the age of 16 with awe, and I fondly determined to be a lawyer."[71] The power of Blackstone's *Commentaries*, even in war, was immense. We have seen that Blackstone took a dim view of Americans in their revolt, but this did not lessen his influence as a legal source and inspiration. Two years later, while reading law with a practicing lawyer in Poughkeepsie—in his native Duchess County, New York—Kent read "Grotius and Puffendorf in huge folios, and made copious extracts."[72] Kent continued recounting his experiences: "My fellow students were more gay and gallant, thought me very odd and dull in my taste. I was free from all dissipation, and chaste as pure virgin snow.... I abridged Hale's history of the common law, and the old books of practice, and read parts of Blackstone again and again."[73] Grotius, Puffendorf, Hale, Hume, Blackstone—Kent read and was inspired by every one of them. While other students of the same time read the same texts, few took it as seriously as Kent. He entered the practice of law in 1785 and became one of America's most distinguished jurists and legal scholars.[74] His description is typical of the life of the "average" law student in Colonial and Revolutionary America. For those who could afford it however, England or elsewhere in Europe still offered the best education available in the law.

Another young American law student, better known than Kent, also left his reflections on studying the law. Thomas Jefferson studied a generation before Kent when America was still colonial. In fact, Jefferson was even too early for Blackstone's *Commentaries*. Like Kent, Jefferson was a bit out of the ordinary. Jefferson was wealthy and from a prominent family, and he had an unusual mind, capable of digesting and retaining enormous amounts of information. But, unlike Kent, Jefferson was wholly at ease in society. In fact, society often sought him out instead of the other way around.

The amount of time Jefferson spent studying law with George Wythe (before Wythe was a professor of law at William and Mary) is a topic of some debate. Jefferson himself never fully clarified that he studied from any particular time to another, but it is nonetheless safe to say that Jefferson spent around three years studying in Williamsburg with Wythe after he graduated from William and Mary in 1762. For our purposes, it is not so much the length of time but rather the authors studied with Wythe that are important. The continuity of legal practice relied on the continuity in legal training and preparation. Again, with Jefferson, his experience might not be typical in the sense of his extraordinary abilities. Yet, the similarities are important to establish an awareness of the authors and titles that were widely studied during this period that saw the formation of the United States.

Jefferson purchased numerous books while a student under Wythe, although he no doubt had access to Wythe's library collection as well. In addition to the usual names of Grotius, Coke, Puffendorf, and Hale, Jefferson also included Robert Richardson, Joseph Harrison, William Russell, and several "pocket companion" type books by anonymous authors dealing with the practical workings of the court system, especially in Virginia.[75]

John Adams, like Thomas Jefferson, was not the usual law student either. Far more industrious than most, Adams read voraciously and heartily once he determined to be a lawyer; Adams "worked his way through the philosophers of the Enlightenment, who spoke so much in jurisprudential terms. Justinian, Vinnius, Bracton, Coke, Bolingbroke, Montesquieu, and Rousseau mingle in the early diaries that record his reading."[76]

Young John Adams, when he was twenty-five, recorded a list of names and topics of reference that even he acknowledged few of his colleagues both-ered with. In 1758, Adams wrote: "Few of my contemporary beginners in the study of the law have the resolution to aim at much knowledge in the civil law. See me distinguish myself from them by the study of the civil law in its native language."[77] Adams's prodigious learning and reading was filled with authors such as "Coke, Lillie, Hawkins, Justinian, Vinnius, Van Muyden, Wood, Cowell, Hale...."[78] When Adams inquired for advice on the study and practice of law while still a student, he received a rather startling response from a practicing attorney, Mr. Gridley. One item which no doubt caught Adams's attention was "...not to marry early; for an early marriage will obstruct your improvement.... Another thing, is not to keep much company, for the application of a man who aims to be a lawyer must be incessant; his attention to his books must be constant."[79]

Interestingly, nearly thirty years later, Adams's son John Quincy Adams, himself a law student, had a much different take on one of his father's favorite authors: "This day got through my folio of Lord Coke which has been hanging heavily upon me these ten weeks. It contains a vast mass of law learning, but heaped up in such an incoherent mass that I have derived very little benefit from it—indeed I think it a very improper book to put into the hands of a student."[80]

What was so remarkable about John Adams was that much of his legal training was self-directed, a remarkable undertaking that would have ended a promising law career for most students. Adams, however, was not most stu-dents. Another striking aspect of Adams's list was the number of books he had available to him. It would have taken considerable resources and effort to amass such a collection in Colonial America. The effort must have been monumental, the results we are all familiar with.

A description of legal education for the less well-off student was pro-vided by Hugh Blair Grigsby. Writing in 1860 (looking back to the turn of the nineteenth century), Grigsby summarized the thin veneer of legal edu-cation which masked a greater understanding of human nature, upon which many American lawyers relied rather than upon legal knowledge. Grigsby wrote:

> He [a student] was of that substantial class of lawyers who, having received an elemen-tary grounding in Latin and mathematics in the schools of the time, entered the clerk's office and served a term of duty within its precincts. He was thus well versed in the ordinary forms of the law and with the decision of the courts in leading cases. With such men as a class there was no great intimacy with the law as a science. As long as the case lay in the old routine, this class of lawyers would get along very well; but nov-elties were unpleasant to them.[81]

This last comment was fascinating. In many ways, an argument can be made that if one's case went beyond the proscribed boundaries of existing legal nomenclature, a judge and attorney had little choice in trying a case. Again, it points to the veneer of legal thought that existed in some parts of the United States.

A more upbeat assessment concerning the learning process of someone of affluence, can be found in a reference by John Quincy Adams. Writing in his diary concerning his legal tutor Theophilus Parsons (a prominent Boston attorney) in 1787, the young Adams wrote:

> It is of great advantage to us to have Mr. Parsons in the office. He is in himself a law library, and as proficient in every useful branch of service; but his chief excellency is, that no student can be more fond of proposing questions than he is of solving them. He is never at a loss, and always gives a full and ample account, not only of the subject proposed, but of all matters which have any intimate connection with it. I am persuaded that the advantage of having such an instructor is very great, and I hope I shall not mis-improve it as some of his pupils have done.[82]

Adams saw the pupil as an integral part of the learning process, a pro-active member of a team. Much like higher education itself, most students get out of it what they put in it. It is interesting to note that John Quincy Adams rejected a nomination to the Supreme Court in 1811 by President James Madison. The seat was eventually filled by the influential New England legal scholar Joseph Story.

This chapter is an overview of a centuries-long struggle to establish a separate legal profession in England, and a similar struggle which fortunately did not take as long in the United States. It should be remembered that it was not until the twentieth century that American law schools became the formalized, American Bar Association approved, schools that we think of today. In a lecture delivered in 1921, Charles Hepburn stated:

> We may be at the dawn of a day when organized university law schools, equipped with trained teachers of law, and organized bar associations, moved by their historic interest in the professional training of American lawyers, and following the constructive ideals of forward looking leaders of the Bar, will cooperate effectively in a common cause.[83]

2

The Constitutional Convention and *The Federalist* Papers

A Revolutionary Preview

At its base, the American Revolution was a giant, and deadly, debate about British law. And rather than in the debate room it was decided on the battlefield. This of course ensured that the conflict would always be more focused on the military than the halls of learning. Given this reality, it is difficult to concentrate on the Revolutionary period in terms of anything other than the military approach. Yet churning just below the surface was every other aspect of daily life—and this included law. The debate over law during the years of conflict occurred at the theoretical level primarily in the Continental Congress. The American Revolution did little to clarify the place of law in the new American states. In fact, if anything, it complicated the situation. The guiding legal document of the Revolutionary period, the Articles of Confederation, was wholly inadequate to governing the colonies/states. For the average citizen, with the obvious change of allegiance away from George III, the business of law was primarily unchanged at the state level. The debates which enveloped Congress looked towards a national law, an overarching law that would connect all thirteen states into a system of legal understanding and operation that would produce a country operational on the world stage. The Articles of Confederation, not formally adopted until March 1781 (seven months prior to the Yorktown victory), proved woefully inadequate from a legal perspective to govern the new nation. The union of states that emerged at the end of the war were more appropriately styled the "united states" rather than the "United States." This failure would lead directly to the Constitutional Convention in Philadelphia in 1787, where the topic of law was heartily debated. Only after the Constitutional Convention could they be truly united, in a way they never were before under a system of law recognized by all. It also led to a national judiciary headed by a Supreme

Court. The Constitution, followed by *The Federalist* papers, produced the greatest disquisition on American law up to that point.

The decade leading to the Constitutional Convention of 1787 was fraught with starts and false starts in relation to the determination of American governmental sovereignty. There clearly is no doubt American leaders thought long and hard, some to the point of obsession, about the legal and constitutional relationship between Britain and America. Most of these leaders viewed the colonies as singular, rather than plural, which caused many problems leading up to 1787; indeed, "the colonial assemblies slowly managed to obtain in practice the authority that Crown officials denied them in theory."[1] These moves by the individual colonial assemblies reinforced the notion of un-united colonies in the face of Britain.

On February 8, 1825, James Madison, in retirement at Montpelier, wrote a letter to Thomas Jefferson, in retirement at Monticello. In the letter, Madison wrote that he had "looked with attention over your intended proposal of a text book for the law school," presumably at the new University of Virginia.[2] Madison, a co-founder of the University of Virginia with Jefferson, was highly involved in the curriculum planning and his input on law, though he was not a lawyer himself, was indicative of his standing in the early republic as the Father of the Constitution. Furthermore, it highlights the importance Jefferson felt should be attached to a law school in that it should teach and prepare students to work within the framework of the Constitution, not quite forty years after it went into effect. In other words, Jefferson was looking to teach the practice of American law. There was no more qualified person, lawyer or non-lawyer, to offer guidance than James Madison.

In the letter, Madison noted it was difficult to "find standard books that will be both guides and guards for the purpose" of protecting American liberty and the political system.[3] Madison noted, "[Algernon] Sidney and [John] Locke are admirably calculated to impress on young minds the right of nations to establish their own governments ... but afford no aid in guarding our republican charters against constructive violations."[4] Madison proposed *The Federalist* papers, of which he was a co-author, as being "regarded as the most authentic exposition of the text of the federal Constitution."[5] Madison even noted that *The Federalist* papers were being used as a text book at two colleges: "those of Harvard and Rhode Island [presumably Brown University]."[6] This letter obviously reflects the mature James Madison and his view of law in the new century. To understand Madison as he viewed America and the development of its law, we need to return to Philadelphia in 1787.

The whole idea behind the Constitutional Convention of 1787 was to create a nation. The Articles of Confederation had failed to bring the new states into closer political cooperation with a central vision or focus. The territorialism which existed among the states extended to nearly every aspect of life. This included law, economics, and cultural/societal ideas; the states were fragmented. And there were many statesmen who saw this as a good arrangement. Patrick Henry, Samuel Adams, and Richard Henry Lee were just three examples.

There were several attempts to make the union stronger, notably the Annapolis Convention of 1786. These attempts all failed. The two leaders of the Annapolis convention, James Madison and Alexander Hamilton, rather than accept defeat, actually called for a larger, more orchestrated gathering to occur in Philadelphia in May 1787. Madison had spent the years prior to 1787 deep in study at Montpelier. He undertook a systematic overview of nearly two thousand years of Western history focusing on government, law, and human nature. These studies resulted ultimately in what came to be known as the Virginia Plan at the Philadelphia Convention. But, in 1785–1786, with the failure at Annapolis, they were just the notes and musings of a very wealthy young man with seemingly little else to do.

The Virginia Plan and the Law

The plan that James Madison brought with him to Philadelphia in May 1787 was put forward to get the Convention started. It was offered as something to get discussion and debate initiated. It must have been hard for Madison to see what he knew very well was more work and effort than anyone else expended used as both kindling to ignite discussion and as a foil for others to attack. While section eight of Madison's plan called for a national judiciary, it did not describe what a national judiciary would do until section nine, which outlined that:

> a national judiciary be established to consist of one or more supreme tribunals, and of inferior tribunals to be chosen by the national legislature.... That the jurisdiction of the inferior tribunals shall be to hear and determine in the first instance, and of the supreme tribunal to hear and determine in the [last] resort, all piracies and felonies on the high seas, captures from an enemy; cases in which foreigners or citizens of other states applying to such jurisdictions may be interested, or which respect the collection of the national revenue ... and questions which may involve the national peace and harmony.[7]

In his plan, Madison clearly had in mind a separate national judiciary which was completely lacking in the Articles of Confederation. Aside from the fact that the Virginia Plan called for one or more supreme tribunals, the outcome of Article III of the Constitution was remarkably close to the plan Madison had envisioned.

It has often been pointed out that Madison was not a lawyer by training. While true, his vast reading and research included forays into the depths of legal scholarship. He had much more understanding of the law than most practitioners who passed the bar and received a license to practice. Madison was more than prepared to devise a plan of national legal adjudication. In the years leading up to the Constitutional Convention, Madison wrote in numerous letters his views (the result of his vast research) concerning a national legal system.

In an August 1785 letter to Caleb Wallace of Kentucky, Madison gave an overview of his thinking about a national Constitution in response to a question from Wallace. Among the various attributes Madison saw as necessary was one dealing with a judicial department, which, according to Madison, "merits every care."[8] Madison saw the best role of an independent national judiciary as "maintaining" private rights against all the corruptions of the two other branches of government; corruption which gives a reputation to the whole government which it (the judiciary) is not in itself entitled to.[9] Madison pointed to the role of the national judiciary in Britain and saw an example for how a national judiciary could work as a check on the misbehavior of the other branches of government. Madison did acknowledge possible misbehavior of the judicial branch though. He wrote that "the states seem to have seen the necessity of providing for impeachments [of judges] but none of them to have hit on an unexceptional tribunal."[10] To Madison's view, judicial misconduct was rare at the state level. On April 16, 1787, one month before the start of the Constitutional Convention, Madison wrote to George Washington concerning his thoughts about a national judiciary:

> The national supremacy ought also to be extended as I conceive to the judiciary departments. If those who are to expound and apply the laws, are connected by their interests and their oaths with the particular states wholly, and not with the union, the participation of the union in the making of the laws may be possibly rendered unavailing.[11]

Madison saw a grave threat to the national union of states by not having a national judiciary. He felt state judges, who were unaffiliated with the union, would be less apt to render opinions with the national well-being in mind. For Madison, this national affiliation also had to come in the form of an independent separate branch of the government. Madison's extensive study of history, and the recent experience with the Articles of Confederation, clearly showed that judicial independence was paramount for the effective operation of a republic.

The Constitutional Convention

Before the topic of a national tribunal or judiciary, ultimately a supreme court, could be discussed, the uneasiness of the supremacy of national law over state law had to be dealt with. Naturally, no straightforward answer was found to appease every delegate in Philadelphia in 1787. Still, for the creation of a national court to be part of the new proposed government, the debate over supremacy had to occur. Multiple times throughout the Convention this topic arose. It has already been seen that Madison's Virginia Plan called for a national court. On June 13, 1787, the Committee of the Whole, reporting on the Virginia Plan, first indicated that the new government would contain a judiciary, along with the two other branches of government. "Resolved, that it is the opinion of this committee that a national government ought to be established, consisting of a supreme legislative, executive, and judiciary."[12] That was also an explicit acknowledgment that the Articles of Confederation, lacking these three distinct branches of government, were not going to be the outline of government for the new nation any longer.

The concern over the supremacy of national law first occurred, according to Madison's notes, on June 15, 1787. Delegate William Paterson (a future Supreme Court justice) in presenting his New Jersey Plan, proposed that "a federal judiciary be established to consist of a supreme tribunal."[13] Following this, Paterson dealt with the supremacy issue:

> All acts of the United States in Congress made by virtue and in pursuance of the powers … vested in them, and all treaties made and ratified under the authority of the United States shall be the supreme law of the respective states so far … as those acts and treaties shall relate to the said states or their citizens, and that the judiciary of the several states shall be bound thereby in their decisions, anything in the respective laws of the individual states to the contrary notwithstanding.[14]

This concept was prevalent in the 1783 Paris Peace Treaty ending the American Revolution. The Treaty, approved by the Continental Congress following the Articles of Confederation, proved to be particularly prone to being ignored by the states. In fact, some states passed laws directly in contradiction of the Treaty. Paterson, Madison, and many of the mature Founders saw this as an embarrassment. The opposing view saw this from a "states' rights" perspective, not a national perspective. During the Convention, it thus became more critical than ever to ensure that a proper understanding of the supremacy issue existed among the states. Whether they agreed or not was another matter.

Three days later, on Monday, June 18, the Convention debated the two major plans—the Virginia Plan and the New Jersey Plan. Alexander Hamilton took the floor and made an extended speech in favor of most of the Virginia Plan. Particularly, Hamilton took on the topic of supremacy of the national law. In Hamilton's view, "All laws of the particular states contrary to the Constitution or laws of the United States [are] to be utterly void."[15]

The next day, Tuesday, June 19, Madison himself took the floor in a discussion of the New Jersey Plan to point out how many egregious violations of the Articles of Confederation had occurred. Specifically, Madison pointed to the number of states that had separately waged war or made treaties with Native American tribes. This was completely in opposition to the Articles yet it was occurring daily. Madison saw this as one of the greatest weaknesses of a weak document (the Articles). Madison also saw this pattern of flaunting national law as liable to continue under the New Jersey Plan which was not, in his view, strong enough in its language regarding the supremacy of national law. "He [Madison] observed that the [New Jersey] Plan ... [omitted] a control over the states as a general defense of the federal prerogatives."[16]

On Tuesday, July 17, Luther Martin of Maryland put fashion to the language by proposing the following:

> That the legislature of the United States made by virtue and in pursuance of the articles of union, and all treaties made and ratified under the authority of the United States shall be the supreme law of the respective states, ... and that the judiciaries of the several states shall be bound thereby in their decisions, anything in the respective laws of the individual states to the contrary notwithstanding.[17]

Interestingly, Martin would refuse to sign the Constitution as he felt it gave too much power to the national government.

On Thursday, July 26, the notes and scattered jottings of the delegates were gathered and presented to a Committee of Detail who were charged with fashioning a draft working constitution over the next two weeks while their colleagues enjoyed a break. This committee crafted the following language concerning the supremacy of national law and a national tribunal:

> Resolved, that the legislative acts of the United States, made by virtue and in pursuance of the articles of union [the Constitution], and all treaties made and ratified under the authority of the United States, shall be the supreme law of the respective states, as far as those acts or treaties shall relate to the said states, or their citizens and inhabitants; and the judiciaries of the several states shall be bound thereby in their decisions, anything in the respective laws of the individual states to the contrary, notwithstanding.
>
> Resolved, that a national judiciary be established, to consist of one supreme tribunal.[18]

These two resolutions, by mid-summer, were already very recognizable compared with what we know today as the final product. This draft, after being prepared by the Committee of Detail, was presented to all the delegates on their return from break on August 6, 1787. It would be John Rutledge, the chair of the Committee of Detail (and future Supreme Court justice), who suggested the final form of Article VI concerning national law on August 23. His proposal is what we read today with a minor variation.

In that same Committee of Detail, the outlines of Article III, dealing with the Supreme Court and the national judiciary, were dealt with as we have seen. When the delegates returned from their two-week recess on August 6, they were presented with language which very nearly matched what eventually came to be in the Constitution.

Bending the rule of secrecy slightly, Madison gave Thomas Jefferson, who was serving in France as the American ambassador, a preview of the probable outcome of the convention before it ended. Writing on September 6, 1787, eleven days before the convention formally ended with the public release of its work, Madison told Jefferson that "a government will probably be submitted to the *people of* the *states* consisting of … a regular *judiciary* establishment [emphasis in original]."[19] Madison's letters during this period are filled with language musing on the nature of the judiciary. Writing again to Thomas Jefferson on October 24, 1787, Madison envisioned the role of the national judiciary thus: "It may be said that the judicial authority under our new system will keep the states within their proper limits, and supply the place of a negative on their laws. The answer is, that it is more convenient to prevent the passage of a law, than to declare it void after it is passed."[20] Madison found endless opportunities to plumb the depths of a fast-approaching federal government with a separate judiciary. (Madison would write about the judiciary in *The Federalist* papers, numbers 47, 48, and 49.)

On June 20, 1788, Madison, a delegate to the state ratifying convention in Virginia, gave a lengthy speech in defense of the judiciary as proposed in the Constitution. Madison pointed to issues arising directly from the Constitution as within the prevue of the federal judiciary, likewise, cases involving ambassadors, or cases where the interests of the United States were at issue.[21] Naturally, cases where two states were party against each other were within the area of consideration of the federal judiciary (which under the proposed Constitution only consisted of a supreme court). Madison envisioned what would be the topic of *Chisholm v. Georgia* in 1793 (and lead directly to the passage of the Eleventh Amendment): whether citizens could sue another state than the one wherein they resided. Madison foresaw an empire of justice as far as the Congress would reach: "I am of opinion, and my reasoning and conclusions are drawn from facts, that as far as the power of Congress can extend, the judicial power will be accommodated to every part of America."[22] This is Madison at his most expansive; not just from a geographic perspective, but from the perspective of national government and especially national law. Naturally, many opponents of the proposed Constitution saw a threat from a national judiciary, or any aspect of a national government. Madison, like so many others in support of the Constitution, found these arguments out of touch with the dangers the new nation faced as just a weak, loosely organized collection of states.

The Federal Judiciary in The Federalist *Papers*

The Federalist papers reviewed every aspect of the proposed Constitution. The series of eighty-five essays, written by Alexander Hamilton, James

Madison, and John Jay, were published in New York City newspapers between October 1787 and August 1788. While the topic of a federal judiciary was mentioned in several of the other essays, only six were devoted exclusively to the topic. All were written by Alexander Hamilton. The six essays dealing expressly with the federal judiciary, numbers 78 through 83, appeared first in book form before being published in the newspapers. The celebrated first edition of *The Federalist* papers published in New York by McLean, appeared in advance of the last eight essays appearing in the press. It points to the fact that Hamilton wrote these well ahead of their final appearance in the press. As we have seen, the main arguments posed by opponents of the proposed federal system were concerned with the status of state judiciaries in the new federal government and in particular about jury trials decided within a particular state.

The Founders faced two momentous decisions in the aftermath of achieving independence. First, were they to have a country? Meaning were they to have a true, authentic national government which was not liable, at least in theory, to the petty jealousies that existed during the Revolution and required the intervention of monarchies (France and Spain) more tyrannical than the one the Americans were revolting against? Secondly, if the answer to the first question was affirmative, then it immediately became a question as to what type of government they would have given the failure of the Articles of Confederation. And, within the answer to the second question, presuming a written Constitution, how was it to be enforced, and more importantly, interpreted? It fell to Hamilton, in his six essays in *The Federalist* papers, on the federal judiciary and the Supreme Court, to answer this.

Hamilton began number 78 indicating that since the need for a federal judiciary was thoroughly manifested by the experience of the Articles of Confederation, that he would then only look at "questions which have been raised being relative to the manner of constituting it, and to its extent."[23] Hamilton went on to clarify his statement: "The manner of constituting it seems to embrace these several objects: 1st. The mode of appointing the judges. 2nd. The tenure by which they are to hold their places. 3rd. The partition of the judiciary authority between different courts, and their relations to each other."[24]

In this opening essay, Hamilton made one of the more famous comments concerning the Court: "The judiciary ... has no influence over either the sword or the purse; no direction either of the strength or of the wealth of the society; and can take no active resolution whatever."[25] Hamilton argued, unlike the executive (sword) and legislative (purse), the judiciary can have no physical way of threatening the government or society overall. In fact, some opponents saw this as a reason for not having a federal judiciary, as we have seen. Hamilton, however, countered such thinking by saying that this was precisely why the Court was needed. Looking at the Court's lifetime appointments, Hamilton reasoned: "That as nothing can contribute so much to its firmness and independence as permanency in office, this quality may therefore be justly regarded as an indispensable ingredient in its constitution, and, in a great measure, as the citadel of the public justice and the public security."[26] Hamilton also pointed out unequivocally that the Supreme Court was the arbiter on Constitutional issues. The courts, Hamilton wrote, have a duty "to declare all acts contrary to the manifest tenor of the Constitution void."[27]

Hamilton acknowledged that this power was uncomfortable to some. In fact, some rejected the Constitution outright because they felt this power, while not explicit, was nonetheless understood. Article VI, while oblique, is fairly clear that federal law was supreme and the Supreme Court can act accordingly. From this starting point, Hamilton proceeded to discuss his understanding, and by extension, all proponents of the proposed Constitution. Immediately, Hamilton stated: "There is no position which depends on clearer principle, than that every act of a delegated authority, contrary to the tenor of the commission under which it is exercised, is void."[28]

This seemed simple enough. However, not everyone saw it that way. Hamilton based his thinking on the simple premise that in a relationship such as existed in the United States in 1787, with a failed central government and a newly independent country about to splinter into jealous factions based on regional rivalries, they had one chance to get it right. If the current effort failed, the United States would have proven the "wise men" of Europe, who saw the American experiment as juvenile at best, correct. Hamilton and his supporters saw a written constitution as the best guarantee against the encroachments of an over-zealous legislature or executive. Naturally, Hamilton and the other Federalists who supported the Constitution never fully imagined the Supreme Court, or any inferior court, as being overtly political.

Hamilton saw the Court as a "bulwark of a limited Constitution against legislative encroachments" rather than as most opponents saw it, which was as an unelected body out to dismantle the will of the people.[29] For Hamilton, the Court was the protector of the Constitution, not the legislature—the people could not always be trusted to do the right thing in electing the legislature. The Court was appointed for life terms; they were free from political intrigue (or so he claimed); and they did not have to constantly think about the next election. Similarly, "next to permanency in office, nothing can contribute more to the independence of the judges than a fixed provision for their support."[30]

Hamilton was also interested in longevity. He argued there was no reason to put age limits on Supreme Court justices as some states were already doing.

He felt a life appointment was proper and necessary for such a deliberative body as the Supreme Court. Furthermore, with life expectancies rather short in the overall scheme, he saw the prospects of a Court filled with antiquarian judges highly unlikely.[31]

Hamilton approached the main topic with his opponents in essay eighty. Attempting to frame the outline of the essay, he began by listing what proponents of the proposed Constitution saw as the proper role, the jurisdiction, of the federal judiciary, and the Supreme Court. Hamilton wrote:

> It seems scarcely to admit of controversy, that the judiciary authority of the union ought to extend to these several descriptions of cases: 1st, to all those which arise out of the laws of the United States...; 2nd, to all those which concern the execution of the provisions expressly contained in the articles of union; 3rd, to all those in which the United States are a party; 4th, to all those which involve the PEACE of the CONFEDERACY...; 5th, to all those which originate on the high seas ... [emphasis in original].[32]

Federalist 80 contains another often-quoted part of *The Federalist* papers. In seeking to argue the necessity for a singular, federal power, Hamilton stated, "Thirteen independent courts of final jurisdiction over the same causes, arising upon the same laws, is a hydra in government from which nothing but contradiction and confusion can proceed."[33] The threat of so many voices trying to run a government would be simply leaving the national government as it stood in 1788, with the Articles of Confederation. The Articles had proven, by 1788, to be worthless as a governing document for a new country.

In essay 81, Hamilton took up the complaint that the Supreme Court would be superior to the legislative by the fact that it could declare laws unconstitutional, thus overriding the will of the people, as already seen. Hamilton found this concern unsubstantiated. Hamilton was convinced, however, "that the Constitution ought to be the standard of construction for the laws, and that wherever there is an evident opposition, the laws ought to give place to the Constitution."[34] Perhaps this went without saying in the essay, but Hamilton reiterated the point many times to ensure the message was not lost.

Summing up his argument, Hamilton ended with an overview of what had been established thus far:

> The amount of the observations hitherto made on the authority of the judicial department is this: that it has been carefully restricted to those causes which are manifestly proper for the cognizance of the national judicature, ... that the Supreme Court will possess an appellate jurisdiction, both as to law and fact, ... that this appellate jurisdiction does, in no case, *abolish* the trial by jury; and that an ordinary degree of prudence and integrity in the national councils will insure us solid advantages from the establishment of the proposed judiciary ... [emphasis in original].[35]

Hamilton here used an exquisitely crafted phrase—"an ordinary degree of prudence and integrity"—to not just show off his writing skills; he was also acknowledging the fact that while it did not take much in the way of the "good" aspects of human nature to keep the government honest, it was entirely possible, maybe even likely, that at some future date the "bad" aspects of human nature could derail the "solid advantages" of an honest government, in this particular case, a federal judiciary. What was intriguing, is that Hamilton left out whether or not an intentional manipulation of the levers of government were also possible.

In the opening of essay 82, Hamilton admitted that only time could answer some of the criticisms leveled against the proposed federal judiciary: "Time only ... can mature and perfect so compound a system, can liquidate the meaning of all the parts, and can adjust them to each other in a harmonious consistent whole."[36] Hamilton realized this commentary would sway no one, and immediately set into his argument once again. He sought to persuade opponents concerned with the role of the federal judiciary that states would lose none of their existing authority, "unless it appears to be taken away in one of the enumerated modes."[37]

The final *Federalist* essay dealing with the Supreme Court and the federal judiciary was number 83. It is the longest essay and covers trial by jury. Clearly, given the length of the essay, this was an important topic. Hamilton stated that it was really misinformation that had fueled the concern: "The disingenuous form in which this objection is usually stated has been repeatedly adverted to and exposed, but continues to be pursued in all conversations and writings of the opponents of the plan."[38]

Essay 83 had Hamilton angrily admonishing those who spoke or printed such outright false claims. Hamilton fully knew that trial by jury, in both civil and criminal cases, was a cherished tradition. He certainly knew it was one of the indictments against King George III in the Declaration of Independence. Hamilton no doubt recalled the outrage it had caused and wanted to avoid at all cost a similar fate for the Constitution. Hamilton pointedly asked: "If it is consistent with common-sense to suppose that a provision obliging the legislative power to commit the trial of criminal cases to juries, is a privation of its right to authorize or permit that mode of trial in other cases?"[39] The right to jury trial was seen as the best guarantee against arbitrary use of power by the authority of the court. "In the harsh criminal procedure of the day it was only the jury that could dispense the leaven of mercy, and in civil proceedings it functioned as an immediate corrective for the lack-leaned or overbearing judge."[40] This applied to civil and criminal cases in the colonists' view. And Hamilton certainly appreciated that. Amendments Six and Seven to the Constitution (within the Bill of Rights) attempted to further define and address the concern.

At the Constitutional Convention, while jury trial was specifically called for, jury trial for criminal cases, while not called for, was not prohibited either.

That was Hamilton's argument in *Federalist* 83. However, the problem, as encountered in 1787 in Philadelphia, was "the difficulty ... in attempting to lay down a general rule."[41] As opposed to criminal trials, civil trial proved more cumbersome to apply one approach to. "The practice in the different states varied, and there were some equity and maritime cases in which juries were not admissible."[42]

One of the main reasons opponents obsessed over the issue of trial by jury for so long was that it formed one of the argument points in the Declaration of Independence, as already mentioned. For decades prior to the Revolution, trial by jury had been the standard for protecting the rights of the accused. In the years immediately preceding the American conflict, the right was, from the American perspective, compromised. Thus, it became one of the charges included in the Declaration upon which the Americans placed the justifications for independence. Furthermore, to the "average" Englishman, trial by jury was part of their heritage stretching back over a millennium, to a time when the Saxons, before the arrival of the Normans in 1066, ruled the scattered kingdoms that eventually coalesced into England.

With the completion of *Federalist* 83, the debate over the federal judiciary had nearly run its course. There was nothing left to say, only new ways of saying it, which was wasted breath. Virtually no one by the spring of 1788 was without an opinion on how they would vote on the new Constitution if given the chance. That chance was available to a very select few, but that was another issue.

Among the voting elite would be most of those who made some of the strongest arguments for and against not just the Constitution, but for and against the federal judiciary. All those opinions were grounded in genuine concern for the country and in the experiences of the American War for Independence and the ineffectiveness of the Articles of Confederation. The moment had arrived, and the voting would begin. Delaware cast the first affirmative votes on December 7, 1787, thus becoming forever the first state to ratify the new Constitution. The opposition, had only begun to fight, however.

Opponents

Less than a month after the proposed Constitution was signed, a letter appeared in the Philadelphia *Independent Gazetteer* on October 5, 1787. Written under the name of "Centinel" (Samuel Bryan), the writer sought to show his readers the despotic nature of the proposed new government. Writing specifically about the Supreme Court, Centinel wrote that, per Article III: "the objects of jurisdiction, ... are so numerous, and the shades of distinction between civil causes are oftentimes so slight, that it is more than probable that the state judicatories would be wholly superseded; for in contests about jurisdiction, the federal court, as the most powerful, would ever prevail."[43] This language, while genuine, was very symptomatic of most criticism of the proposed Constitution, and specifically of the national judiciary usurping the power of the state courts. As probably the worst type of insult Bryan could imagine, he compared the power of the federal judiciary under Article III to the English courts. "Every person acquainted with the history of the courts of England, knows by what ingenious sophisms they have, ... extended the sphere of their jurisdiction."[44]

The role of state courts relative to the Supreme Court clearly raised many questions during the ratification period. Symptomatic of that writing was an unknown writer by the name of "A Democratic Federalist." Writing on October 17, 1787, in the Philadelphia *Pennsylvania Herald*, he wondered, "In case of a *conflict of jurisdiction* between the courts of the United States, and those of the several commonwealths, is it not easy to foresee which of the two will obtain the advantage [emphasis in original]?"[45]

Samuel Osgood, writing to Samuel Adams on January 5, 1788, noted with grave concern the power of the proposed federal judiciary headed by a Supreme Court. After raising numerous issues of perceived federal strength at the expense of individual liberty, Osgood ended by lamenting, "I am doubtful whether any instance can be found, where a free people have voluntarily established, so great and so important a supreme judicial court."[46] While not in and of itself a direct attack on the judiciary, Osgood's comment was meant as a warning, not complete praise.

At the Pennsylvania state ratifying convention, those opposed to the Constitution published their concerns in the Philadelphia *Pennsylvania Packet* on December 18, 1787. With the familiar theme of an overpowering federal judiciary, they wrote:

> The judicial powers vested in Congress are also so various and extensive, that by legal ingenuity they may be extended to every case, and thus absorb the states judiciaries, and when we consider the decisive influence that a general judiciary would have over the civil polity of the several states, we do not hesitate to pronounce that this power ... would effect a consolidation of the states under one government.[47]

These were significant arguments and genuinely felt. The proponents however, much as they did during similar debates during the Continental Congress period, held that for a true nation to exist, power had to reside on a national level; that much was uncontestable.

Interestingly, a writer known to history as "Civis Rusticus," writing in the Richmond *Virginia Independent Chronicle* on January 30, 1788, sounded a very similar theme concerning access to the law based on class status. Rusticus wrote "the rich here, as in all other countries, will have an advantage over the poor, in all cases where the services of eminent and learned men are to be commanded by the influence of money."[48]

George Mason, writing in the Alexandria *Virginia Journal* on November 22, 1787, sounded a nearly identical theme, "The judiciary of the United States is so constructed and extended as to absorb and destroy the judiciaries of the several states ... [and] as in England, ... enabling the rich to oppress and ruin the poor."[49] In reply to Mason's assertions, future Supreme Court justice James Iredell, writing as "Marcus," wrote in the Virginia *Norfolk and Portsmouth Journal* on February 27, 1788: "How is this the case? Are not the state judiciaries left uncontrolled as to all the affairs of *that state only*? In this, as in all other cases, where there is a wise distribution, power is commensurate to its object. With the mere internal concerns of a state, congress are to have nothing to do [emphasis in original]."[50]

Colonial courts relied heavily on juries. This is one reason Hamilton felt compelled to include the subject as part of *Federalist* 83, as opponents of the proposed Constitution saw a threat to the jury system. This was not an immediate response to situations the colonists found from the beginning. As an example, in Massachusetts, the jury system slowly came into being over the course of the seventeenth century, which corresponded with the loosening of the control of the church in such matters. "As the churches lost much of their power to influence civic and economic behavior, the courts assumed a role that assisted social integration."[51] In many of these instances, decisions were increasingly based on the English common law combined with locally accepted patterns of behavior. This was especially true after more colonists had the opportunity to become familiar with the common law. "Law must be an organic force, not a static one, or it eventually ceases to be law."[52] This sense of organic law only continued to build during the eighteenth century. Even with a greater reliance on common law, colonists continued to increase their maturity with law to the point whereby after the Revolution America was ready, after several false starts, to embark on an American law leading directly to the Supreme Court.

Many opponents of the Constitution who viewed the judiciary from a negative perspective relative to state law, saw the absence of a guarantee to a jury trial as one of the greatest omissions possible. The eminent jurist James Wilson, future Supreme Court justice, defended this by arguing that the multitude of cases providing a jury trial varied so considerably by state that it would have been impossible to transfer that into the new Constitution. James Wilson's speech at a public meeting on October 6, 1787, concerning trial by jury, included:

> Another objection that has been fabricated against the new constitution, is expressed in this disingenuous form—"the trial by jury is abolished in civil cases." I must be excused ... if upon this point, I take advantage of my professional experience to detect

the futility of the assertion. Let it be remembered then, that the business of the federal convention was not local, but general; not limited to the views and establishments of a single state, but co-extensive with the continent, and comprehending the views and establishments of thirteen independent sovereignties.[53]

Hamilton would deal with this issue in *Federalist* 83, as mentioned. The issue may appear as something of an academic debate, but trial by jury was one of the most cherished aspects of American and English law. The writer known as "A Democratic Federalist," in the Philadelphia *Pennsylvania Herald* on October 17, 1787, found Wilson's defense argument less than convincing. He characterized Wilson's reasoning as "extremely futile."[54]

In a great bit of foreshadowing, a writer known as "Cincinnatus"—likely Arthur Lee—wrote a similar reply to James Wilson concerning the jury issue. In the *New York Journal* on November 1, 1787, Cincinnatus wrote, referencing the famous case of the printer Peter Zinger: "Thus, if the president, vice-president, or any officer, or favorite of state, should be censured in print, he might effectually deprive the printer, or author, of his trial by jury."[55]

As a counterpoint, a writer known simply as "A Citizen of America"— Noah Webster—wrote in Philadelphia on October 17, 1787, that the story about abolition of trial by jury was a fiction concocted by alarmists. Citizen of America wrote, "The fact is, that trial by jury is not affected in *any case*, by the constitution, except in cases of impeachment, which are to be tried by the senate.... The insinuation therefore that trials by jury are to be abolished, is groundless and beyond conception, wicked [emphasis in original]."[56] Clearly, opinions and emotions ran high on both sides. Indeed, even Thomas Jefferson, in France as ambassador, felt the need for a guarantee of trial by jury in the Constitution. The concept of trial by jury was wrapped up in the larger issue of a Bill of Rights, which was taken up by the first Congress. Trial by jury would be guaranteed by the Sixth Amendment.

The draft Constitution of August 6, 1787, had the issue of trial by jury squarely dealt with: "The trial of all criminal offenses (except in cases of impeachment) shall be in the state where they shall be committed; and shall be by jury."[57] This language appears nearly verbatim in the final version of the Constitution, Article III. It would be strengthened by the Sixth Amendment in the Bill of Rights. In an era of more territory than states, the Convention even considered a clause ensuring a jury trial for crimes committed in a territory without a distinct state government. This is yet another indication of how important this concept was to the delegates and Americans at large.

In a speech in Edenton, North Carolina, on November 8, 1787, Hugh Williamson, a signer of the Constitution, stated that, "the objects that are now to be submitted to the Supreme Judiciary, ... are those which naturally arise from the constitutional laws of Congress."[58] His comments were reprinted in the New York press in February 1788. Williamson can be seen as trying to neutralize concerns some had over the potentially expansive powers of the Supreme Court. Williamson, as many supporters of the proposed Constitution argued, focused on the national power of the court, not the imagined power over the states. In anticipation of Brutus's arguments four months later, Williamson stated that complaints about the power of the Supreme Court were unfounded: "This objection appears to have the greatest weight in the eyes of gentlemen who have not carefully compared the powers which are to be delegated with those that had been delegated to Congress."[59] This is because "the powers of judiciary naturally arise from those of the legislative."[60]

Williamson was arguing that many of the expressed powers enumerated in the proposed Constitution already existed in theory in the Articles of Confederation—a document that, while approved by all the states, was generally ignored.

Brutus

One of the more sustained criticisms of the Supreme Court came from the writer known as "Brutus." In Brutus' essay eleven, from the *New York Journal* of January 31, 1788, Brutus lashed out at the proposed powers of the federal judiciary, especially the Supreme Court. According to Brutus, he has "not met with any writer, who has discussed the judicial powers with any degree of accuracy."[61] In January 1788, the *Federalist* essays dealing specifically with the Court had yet to be published. So, the main newspaper argument on behalf of the federal judiciary was still to come. The Anti-Federalist position essentially "owned" the argument in the beginning. The proponent side of the judiciary debate, aside from James Wilson in October 1787, had not been fully articulated. Brutus was not unaware of the great potential power of the Supreme Court; he pointed out that the Court would answer for every aspect of the new American government proposed by the Constitution. Brutus wrote: "The real effect of this system of government, will therefore be brought home to the feelings of the people, through the medium of the judicial power."[62] Brutus also pointed out the centrality of law in America and under the proposed Constitution. As with all aspects of human government, Brutus was particularly concerned with those who are entrusted with power using it appropriately—he wanted to ensure that the judges would "exercise [power] for the general good."[63] However Brutus saw the state judiciaries as particularly vulnerable: "Though I am not competent to give a perfect explanation of the powers granted to this department of the government, I shall yet attempt to trace some of the leading features of it, from which I presume it will appear, that they will operate to a total submission of the state judiciaries, if not, to the legislative authority of the states."[64] As we have seen, this was a constant, well-articulated concern of those opposed to the proposed Constitution. Even some who supported the Constitution had similar, though less strident, concerns.

The writer known as Brutus wrote again on the power of the Supreme Court. In two separate essays, published a week apart in the *New York Journal*—on February 7 and 14, 1788—he laid out increasingly familiar language concerning the great power of the proposed Supreme Court. In fact, the arguments raised by Brutus have been used against the Court ever since. Brutus, and those who thought as he did, saw the issue of the Court in very human terms. They were not concerned with the Court responding to, and judging cases of law that were clearly presented, without room for equivocation. What Brutus, and many ever since, bemoaned was the area of law which is not black and white, the area of law which enriches lawyers and bankrupts those accused. The gray area, the soft middle, the parts of law open to interpretation are what Brutus and many Anti-Federalists feared. Their fear was that human judges, given a coalition of like-minded colleagues with whom to adjudicate, would fall prey to human nature and follow their instinct to rule in favor of their personal interest. As Brutus would write:

> I showed, that the judicial power of the United States ... would be authorized to explain the constitution, not only according to its letter, but according to its spirit and intention; and having this power, they would strongly incline to give it such construction as to extend the powers of the general government, ... to the diminution, and finally to the destruction, of that of the respective states.[65]

Part of the argument, as Brutus saw it, was the loss of power of the legislature, the voice of the people. If the Supreme Court "has the power ... to determine all questions that may arise in the course of legal discussion, on the meaning and construction of the constitution," then what would become of the so-called *vox populi* (the voice of the people)? In essence, how could the people be said to possess power through the legislature if the Supreme Court could declare null and void actions of the legislature?

Brutus further set forth to deconstruct the preamble to the Constitution. He sought to show how the simple, yet powerful, words of the opening paragraph contained the dimensions of the power the Court would have. The simple phrase "to ensure domestic tranquility," for instance, Brutus saw as containing within "its spirit ... to subvert and abolish all the powers of the state government, and to embrace every object to which any government extends."[66] Brutus summed up his thoughts in the following manner: "From these remarks it is easy to see, that in proportion as the general government acquires power and jurisdiction, by the liberal construction which the judges may give the constitution, will those states lose its rights, until they become so trifling and unimportant, as not to be worth having."[67] On the same date (February 7, 1788) that Brutus was publishing his essays, George Washington was writing to the Marquis de Lafayette. Writing from Mount Vernon, Washington's letter emphatically seemed to counterbalance Brutus's essay. There is no indication whatsoever that Washington was aware of Brutus's thoughts, though, when he wrote: "That the general government is not invested with more powers than are indispensably necessary to perform the functions of a good government; and consequently, that no objection ought to be made against the quantity of power delegated to it."[68] The difference between Brutus and Washington was their audience. Brutus wrote for the literate public; whereas Washington wrote for one high-strung Frenchman whom he saw as a son. Whether Washington would have been as demonstrative in a public letter is unknown, yet, his definitive declaration was certainly as well-meaning as Brutus's.

On February 21, 1788, Brutus continued his examination of the Constitution and the Supreme Court. Specifically, in an end-of-February essay, Brutus cautioned against the specter of a citizen of one state suing another state. As Brutus wrote, "The situation of the states will be deplorable. By this system, they will surrender to the government, all the means of raising money, and at the same time, will subject themselves to suits at law, for the recovery of the debts they have contracted in effecting the revolution."[69] This topic will be covered in much greater depth later during the case of *Chisholm v. Georgia* (1793)—a decision which directly led to the passage of the Eleventh Amendment. The central argument, without getting too far ahead, was that debts contracted during the Revolution should be paid by the debtor, which in many cases were the states. Many claimed they should not be held liable for debts incurred during the War as they were agreed to under a quasi-governmental setting. The proponents of the Constitution saw this as hair splitting. For a legitimate government to emerge from the quagmire of the 1780s, debt incurred by obligation had to be held sacrosanct, if for no other reason than to ensure the sanctity of contracts in the future. This topic will be reviewed in Chapter 5.

One writer contrary to Brutus was James Winthrop. Writing as "Agrippa" in the Boston *Massachusetts Gazette* on February 5, 1788, he argued for a Supreme Court of exceptionally limited scope:

> The judicial department shall be confined to cases in which ambassadors are concerned, to cases depending upon treaties, to offences committed upon the high seas, to the capture of prizes, and to cases in which a foreigner residing in some foreign country shall be a party, and an American state or citizen shall be the other party.[70]

While Brutus was publishing his essays, a writer known as "The Impartial Examiner" was drawing similar conclusions. In an essay published in the Richmond, Virginia, *Independent Chronicle*, on February 27, 1788, The Impartial Examiner wrote: "The Supreme Court is another branch of federal authority, which wears the aspect of imperial jurisdiction, clad in dread array, and spreading its wide domain into all parts of the continent."[71] Indicating the raw newness of a Supreme Court, The Impartial Examiner continued: "Here is a system of jurisprudence to be erected, no less surprising than it is new and unusual. Here is an innovation, which bears no kind of analogy to anything, that Englishmen, or Americans, the descendants of Englishmen, have ever yet experienced."[72]

Brutus also found fault with the Supreme Court's original jurisdiction in cases involving ambassadors and foreign ministers. Brutus pointed out that foreign representatives have certain privileges already under international law and the law of nations. "The meanest servant of an ambassador is exempted by the law of nations from being sued for debt."[73] What Brutus saw as problematic was a scenario where a citizen filed a suit against a foreign representative or their staff, and thus was drawn into a Supreme Court case at great expense to the bringer of the suit. Brutus found this excessive for instances that may involve small debts and could be handled at a lower level rather than automatically going to the Supreme Court.

Brutus further found cause with the Supreme Court's appellate power, especially concerning criminal cases. Brutus wrote, "I believe it is a new and unusual thing to allow appeals in criminal matters. It is contrary to the sense of our laws, and dangerous to the lives and liberties of the citizen. As our law now stands, a person charged with a crime has a right to a fair and impartial trial by a jury of his country, and their verdict is final."[74] Brutus saw these as impacting defendants negatively. Suppose someone accused of a crime was acquitted. In Brutus's reading of the proposed Article III of the Constitution, this defendant could then be liable to another trial if the losing prosecutor appealed to the Supreme Court. The double jeopardy amendment dealt with this issue in the Bill of Rights. Brutus reflected "I can scarcely believe there can be a considerate citizen of the United States, that will approve of this appellate jurisdiction, as extending to criminal cases."[75] Brutus was quite prescient, predicting that American law, as outlined in the proposed Constitution, would become "intolerably burthensome, intricate, and dilatory" if, as proposed, the administration of justice would advance as suggested.[76] Brutus saw little wrong with the way justice was administered at the state level. In fact:

> This method would preserve the good old way of administering justice, would bring justice to every man's door, and preserve the inestimable right of trial by jury. It would be following, as near as our circumstances will admit, the practice of the courts in England, which is almost the only thing I would wish to copy in their government.[77]

Up to this point, every argument encountered has been, as far as is known, by a man. Mercy Otis Warren was a force to be reckoned with. A sister of James Otis (of the Writs of Assistance case in 1761), she was married to the influential James Warren. A friend of Abigail Adams, Mercy Warren was also a well-known historian, playwright, and essayist. Writing from Boston in February 1788, under the name of "A Columbian Patriot," she expressed her doubts about the proposed Constitution and the role of the federal judiciary. She wrote:

> There are no well defined limits of the judiciary powers, they seem to be left as a boundless ocean, that has broken over the chart of the Supreme Lawgiver..., and as they cannot be comprehended by the clearest capacity, or the most sagacious mind, it would be an Herculean labor to attempt to describe the dangers with which they are replete.[78]

While not specific, Mercy Warren leaves no doubt she is not a proponent of the new Supreme Court as proposed. One area where she does go into detail is jury trial. Her comments also show her extensive knowledge of legal matters (it is worth noting that Mercy's great-great-grandson was Charles Warren, a famed legal scholar and historian of the Supreme Court):

> The abolition of trial by jury in civil cases—This mode of trial the learned Judge Blackstone observes, 'has been coeval with the first rudiments of civil government, that property, liberty and life, depend on maintaining in its force the constitutional trial by jury.' He bids his readers pause, and with Sir Matthew Hale [a noted legal historian] observes, how admirably this mode is adapted to the investigation of truth beyond any other the world can produce.[79]

During the battle over ratification of the Constitution, when essays and articles were being written weekly, when *The Federalist* papers were saturating the

Stained glass window dedicated to the memory of legal scholar and historian Charles Warren, "Spirit of Law I," 1959. By Napoleon Setti (Washington National Cathedral).

public sphere, no writer attacked the Supreme Court, and Article III which created the Court, more than Brutus. Perhaps it is fitting to give the last word to this unidentified writer, clearly learned in the law, who waged an anonymous campaign to alter the level of support for the proposed Constitution. In March 1788, in one of his last appearances in print, he wrote, "perhaps nothing could have been better conceived to facilitate the abolition of the state governments than the constitution of the judicial."[80]

On June 19, 1788, George Mason embarked on a quixotic journey concerning the federal judiciary at the Virginia state ratifying convention. Similar to Brutus, George Mason, at the convention in June 1788, stated, "when we come to the judiciary, we shall be more convinced, that this government will terminate in the annihilation of the state governments."[81] Mason, a delegate to the Philadelphia convention in 1787 (he did not sign the final version), questioned the role of state judiciaries under the Supreme Court. Mason stated, "I should not tell my sentiments upon it [the Supreme Court], did I not conceive it to be so constructed as to destroy the dearest rights of the community ... what is there left to the state courts. Will gentlemen be pleased, candidly, fairly, and without sophistry, to show us what remains?"[82]

Mason, and those of his persuasion, were greatly troubled by the specter of federal treaty obligations being imposed on states against their will. At the time, in 1788, this meant the 1783 Paris Peace Treaty, and others which could be similar, requiring states to follow laws they did not agree with, specifically treaty requirements respecting the rights of British creditors and former loyalists. Most states openly violated the provisions and maintained discriminatory laws in place in direct violation of national treaties passed by the Continental Congress, still technically the governing body of the United States. Mason voiced this point when he said that "there is not, in my opinion, a single British creditor, but who can bring his debtors to the federal court."[83] To a greater or lesser extent the arguments used by opponents of the proposed Constitution, when considering the national judiciary and the Supreme Court, were remarkably similar. The feelings, fears, and frustrations ran high among those opposing the Constitution. Some saw it as a betrayal of the fight for independence.

Another compelling point Mason brought, as did many of his supporters, was how would the Supreme Court enforce its decisions over states? Mason thought that the Court could not. And therefore, "a power which cannot be executed, ought not to be granted."[84] In other words, Mason was arguing that it was absurd to give the Supreme Court power it could not enforce. Yet, for proponents of the Court, this issue was the bedrock of a unified country; and recent events under the Articles of Confederation, which lacked a national judiciary, proved the necessity of such a court. Future Supreme Court Chief Justice John Marshall pointed this out in his speech before the Virginia state ratifying convention. On June 20, 1788, Marshall stated, the inclusion of a national judiciary was "a great improvement on that system from which we are now departing. Here are tribunals appointed for the decision of controversies, which were before, either not at all, or improperly provided for."[85]

At the North Carolina state ratifying convention, on July 29, 1788 (after the Constitution had already formally gone into effect), Samuel Spencer noted some of the arguments that opponents had been making—federal law being higher than state law, and the issue of trial by jury. Spencer put his argument thus: "In the clause that has been read, it is ascertained that criminal cases are to be tried by jury, in the states wherein they are committed. It has been objected to that clause, that it is not sufficiently explicit. I think that it is not."[86] Spencer pointed out that one of the grievances against Britain during the Revolution was opposition to those charged with a crime being sent to Britain for trial in some cases. As Jefferson put it in the Declaration of Independence: "For depriving us in many cases, of the benefits of trial by jury; for transporting us beyond seas to be tried for pretended offenses." Spencer argued that more precise language should be included in the Constitution; he got his wish later in the Bill of Rights.

William Davie, speaking in North Carolina the day after Spencer, was more accepting and supportive of the Constitution, especially the federal judiciary. Reflecting on the power of the Supreme Court in cases of citizens of one state in suit against citizens of another, Davie stated: "Without a general controlling judiciary, laws might be made in particular states to enable its citizens to defraud the citizens of other states. [Further, states] might pass the most iniquitous laws, procrastinating the payment of debts due from their citizens."[87] Respecting suits between citizens of different states, Davie summarized, "the security of impartiality is the principal reason for giving up the ultimate decision of controversies between citizens of different states."[88]

Conclusion

Like a set of nesting dolls, the drama of the fight over a national judiciary and a supreme court was part of the larger drama of the writing and passage of the Constitution, which in turn was part of the larger drama resultant from the American War for Independence, which finally, was part of the much larger global angst of the eighteenth century. This should not be surprising, history did not happen in a vacuum and it should not be understood as such.

The struggle over the judiciary, if we use an arbitrary date, started with the Constitutional Convention, which began on May 25, 1787. Under this scenario, it could be seen to have ended when the required ninth state (New Hampshire) ratified the Constitution on June 21, 1788, thus making the Constitution, along with Article III and the federal judiciary and the new Supreme Court, the law of the land. The next step was for the new government to physically assemble and start business on March 4, 1789. One of the most important pieces of legislation to face the new Congress, for our purposes, was the creation of the federal judiciary as called for in Article III of the new Constitution. That piece of legislation, a landmark of the first Congress of 1789–1791, was the Judiciary Act of 1789. It is this Act that the next chapter will be concerned with.

3

The Judiciary Act of 1789

The Judiciary Act of 1789 was an immense piece of legislation—size-wise and policy-wise. This makes sense given the enormity of the task of creating the federal judiciary as called for under Article III of the new Constitution, and time was of necessity. The new United States was operating and the legal infrastructure it needed to function had to be in place. The first federal Congress, 1789–1791, had the task of preparing the multitude of bills necessary to make the law (after signature by the president) to set in motion the working government.

Overview

The outline of how the Judiciary Act moved through Congress is well documented. On May 11, 1789, the Senate Judiciary Sub-Committee had debated enough to draft a bill. On June 12, 1789, the full Senate Judiciary Committee met to debate the draft bill. The large-scale printing of the draft bill occurred on June 15, with both Senate and House members receiving copies.[1] The Senate passed their version on July 17 and sent it to the House for consideration.

On July 23, 1789, the printer Thomas Greenleaf delivered one hundred copies of the Senate-passed Judiciary Act to the House for debate.[2] The House took until September 17 (exactly two years after signing the Constitution in Philadelphia) to finally pass their version of the Senate's version. The House and Senate resolved their differences within a week and President Washington signed the Act into law on September 24, 1789.

James Madison, the "Father of the Constitution" and congressman from Virginia, would play an outsized role in the first Congress, just as he did at the Philadelphia convention in 1787. Not surprisingly, Madison's enemies tried to keep him from political office, much as they tried to derail ratification of the Constitution in the Virginia state ratifying convention. Once again,

Madison's chief opponent, the arch Anti-Federalist Patrick Henry, did his best to keep Madison out of the new government. Henry, according to Madison's friend and colleague George Turberville, even went so far as to declare when Madison was a Senate candidate—in typical Henry theatrics—that a victory for Madison as Senator "would terminate in producing rivulets of blood throughout the land."[3] Such ridiculous language did actually keep Madison from being chosen as a senator from Virginia, but did not preclude him from winning election as a representative, although not for Henry's lack of trying to prevent that election too. Being a representative rather than a senator probably worked out better in the long run as most of the nuts and bolts of getting the required legislation actually began in the House of Representatives. The new House of Representatives reached a quorum in New York on April 1, 1789, with Madison among the first to arrive. Madison's superior knowledge of the Constitution and the Congress would be of great benefit later during the debate on the Bill of Rights—the first ten amendments to the Constitution.

While the Senate can be said to have initiated more legislation in the first Congress, it was far from a contest. Historian George Galloway wrote this overview of the subject:

> The House and Senate divided the honors in originating [the] vast legislative output. The bills creating the new departments, the financial measures, the tariff bill, and the bill for the assumption of the state debts started in the House of Representatives.... The Senate took the initiative ... for incorporating the first bank of the United States, and it originated the procedure for the organization of new states and territories. The Senate also took the lead in the measures establishing the judicial courts of the United States, regulating their procedure, and providing for the punishment of crimes against the United States.[4]

With the House of Representatives safely guided by Madison, the Senate debate on the federal judiciary would find two capable leaders in Senator Oliver Ellsworth of Connecticut and Senator William Paterson of New Jersey. These two men, both future Supreme Court justices (Ellsworth as chief), would shoulder the burden of crafting and marshaling the forces necessary for the passage of the Judiciary Act. In fact, in many ways, the Act was a direct result of their work; Ellsworth and Paterson, whose contributions will be reviewed, can rightly be hailed as the "Fathers of the Judiciary Act" as surely as Madison is the "Father of the Constitution."

The subcommittee responsible for developing a working draft consisted of Senator's Paterson and Ellsworth, and Senator Caleb Strong of Massachusetts. This subcommittee of the Senate Judiciary Committee took up their work by early May 1789. Within a month, the sub-committee had produced a working draft from which the full Judiciary Committee began to debate. Within a week, the full Senate was debating the draft.

Perhaps the Senate was the best place, whether by coincidence or planning, to have started the legislation on the federal judiciary. As has been pointed out, Senator's Ellsworth and Paterson were two of the most capable of legislators and two of the most capable legal statesmen serving in the Congress. As future Supreme Court justices, they were particularly well situated to be present at the creation of the branch of the government that they were to eventually lead. Whether either man wrote the legislation with an eye toward leading the federal judiciary is doubtful though.

Inevitably, the heavy hand of Patrick Henry, who had maneuvered to keep Madison out of the Senate, was immediately felt. Henry's two choices as Virginia senators, Richard Henry Lee and William Grayson, both nearly as vociferous as Henry, introduced a plan that would have severely limited the lower federal courts. The two Senators "proposed to limit the jurisdiction of the lower federal courts to admiralty cases. Thus, the state courts would be the trial courts of the federal system and, except for admiralty, all issues would come to the Supreme Court either on appeal from the states or as an original trial."[5] This may seem innocuous, but it would have left the federal courts with little to do. Both the Senate and the House rejected this plan. Other plans, of varying seriousness, were put forward and quickly rejected. Oliver Ellsworth's proposed plan was the result of compromise thinking, just like the Constitution itself. Ellsworth sought to find common ground with the Anti-Federalists who opposed the Constitution, and Article III, from the beginning. This was essential for moving the country forward, and Ellsworth was mature enough to put the most tasteless aspects of partisanship aside. Ellsworth's plan first and foremost assigned federal court jurisdiction to "cases 'arising under' the Constitution, laws, or treaties" as the province of state courts, "and appeal to the Supreme Court *only* 1) from *final* decisions in the *highest* court of a state, and 2) where the state court had ruled *against* the federal law in question [emphasis in original]."[6]

As debates in Congress over the federal judiciary began, it raised a multitude of questions right from the start. Those questions engaged the members of Congress, as well as the public. Daniel Carroll, writing on May 22, 1789, as discussion was just getting underway, wondered if an alcohol tax, or stamp tax (a great irony given the role of the British Stamp Act of 1765 in America) was needed to fund justice in the United States? Carroll wrote, "Would not an excise on ardent spirits, foreign and domestic be advisable? Stamp duties I hope may be collected to defray the expense of the federal judiciary."[7]

Significantly, Ellsworth placed issues of non–Americans, or out of state citizens, in the jurisdiction of federal courts, but only where a five-hundred-dollar minimum was at stake. "This provision eliminated at one stroke about half the British debts from federal court, including all of the smallest ones most troubling to Anti-Federalists."[8] For an appeal to the Supreme Court, a two-thousand-dollar threshold was established. Finally, only appeals on a writ of error could be entertained by the Supreme Court, thus ensuring only questions of law would be considered on appeal, not questions of fact, thereby ensuring "no jury verdicts would be overturned."[9] The statement in Article III of the Constitution dealing with the power of the Supreme Court to have appellate jurisdiction for both law and fact struck many as an attempt by the federal government to intrude on state judicial affairs. It was feared that this provision, without some modification, "would enable the rich litigant to abuse the poor litigant. Furthermore, it would deprive litigants of trial before a jury drawn from the same locality as the commission of the crime."[10]

Both of these points were raised before by opponents of the Constitution. By having jury decisions reviewed by the federal government (Supreme Court) on appeal, many felt that local control of such a basic right was being lost. This was one argument which was leveled against King George III in the Declaration of Independence. Secondly, the whole issue of citizenship was another favorite topic of opponents of the Constitution who saw an erosion of state sovereignty by the ability of non-state citizens, or non–Americans, to sue their citizens in federal court. Worst of all was the fear that a citizen of one state would sue another state—this would be an area where the Supreme Court would have original jurisdiction and will be covered in Chapter 5. These were genuine fears and they caused years of debate and maneuvering for power.

The Senate

Senator Oliver Ellsworth of Connecticut, a future Supreme Court chief justice, can be given the principle role in bringing the strong theoretical writing of Alexander Hamilton in *The Federalist* papers in favor of the federal judiciary into practical form through his role in the Senate.[11] Ellsworth was particularly well suited to be in this position. In 1788, he was a proponent of ratification and a delegate to the Connecticut state ratifying convention (and in Philadelphia for the Constitutional Convention) for the new Constitution. By no means concerned with the threat of too much federal judicial power at the expense of the states, Ellsworth argued that a strong judiciary should in fact have the most latitude relative to the power of Congress. States by inference (as Ellsworth commented) would not have to be unduly concerned with Congress enacting unconstitutional legislation (thus presumably infringing on state sovereignty). "If the United States go beyond their powers, if they make a law which the constitution does not authorize, it is void; and the judicial power, the national judges, who to secure their impartiality are to be made independent, will declare it to be void [very similar in language to *Federalist*

78]."[12] However, Ellsworth continued, the issue which could not be countenanced by opponents of the proposed judiciary was the fact that "if the states go beyond their limits, if they make a law which is an usurpation upon the general government, the law is void, and upright independent judges will declare it to be so."[13]

The Oliver Ellsworth and William Paterson judiciary plan in the Senate had several major points. First, restrictions limited the jurisdiction of the federal courts to cases directly relating to constitutional issues that had first been heard by state courts and subsequently appealed to the Supreme Court, only if the state court had ruled against the federal law in question.[14] This again related to the issue of the Supreme Court reviewing the facts of a case, something opponents of a strong Court could not tolerate as they feared the overturning of jury decisions. They saw the Court's review of case facts as a clear violation of state sovereignty. This was in part a holdover of the ancient common law concept of trying a case where the crime occurred, as opposed to some remote location removed from the locus of the facts.

A second major feature of the Ellsworth plan allowed for "out-of-state" citizens to have their cases heard directly in a state court if the case involved less than $500.00, thus removing most repayment issues out of federal control and into state control. This became a controversial issue when the federal government no longer had power over half of the claims filed against Americans. The Paris Peace Treaty of 1783 clearly stipulated that no impediments would stand between a British creditor and his American debtor. Only a powerful federal judiciary could enforce this policy and now it was taken out of federal control and placed in state control. For obvious reasons, this worried many British creditors and many American proponents of a strong central government. The Court was therefore thrust into a position in these cases of having its decision play a major role in United States foreign policy. Supreme Court cases involving British creditor claims would occur throughout the 1790s.

The overall goal of the United States, if state courts heard British creditor cases, was to enhance its reputation as a serious, respectable nation, founded on a constitutional basis which could ensure that contracted debts would be fulfilled. A major part of the foreign policy initiative of the United States sprang from a two-pronged system. Hence, not only would the United States gain recognition on a national level, but from a domestic standpoint the shared responsibility of economic standardization would tend to bind the population together. In a sense, domestic and foreign economic initiatives would essentially be one.

Finally, in a further attempt to mollify the proponents of state-centered jurisprudence, the Supreme Court appellate jurisdiction would be limited to those appeals granted through a "writ of error only."[15] A writ of error refers to an order (writ) from the appellate court (in this instance the Supreme Court) to the court of record (where the initial case was tried) to relinquish the proceedings of a case for appellate review for possible errors of law. In essence, this meant that the verdicts of state juries could not be called into question and thus their convictions in cases could not be overturned by the federal judiciary, thus in theory maintaining state sovereignty. This clause therefore ensured the supremacy of state court decisions and only allowed for federal review in cases where established proceedings were not followed.

The Anti-Federalist opponents of the Act in the Senate (mostly the same Anti-Federalist members who opposed ratification of the Constitution a year earlier) were thrilled with the measure of sovereignty they could retain for individual state judiciaries. The Federalists in the Senate (mostly those who supported ratification of the Constitution a year earlier) were just as anxious to create a federal judiciary that had the ability to bring some order out of the chaos of federal jurisprudence. Without order, the essence of the *United States* would be dramatically reduced because no solidifying quality of law would be present.[16]

Most Federalists believed they had compromised too much for the passage of the Judiciary Act and thus saw it as a temporary measure subject to modification in the near future.[17] (This is similar to what James Iredell argued for opponents of the Constitution to take solace in earlier in the process— changes were possible.) Congressman Fisher Ames commented the Act would be "a short experiment [that] will make manifest the proper alterations."[18] This commentary, short of condemnation, but hardly a ringing endorsement, in a certain manner foreshadowed the development of the Court during the 1790s, when it appeared to lack the total conviction (demonstrated in the political squabbles over the Judiciary Act) to assert the power granted it.

As provided by the Act, each state would be assigned a district court staffed by one federal judge. Each state would also be part of a circuit within which a circuit court would sit. This court would have assigned staff; further, each Supreme Court justice would be assigned a circuit and would ride this circuit at prescribed intervals. In theory, this would bring members of the Supreme Court to the people of the country, thus strengthening the bond between the people and the federal government establishment.[19]

This personal interaction also served to "humanize" the federal system, in essence making physical the "We the People" preamble of the Constitution to an extent everyone could see and thus would hopefully understand. On the negative side, circuit riding would also become one of the bitterest aspects of service on the Supreme Court, and justices routinely complained about the arduous travel.

James Sullivan wrote to Elbridge Gerry in March 1789, "The freedom of the people depends so much upon the proper arrangement of this part [the judiciary] of the Government."[20] The creation of circuit courts was reminiscent of the military districts utilized during the Revolution. The idea for circuit courts, where Supreme Court justices traveled twice yearly on their appointed Circuit, was a reflection of the English practice wherein, "Judicial personnel of the court of Westminster [traveled] to dispense justice in the country, sometimes but not invariably in association with local officials."[21] In this way, the Supreme Court carried the mantle of national government. Senator Paterson of New Jersey commented in 1789 that the circuit courts would bring "law to their [citizens] homes, courts to their doors, [and] meet every citizen in his own state."[22] Similarly, Chief Justice John Jay, in his charge to the grand jury of the circuit court in New York in 1790, intoned the purpose of his presence on circuit was to bring "justice as it were to every man's door."[23] In short, there was a greater likelihood that a person would see a Supreme Court justice than any other member of the national government on a somewhat regular basis. For example, Chief Justice Jay, when on circuit, was probably better known (although Washington was obviously well traveled), by appearance, than either of the heads of the executive or legislative branches.

This brought the meaning of the national government to the people in a way the executive and legislative branches could not. Through this, communities actually saw the government at work, not only dispensing justice, but, more importantly, pulling the loose threads of confederation more tightly together. Nathaniel Sargent wrote to John Adams in April 1789 that the Supreme Court, through circuit riding, would "strengthen government in [the] extreme parts."[24] Justices on circuit frequently reminded listeners through their grand jury charges of "the benefits to be derived from—and obligations owed to—the federal government, including the federal courts."[25] In a manner of speaking, it created a legal culture which everyone could participate in and come to see as their own.

The Grand Jury Charge

The power of the grand jury charge should not be overlooked either. Given that the six justices ventured out twice a year on circuit duty, it would be interesting to compare the style and tonal quality of the charges. No doubt some element of drafting a grand jury charge would take in the local issues which the justices would face in any given area. The political aspects of a grand jury charge, if they were ever political, would indicate too the engagement of the justices to tailor their comments to the particular area and thus perhaps "focus" their remarks. "It was in the performance of their circuit duties and in particular in presenting charges to the grand juries that the Justices took sides on some of the political issues of the day, and it was here that the first friction arose between the federal Judiciary and the state agencies that were jealous of their rights and prerogatives."[26]

With the population stretched across the vast expanse of the eastern seaboard and west to the Mississippi River, cultural connections on a national scale were generally absent. The one element all the disparate culturally affiliated groups (admittedly not the Native Americans or the enslaved) could identify with was a government which bound them together. The Supreme Court would bear the burden of binding together the unbound notions of the federal government through the judiciary. Without this adhesive function, disparity would likely reign in the administration of justice. Furthermore, how could the people even know what judicial system they lived under if the judiciary did not come to them? As the *Albany Register* commented in January 1789, "Have we not neglected to secure to ourselves the weighty matter of judgment or justice, by empowering the General Government to establish one supreme, and as many inferior courts as they please, whose proceedings they have a right to fix and regulate as they shall think fit; so that we are ignorant, whether they will be according to the common, the civil, the Jewish or the Turkish law?"[27] Over the long term, this may well have been the finest contribution of the Supreme Court during its first decade. The Supreme Court, through the justices on circuit, helped to define the parameters of the American constitutional system of jurisprudence to which all were responsible. Everyone, regardless of whether they came from Europe, Asia, South America, or points in between or beyond, theoretically were bound together by one government, and one set of rules. This idea of uniformity played a central role in the creation of the judiciary. The underlining theme of those who advised Congress in 1789 was to ensure the system "would be uniform throughout," and "that every state would be obedient to it."[28]

Conclusion in the Senate

Senator Ellsworth was fully aware of the immense appellate power granted the Supreme Court and what this potentially meant for lower federal courts and state courts. Senator Ellsworth proposed "limiting the Supreme Court's jurisdiction to specific situations in which there was an obvious and direct interest in assuring a federal court review of a particular issue."[29] Concerning the state courts, Senator Ellsworth's plan stated, "The Court's appellate authority over state courts extended to specific issues governed by positive, written federal laws."[30]

The conclusion of section twenty-five of the Judiciary Act of 1789 reflected Senator Ellsworth's concern over the appellate power. It read in part, "no other error shall be ... regarded as a ground of reversal in any such case as aforesaid, than such as ... immediately respects the before mentioned questions of validity or construction of the said constitution, treaties, statues, commissions or authorities."[31] To further clarify the Supreme Court's appellate authority over lower federal courts, the Supreme Court was "given a general authority to review all legal issues regardless of whether they were controlled by written federal law, written state law, or the unwritten common law."[32] In the delicate balance of federal versus state judicial power, Senator Ellsworth attempted to craft legislation "to defuse all possible objections."[33] The Supreme Court would be limited "to a narrow range of clearly defined federal laws" when reviewing state court legal issues, not factual issues.[34] This ensured a reasonable area of state court autonomy would be respected. It was a compromise of necessity, "wholly sensitive to the variety of criticisms that had been directed at the judicial."[35]

The final product of the Senate committee which eventually became the Judiciary Act of 1789 was sent out to distinguished jurists for comment in draft form. It was not generally well received, in its particulars, predictably given the power granted the federal judiciary at the expense of the states. As an example, John Dickinson and Gunning Bedford, Jr. (both signers of the Constitution) were both highly regarded attorneys and political leaders in Delaware (Dickinson was also associated with Philadelphia) who read and commented on the draft bill. Both men were highly learned in legal theory and practice. Dickinson was one of the most learned in the new country, having spent several years studying at the Inns of Court (Middle Temple) in London where only the most talented and wealthy of American sons were sent in the pre–Revolutionary era. Dickinson, in a letter to another prominent Delaware attorney, George Read, commented that he found the draft "the most difficult to be understood of any legislative bill I ever read."[36] Gunning Bedford, on the other hand, felt it a "noble work," although he too had difficulty in following the reasoning at times.[37] Edmund Randolph of Virginia, soon to be the first attorney general, commented in a similar way concerning the jurisdiction of the Supreme Court as having been described in the Judiciary Act as "inartificially, untechnically and confusedly worded."[38]

The House of Representatives

On May 10, 1789, Joseph Jones likened the new government to a great machine, whose engine was the judiciary. Writing to James Madison, Jones stated: "The organization of the judiciary which the senate had undertaken will I apprehend be found a labor of great difficulty—one important object should be invariably pursued which is not to incur more expense than is indispensably necessary for moving smoothly forward the great machine."[39] The work on the judiciary was followed with great interest by those not involved in the process. Writing on May 28, 1789, Joseph Jones asked James Madison "if you can pray give me a sketch of what is intended" for the judiciary?[40] Part of the reason for such interest in the federal judiciary was that of the three branches, the judiciary was most prone to impact, directly or indirectly, each state. The executive and legislative branches certainly had the possibility of impacting the states, but with control of elections, each state had some leverage to bring to bear on these two branches of the government. That was not, however, the case with the federal judiciary. And hence, the great interest in what was being planned in Congress in 1789.

Two months later, Jones (an Anti-Federalist Virginian politician and attorney who graduated from the Inns of Court in 1751) made an observation that others had considered. It has been mentioned that the Judiciary Act of 1789 was an immense piece of legislation—both in terms of length and scope it undertook to define, which was nothing less than the entire federal judiciary. Jones, writing to James Madison on July 3, 1789, observed:

> I have seen a copy of the bill establishing the judiciary and from the cursory reading I have given it the different powers and jurisdictions of the Courts would have been more clearly seen had they been taken up in several bills, each describing the province and boundary of the court which it particularly applied ... in so extensive a country as the United States every precaution, consistent with the right of appeal, should be interposed to prevent inconvenience and legal oppression.[41]

According to Jones, he too thought the legislation was too immense and unwieldy a document. He envisioned a separate bill for each court established to include their unique areas of operation. This would have perhaps made the federal judiciary clearer, but it would have put an overwhelming burden on the Congressmen. Separate bills would have been more prone to manipulation and influence peddling. While hard to imagine, even in the first Congress, these threats existed. Plus, the time necessary to individually piece together the federal judiciary was not available, it clearly had to be an omnibus piece of legislation to get the country moving and working.

In a lengthy letter to Thomas Jefferson, still in France as the American ambassador (and not a disinterested party to the new government), James Madison, on June 30, 1789, alluded to the difficult work pertaining to the creation of the judiciary. "The Senate have in hand a bill for the Judiciary Department. It is found a pretty arduous task and will probably be long on its way through the two houses."[42] Jefferson was someone Madison could write to in a familiar style. With Jefferson, even 3,000 miles away, Madison did not have to guard his language. His assessment of the situation in Congress Jefferson both welcomed and encouraged. With the federal judiciary, Madison was aware of the difficulties and pitfalls associated with bringing such an organization to life. As pointed out above, the federal judiciary was far more problematic than the legislative and executive branches as far as the states were concerned. While Hamilton in *Federalist* 78 likened the Supreme Court to a powerless and penniless vagabond, the Court was certainly more than that— or at least had the potential to be more, much more.

Surprisingly, Madison sent a copy of the draft Judiciary Act bill to Edmund Randolph. Randolph, who introduced Madison's Virginia Plan to the Constitutional Convention in May 1787, would refuse to sign the final product of the Convention. Yet, he still held power in Virginia and was someone Madison held cordial relations with (and who became the United States attorney general). Madison sent the draft bill before the House had even begun debate. The parcel to Randolph was dated June 17, 1789. In fact, Madison had not even officially commented on the bill as a congressman. Whether Madison was inviting comments from Randolph is unknown, but it could hardly have been imagined that Randolph, a staunch "states' rights" proponent, would have been overly enthusiastic about the draft Judiciary Act bill and the proposed power of the federal judiciary.[43]

A month later, on July 18, 1789, Madison wrote to Wilson Cary Nicholas, a Virginia politician and future senator, "The Judiciary bill has got through the Senate but is not yet before the H[ouse] of Rep[resentatives]."[44] Madison spent several weeks informing his colleagues that the judiciary bill was not yet at the House, and had only got through the Senate. It would seem to indicate the length of time necessary considering the effort that Madison expended keeping up with its whereabouts. Madison certainly knew the level of opposition to the bill and knew a potentially long debate would be had in the House. This would only postpone the actual creation of the federal judiciary, something Madison was not inclined to agree with. A functioning government was needed, now. For Madison, the "Father of the Constitution," when the judiciary bill finally arrived in the House on July 20, 1789, it was nearly two years since the Constitution had been drafted in Philadelphia, and a year since the debate in the Virginia state ratifying convention. The time, for Madison and the country, had arrived.

Two weeks later, on July 31, 1789, Madison wrote to Anthony Wayne with an optimistic outlook on the pending Judiciary Act arriving at the House. While the Senate had finished its work on the Act, the House did not take up the measure for several weeks. Perhaps it was because the legislation was so massive, and contained so many difficult issues, that the House avoided having to deal with it until it had no choice. Madison told Wayne, "the subject next in order is the judiciary establishment which is pregnant with perhaps still greater difficulties; but being sent from the Senate in the form of a digested bill, where it is hoped produce less discussion and delay."[45] Clearly, Madison was counting on the fact that the Senate, having given the legislation a thorough debate, would expedite discussion in the House. Madison was intimately aware though of the great difficulties with which the legislation was "pregnant." He, more than most congressman, would have been aware of the stakes involved.

The idea of having the state courts serve as the inferior federal courts came up in the House as it had done earlier in the Senate debate. The idea was that by eliminating the federal inferior courts, the states would somehow retain more of their sovereignty relative to the federal government. As has been pointed out, the federal judiciary was in many ways the more immediate threat to the states as envisioned by the Anti-Federalists. For them, their unique systems of state law and justice would be threatened in a way Congress or the executive could not replicate. The insertion of the state courts in the federal judiciary by elimination of the inferior courts would be one way, as many Anti-Federalists saw it, of maintaining some semblance of state involvement in federal matters pertaining to the judiciary.

When debate opened in the House in late July 1789, Virginia Congressman James Madison had, not surprisingly, strong views on the need to maintain the creation of inferior courts as called for in the Constitution. Madison stated:

> To make the state courts federal courts, is liable to insuperable objections. Not to repeat that the moment that is done, they will from the highest down to the county courts, hold their tenures during good behavior, by virtue of the Constitution. It may be remarked that in another point of view, it would violate the Constitution by usurping a prerogative of the supreme executive of the United States. It would be making appointments which are expressly vested in that department.... But laying these difficulties aside, a review of the Constitution of the courts in many states will satisfy us that they cannot be trusted with the execution of the federal laws ... that to make the federal law dependent on them, would throw us back into all the embarrassments which characterized our former situation.[46]

This was brilliant Madison. He needed to point out only a few of the anomalies which would occur if the state courts entered the role proposed by the Anti-Federalists. Every appointment would be for life; every judge would have to be appointed by the president as called for by Article III, not to mention the quality of the judges (something Madison does not mention but was aware of). After just a few points, Madison almost seemed to be throwing up his hands in disgust. After two years of debating the Constitution, this was not the time or place to renew old arguments. Although the Bill of Rights would soon be created, Madison was not about to allow changes in the document so recently passed. The idea of state judges ruling on federal issues was absurd to Madison and his fellow Federalists (supporters of the Constitution, not the political party).

Comparing what some were calling for to the failures of the Articles of Confederation was Madison's frustration coming out. After all the young nation had been through, was that really what the opposition wanted? Could anyone really, honestly, advocate for going back to the days when, as Madison put it, an "embarrassment" hung over the American government? The Founders were fond of saying the eyes of the world were upon America as a beacon of hope and freedom. There was no doubt some truth to this. But equally as valid, were the eyes who were looking to see if self-government could actually work. Could the Americans truly bring together thirteen separate nations and form one functioning nation? For Madison and his followers, this had to happen; it was no longer optional if a nation was to emerge from the ashes of the American War of Independence.

Even with Madison's strong rebuke of the idea of state courts as inferior federal courts, some of his correspondents still wondered about the prospect. On August 3, 1789, Edward Carrington wrote to Madison, "The result of my reflections, is, that the state courts, where they are well established might be adopted as the inferior federal courts."[47] Carrington continued, "Such an arrangement would save immense expense; would occasion little innovation in the ancient forms of judicial proceedings amongst the people, and would also, without difficulty, accommodate jury trials in matters of fact, to the wishes of each state, as everyone would retain its own usage."[48]

The newspaper *The Gazette of the United States* took much the same approach towards state courts working on federal issues: "The simple self-evident proposition, that the means ought ever to be commensurate with the end designed, points out the need of a national judiciary."[49] The editorial continued:

> The perfect propriety of having a national judiciary, to interpret the laws made by a national legislative; and to decide upon the causes which naturally come within the cognizance of those laws, intuitively produces conviction in the mind, from only a cursory glance of the subject; and that this establishment, co-equal with the objects it involves should also be co-existent with those objects.[50]

The *Gazette*, which was a Federalist leaning newspaper, made a compelling case for keeping federal cases with federal courts, and state cases with state courts. In a certain measure, the whole issue of inferior federal courts being replaced with state courts was an attempt to argue Article III of the Constitution one more time.

While it has been shown that the Judiciary Act of 1789 was a compromise document, and thus a lengthy document as well, it should come as no surprise that agitations for reform began almost immediately after it was signed by President Washington. Reflecting that thinking, Secretary of State Thomas Jefferson, who wrote draft topics for President Washington's message to Congress on December 8, 1790, included some thoughts on reform. Jefferson provided the President with the following suggestions for his address to Congress:

The laws you have already passed for the establishment of a judiciary system have opened the doors of justice to all descriptions of persons. You will consider whether improvements in that system may yet be made; and particularly whether an uniform process of execution, on sentences issuing from the federal courts, be not desirable through all the states.[51]

President Washington used Jefferson's suggested language without change in his address to Congress.

Reflection

Legal historian Julius Goebel has written that the Judiciary Act "must be viewed in a political context as an instrument of reconciliation deliberately framed to quiet still smoldering resentments, in a juristic context it is a document of less fugitive nature and one of great historical depth."[52]

While the Judiciary Act of 1789 was a massive document, it contained three major developments that have been referred to. The first dealt with the idea of using state courts as inferior federal courts; the second was the issue of citizenship and foreign aliens in disputes; the third dealt with the creation of districts on a federal level. We have seen that the first two issues reflected state concerns over sovereignty, and to a lesser extent budgetary constraint over inferior federal courts. The district court plan was however one of the truly ingenious solutions to the problem of a large geographic territory. Julius Goebel has described it as:

The districts were grouped into three circuits: the eastern, the middle and the southern—a division of the country that had been used for military administration in the first year of the Revolution. In each district there were to be held annually in the spring and fall two courts to "consist" of any two Justices of the Supreme Court and the District judge.[53]

The district concept had its roots in English law, as did much of what America created, however much it differed in the outcome. The English idea was that judges of England's highest court at Westminster would travel the country on a regularly defined schedule, thus bringing the power and majesty of the monarch (or federal government in America's case) to "ordinary" people. This was highly effective in England. England, small geographically compared to the United States, which seemed to expand at every turn, made effective use of the circuit court system and found it quite useful in connecting the country.

Historian Goebel saw several main points in the Judiciary Act that served to deflect criticisms from the Anti-Federalists over certain provisions of the Constitution. Among those identified, Goebel listed a:

due regard to antifederalist criticism of a federal system by fixing a minimum above $500 (exclusive of costs) for civil actions in law and equity; by forbidding arrests of defendants in one district for trial in another; and by limiting actions by original process against an inhabitant of the United States in any district other than where he might be an inhabitant.[54]

Goebel clearly saw the Act for what it was—a further compromise measure and outgrowth of the Constitutional Convention and the subsequent approval of the Constitution by the states.

This is a sentiment born out in a comment made in 1792 by historian David Ramsey: "It is perhaps not difficult to say which is the most arduous task, that of the convention who framed the Constitution, or of the first legislatures to whom it will appertain to mature and perfect so compound a system, to liquidate the meaning of all parts, and adjust them to each other in a harmonious and consistent whole."[55] Ramsey, an astute observer of the unfolding of history occurring around him, wondered not only which gathering, the Constitutional Convention or the First Congress, had the more difficult task relative to establishing the new nation. Beyond that, Ramsey also wondered which gathering would be remembered more in history? Whose constitutions would be received more with applause?

Before the debates even began, an attuned young woman expressed her reflections on the rapidly evolving momentum towards a federal government. Abigail Adams Smith, the daughter of John and Abigail Adams, wrote to her brother John Quincy Adams, on August 20, 1788, from her home in New York. She was desirous to let him know she was aware of developments concerning their father:

> Col. Lee from Virginia, a nephew of the Mr. Lee's, and a member of [the Continental] Congress told me the other day that it was his opinion, and the opinion of others, and, he spoke as a Southern man, that the offices of Vice-President and Chief Justice, would lay between my father and Mr. Jay, that he wished my father might be appointed to the latter and accept of it, for he esteemed it next to the Presidentship the most respectable under the new government.... I wish our dear father to consider well as he no doubt will, before he decides against accepting it.[56]

The younger Abigail seemed to have doubts whether her father would accept the position of chief justice. Perhaps in her letter to John Quincy she was hoping to encourage him to speak to their father.

Further Thoughts

Much like the Constitution itself, the Judiciary Act of 1789 generated profound feelings and viewpoints. As such, it seems it would be beneficial to examine a few more of the polemics generated by this piece of legislation. In summarizing the Judiciary Act of 1789, legal historian Charles Grove Haines wrote:

> Although the records of the debates on the measure are rather meager, it seems that the two features of the act which caused later criticisms and controversies were approved with little comment. One of these was the provision which required the Supreme Court Justices to travel and to try cases on the circuits, many of which would later come before them again on appeal. The other was the twenty-fifth section of the act which regulated appeals to the Supreme Court.... The grant of this authority to the federal courts is not so clear and specific as is frequently inferred from the language of the section.[57]

Any historical narrative is enhanced by the words of those who participated in the events written about. They offer the documentary evidence for an author to make the description authentic and original. While this book has already offered a glimpse of those involved with the early judiciary, it has leaned somewhat disproportionately towards the more familiar names. This section seeks to offer the observations of some of the lesser known figures from the 1790s and the creation and development of American law.

While genuine historical characters can be easily identified, there were a not insubstantial number of writers who sought anonymity even though expressing their opinions. One well known approach to this was an essay signed with a pseudonym—nearly always a classical name referencing some ancient figure with whom the writer wanted to invoke an intellectual kinship. Another approach was the unsigned editorial or opinion piece in a newspaper. Then as now, opinion pieces tended to tack along the ideological leanings of the newspaper in which the piece was published.

One example of a particularly harsh assessment of the proposed American legal system as envisioned by the Constitution was published, anonymously, on January 5, 1789, in the *Albany Register*. Conjuring up images of centuries past religious inspired injustice, the writer wondered whether the new American system would be based on those concepts that led our distant ancestors to slaughter one another in the name of "god" law? The writer opined that the Constitution offered no sense of mercy from the secret and barbaric rites practiced during the inquisition or the ancient laws found in the Bible.[58] The writer identified with a strong element in the American approach for a non-religious foundation for law. The writer also was concerned that the secrecy and brutality surrounding such non-secular cases would lead to an inefficient system and one biased from the very start. At its base, the writer's argument was how to trust government and how to trust human nature. The writer argued, "Have we not neglected to secure to ourselves the mighty matter of judgment or justice, by empowering the general government to establish one supreme, and many inferior courts as they please, whose proceedings they have a right to fix and regulate as they shall think fit."[59]

As we have seen, many salient arguments existed during the period of the writing of the Judiciary Act of 1789. Some felt concern over the lessening of the power of state courts and indeed some felt state courts should act as the inferior courts called for in the Constitution. Others were concerned about the expense associated with inferior courts. Jeremiah Hill, writing to George Thatcher (both of Maine), on March 4, 1789, noted that "some perhaps will find fault at the expense of so many officers, but what will it signify to make laws except there is somebody to put them in force."[60]

In contrast to concerns about the high costs of the judiciary as proposed during debate in 1789, Robert R. Livingston found the judiciary system to be "both cheap and expeditious."[61] Livingston found the proposed system to be a great value when considering the vast expanse of territory covered by the American legal system.

Well known Massachusetts politician Elbridge Gerry, received a letter from James Sullivan, dated March 22, 1789. Sullivan expressed doubts about not just the federal court system, but about those leaders who devised the system. Sullivan wrote Gerry asking for him to offer his thoughts concerning the judiciary:

> I wish you to write me as you have leisure respecting the ideas entertained on the judicial department. The freedom and liberty of the people depends so much upon the proper arrangement of this part of the government that I feel anxious about it. You ask why I am anxious since there are so many men in Congress who understand the matter better than I do?[62]

Sullivan, not invited to the national convention in 1787 or to the Massachusetts state ratifying convention, was not impressed with the quality of those making decisions about the future American legal system. What was amusing, was the fact that Gerry apparently told Sullivan that those involved in preparing the bill to bring life to Article III of the Constitution had a better understanding of the issues involved and he (Sullivan) should not worry. Apparently Sullivan took this slight as it was intended.

A week later, on March 29, 1789, Sullivan again wrote to Elbridge Gerry expressing his further disapproval of the proposed Judiciary Act. Sullivan wrote, "I have seen a sketch of a plan which I do not like. That there should be an [federal] inferior judge in each state vested with admiralty, common law, and chancery powers. I do not like the mixture."[63]

Among the more repeated criticisms of the Judiciary Act was the travel required to obtain a hearing on a case. This was no small point given the immense distances involved between some states and the federal capital. The approach the drafters of the Judiciary took in an attempt to remedy this was to devise a series of circuit courts around the country which would be staffed by one Supreme Court justice and one circuit judge who resided in the vicinity of the court. The problem with this was it took the responsibility for travel off the litigants and placed it on the justices themselves. This was immediately disavowed by the justices. Yet, it was something they had to deal with until modifications to the Act were undertaken.

Nathaniel Peaslea Sargent wrote to John Adams (then serving as vice president) on April 25, 1789, and offered a regional perspective on the prospect of law being dispensed at great distance. "Perhaps nothing will disturb [the] New England people more than to make their litigations lengthy and expensive."[64] Sargent nonetheless saw a dedicated judiciary as indispensable to a national government, "nothing in my view of things tends more to strengthen government in [the] extreme parts, than sometimes to have a court ... among them."[65]

Delaware Senator Richard Bassett wrote to Benjamin Chew in June 1789 that while the work in the Senate on the Judiciary Act was tiring, it was necessary. According to Bassett, "The establishment of the judiciary has engrossed the attention of a few of us for some time. It is an intricate and laborious work, and I think I may venture to say our happiness as a people very much depends on this system."[66]

Bassett gave voice to a theme much agreed with at the time but rarely fully articulated: a national legal system was the key to American development during the post–Revolutionary War period. America, above all else, needed stability. Only with some type of structured government and law could America ever hope to advance beyond the chaos of post–Revolutionary America and the disaster of the Articles of Confederation government. Bassett and others were well aware that a national congress or a national executive (both of which existed under the Articles of Confederation) were within grasp and the states already had some experience, to a greater or lesser extent, during the war. What was completely new was a national judiciary. During the years of war with Britain, a national judiciary would have been nearly impossible to create. Each state was too jealous of its new-found freedom and rights to think seriously about a national tribunal passing judgment on its actions. By 1789 though, it was widely understood that Article III of the new Constitution, while the shortest, was also the most powerful.

An anonymous writer, known as "Americanus," wrote in an essay published on June 10, 1789, in the *Gazette of the United States*, that a national judiciary was "necessary to secure the life, liberty, and property of the subject, and ought to be placed in a distinct and separate body."[67] Americanus thought the demands of the nation should outweigh those of the states, "that in framing the judiciary system, a sacrifice of local views and partial prejudices, will be found peculiarly necessary."[68] Gunning Bedford, Jr., of Delaware referred to the Judiciary Act as the framework "upon which the most grand and elegant superstructure of jurisprudences is to be built."[69]

Bedford touched on the idea of common law in his June 24, 1789, letter to fellow Delawarean George Read. Bedford wrote, "What then, is the common law and statute law of the United States? It is difficult to answer. Yet the dignity of America requires that it be ascertained, and that where we refer to laws they should be laws of our own country."[70] Bedford added for good measure that 1789, with a new Constitution, represented a "moment for legal emancipation; as the foundation is laid [Constitution] so must the superstructure [Judiciary Act] be built."[71]

William Bradford, Jr., writing to Elias Boudinot of New Jersey, suggested in a June 30, 1789, letter that "the system [Judiciary Act] does not meet with approbation from any professional gentleman."[72]

William Maclay, a senator from Pennsylvania, kept a diary which presumably he shared with no one at the time. His diary has come to form the basis of some of the most unique perspectives on this time period and the founding of the American legal system. His June 29, 1789, entry expressed his feelings over Senator Ellsworth who was widely seen as the intellectual force behind the Judiciary Act. Maclay wrote his views about a Senate session he had just attended. He confided to his diary, "I made a remark where Ellsworth in his diction had varied from the Constitution. This vile bill [Judiciary Act] is a child of his, and he defends it with the care of a parent, even with wrath and anger. He kindled as he always does when it was meddled with."[73] Maclay continued in this particular entry to confide to the privacy of his diary how Ellsworth and his lieutenant William Paterson of New Jersey manipulated debates to protect the specifics of the Judiciary Act.

Tristam Lowther, writing to future Supreme Court justice James Iredell, pointed to a peculiar fact impacting the Judiciary Act in a July 1, 1789, letter. Noting the lack of lawyers in the Senate as opposed to the House, Lowther wrote, "It was principally drawn up by a Mr. Ellsworth from Connecticut but it is supposed considerable alterations will be made in the bill before it passes both houses; there are not many lawyers in the senate but they compose three-forths of the representatives."[74]

William Maclay, perhaps due to his suffering severe bouts of rheumatism, continued to obsess on the terrible aspects, as he saw it, of the Judiciary Act. In his diary entry for July 2, 1789, after complaining about his poor health, he too noted the role lawyers would play in the passage of the Act. He wrote:

The bill was taken up for the Judiciary, I really dislike the whole of this bill, but I endevoured to mend it in several places and make it as perfect as possible, if it is to be the law of the land; but it was fabricated by a knot of lawyers [Ellsworth and Paterson] who join here and try to run down any person, who will venture to say one word about it.... It was in vain to attempt anything, the people who were not lawyers on a supposition that lawyers knew best, would follow the lawyers, and a party were determined to push it.[75]

Robert Morris, writing to Francis Hopkinson on July 13, 1789, picked up on the disparity of lawyers in the House as opposed to the Senate and speculated on the changes to be expected when the proposed Act reached the lower chamber for review:

> The Bill has been securely handled and many alterations made, I suppose it will find its way to the House of Representatives this week, … and as there is no less than two and twenty lawyers in that House I expect they will turn and twist this poor bill until they send it back to its parents as unlike the original as law language will permit.[76]

Morris' use of descriptive language—the Senate being the parents of the bill and the high number of lawyers in the House—was echoed by others during the same time who saw the proposed Judiciary Act as a child which germinated in the Senate but that the voracious lawyers of the House would nearly devour and recast in some alien form.

Two days later on July 4, Maclay wrote a letter to fellow Pennsylvanian Jared Ingersoll. Maclay continued to argue that his Senate colleagues, especially Ellsworth and Paterson, were driving the debate and passage of the Judiciary Act in a very heavy-handed manner. Maclay complained to Ingersoll:

> I have seen in a gentleman's letter a clause, which mentioned your opinion as being rather unfavorable to the bill for establishing the Judiciary of the United States. I really fear that a prevailing disposition, to treat everything with great respect, that proceeds from the new congress will prevent our obtaining that free information, which alone can be useful to us at present. I have generally (except in Senate) been cautious of delivering any opinion about it. I wished men to come forward without any bias whatever.[77]

Maclay wrote with some strong language and criticism against Ellsworth and Paterson (although not named specifically). His apprehension for both the Judiciary Act and some of his fellow senators was palpable. Maclay even went so far, in the privacy of his diary, to criticize President Washington, writing that "he showed a peevish obstinacy" when it came to the Judiciary Act.[78]

Diaries almost always make for fascinating, informative, and sometimes entertaining reading. It is engaging speculation to wonder whether a diarist anticipated their work being read and commented on centuries after they wrote it. The same speculation holds true for Maclay.

John Sullivan, writing to John Langdon on August 18, 1789, in New Hampshire, expressed continuing concern over the cost of a national judiciary. It was clear from an early point that the federal judiciary would be one of the larger line items in the federal budget. Sullivan wrote:

> I think … the system will be expensive for a government not only poor, but deeply involved in debt; and will create jealousies, and uneasiness among the people; and might have been so contrived as to have equal justice with much less expense; when I consider the expense of our national government, and compare it with the probable resources; … I fear that it cannot long be supported in its present form.[79]

As with other arguments raised by the Anti-Federalists during the debate over the Constitution in 1788, especially over Article III pertaining to a federal judiciary, some writers brought those arguments forward a year earlier and used them to attack the proposed Judiciary Act. One such writer, known as "Centinel Revived"—in his number twenty-six essay, published on August 27, 1789, in the Philadelphia *Independent Gazette*—took issue with the power of the federal judiciary at the expense of the states. In an argument, which could easily have been seen as against Article III of the Constitution, Centinel wrote concerning the Judiciary Act:

> The Judicial powers vested in Congress are also so various and extensive, that by legal ingenuity they may be extended to every case, and thus absorb the state judiciaries; and when we consider the decisive influence that a general judiciary would have over the civil polity of the several states, we do not hesitate to pronounce that this power, unaided by the legislative, would effect a consolidation of the states under one government.[80]

A little over a week before the Judiciary Act passed Congress, Elbridge Gerry, writing to John Wendell, expressed his displeasure with the whole system of federal courts as designed. Gerry wrote:

> The judiciary bill is now under consideration of Congress. This department I dread as an awful tribunal. By the constitution the judges are completely independent, being secure of their salaries and removable only by impeachment, not being subject to discharge on the address of both Houses as is the case in G. Britain. The courts have cognizance of common law equity and exchequer causes and also those of maritime and admiralty jurisdiction.[81]

Gerry sums up the main opposition to the federal court system as envisioned in the Judiciary Act: it was too powerful. Gerry also pointed out how the American system was constantly compared to the British system. It was after all the system the Americans knew best (and many admired). The links and lineal descent of American law undeniably lie in the England of old.

The *Gazette of the United States* reported on the progress of the Judiciary Act on September 17, 1789, by referencing Gerry's perspective during his debate in the House. The *Gazette* reported:

> Mr. Gerry then rose, and stated a number of objections against passing this bill—these went to its principles and operation [presumably similar in content as in his letter to Wendell]. But he further observed, that as it is acknowledged the bill is an experiment, and as it has been precipitated through the House he wished if it did pass, that a clause to limit its duration might be added.[82]

Gerry, a seasoned politician and signer of the Declaration of Independence, was well aware that all legislation is experimental in the sense that it can always be revisited, whether by Congress itself, or the courts.

A young law student at the time, John Quincy Adams confided to his diary that he attended the debates in the House over the Judiciary Act, but "did not perceive any extraordinary powers of oratory displayed by any" of the representatives, including Gerry.[83] As Adams knew, by this late date, there was very little new that could be offered; "The eloquence had all been exhausted, but the spirit of contention still remained."[84]

In the long-heated debates over the salaries of judges, which naturally included a discussion of all federal officials, the debate became one of determining the amount of money necessary to live in various parts of the country. One area did not necessarily equate to another. Living in rural Maine or Georgia was significantly less than keeping a home in Boston or Charleston. An anonymous writer, known as "Cincinnatus," writing in the *Herald of Freedom* in Boston, wrote on October 2, 1789 (after the Judiciary Act had been signed by President Washington),

> The idea of purchasing members of Congress and judges, into integrity and uprightness, is quite unnatural and absurd; if we look round the world, we shall find men of greatest estates to have been the most unjust, cruel, and oppressive. It is true that small and trifling sums may not always purchase rich men to fraud, but it is as true, that where the heart of a man is fixed upon gain, that however rich he is, he will cheat, meanly cheat, for a trifle.[85]

James Sullivan reacted angrily to judicial compensation in an October 11, 1789, letter to Elbridge Gerry, "The compensation act is very disgusting indeed. The people say they can never pay such salaries. On a computation, they say there are not ten men in the United States who have an income from estates equal to what is given the judges."[86] The whole idea of paying for justice seems to have escalated more after President Washington signed the Act into law. Not being able to alter the Act to their liking, opponents honed in on something everyone could relate to: money. The extended debate did little to alter the best venue for aggrievement available to opponents to deride the Act.

A year after President Washington signed the Judiciary Act into law, an essayist in the *Independent Chronicle* published an article entitled "Federal Government." The author was unsparing in criticism concerning the federal judiciary:

> It is time, the members [of Congress] have by adopting an extensive, expensive, perplexing, and distressing JUDICIARY SYSTEM.... Can any reasonable person suppose it necessary to introduce into this country, so intricate and tedious a Judiciary system, as is adopted by Congress; whereby every tradesman, merchant and farmer, are exposed, through a long train of Courts, to the most enormous costs in maintaining their most simple demands [emphasis in original].[87]

On the same day that he signed the Judiciary Act into law (September 24, 1789), President Washington sent the names of the six men he sought to nominate to the Supreme Court to the Senate for consideration and confirmation. All were approved straight away. It is worth noting, that Washington received much unsolicited advice about whom to nominate to the Court. From all corners of the country, letters poured into the President. In the end, he seems to have kept his own counsel, by and large. Not being a jurist, or particularly well-versed in legal matters, Washington no doubt sought some advice. He was, after all, staffing the Supreme Court of the United States and the federal judiciary at large, a task not to be taken lightly and not to be staffed with "lightweights." Washington took great care to pick seasoned jurists and geographically diverse nominees.

Naturally, not all appointments were equally well received. As an example, when the officials in Massachusetts learned that William Cushing, chief justice of the Massachusetts Supreme Judicial Court, was to be nominated for the Supreme Court, they were honored. Then, it was realized that there was a political backstory to Cushing's appointment. By vacating the state bench, Governor John Hancock, an Anti-Federalist (party affiliation, not against the Constitution) would be able to appoint a replacement for Cushing, a reliable Federalist in a state which would have adherents to that party long after it had died. In fact, Christopher Gore (a Massachusetts politician) wrote to New York Senator Rufus King stating, "The Chief Justice [Cushing], now 56 years of age, cannot long be an active member of the Court, and he has new habits and new modes of legal decision to acquire."[88]

With the enactment of the Judiciary Act of 1789, the Supreme Court became the branch charged as the main expositor of the outlines of American constitutionalism. The Court would have the power to hear appellate cases from both state and federal courts. This did not please all those involved in the negotiations concerning the Act. The Court would therefore be forced to operate with the handicap of significant opposition to its mandate. Unlike the two other branches of government, the Court would, relatively speaking, have to lay its foundation amidst powerful competing interests.

The Court, however, would waste little time in fulfilling its obligation to provide the continuity required for constitutional development. The Court will be shown to have struck a remarkably independent tone and course regardless of political pressures. Subsequent chapters will analyze how the Court approached, digested, and adjudicated the beginning of a system of written law largely untried up to that time. The problems engendered in the factional creation of the Court through the Act, while they did not dissipate, became neutralized by the exigencies of creating the Court system through the Act. The Judiciary Act codified the concept of a singular branch of government dedicated to the interpretation of the Constitution. What had been debated concerning the parameters of constitutional jurisprudence had become law.

The nearly twenty–year struggle for an independent American government had reached an end. What was to happen no one could know for certain.

All that had been said, printed, and written, about the new government was now history. While the similar themes would still be reenergized over the next decade (1790s) up and down the federal government structure, the basic outlines of the new system had been achieved. Rather than theory, there was now the practical. The year 1789 marked a turning point as surely as 1776 in American history. All three branches were released and work began to bring the government into full operation. Going forward, this book will look exclusively at the Supreme Court and to a lesser extent the federal judiciary during the 1790s. To begin that process, it will first be helpful to know the individuals involved. Given that most of the members of the Supreme Court are less than household names today, an overview in the form of mini-biographies will be presented in Chapter 4.

4

Important Individuals
1789–1800

On September 24, 1789, President George Washington nominated six jurists to seats on the newly created Supreme Court of the United States. Washington personally wrote each appointee appealing to their judicial wisdom, sense of patriotist, and devotion to the public good. In each letter, Washington commented on the importance of the judicial branch. Washington, writing from personal conviction about the place of law in society, also attempted to inflate the role to sell the appointment. The president chose this approach as any delay in staffing the Court would be not only embarrassing, but unnecessarily time consuming in relation to the overall need to ensure that the machinery of the Constitution was functioning. It is clear that Washington was aware of the respect and role which the Supreme Court would, and should, have in the new nation.

At first glance, the thirteen men appointed to the Supreme Court by Presidents Washington and Adams between 1789 and 1800 all seem one part of a whole. White, male, highly educated, Protestant, American gentry if not aristocracy; the list could go on. Yet, just below the surface some differences are perceptible. Still, while these differences are what makes each man an individual, the similarities account for the sense of cohesiveness they brought to the Court.

In total, every nominee was a Founding Father; some were more involved than others, but each one had contributed to the founding of the new nation. All were also leaders in their home states. All were considered to be of the highest character. Six had served in the Continental Congress (Chase, Ellsworth, Rutledge, Wilson, Blair, Paterson), two signed the Declaration of Independence (Wilson, Chase), four signed the Constitution (Rutledge, Blair, Wilson, Paterson), and one was one of only six men to sign both the Declaration and the Constitution (James Wilson). They were all approved by the Senate when nominated.

President Washington took great care in nominating individuals whom he felt represented the best the American legal system had to offer. Not trained in the law himself, Washington nonetheless understood the importance of the vital role law played within any society. His nominations, whether confirmed or not, were designed to assure the public of the stability of the new government. As historian James Perry has written: "In sum, President Washington's first nominations to the Supreme Court were made after careful consideration of appropriate criteria and after extensive consultation with those who knew the candidates."[1] The mini-biographies in this chapter will provide a snapshot of each individual man while not losing sight of the qualities which brought a sense of mission to the Court when they were all carrying out their official duties, both when the Court was meeting as such and on circuit duty, where each justice spent part of the year. This requirement, a feature of the 1789 Judiciary Act, would prove to be a most contentious aspect of being a justice in the days before motorized travel and instant communication.

The early Justices were devoted to the well-being of the United States and of the stability of the Constitution as the foundation of American life. These twelve men were not only guiding the young republic, they were guiding the future republic as well. Their backgrounds prepared them to see America not only in the moment, but in the "becoming"; an America constantly unfolding and pressing ahead into the future of not some unknown path, but a path articulated in a document (the Constitution) of which they were the arbiters. In total, the Supreme Court would adjudicate as arbiters just sixty-one cases before 1801.[2]

It is crucial to know these men because most of what we read, hear, or learn about them is void of any reference to their humanity. We forget these were living, breathing, human beings just like us. We tend to sense the black robe (they wore them in the beginning just like today—although during the 1790s some justices wore distinctively English inspired robes; some with fur trim and with bold colors) and instinctively withdraw or suspend our critique of them as people because the robe has a certain impression of majesty about it, much like a religious figure in vestments of some sort. The robe is meant to announce to those who observe it that they should maintain a certain amount of awe, to cease questioning, to respect the wearer and his announcements; unless we can get beyond undue reverence concerning the early republic, these early justices are doomed to eternal obscurity.

The Six Original Court Appointees

After passage of the Judiciary Act of 1789, President Washington was obliged to nominate six potential Justices to the Supreme Court for the Senate to consider. In a brief note to the Senate, Washington nominated John Jay as chief justice, and James Wilson of Pennsylvania, John Rutledge of South Carolina, William Cushing of Massachusetts, Robert Harrison of Maryland, and John Blair of Virginia as associate justices. All were eminently qualified. All were nominated and duly appointed with the exception of Robert Harrison, who became the first nominee to refuse his nomination (he cited ill health). Harrison wrote to Washington, "On no occasion of my life have I been under an embarrassment so painful. It is at length with a difficulty almost inconceivable, after revolving every circumstance, and after many days and nights of anxious solicitude, that I have come to a final determination that I cannot but decline the appointment."[3] Harrison, who would be dead in less than a year, noted "that as a judge solicitous to discharge my trust, I must hazard, in an eminent degree, the loss of my health, and sacrifice a very large portion of my private and domestic happiness."[4] Aside from his personal health, Harrison noted the physical vigor, in addition to the intellectual, that was necessary to be a justice riding circuit. This was the first instance, and by no means the last, of the issue of circuit riding putting a nominee off accepting appointment to the Court. Curiously, before Washington and Harrison exchanged correspondence, an anonymous writer known as "Civis" wrote to Washington promoting Harrison for the Supreme Court. On September 1, 1789, Civis wrote:

> He is aware that from the retired habits of Col. Harrison, that he is not well known throughout America as many men of high characters who perhaps are not near so perfect; …when out of the chair of justice he returns home the most recluse citizen unknown to all but his neighbors and friends, that his virtues and abilities are not hidden…. If this appointment takes place the state of Maryland will lose the best man in it, there is no one who can represent him as a judge and perhaps the citizens would have cause to regret the removal, but the writer is one of those men who always will wave local considerations for the good of the whole.[5]

On the whole, a strange letter. Whether Washington was influenced by it (more than likely not) he did receive it and catalog it with his collection of correspondence. In Harrison's place, Washington nominated James Iredell of North Carolina.

George Washington was a president of many firsts. Of course, everything he did as president was a first for a president—except living in the White House. As such, this list of firsts contains Washington being the first president to be solicited by office seekers, in particular job seekers for judiciary posts. On August 30, 1789, Georgia Governor George Walton wrote President Washington that although he had been "employed in the service of America … almost without interruption, since the commencement of the public meetings and discussions which led to the Revolution, I do not recollect ever to have solicited an appointment."[6] Walton felt that the new Congress in New York

Chief Justice John Jay of New York (Morristown National Historical Park).

had an inaccurate view of his enthusiasm about federal work: it has "been suggested that my desire of serving in the Judiciary of the Union might be doubted at New York."[7] Governor Walton was interested in the position of judge of the District of Georgia. He was not appointed.

In the president's home state of Virginia, Meriwether Smith sought to approach Washington about employment. "Permit me to interrupt you for a moment in soliciting a favor for myself," Smith began.[8] As with Governor

Walton, Smith saw himself as a supporter of the Revolution from the beginning. Now, in his declining years, he sought a suitable government post. Smith wrote: "I make application to you, for some honorable and lucrative employment under the government, suitable to my declining years, which, by the causalities to which my fortune and family have been exposed under the Revolution, would be highly acceptable and convenient to me."[9] Smith, like Governor Walton, sought a position in the judiciary. Smith, again like Governor Walton, received no appointment.

The original six appointees—Jay, Cushing, Rutledge, Blair, Wilson, and Harrison/Iredell—were all men personally acquainted, to greater or lesser extents, with Washington. Like many later Presidents, Washington sought to geographically balance Court membership. There were many good reasons for this. Rough balance would ensure the composition of the Court would not unduly favor one section or state unfairly. It also ensured that the Justices would share in both long and short rides to their circuit courts, thus ensuring relatively equal shares of discomfort during the arduous circuit court duty. Many were watching the list of nominees submitted by the President. One observer was Abigail Adams, wife of Vice President John Adams. Abigail Adams was well known for her interests in government and as a letter from 1789 to her sister Elizabeth Smith Shaw indicates she was following events closely. On September 27, Mrs. Adams wrote:

> I am fearful of touching upon political subjects yet perhaps there is no person who feels more interested in them, and upon this occasion I may congratulate my country upon the late judicial appointments, in which an assemblage of the greatest talents and abilities are united, which any country can boast of. Gentlemen in whom the public have great confidence in support of our government.[10]

John Jay

Heading President Washington's list was John Jay of New York as chief justice. Washington and Jay were effusive with each other in their mutual praise and commendation in letters concerning Jay's appointment. In typical eighteenth-century fashion, Washington, informing Jay of his appointment, wrote on October 5, 1789, that he, "did a grateful thing [for] the good citizens of these United States" by appointing Jay.[11] Jay, for his part consenting to the appointment, wrote that those accepting positions of importance "derive honor not only from their offices, but from the hand which confers them."[12] Jay took his oath on October 19, 1789, which was administered by Richard Morris, chief justice of the supreme court of the state of New York.

Jay's sister-in-law, Catherine Ridley, wrote to congratulate him on November 4, 1789. She had a request for Jay as well. She asked if he, now chief justice, would consider her husband Matthew for a position of clerk to the Supreme Court. Mrs. Ridley wrote:

> A tedious fit of illness and a relapse since has deprived me of that pleasure [writing sooner] and congratulating you on your late appointment, which from the general satisfaction it gives is very flattering to all your friends.... You will I hope excuse the application it leads me to make, it's with reluctance I assure you, knowing your delicacy on that subject that I do it, but my desire if I live to have it in my power to be nearer my friends encourages me to it ... and if this does not meet your approbation it need go no farther, being entirely between ourselves, Mr. Ridley left me before I knew there would be a clerks place to be disposed of for the Supreme Court.[13]

Mrs. Ridley assured Jay that the main reason for her request was the desire to maintain a stable home life for her family. A clerk position would allow her husband to have a type of job in the law that did not necessitate travel away from home, unlike many others who practiced law in Maryland which "obliges those of the profession to be almost entirely from their families."[14] Jay replied a week later that he was not averse to considering her proposal. Writing on November 11, 1789, Jay noted:

> Your wishes are natural, and correspond perfectly with mine.... In my judgment, the place in question will not be worth 200 a year, that alone will not afford a living, how is the deficiency to be supplied; or how are the local advantages which in case it should be attainable you would relinquish for it to be compensated by professional or other pursuits here?[15]

Of the thirteen men who served on the Supreme Court before 1800, John Jay is likely the best known today. The three most important achievements in John Jay's life were being co-author of *The Federalist* papers; participating as one of the negotiators for the Paris Peace Treaty of 1783, ending the American Revolution; and being the first chief justice of the United States Supreme Court. Before arriving at those momentous aspects of his career, he, like everyone else, started small.

The story of the Huguenots of France is very much part of the story of the Jays. The immediate family had its roots in La Rochelle, France (a major Huguenot city). Jay's grandfather, Augustus Jay (1665–1751), emigrated to America in the late seventeenth century, arriving in South Carolina and quickly moving to New York City in about 1688. His departure from France was in direct response of Louis XIV's revocation of the Edict of Nantes of 1685 (which was not easy as the revocation prohibited people from fleeing). In fact, young Augustus was away on business when the revocation was enacted and his parents and siblings had already secretly fled to England. Augustus found himself homeless and destitute (and technically prohibited from leaving) when he returned to France but quickly left clandestinely for America through a network of friends. Years later, in his memoirs, John Jay referred to the revocation as the "detestable proceedings."[16] Augustus seems to have effortlessly become a part of his new home in New York and joined the French Protestant Church. In 1725 a clerical dispute drove Augustus Jay into the Anglican Church which became the Jay family religion going forward. Augustus and his wife Anna Bayard had four children that survived. Their son, Peter—John's father—was born in 1704. Peter, like his father and other family members, was trained as a merchant. In 1728, he married Mary Anna van Cortland. John Jay was born the eighth child of Peter and Mary on December 12, 1745, in New York City. His parents would relocate to Rye shortly afterward. Somewhat prophetically for a future chief justice, John Jay was named John after his aunt's husband, John Chambers, a justice of the supreme court of the colony of New York. Listening to vivid family stories about persecution and religious intolerance as a child left a lifelong impression on Jay, who was one of the most outwardly traditionally religious Founders.

At the age of six, Jay was sent to a grammar school kept by the Reverend Stoope in New Rochelle (the city's roots stretched back to the French city of La Rochelle). At an early age, John Jay impressed his parents and teachers by taking "to learning exceedingly well."[17] Jay stayed with the Reverend Stoope three years before returning home for private tutoring and entering college. In May 1764, Jay graduated top in his class with a Bachelor of Arts degree. He had by this point already decided on pursuing law as a career. Without delay, Jay entered the law office of Benjamin Kissam to commence his legal studies. After three years of study and practical experience, Jay was admitted to the bar in 1768. His reputation for hard work, sound reasoning, and strong principles (and his father's network of associates), gained Jay a lucrative business practice in short order. Jay's first big assignment on the public stage came in the early 1770s when King George III appointed a commission to adjudicate the boundary dispute between New York and New Jersey. The commission appointed Jay to be the secretary. On April 28, 1774, Jay married Sarah Livingston, daughter of the soon to be first non-royal governor of New Jersey, William Livingston.

John and Sarah Jay's honeymoon was short lived. News reached the colonies of the new British law called the Boston Port Bill scheduled to take effect in May of that year. The Port Bill closed the port of Boston as punishment in part for the Boston Tea Party. On May 16, 1774 (three weeks after they wed), prominent men of New York City met to discuss the turn of events in Boston and what implications this bill could have on New York. This gathering produced a committee of fifty to work with the other colonies on a joint response to Parliament. John Jay, still a newlywed, was appointed to this committee.

On September 5, 1774, John Jay took his place among the delegates who gathered in Carpenter's Hall in Philadelphia for the First Continental Congress. Jay was one of the youngest delegates—if not the youngest—to be a representative of his colony; he was 28. Jay was appointed to multiple commit-tees and quickly earned a reputation as a good writer and even better thinker.

Jay made the most of his first experience with national issues, and impressed nearly all the delegates with his energy and determination. He was subsequently elected to the post of delegate to the Second Continental Con-gress meeting in May 1775. Jay's national career was cut short however when he returned home to help draft the New York state constitution.

Under the new state Constitution of New York in 1777, Jay was named the chief justice of the state supreme court. He was offered the governorship, but declined, saying he felt he could best serve New York by being a part of the judiciary, and not the executive branch. Staying on the court allowed Jay to continue in the realm which suited his education and abilities. For over two years Jay worked at this position while no longer being a member of the Continental Congress (and missing his chance to be a signer of the Declara-tion of Independence). In late 1778, Jay was recalled back to Congress and made its president. Upon this distinction, he resigned as chief justice of New York.

On September 27, 1779, the Continental Congress selected their presi-dent, John Jay, to be the next minister plenipotentiary to Spain. Jay's voyage to Spain was not without incident. John and Sarah left Philadelphia on the *Confederacy*, at the end of October 1779. The ship had problems just getting out of the Delaware River and into the Bay and Atlantic. Then, a fierce storm nearly sank the ship, leaving it virtually helpless in the ocean. It limped to Martinique where the Jays were immediately placed on the French ship *Aurora* to continue their journey. That ship was forced to change course after being chased by a British warship off of France and instead docked in Cadiz, Spain. The original idea was to have the French introduce Jay to the Spanish. Spain was not overly open to acknowledging American independence. For Jay however, American independence was an established fact, never mind the war being fought. The Spanish, colonial masters themselves, were not so convinced independence was a suitable course for colonies to pursue. They wanted proof America was ready to go its separate way; Jay could not provide proof. Spanish officials treated Jay accordingly, "Pains were taken to prevent any conduct towards me that might savour of an admission or knowledge of American independence."[18] He did manage to secure a small loan for the Americans from Spain though.

Amidst the fast-paced flow of events occasioned by the end of the fight-ing after Yorktown, Jay received a letter from Benjamin Franklin in Paris in May 1782 asking him to proceed to join him in preparation for anticipated peace negotiations with England. His move to Paris would mark a new aspect of his career and a further enhancement of his credentials. Jay was instru-mental in urging direct negotiations with Great Britain against the advice of the Congress which recommended letting France take the lead—a directive that rankled Jay's nationalist impulses. The greatest achievement of his time in Europe was the Paris Peace Treaty of 1783. It was his one true accomplishment of nearly five years overseas.

Jay returned to New York with Sarah on July 24, 1784, five years after they left. When he stepped off the ship he was hailed as though a conquering hero. There was little rest for the weary though as Congress had appointed Jay to the office of secretary of foreign affairs. Jay immediately accepted, despite his fatigue. Jay dutifully fulfilled this role for three years, eschewing larger domestic issues facing the newly independent United States. Jay was not involved with any convention or committee work leading up to the Constitutional Convention in 1787; in fact, his political enemy, Governor George Clinton, maneuvered to prevent Jay from being part of the New York delegation to Philadelphia in 1787—and thus Jay missed being a signer of the Constitution too.

In the midst of being the foreign affairs secretary, and marginalized by Clinton, Jay was approached by Alexander Hamilton about a project he (Hamilton) had developed to bolster the chances of the newly drafted Constitution being ratified by the state of New York. *The Federalist* papers, a series of 85 essays written by Hamilton, Jay, and James Madison, over the course of about seven months from October 1787 to the summer of 1788, were something of an owner's manual for the new, proposed, Constitution. Unfortunately, Jay was taken sick with severe rheumatism and contributed only five essays: numbers 2, 3, 4, 5, and 64. Each essay dealt with foreign influence and the need to have a union of states with a central government rather than a confederation. Hamilton considered Jay a great catch for *The Federalist* papers project, as Jay was by far the most notable of the three writers in 1787, even though their identity was secret.

Jay's big role on the national stage occurred with the creation of the new government under the Constitution in 1789. As chief justice, Jay can be credited with creating a body that had limited precedent in Britain and only slight instances within the states as appeals courts. He tried most notably several loyalist cases and British creditor, pre–War, cases. In his first jury instructions as chief justice, Jay sounded a familiar theme of inclusive sacrifice for the greater good. These instructions are considered a classic exposition of American law. (See Appendix C.) Specifically, Jay was concerned about repayment of British debt contracted before the Revolution and the ways states were ignoring the provisions of the 1783 Treaty calling for repayment of contracted debt. Jay was intimately aware of the issue not just from the standpoint of his work on the Paris Peace Treaty ten years earlier as a negotiator, but also through his work on the Court. Not only did these cases highlight the extent to which states were going to ignore the Treaty, it also illustrated the level of animosity which some states displayed accepting the supremacy of federal law as established through the Constitution.

When John Jay rejected President Adams's appointment to the position of chief justice in 1801 (which would have been his second time in the role of chief), he cited the lack of respect the Court had endured during the previous ten years. (See Appendix D.) He had a point. The Court, as a joint creation of the legislative and executive branches, had become a tennis ball. The high turnover rate of justices due to a variety of reasons, and the sometimes-lackluster talent chosen by Presidents Washington and Adams, all conspired to render the Court a challenge not worthy of the highest legal minds in the country. Jay was a prime example of this. He was unquestionably one of the finest legal minds in the nation but shied away from serving a second time as chief justice. The man who ultimately became chief, John Marshall, known today as the "Great Chief Justice," had a legal education that was the envy of no one. Naturally, at the time, legal education was something we tend to put in quotations today, as a system of legal study did not formally exist as we know it; still, there was a system and it worked for the time. Marshall, however, did not even excel at what was standard for the time. There is no question though that Marshall rose to the challenge, though that is beyond the survey of this book. To return to John Jay, the *Aurora* reported on February 3, 1801, that Jay's rejection of his appointment to the Supreme Court for a second time had "staggered the malcontents. In fact, it was as astounding to them, as if the earth had opened a cavern before them, and threatened to swallow them up."[19] The *Aurora* was reporting on the political aspects of Jay's rejection; further indication of just how politicized the Court had become.

Despite all the issues, Jay still held the Court in esteem. According to John Jay's son, William, joining the Supreme Court in 1789 was a great milestone in his father's life. Remembering the episode, William Jay wrote:

> His emotions on the present occasion, though more unmixed than before, must still have been strongly excited. He now saw his country in the enjoyment, not only of peace and independence, but of a wise, equal, and energetic government; and after having long deplored those aberrations from justice and good faith which had tarnished the luster of the American confederacy, he found himself called to apply his own inflexible principles of right, not only to private controversies, but likewise to such as involved the obligations of treaties, and the honor and interests of the nation.[20]

John Rutledge

John Rutledge was born in Charleston, South Carolina, in 1739, by most accounts on September 18. He was born into two aristocratic plantation families (Hext and Rutledge) and had his life planned for him from an early age due to his advantageous birth. Aside from operating a large plantation, the family business was law and statecraft. Many members of Rutledge's extended family practiced law and many were involved in the political affairs of the colony.

After private tutoring, first with his father, and after his father's death with the Reverend Andrews, rector of Christ Church Parish, Rutledge read law with James Parsons before heading to London to study law at the Inns of Court in London.[21] Specifically, John Rutledge studied at Middle Temple and was admitted to the English Bar in 1760 (the same year incidentally that George III ascended the throne). Returning to South Carolina, Rutledge quickly settled into life as an aristocratic planter. In fact, he acquired his first clients before he ever returned to Charleston. Due to his birth, Rutledge was destined for more than the daily drudgery of law office work. In quick succession, Rutledge was elected to the Commons House of Assembly and then to represent South Carolina in the Stamp Act Congress which met in New York on October 7, 1765. Rutledge was the youngest member of Congress at 26.

As one of the older justices appointed by President Washington in 1789, Rutledge studied law before the arrival of William Blackstone's *Commentaries on the Laws of England*, which began arriving in the colonies in the late 1760s. In fact, Rutledge held the post of attorney general of the colony of South Carolina before Blackstone's study arrived in the colonies. Like all aspiring lawyers in the pre–Blackstone era though, Rutledge did study *Coke on Littleton* and all the musty law tomes which had accumulated at the Inns of Court before his arrival as a student.

Rutledge began his career as a national statesman, like so many others throughout the colonies in that generation, in the Stamp Act Congress of 1765. This was the first real test of the colonies' ability to come together as a collective to oppose British governance. Furthermore, like most, Rutledge saw that the way forward for the colonies was still as members of the British Empire. In the Stamp Act Congress, he was tasked with drafting a petition to the British House of Lords, laying out in detail the colonies' objections to the Stamp Act itself. From this point forward American and British relations would spiral downward to the point of war. At every step along the way, John Rutledge was part of the debate for his home colony of South Carolina.

In 1774, he represented South Carolina in the First Continental Congress, which met in Philadelphia. Again, as with many of his colleagues, even after almost ten years of disagreement with Britain, they still hoped for an amicable solution whereby the colonies would remain part of the Empire. These hopes were quickly dashed in April 1775 in Concord, Massachusetts, and the colonies started to organize themselves politically for war and independence. South Carolina elected John Rutledge their first state president. In fact, so powerful was Rutledge's post that he was often referred to as the dictator, assuming extraordinary power to conduct state business during the Revolutionary crisis.

One example of Rutledge's approach to the War is seen in a letter to Major General Lincoln on September 10, 1779. Rutledge, writing about southern strategy, saw several cities as necessary for the Americans to neutralize. Rutledge wrote, "The reduction of St. Augustine and destroying the town and castle..., appear absolutely necessary, for the security of Georgia and this state [South Carolina] and would, probably, ensure their future tranquility.... I therefore cannot avoid proposing an attack by the forces under your command, in conjunction with those of our ally, on St. Augustine." Rutledge argued that prisoners of war should "be delivered up, to the executive authority of this state, to be treated according to our law." Finally, Rutledge felt it "just that all property which belonged to the inhabitants of this state should be restored to them, or payment of reasonable salvage."[22] In another letter, Rutledge talked of receiving 50,000 pounds of gun powder and 7,000 muskets with bayonets.[23]

During the War, Rutledge never held a national military post. He served in the Continental Congress, and then as governor of South Carolina through a series of mostly disastrous confrontations with the British. In fact, for one year, Rutledge was in exile in North Carolina due to the British presence in his state. Another aspect that made the Carolina's so difficult to govern during the Revolutionary years was the side conflict occurring between the warring Scots clans who were agitated for and against the British and Americans. Ancient Scots clan warfare (which the migrants brought with them from Scotland when they came to the colonies) put the southern conflict into an entirely separate dimension.

Author David Ramsay is the source for much of the information concerning John Rutledge during his years as governor of South Carolina. Ramsay's *History of The Revolution of South Carolina, from a British Province to an Independent State*, published in 1785, relied on first hand accounts and access to state papers to fashion his depiction of Rutledge and of the extraordinary powers given to him by the South Carolina Assembly. Ramsay did not use the term "dictator," but once it was used, whether to criticize Rutledge or condemn the Assembly, it stuck. The specific ordinance of the Assembly which is often seen as granting extraordinary power to Rutledge, passed on February 3, 1780, allowed the governor and his council:

> A number of specific powers, namely, to embody the militia and provide for the support of the families of poor militiamen during service; to stop vendues [public auctions], commercial transactions, and the proceedings of the Court of Common Pleas.... Furthermore, the faith and credit of the state were pledged for any expense the governor and the Council might incur in carrying out the ... powers.[24]

Rutledge certainly enjoyed expansive powers as governor, however, he is credited with using them, in the aggregate, judiciously. Among his actions, he "suspended the laws making state and Continental paper money legal tender; he issued a proclamation against plundering and sought to put a stop to the outrages that were being committed by partisans and outlaws; he appointed magistrates and ordinaries; ... and above all he made strenuous efforts, with varying success, to enforce the militia laws and to organize a body of regular troops."[25] In total, during the War, Rutledge held a variety of positions in state government besides governor; among them, delegate to the Continental Congress, member of the South Carolina Council of Safety, and president of the South Carolina House of Representatives.

At the Constitutional Convention of 1787, Rutledge approached the proceedings along a line of argument that went generally with a states' rights reasoning philosophy. Rutledge was a prominent member of the prominent South Carolina delegation and played a leading role among the handful of leaders who dominated debate during the long months over the summer of 1787. Throughout the Convention Rutledge served on numerous committees, among them were compromise on representation, detail, apportionment, and interstate comity and bankruptcy.

Rutledge was extremely pro-slavery during the convention. As a southerner, this could have been expected. Yet Rutledge went beyond many of his fellow Southerners in his views to ensure that "the states not interested in that property and prejudiced against it" did not gain more power than those states which did have an interest in slavery.[26] In fact, Rutledge saw the slavery question as not about "religion and humanity" but rather whether the south would be part of the union.[27] As James Madison recorded in his notes, Rutledge stated: "If the convention thinks that North Carolina, South Carolina, and Georgia will never agree to the plan, unless their right to import slaves be untouched, the expectation is vain."[28]

Yet, Rutledge was a proponent of the supremacy of the proposed federal Constitution. Rutledge even suggested the language, "This Constitution and the laws of the United States made in pursuance thereof, ... should be the supreme law of the several states and of their citizens and inhabitants."[29] Rutledge also was in favor of expanding suffrage. He felt that suffrage should be open to more than freeholders. Again, as James Madison recorded in his notes, Rutledge stated that "restraining the right of [suffrage] ... a very unadvised one. It would create division among the people and make enemies of all those who should be excluded."[30]

Rutledge was not in favor of making a general address to the people of America by the delegates upon the drafting of the proposed Constitution when the convention finished its work in September 1787. Rutledge felt it would be premature to address American citizens about a proposal, which the new Constitution was at that point. It still had to be ratified by the separate states. Furthermore, Rutledge felt the Continental Congress should make any pronouncement as it was the legal body still in place representing the American public—however limited that public was.[31]

President Washington nominated John Rutledge of South Carolina as senior associate justice. An imminent jurist with impeccable educational attainments, Rutledge's commission was dated September 26, 1789. In a letter three days later to Rutledge, the President squarely set forth his view on the nature of the new federal judiciary. Washington acknowledged the adhesive quality of law to a society when administered uniformly. This bonding quality of law was one of Washington's most descriptive explanations of law as a unifying force. Writing from the capital in New York on September 29, 1789, Washington wrote:

> Regarding the due administration of justice as the strongest cement of good government, I have considered the first organization of the judicial department as essential to the happiness of our citizens, and to the stability of our political system....
>
> In any event I concluded that I should discharge the duty which I owe to the public by nominating to this important office a person whom I judged best qualified to execute its function—and you will allow me to repeat the wish that I may have the pleasure to hear of your acceptance of the appointment.[32]

Rutledge's acceptance response to the president was as solicitous as was the President's original letter. Claiming that his original plans in 1789 centered on retirement rather than service, Rutledge conceded that Washington's high opinion of him required him to accept. Rutledge replied to the President on October 27, 1789: "I esteem it highly honorable, to be selected as one of the fittest characters to fill the supreme judicial department, and associated with gentlemen of such ability and integrity as those whom you have chosen for that purpose."[33]

Among the original seven appointees, Rutledge is the only one who accepted his nomination but never heard a case as an associate justice. After the first three terms of the Court, where no cases were heard, Rutledge was appointed chief justice of the Court of Common Pleas for South Carolina. He resigned from the Supreme Court (March 5, 1791) before he ever acted upon a case—although he did attend to some perfunctory duties while a justice and during circuit travels. Rutledge wrote to the President: "This state [South Carolina] having thought proper to create the office of chief justice, and offer it to me, and the peculiar circumstances of the appointment being such that I conceive I could not with any propriety refuse it, I beg leave to enclose, and resign, my commission, of an associate judge of the United States."[34]

Four years later, in 1795, after a none-too-self-serving letter to the president, Washington again appointed Rutledge to a seat on the Court, this time as chief justice. After John Jay resigned to become governor of New York, Washington made a recess appointment of John Rutledge on July 1, 1795. Rutledge had actually sent a letter to Washington expressing his willingness to accept the chief justice position should it be offered. This may seem self-serving, and no doubt it was to an extent, but Washington was always interested in actually knowing beforehand whether potential nominees would accept a posting so as to avoid the public embarrassment of someone rejecting an offering of a post. So, in a way, Rutledge's letter was just what Washington wanted to hear.

Unfortunately, the president let his conviction get the better of him. He received numerous bits of advice concerning Rutledge and his fitness for office. All of these were negative as to Rutledge's ability, due to an increasingly debilitating mental state, to carry out his duties as chief justice. In the end, Washington kept to his own counsel and put Rutledge's nomination forward.

Before his nomination was acted upon by the Senate in December 1795, Rutledge made the huge mistake of making indecorous remarks concerning the recently concluded Jay Treaty, which President Washington and the Federalists were trying to round up support for. It was a controversial agreement which many Americans saw as being too favorable to the British.

While Rutledge did sit as chief in a recess appointment and delivered opinions, he never sat with Senate approval (his time on the Court will be covered in Chapter 6). When his nomination came up in December 1795, the Senate rejected his appointment (the first rejection of a Supreme Court nominee), in part for his vocal denunciation of the Jay Treaty and because, some observed, Rutledge had begun to exhibit frequent episodes of unstable mental health. In fact, Rutledge tried to kill himself the day after Christmas 1795.

Reflecting on the whole matter in the new year, Gabriel Ford, scion of one of northern New Jersey's most powerful families, wrote to his brother Timothy on January 13, 1796. Timothy Ford, having moved to Charleston a decade earlier with his brother Jacob and sister Elizabeth and her husband Henry William De Saussure, was uniquely situated to report on the tribulations surrounding John Rutledge. Gabriel, writing from his home in Morristown, responded to the news his brother was sending:

> I expressed some joy to Mr. D[e Saussure] that the Senate had rejected the nomination of Mr. Rutledge whose wild, intemperate speeches had sunk him as an able statesman quite below mediocrity, for I could not credit the reports of his infirmity. It is since then established by a paragraph in one of your papers that disarms me of my former opinion and I am ready to believe freely that when in health he was the able, profound, good man which so many of you represented him to be.[35]

Gabriel Ford was clearly up to date on current topics concerning John Rutledge and his ill-fated nomination as chief justice. Ford's comment on statesmanship

Charleston, South Carolina, home of John Rutledge, date unknown (Historical American Buildings Survey).

was a reference to Rutledge's attack of the Jay Treaty—a treaty the Ford family would likely have supported.

In trying to avoid a public relations disaster, Washington only created one; and it got larger when Associate Justice John Blair resigned in early 1796. Washington now had two vacancies to fill on the Court. Once again, trying to move quickly to fill the Court's seats, Washington sought to elevate Associate Justice William Cushing to chief and nominate Samuel Chase of Maryland as an associate justice. (Even if this had worked out, it still would have left one seat vacant due to Cushing's elevation to chief.) The Senate confirmed both Cushing and Chase but Cushing, claiming ill health, declined the chief's role but kept his associate justice seat. With the chief's seat once again vacant, Washington turned to Connecticut Senator Oliver Ellsworth, which proved successful.

Washington seemed to lose his good sense of political awareness when Jay resigned as Chief Justice in 1795. This was partly due to the expediency of the situation. Rutledge was a known entity with unquestionable credentials. However, Rutledge also had a noticeable mental illness that at the time was difficult to diagnose but not difficult to observe. Washington ignored this, and the advice of others who cautioned him to think twice about Rutledge. Washington had to know the Senate vote on Rutledge as chief would not be easy or unanimous. This Senate rebuke was a painful public rejection for the president.

In summing up John Rutledge, his contributions to the American cause were unquestionable. Yet, he suffered overtly from the same petty jealousies that doomed the Articles of Confederation. In turn, the sniping of pro-state delegates to the Constitutional Convention in 1787 had no greater champion than Rutledge. He did manage to compromise occasionally, but he was conscious of, in his view, not short-changing South Carolina. There is a fine line between compromise and saying no; Rutledge seemed to have straddled the line with great finesse. Leon Friedman concludes a short biography of Rutledge by stating: "Though he participated in all great events of his time, he lacked the vision, ability, and power of Hamilton, Madison, or Jefferson.... While many members of the Virginia aristocracy concerned themselves with the general welfare of the nation, the South Carolinian leaders looked only to their own constituents."[36]

William Cushing

Like every other member of the Supreme Court, William Cushing enjoyed the advantages of a distinguished birth. Both his mother's and father's line had deep roots in the New England area, Boston specifically, for nearly a century before he was born. Both sides as well had distinguished ancestors who added to the weight of expectation into which William Cushing was born. As Herbert Johnson wrote in a short biography of Cushing: "Social and political connections being an important aspect of office holding [in] the Bay Colony, it was a foregone conclusion that one-day young William would succeed to the positions of his ancestors as one of the leaders of his native province."[37]

William Cushing was born on March 1, 1732 (less than two weeks after George Washington in Virginia), in Scituate, Massachusetts. He would have the distinction of being the longest-serving of President Washington's original appointees to the Court. Like his peers, Cushing was highly educated, with a degree from Harvard and an honorary degree from Yale. He also read law with notable Boston lawyer Jeremiah Gridley. Cushing was admitted to the bar in 1755. Cushing's private legal practice was not successful and he turned to the judiciary where he succeeded his father as an associate justice of the Superior Court in Boston in 1772.

This was a time fraught with incredible energy in Boston over the quickly rising colonial government debate with Britain. The Boston "Massacre" and the Tea Party had both occurred by the time Cushing married Hannah Phillips in 1774. Cushing had a remarkable career given the incendiary nature of Boston at the time he was beginning his first judicial post. After all, Cushing was appointed to his first judgeship by the Royal Governor Thomas Hutchinson and thus was clearly working for the British government. In the same year of his marriage (1774) Cushing's hand was forced; was he to side with the Crown or the rebels in the Massachusetts legislature? Cushing seems genuinely to have agonized over this and at the last moment chose the rebel side, thus sealing the fate of the rest of his life. He is still viewed as a lukewarm Revolutionary at best. Nevertheless, he made his decision and stuck with it.

Cushing was the only one of his judicial colleagues on the Superior Court to side with the new revolutionary Council of State in 1775 when that body declared itself the new government of Massachusetts. When the new Superior Court of Judicature was organized in 1775 (a court Cushing would soon lead), John Adams was appointed the chief justice. Adams wrote to Cushing: "But be assured that no circumstance relating to that appointment has given me so much concern as my being placed at the head of it, in preference to another, who in my opinion was so much better qualified for it and entitled to it."[38] Adams held the new position barely a year, never having actually performed his duties, as Massachusetts, and the colonies, careened towards war and independence. After Adams resigned from the Superior Court, Cushing was appointed chief, a role he would fulfill for the next twelve years through war, independence, and the start of a new country with the Constitution.[39]

William Cushing spent the entire Revolutionary War as a judge. He did occasionally take on representative roles to help write the state constitution or to help ratify the federal Constitution in 1788. But, Cushing was a jurist, a judge; he was not a fighter or revolutionary in the John Adams mold, and certainly not in the Samuel Adams mold. It was this steady hand at the judiciary

which, in part, led President Washington to nominate Cushing to be one of
the first six appointees to the Supreme
Court.

Rather than charting a career in
post-colonial government, Cushing
provided a steady hand on the judiciary in Massachusetts during extremely
trying times. While Cushing did not
participate in any of the major events
of the Revolutionary Era (Continental
Congress, military posts, diplomatic
work), his unwavering commitment to
the legal process, even during the most
unstable times, ensured a framework
upon which to expand the rapidly ad-
vancing ideas of post–War America.
This may seem to make him an odd
choice for a seat on the Supreme Court.
Yet, it was precisely his steady, work-
a-day approach to being a judge that
prevailed upon President Washington
to make Cushing an associate justice.

Justice William Cushing of Massachusetts (Morristown National Historical
Park).

In fact, those very qualities that led Cushing to be such a long serving judge
in Boston played out on the Supreme Court as Cushing was the last surviving,
and longest serving, member of Washington's first six nominees.

After receiving his official letter of nomination from President Washington, Cushing responded to the president as follows:

> You condescended, sir, to consider the judicial system as the chief pillar of our national
> government, and kindly to say, that you have nominated to that department such men
> as you conceived would give dignity and luster to our national government. I should
> be glad if my poor abilities could in any measure give ground for such a hope respecting
> myself; but I beg leave to say, that my wish has been from the beginning, to have such
> a national government take place, as should effectively secure the union, the authority,
> the peace and prosperity of these states. And since you have been pleased to express a
> desire of my ready acceptance of the office, I do now, with the greater confidence, but
> hoping for your candor, of which I shall stand in need, declare my acceptance of it.[40]

In a letter from February 2, 1792, Cushing offered a glimpse of the hardships the justices faced while traveling on circuit duty. Writing to President
Washington, Cushing stated:

> I take the liberty to inform you … [that] I have had the misfortune to be stopped here,
> since Friday last, by a bad cold attended with somewhat of a fever…. The traveling is

difficult this season. I left Boston the 13th of January in a phaeton, in which I made out to reach Middleton as the snow of the 18th began, which fell so deep there as to oblige me to take a sleigh, and now again wheels seem necessary.[41]

When President Washington was looking for a chief justice after the John Rutledge fiasco he turned to William Cushing—without first gauging his interest. Washington actually nominated Cushing as chief and placed his name before the Senate where it was immediately ratified on January 27, 1796. When notified, Cushing considered the post, but ultimately turned down the chief position and remained as an associate justice.

Unlike some of his colleagues, "there is no spectacle of an instant leap from obscurity to fame."[42] Cushing had perhaps one of the most boringly predictable lives of any of the justices, both prior to and during his tenure on the Court. Not that that was a bad thing; continuity and consistency are highly valued qualities both in revolutionary times and during peaceful times. Put in a slightly romantic fashion, Cushing can be likened to a tree—"such a life is of necessity one of slow and steady growth, like that of the oak, ring on ring."[43]

After over twenty years on the bench, Cushing could claim to have been involved in some of the most foundational cases to come before the Court during its formative period. Cushing was the first Supreme Court justice to administer the oath of office to a president in March 1793. Cushing ruled in cases involving state sovereignty, constitutional supremacy, and admission of evidence in criminal cases. These decisions will be covered in the appropriate chapters corresponding to the period in which they were decided.

Former president Thomas Jefferson, in retirement at Monticello, made a point in an 1810 letter to Attorney General Caesar A. Rodney about a replacement for Cushing after his death. It was a sad commentary that Cushing, the last surviving member of the first six nominees to the Court by President Washington, would serve long enough to see his seat become little more than political fodder, something that genuinely would have surprised him, and George Washington, in 1789 when he was first appointed. In the September 25 letter to Rodney, Jefferson (who became a hyperpartisan during his presidency) relished the opportunity to have a majority of justices who supported his Republican party perspective. He wrote: "The death of Cushing is therefore opportune as it gives an opening for at length getting a Republican majority on the supreme bench. Ten years has the anti-civism of that body been bidding defiance to the spirit of the whole nation, after they had manifested their will by reforming every other branch of the government."[44] Concerning the lack of common law procedure or practice in New England, and as a swipe at the dreaded Federalist Party, Jefferson wrote to Rodney, "There is not, and never was an able one [lawyer] in the New England states. Their system is *sui generis* [unique], in which the common law is little attended to."[45]

John Blair

John Blair of Virginia was born in Williamsburg in 1732, the same year as Washington. He graduated from the College of William and Mary in 1752. Family wealth allowed Blair to travel to England where he studied law at the Inns of Court (Middle Temple), graduating in 1754. While in England, young Blair had the privilege to have as a mentor family friend Robert Dinwiddie, former governor of the Virginia colony. Upon his return, he was elected to the House of Burgess in 1766 to represent the College of William and Mary, and he followed that body as it revolted against British rule. Blair was not a "flaming" radical and never served in the military. Blair worked primarily in the Virginia state courts during the American Revolution and was appointed a delegate to the Philadelphia Constitutional Convention in 1787 and signed the final draft produced by the Convention. Blair was first appointed to the Virginia Supreme Court of Appeals in 1789 but declined after he became one of President Washington's first six nominees to the new Supreme Court, to which he received his commission in September 1789. John Blair wrote to Washington that "I have determined to make an experiment, whether I am able to perform the requisite services."[46] Like most of the other appointees, Blair was concerned about the circuit riding duties. Traveling circuits would require extended absences from one's family, exposure to the elements, lodging with strangers in strange inns, and eating questionable food on a daily basis. Given all the negative aspects of the job, Blair consented only because it was Washington who was asking. Justice Blair had the distinction of being the judge whose presence allowed the Court to conduct its first business with his arrival on February 2, 1790, in New York. His arrival allowed for a quorum to be reached.

James Wilson

A substantial claim could certainly be made that James Wilson was the most interesting and unique member of the early Supreme Court. As one of only six men to sign both the Declaration of Independence and the Constitution, Wilson was clearly a Founding Father.[47] His education and intellectual attainments marked him early in life to be a leader and a mentor of not just men, but mankind. Yet, with all of that in the credit column of his life's ledger book, he still came to die penniless in an obscure tavern in North Carolina while on the run from bill collector's when he was fifty-six.[48]

James Wilson was born on September 14, 1742, in Fifeshire, Scotland. Early in life Wilson exhibited an innate intellectual bearing which was well incubated during the heady days of the Scottish Enlightenment. His studies

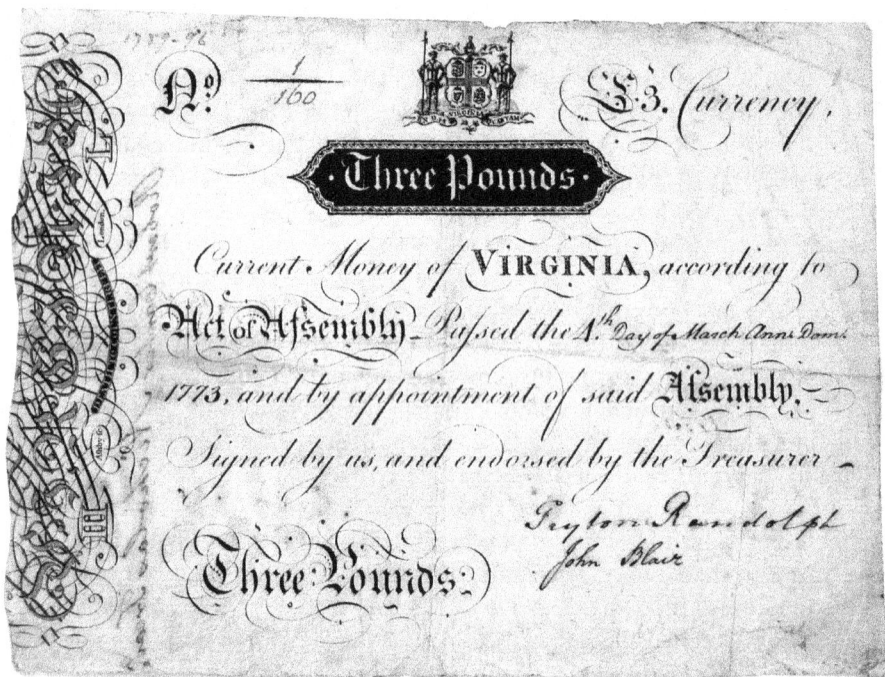

Signature of future Supreme Court justice John Blair on a 3-pound note, 1773. The note is also signed by the first president of the First Continental Congress, Payton Randolph (Morristown National Historical Park).

prepared him for his migration to the American colonies in 1765, after graduating from Saint Andrews University. He settled in Philadelphia and began to study law. Fortunately for Wilson, he was accepted to study with John Dickinson, a highly learned and capable attorney who himself became a Founder. After successfully practicing law for a number of years, Wilson was eager to lend his voice to the growing crisis between the colonies and Britain. In 1774, the same year as Thomas Jefferson's pamphlet *The Rights of British North America*, Wilson wrote his own pamphlet called *Considerations on the Nature and Extent of the Legislative Authority of the British Parliament*. Wilson was elected to the Second Continental Congress and continued to prosper in his legal practice. In the early 1780s he began to become involved with land speculation, and in less than 20 years he would be dead, buried in a pauper's grave.

In the vast North American continent, land speculation was not uncommon—in fact quite a few Founders engaged in the practice. Certainly, men of means were engaged, and over extended, in the contest to create wealth and determine western settlement and expansion. Men from all economic strata engaged if they could; from those at the top, like George Washington, to those unnamed of lesser financial standing, all entered the frenzied market. It produced some immense fortunes, but more likely it created financial hardship and burden. For James Wilson, sadly, the latter occurred.

It was also during these 11 years between 1776 and 1787 that Wilson became heavily involved with the banking and land speculation that would ultimately lead to his downfall. He was a director of the Bank of North America when banks were not viewed favorably at all. In fact, Wilson was occasionally the target of vandals and mob violence by those who saw banks as the bastions of the moneyed elite.

Even when he was appointed to the Supreme Court in 1789, there were signs of trouble in his shaky financial portfolio. As early as 1782, Wilson was bargaining over the price of furniture he was selling to satisfy a debt. In a letter of February 9, 1782, Wilson wrote "On reconsidering, more maturely, the [language?] of my last letter to you, I am apprehensive that your reassessing the appraised value of the furniture, as it will not discharge the whole of your demand, may [?] some legal difficulties in the [?] which it may be necessary to take for reassessing the remediation of the debt."[49] Wilson was concerned that the appraised value of the furniture was not high enough to eliminate the debt owed to his creditors and therefore was looking to have the appraisal reconsidered.

Eleven years later, Wilson, now a Supreme Court justice, entered an agreement with William Bingham on July 17, 1793. Wilson borrowed £5,013 to be repaid, with interest, by February 1, 1794. This brief seven-month loan was to be repaid at £5,506, meaning the original loan carried an approximate ten percent interest rate.[50] Wilson's practice of staying one step ahead of one creditor by engaging another creditor lasted nearly 15 years and presented a sorry commentary on the life of someone so brilliant. This was someone forced to sell his household furnishings to cover the debts incurred in land speculation and other investments in the highly turbulent financial world of post–Revolutionary America.

It seems almost incongruous that such a uniquely brilliant legal mind would descend into financial ruin. Of course, not all the blame for his collapse can be placed at Wilson's feet. The unimaginably chaotic financial world of post–Revolutionary America was nearly indecipherable and some elements of Wilson's collapse were certainly out of his control. However, in the late 1770s and for the next decade, Wilson was simply one of the greatest theoretical legal thinkers in the United States.

During the Second Continental Congress, Wilson was a reliable voice for an independent United States before and after the Declaration of Independence. His arguments invariably centered on legal reasoning, generally formulated on the grounds that Britain abrogated their legal duties to the colonies. Wilson was perhaps the best prepared to follow this line of thought. For Wilson, the law was paramount. Without law, there would be no liberty; without liberty, no law. The two concepts or perspectives were fused, and to Wilson they formed the essence of the American colonial revolt.

More significant was Wilson's conception of natural law versus human law. To Wilson, natural law constituted some impenetrable law that existed outside the realm of human law; for him, and ultimately America, human law and liberty were what was at stake in the struggle with Britain. While George Washington is given more than his fair share of credit for the military victory over Britain, Wilson is all but forgotten for his victory over the concepts of the Declaration of Independence, which he did sign. In other words, Wilson, due to his intense involvement in the American political process between 1776 and 1787 (the years of the Declaration and the Constitution), can be seen as the victor in the struggle to find the foundation of American liberty: human law. Those 11 years saw *Nature's God* in the Declaration become *We The People* in the Constitution. "It was Wilson who wrote the intellectual threads of his generation into a theory of popularly based government combined to the rule of law."[51]

Wilson strove throughout his life to bring together the various elements of an emerging American consciousness. "Wilson attempted to blend the ideas of liberty and the rule of law with the new idea of popular sovereignty."[52] He had as much to do with the intellectual underpinnings of the American founding as any man. Wilson not only signed both of America's founding documents, he was instrumental in drafting both. Records indicate he was a seminal figure during the debates in 1776 and in 1787. Wilson's agile mind allowed him to address "the law in broad, often bold strokes that encompassed philosophy, psychology, and political theory."[53] Much of his writing outside the law reflected his research about the law as well. In the new nation, virtue was of paramount importance for being a citizen. Wilson, through his writings, was most closely associated with those who saw citizenship as a "close relationship among public virtue, moral commitment to the public interest, and respect for the will of the people based on their intrinsic good."[54]

WILSON IN 1787

At the Philadelphia Constitutional Convention of 1787, Wilson achieved his greatest public success. He was the second most recorded speaker behind Governor Morris during that hot Philadelphia summer.

During the course of the Convention, Wilson argued for the popular election of members of what became the House of Representatives, while he opposed state legislatures electing Senators. He proposed the executive (president) be a single individual, not a committee; he also felt the executive should be elected directly by the people, not via what would become the Electoral College. As Wilson argued: "If we are to establish a national government, that government ought to flow from the people at large. If one branch of it should be chosen by the legislatures, and the other by the people, the two branches will rest on different foundations, and dissentions will naturally arise between them."[55]

Throughout the summer Wilson engaged in many debates, most of which did not come to fruition in the final document—one which did, has been a source of tremendous controversy ever since. The three-fifths compromise for counting slaves was largely Wilson's idea. That was not a matter of failure on Wilson's part; most contested ideas at the Convention were only adopted in some compromise form—rarely if ever did an individual idea come through the debate process without some alteration if it survived at all. In fact, as one of the more vocal members of the Convention, Wilson recognized that some ideas were dramatically altered and then defeated by the whims of a few states to protect a cherished point-of-view. As James Madison recorded in his notes for Tuesday, June 5, 1787:

> Mr. Wilson took this occasion to lead the committee by a train of observations to the idea of not suffering a disposition in the plurality of states to confederate anew on better principles, to be defeated by the inconsiderate or selfish opposition of a few states. He hoped the provision for ratifying would be put on such a footing as to admit of such a partial union, with a door open for the accession of the rest.[56]

It might seem natural that Wilson, legal scholar that he was, would engage mostly in debates focusing on the judiciary. As is well known, the Articles of Confederation did not have a national judiciary in their composition of the federal government. That was one area the delegates in Philadelphia knew had to be remedied. As such, someone like Wilson was a perfect fit for these debates which touched on sensitive areas of state pride and sovereignty. Taking into account the potential for state squabbling, Wilson and James Madison jointly put forth a resolve on June 5:

> In pursuance of the idea expressed ... by Mr. [John] Dickinson ... the words following "that the national legislature be empowered to institute inferior tribunals." They observed that there was a distinction between establishing such tribunals absolutely, and giving a discretion to the legislature to establish or not establish them.[57]

On June 6, Wilson expressed, perhaps in his most expanded way, his view of federal/state existence and relations. While known as a proponent of a vigorous federal government, Wilson understood the need for state responsibility as well. As recorded again by James Madison, Wilson stated: "The government ought to possess not only first the force, but secondly the mind or sense of the people at large. The legislature ought to be the most exact transcript of the whole society. Representation is made necessary only because it is impossible for the people to act collectively."[58] Wilson was a proponent of a stronger federal government. On July 14, 1787, he presciently observed, "It has never been a complaint against congress that they governed over much. The complaint has been that they have governed too little. To remedy this defect we were sent here."[59]

One of the biggest issues facing the proposed judiciary was the issue of nullification. Could the Supreme Court declare laws passed by Congress unconstitutional? While this prerogative is often seen as having started with the 1803 Supreme Court case of *Marbury v. Madison*, the concept had been around since at least the sixteenth century in English law. Wilson urged that the power to declare laws unconstitutional be included in the written Constitution. While his idea failed to garner support, the concept still remained. He stated on July 21:

> Laws may be unjust, may be unwise, may be dangerous, may be destructive; and yet may not be so unconstitutional as to justify the judges in refusing to give them effect. Let them have a share in the revisionary power, and they will have an opportunity of taking notice of these characters of law, and of counteracting, by weight of their opinions the improper views of the legislature.[60]

Wilson also served on the Committee of Detail which the Convention appointed on July 23 to prepare a draft constitution from the array of resolutions. In fact, of the five members of this committee, three were future Supreme Court members: James Wilson, John Rutledge, and Oliver Ellsworth.

As president of the Constitutional Convention, George Washington no doubt was aware of the makeup of the Committee of Detail and the role it played in fashioning the draft constitution. The efforts on the part of this committee represent the single greatest undertaking by a small group of dedicated delegates who stitched together the variant notions proposed over the preceding three months. To be sure, they embroidered the document with more personal viewpoints than was necessary. Yet, these additions were meant more to smooth out the language, and render sometimes incomprehensible diction, into recognizable language capable of forming a jurisprudence in the form of a constitution.[61] It was a herculean task which is all but lost in attempts to make Constitutional history digestible. If James Madison is rightly hailed as the Father of the Constitution; the Committee of Detail is then the team of doctors who helped birth it into existence.

When President Washington came to appoint members of the Supreme Court, it is interesting to wonder whether he recalled the Committee of Detail and the job they performed. Given that one job prerequisite for a justice to be on the Court ought to be proficiency in understanding the Constitution (although the Constitution makes no such requirement), the President need not have looked any further than the Committee that did the most to structure it. That is why three-fifths of the Committee of Detail's members were appointed to the Supreme Court. Unfortunately, President Washington left no specific reference to this effect.

The Committee of Detail was very important to the overall document being created. While the rest of the delegates enjoyed a ten-day recess from Convention work, the Committee of Detail put together the first working draft of the new constitution. It would fall on the committee to "define the jurisdiction of the federal judiciary more precisely."[62] Thus, this committee, with three future Supreme Court justices, created more than the convention at large—it created the system of American jurisprudence which serves us to this day. Two men, John Rutledge and James Wilson, one southerner and one northerner, were responsible for the draft of the constitution that emerged from the Committee of Detail. As Daniel Stewart has written:

> Rutledge and Wilson thus achieved a creative resolution of the one novel question before the Convention: how to reconcile federal and state powers in an effective structure? Their resolutions left both governments sovereign, both separate, both intertwined, one superior. It was a complex and dynamic resolution, and one that every generation has redefined.[63]

The one area in which the Committee failed to enumerate a judicial prerogative was in declaring laws unconstitutional, a topic that would vex the Court (although most agreed the prerogative existed in theory if not expressly written out) for more than 12 years—even though early instances of its usage predate the famous *Marbury v. Madison* decision of 1803. The final draft of the constitution, prepared by the committee in secret, was printed by publishers John Dunlap and Daniel Claypool for distribution to the delegates to consider upon their return from their ten-day recess.[64]

After the Committee of Detail finished their work, the first working draft of the new proposed constitution was submitted to the convention for review. As one of the five committee members, Wilson was tasked with answering questions from the convention, which began to review and edit the work of the committee beginning on August 7, 1787. The Committee of Detail can be seen as the most effective working group of delegates at the convention. Aside from James Madison, they did more than any other delegates to put the constitution into the form we now recognize. From the jumble of resolutions, utterances, debates, and endless voting, Wilson, Rutledge, Ellsworth, Nathaniel Gorham, and Edmund Randolph (who would ultimately reject the document and refuse to sign it) fashioned the Constitution that has guided the United States ever since. From August 7, the Convention took about a month to edit and revise the work of the Committee of Detail before the Committee of Style wrote the final product. During the month between the Committee of Detail and the Committee of Style, Wilson continued in his role as one of the chief defenders of the draft constitution. After the convention concluded its work in mid–September 1787, and with Wilson's signature on the engrossed parchment, he undertook one more public task in support of the now finalized proposed Constitution. On October 6, 1787, before the first of *The Federalist* papers were published and in what has come to be known as the State House Yard Speech, Wilson gave a muscular defense and explanatory talk to a public audience. It was one of Wilson's finest public performances. Commentators reported that "Mr. Wilson's speech was frequently interrupted with loud and unanimous testimonies of approbation, and the applause which was reiterated at the conclusion, evinced the general sense of its excellence, and the conviction which it had impressed upon every mind."[65] In fact, by the end of the year the speech "had been reprinted in thirty-four newspapers in twelve states and circulated throughout the colonies as a pamphlet."[66]

In December 1791, Justice Wilson approached President Washington about a project he was working on for the State of Pennsylvania, whereby he was digesting the laws of the state for greater understanding and usefulness by citizens. He shared a letter he wrote to the speaker of the house about a possible digest of federal law. (This is something James Kent would complete in 1826.) Wilson wrote:

> By the House of Representatives of Pennsylvania I am empowered to "*digest* into proper *order* and form the laws of that commonwealth"; and "to *report* such a*lterations, additions* and i*mprovements* as the *principles* and forms of the *Constitution* may require."
>
> In this work, I have made some progress; during which it has occurred to me, that a similar work with regard to the laws of the United States might, with propriety accompany that, in which I am engaged.
>
> To *you* it is unnecessary to make any *general* remarks concerning the immense Importance of a good code of municipal law.
>
> There are two circumstances, which induce me to think, that to the United States this subject is *peculiarly* interesting.
>
> 1. Their government is *newly* formed and organized. A good system of legislation introduced into it *now* will have a salutary, a decisive and a *permanent* influence upon its *future* fortunes and character. Good *principles*, at least—principles *congenial* to those of the *Constitution*—should be laid *betimes* as the foundation of subsequent regulations.
> 2. It is of much moment that those principles *established* and *ascertained,* in *complete* and *correct theory, before* they are called farther into *practical operation.* The most intricate and the most delicate questions in our national jurisprudence will arise in running the line between the authority of the national government and that of the several states. A controversy, which happens between two individuals, is considered and determined with coolness and impartiality, like a question of *law.* A controversy, happening between the United States and any particular state in the Union, will be viewed and agitated, with bias and passion, like a question of *politics.* For this reason, the principles and rules, on which it must be determined, should be clearly and explicitly known *before it arises* [emphasis in original].[67]

Courtyard at the back of the Pennsylvania State House (Independence Hall) where James Wilson gave his famous speech, October 1787 (Historic American Buildings Survey).

Robert Harrison

Robert Harrison was born in Charles County, Maryland, in 1745 (his date of birth is unknown). He studied and practiced law prior to the Revolution and became involved in Revolutionary activities from nearly the beginning. He rose rapidly in the army and in May 1776, became a secretary to General George Washington with the rank of Lt. Colonel. He served Washington until the spring of 1781. Thus, he missed the Yorktown campaign which occurred in October 1781, when he was appointed as chief judge of the General Court of Maryland.

Robert Harrison had his share of supporters beyond the president. Alexander Hamilton, who served with Harrison as one of Washington's aid-de-camps, wrote to him at the end of November 1789, upon hearing of Harrison's rejection of an appointment:

> For I consider this business of America's happiness as yet to be done. In proportion to that sentiment has been my disappointment at learning that you had declined a seat on the bench of the United States. Cannot your determination, my dear friend, be reconsidered? ... If it is possible, my dear Harrison, give yourself to us. We want men like you. They are rare at all time.[68]

Robert Harrison's personal letter from President Washington was dated September 30, 1789. With Harrison, Washington picked a good friend and neighbor. Having known Harrison since before the Revolution, Washington felt his "hometown" appointment would be an easy sell. Washington wrote in his official letter to Harrison that "this letter is only considered as an early communication of my sentiments on this occasion."[69]

Responding on October 27, 1789, Harrison admitted that "I cannot but decline the appointment."[70] Harrison remarked and acknowledged that the government is "not yet completely organized."[71] He knew full well his refusal would potentially lead to a delay in the full establishment of the federal government. Harrison, perhaps because of his personal friendship with Washington, was quite candid about why he declined the appointment. Essentially, his family needed him, now more than ever. Harrison found that to accept would be "to desert the interests of those, with whom I am connected by the dearest ties."[72] Without saying it, Harrison was referring to the conditions of the Judiciary Act of 1789 requiring the justices to ride circuit. This mandate was not something to be taken lightly. While it would negatively impact on the justices individually, the collective input, while nearly impossible to measure, was that the Court took the federal government to the people in a way the other branches could not. As Chief Justice John Marshall was to comment several years later, "The judicial department comes home in its effects to every man's fireside; it passes on his property, his reputation, his life, his all."[73]

The case of Harrison was complicated further by his continued inability

Multi-page legal document prepared by Robert Harrison for George Washington as surviving executor of an estate. Filed in Orange County, New York, 1780 (Morristown National Historical Park).

to make a final decision. Although he seemingly rejected Washington, he vacillated in his refusal. On November 14, 1789, James McHenry, a mutual friend of Washington and Harrison, wrote a letter to Washington where he stated that Harrison had asked him to write asking that he (Harrison) "be again in the possession of the commission."[74]

Two weeks later, Washington responded to Harrison with a letter designed in no small measure to impress upon him the pressure of his colleagues. Washington acknowledged that the Judiciary Act needed revision and many members of Congress agreed.[75] Even less than a year into the new government, talk of amending legislation was already common. Most interesting about this letter is the postscript added by the president, which stated: "As it may be satisfactory to you [to] know, the determination of the other Associate Judges of the Supreme Court, I have the pleasure to inform you that all of them have accepted their appointments."[76]

If nothing else, Washington wanted the pressure of Harrison's colleagues to keep him on track and his appointment on time to ensure the Court's readiness. Finally, in a pleading letter on January 21, 1790, two weeks before the Court would first meet, Harrison definitively declined the President's offer. Harrison implored Washington, "I cannot accept the appointment of an associate judge."[77] No further correspondence on the matter was issued.

James Iredell

Born in Lewes, England, in 1751, James Iredell emigrated to America in 1768 and settled in Edenton, North Carolina. Due to his family's harsh financial reality, young James, already exhibiting great potential, was "sacrificed" by the family to try his hand as a colonist. In reality, he had a job arranged for him through family connections and took up the post of Comptroller of Customs, through which he was to partially support his family back in England.

In addition to his work as comptroller, he read law in the office of Samuel Johnston and was admitted to the bar in 1770. He spent the next six years working on honing his legal skills and business sense before beginning serious legal work as a judge in 1777. Iredell was an ardent supporter of the American cause and wrote many essays on behalf of the new American government emerging after declaring independence. In fact, it was as an essayist that he made a name for himself; his strong reasoning abilities and "common sense" went a long way against the likes of the more combustible revolutionaries like Patrick Henry, from neighboring Virginia. Iredell was a member of the Continental Congress, where he and Alexander Hamilton debated general revenue schemes in early 1783. Both advocated for greater national power to raise revenue. Both men were on record early in the tax debate calling for greater national power.[78]

As with many of his closest colleagues in the state and out, Iredell was appalled at the blatant disregard by the states, including his own North Carolina, of the Paris Peace Treaty of 1783 and the language impacting former loyalists and pre–War American debt owed to British merchants. North Carolina,

Letter concerning a court case for a deed, James Iredell, 1782 (Morristown National Historical Park).

much to Iredell's horror, even attempted to pass laws forbidding the state from ever recognizing the Paris Peace Treaty's requirements concerning former loyalists and American debt.[79] Stunned, Iredell continued to publish essays during this period, specifically calling for the strengthening of national laws. In part due to the ill-conceived attempts at legislation on the part of the state, Iredell became more of a vocal supporter of courts having the power over legislatures to declare laws unconstitutional. Although not a delegate to the Philadelphia Constitutional Convention, Iredell was a staunch supporter of the proposed Constitution and fought at the North Carolina state ratifying convention for its passage. During this period, he became best known for his essay "A Reply to the Objections of George Mason." Despite his efforts, and those of other supporters, the first vote in North Carolina to approve the Constitution failed in July of 1788. In November 1789, with the new federal government already operating, the state of North Carolina finally approved the new Constitution.

Thomas Johnson

Thomas Johnson, like George Washington, William Cushing, and John Blair, was born in 1732; he was born in Calvert County, Maryland. He was from a respectable family with ample resources. Johnson read law and was admitted to the bar in 1760. Johnson, like many of his native generation, was an early advocate for American rights and was a delegate to both the First and Second Continental Congresses. He missed being a signer of the Declaration of Independence due to helping to raise a militia in Annapolis. He did serve as Maryland governor for two critical years, 1777–1779. Beyond his work with the militia and the governorship, his efforts during the Revolution and post–Revolutionary period were more focused on his personal business running an iron works. He did reenter active politics in April 1788, when Maryland held its state ratifying convention debating the proposed federal Constitution. Johnson contributed little to the discussion. "One wonders whether Thomas Johnson consciously avoided fame or whether it continually slipped from his grasp."[80]

Thomas Johnson was an odd choice for President Washington. Johnson was certainly a patriot and worked hard for American rights in the years prior to, and immediately after, 1776. But, he was primarily a businessman and not a legal scholar. He was aware of this and tried to reason with the president when notified of his nomination. Johnson was also concerned about the physical requirements of circuit duty. The president assured him that accommodations would be made and that changes to the Judiciary Act of 1789 would be made concerning circuit duties. Johnson was one of the first to rise to George Washington's attention at the Continental Congress, where he was one of the delegates who nominated Colonel George Washington as commander-in-chief of the American army. Johnson followed Washington into the army with his own force which he raised in his native Maryland. Following that venture, Johnson became the first governor of Maryland while remaining active in legal affairs in his state.

Thomas Johnson referencing delivery of goods, 1780 (Morristown National Historical Park).

He replaced John Rutledge as a justice when Rutledge resigned in 1791. Johnson was a recess appointment before being confirmed by the Senate on November 7, 1791. Johnson's greatest qualification for the role of Supreme Court justice seems to have been his association with Washington, especially his work in trade along the Potomac River, something Washington, an astute businessman himself, had worked on since before the Revolution. Other than his loyalty, he had little to bring to the job of a justice.

He served only 14 months, resigning on January 16, 1793, and wrote virtually nothing to be considered a legacy. He seems to have taken the job simply to appease his friend, President Washington. Johnson's resignation led to the growing embarrassment for President Washington over the rapidity of some justices resigning, or, as was the case with Rutledge, never sitting with his colleagues as a justice. The high (and highly public) turnover of staff on the Supreme Court by the end of Washington's first term was a source of concern for him. He felt it not reflective of the dignity of the Court. Furthermore, it placed a stain over the administration of justice which Washington saw as vital to the development of the new nation. Washington wrote to Justice Johnson in a bit of an abrasive tone:

> Besides the difficulty of finding characters to fill the dignified and important station of judge, in whom are combined the necessary professional local and other requisites, the resignation of persons holding that high office conveys to the public mind a want of stability in that department, where it is perhaps more essential than in any other.[81]

This problem showed a weakness of President Washington to misplace his feelings about individuals who in all objectivity should never have been appointed to positions in the government. Sadly, throughout American history this was an all too common occurrence on the part of presidents.

William Paterson

William Paterson was born on December 24, 1745, in County Antrim, Ireland, and brought to America as an infant with his family. The family settled in Princeton, New Jersey. Paterson attended the nearby College of New Jersey where he graduated in 1763 with an undergraduate degree. While at college his classmates included such future leaders as Oliver Ellsworth, James Madison, Luther Martin, Aaron Burr, and others. As a scholar, he quickly and easily gained admittance to study law with one of the most talented lawyers in New Jersey, Richard Stockton. During his time with Stockton, Paterson followed a common practice of keeping a journal or commonplace book, recording the fine points of his study.

THE COMMONPLACE BOOK

William Paterson (1745–1806) is probably best known today, if he is known at all outside a small group of dedicated historians or alumni of the college which bears his name, for the "New Jersey Plan," or the "Paterson Plan," introduced during the Constitutional Convention in 1787.[82] However, far from being a figure known for one shining moment in time, Paterson is in fact someone who had many shining, and some not so shining, moments in the early history of the American Republic. Indeed, Paterson is someone awaiting an updated exploration of his influential career.

Paterson spent much of the 1760s in academic or intellectual pursuits of one sort or another. After taking his undergraduate degree in 1763, he stayed on and completed his graduate work in 1766. Simultaneously, he was apprenticed to Richard Stockton (one of the New Jersey signers of the Declaration of Independence) in the study of the law. Paterson was admitted to the bar in 1769.

One tool in any historian's toolbox is the primary resource. In the case of William Paterson and others of his stature, there are undoubtedly many remaining manuscripts to choose from in various repositories around the country. Determining the type of manuscript to utilize would depend on what one was writing about. While many of these figures are well known today because of their work as adults, it is somewhat unique to be able to study their early lives when they were just beginning to mature into adults. In the case of William Paterson a single ledger or notebook allows us to take the measure of Paterson as he contemplated the legal world of his day and his potential place within that world.

During the mid- to late 1760s the colonies were still very much a part of the British Empire and still celebrating the king's birthday, which they did at the College of New Jersey annually. Whether Paterson participated in these activities is unknown, but he had to have at least known about them. The other issue to keep in mind is that this is precisely the time that William Blackstone was publishing his *Commentaries on the Laws of England*, although few Americans had copies prior to the 1771 printing in Philadelphia. Richard Stockton was known to possess a marvelous library and perhaps had an early British edition of the *Commentaries* for Paterson to study.

Paterson's notebook is serious. There are no doodles or mindless wanderings over pages with a pen which one might expect to accompany a student's notebook. Instead, the erudition which he was already known for and which he would build a career upon is evident throughout. One interesting and somewhat confusing point is on the first page—Paterson wrote his name four times with two different dates. One was "November 29, 1763," the other "June 1769." Given that he was finishing his undergraduate work in 1763 it seems unlikely that the notebook with legal musings was composed then. Conversely it seems odd that the same year he was admitted to the bar (1769) he would have been putting down in print what comes across as mostly beginning law studies. In any event, sometime between 1763 and 1769, Paterson filled this notebook with a variety of legal subjects designed to aid in his studies.

In the notebook, there are several sections with headings for pleas, administration, leases, indictment, juries, jointure, mortgages, appeal, devises, and evidence. Throughout are references to English cases which supply the reasoning and precedent on which Paterson based his argument. Also scattered throughout are areas where Paterson wanted to highlight the importance of a passage, and he identified this with the highly effective hand with a pointing finger symbol. Throughout as well are "Q" and "A" to correspond to the question and answer method which he employed throughout much of the notebook.

A brief sample of Paterson's entries follows (punctuation and spelling have been updated where necessary—all italic or underlined words are in the original):

Q: Were the first principles of the laws known to Pagans?

A: No, for the most learned men among the Pagans knew so little of them, that they had established rules which violate and destroy them. Thus, the Romans too by the same license as other people did too take away the lives of their slaves, and of their own children.

Q: How may we judge of the certainty of the principles of the laws?

A: We may judge of their certainty, by the double impression which such truths ought to make upon our minds, which God reveals to us by religion, and makes us to apprehend by our reason.

Q: What is the nature of man?

A: His nature is nothing else but that being which is created after the image of God and capable of professing that supreme good, which is to be his life and his blessedness.

Q: What is the first law of man?

A: His first law, is that which enjoins him to search after and to love that sovereign good with all the force of his mind and of his heart.

Q: From whence arise all the disorders in society?

A: From man's disobedience to the first law; which commands him to love God.

Q: How many sorts of laws are there?

A: Two, viz, immutable and arbitrary.

Q: What are immutable laws?

A: They are natural, and so just at all times, and in all places, that no authority can either change of abolish them.

Q: What are arbitrary laws?

A: They are those which a lawful authority may enact, change, and [Paterson did not finish the sentence].

Q: Do natural laws regulate both the time past, and time to come?

A: Yes, and nobody can pretend ignorance of them.

Q: Can a mortgage be taken in a Negro slave?

A: Negroes are considered as making part of the personal estate and as such are always taken on in [?] and sold: Therefore, it is natural to suppose, a mortgage taken on a Negro slave would be good. It is certainly consistent with the general principle which regulates slaves, and indeed in every point of light appears highly reasonable— besides, slaves may be sold; it is every day's practice to make bills of sale, which are absolute disposals of them. Now, reasoning from the greater to the less, if a man can make an absolute, he may certainly make a *conditional* alienation of his slave.

Front page of law journal of William Paterson of New Jersey, ca. 1765 (Morristown National Historical Park).

In addition to the question and answer format, Paterson relied on simple note taking. Writing out sections of law and precedent and citing sources. As examples:

> "If a man marries a woman who has a term for years settled on her <u>in trust</u>, the husband may as well dispose of this first, as if the <u>legal interest</u> was in her."

"Where a woman marries a second husband leaving the first, and the second not privy; as to what she acquired during the cohabitation, the C[hief] J[ustice] said he would esteem her as a servant to the second husband, who is entitled to the benefit of her labor."

"One hath power to make a lease for 10 years, and he makes a lease for 20 years, yet in equity this is good for 10 years; and so has been settled several times."

"If a person makes a lease for so many years as he shall live, it is absolutely void for the uncertainty of its continuance."

"If A lets to B for 10 years, who lets to C for 5 years, C cannot surrender to A by reason of the intermediate interest of B but in such case B may surrender to A and after so many years C likewise, because then his lease of 5 years is immediate to the revision of A."

It is apparent Paterson was in part studying Edward Coke. In several places he starts a series of notes by stating "My Lord Coke lays it down for a general rule." References also abound to Bacon—this was probably Matthew Bacon, whose *New Abridgement of the Law* was a common learning reference.

Smaller "notes to self" are found scattered throughout the notebook. One example concerned a section labeled "juries." Paterson wrote, "Judges cannot fine a jury for giving a verdict contrary to evidence." Another entry states, "After a jury is sworn they shall be impounded till they all agree."

It is clear from this brief overview that Paterson in some ways had already formed opinions on certain topics. It is also clear that Paterson was certainly a man of his times with all the apparent prejudices and shortsightedness we associate with the legal profession of that era.

Paterson was admitted to the bar in 1769. His private practice, despite his brilliance, was slow to prosper. He entered the Provincial Congress of New Jersey in 1775 and was part of the team that wrote the New Jersey State Constitution in 1776. He was appointed attorney general for the state and held that position until 1781. He declined service in the Continental Congress due to the burden of being attorney general and due to his now expanding private legal practice. During the early 1780s, when the country faced the end of the Revolution and the turmoil during the mid–1780s leading to the Philadelphia Convention of 1787, Paterson dealt mostly with his by now prosperous legal practice. Paterson's private life changed forever with the calling of the Constitutional Convention in Philadelphia in 1787.

Paterson was elected to represent the state of New Jersey at Philadelphia, and from this point until the end of his life, he was engaged with national affairs at the highest levels—except for a short term as governor of New Jersey. Paterson proved to be an integral part of the Philadelphia Convention. He was most involved with issues impacting large and small state concerns. Most notably, Paterson was behind the New Jersey Plan, which he submitted for consideration on June 15, 1787, a month into the proceedings. The issue of large versus small states impacting federal representation was a contentious one. Under the Articles of Confederation, each state, regardless of size, had equal representation and equal weight in matters of voting. Under the new plan the convention was working with (Madison's Virginia Plan), states were accorded representation and voting power based on population. This naturally put small states at a disadvantage. Paterson's plan called for a unicameral legislature with equal representation of the states. The plan was also more accepting of the existing Articles of Confederation and sought to limit the changes called for by the Virginia Plan. Through the twists and turns of the convention debate process, the New Jersey Plan mutated into the Connecticut Plan, proposed by Paterson's good friend and future Supreme Court colleague Oliver Ellsworth. This plan called for the bicameral legislature with the upper house (Senate), where each state received equal representation regardless of population. Despite having to temporarily leave the Convention to attend to his law practice, Paterson was present to sign the proposed Constitution on September 17, 1787.

After the ratification of the Constitution by the states, Paterson was elected senator from New Jersey. He served one year in the Senate before serving three years as governor of New Jersey. It was during his year in the Senate that he collaborated with Oliver Ellsworth on the Judiciary Act of 1789, as we saw in Chapter 3. In 1793, with the resignation of Justice Thomas Johnson, President Washington nominated Paterson to the Supreme Court; a position he held until his death in 1806.

Samuel Chase

Samuel Chase was born in Princess Anne, Somerset County, Maryland, on April 17, 1741. Following tutoring by his minister father, he read law at the offices of Hammond and Hall in 1759 and was admitted to the bar in 1761. Chase was elected to the Maryland Assembly in 1764 and spent the next 20 years in that body and in the Continental Congress. His time in Maryland politics coincides with all the phases of the American Revolution, and Chase was involved from the very beginning. Chase had an explosive personality, much like Patrick Henry or Samuel Adams. He opposed the Stamp Act and joined the Sons of Liberty to express his displeasure. So ardent was his displeasure that "the mayor of Annapolis and the Board of Aldermen officially condemned him for his attitude and conduct."[83] In 1776, when the Maryland Assembly instructed its delegates to the Continental Congress to oppose calls for American independence, an enraged Chase hurried back to Annapolis, obtained new directions through his persuasiveness for the delegates to vote for independence, and raced back to Philadelphia in time for the vote and to sign the document declaring America free from Britain. (This story has a similar sound as Caesar Rodney riding from Dover, Delaware, to cast his vote for independence.) Chase would serve on nearly every committee in the Continental Congress, making him a well-known member of America's leading politicians.

Chase's manic energy led him into an unsavory episode in the late 1770s. He took advantage of secret information he gathered through one of his committee assignments and attempted to corner the market on flour in an effort to personally profit from the War. This action naturally caused an outcry when it was discovered. He was dismissed from the Maryland delegation and sent home. In a further attempt to "make the issue go away" he was sent to England on a minor diplomatic mission in 1783 by the Maryland governor. His personal financial ventures were similar to fellow Justice James Wilson. They both speculated heavily and both had zero business sense. Chase was forced to declare bankruptcy in 1789.

Chase began to redeem himself by accepting judicial appointments at varying levels in Baltimore before being inexplicably chosen by President Washington for a seat on the nation's highest court. Chase had many detractors, but one supporter counted more than all the detractors combined: George Washington. Why President Washington nominated someone with such a checkered past is open for debate. It was 1796, the president was near the end of his term and was no doubt tired and ready to leave the government. Perhaps he thought Chase would come to realize his responsibilities as a justice and forget his earlier indiscretions. Whatever the reason, Chase took his seat on February 4, 1796, much to the consternation of some of his colleagues. He is still the only Supreme Court justice to have been impeached, which occurred during the presidency of Thomas Jefferson. As a biographer has written: "A fair appraisal of Justice Chase is far from simple. He was an intense patriot given his lights. He was a man of ability, skill, learning, and intellect. But he also was unrestrained, autocratic, violent, and

Justice Samuel Chase of Maryland (Morristown National Historical Park).

headstrong. He was more the advocate than the judge, although on occasion he could be wholly judicious."[84] In total, his years in the service of the judiciary in Baltimore and on the Supreme Court covered 25 years.

Bushrod Washington

Bushrod Washington was the single largest benefactor of the estate of the most famous man in the world. Largely forgotten today, his contribution to two main aspects of American history cannot be overlooked.[85] As a largely loyal colleague of Chief Justice John Marshall on the Supreme Court, Justice Washington was part of some of the most foundation-building cases in constitutional law argued up to that time. Washington also was actively involved in trying to promote his uncle's (President Washington) legacy: first, as a willing partner with John Marshall in Marshall's work as a biographer; and, second, as a grudging partner with Jared Sparks in his project to edit and publish Washington's papers nearly 20 years after Marshall started his work. His contributions are more than enough to warrant a stand-alone biography, and perhaps someday he will be removed from his uncle's shadow long enough for a creditable treatment of his life to be written.

Just months after his uncle's death, Bushrod realized the obligation and trust which he held in his uncle's papers. His scholarly inclinations enabled him to recognize that he had a responsibility to posterity and to those currently alive who would benefit from a more detailed understanding of his Uncle George.

To his friend, Dr. Morse, Bushrod wrote on February 18, 1800 (barely two months after his uncle's death),

> So soon as I found myself the legatee of the papers of my late uncle General Washington, I presumed that the public would expect from me the history of a life so conspicuously employed as he was in the civil and military affairs of this country. Your observations have impressed me very fully with the propriety of having such a history prepared for publication as speedily as circumstances will admit. A diffidence of my own talents for such an undertaking, together with weak eyes and want of time will probably forbid me from attempting it; but I trust that the selection of a fit character may be in my power, and this I shall endeavor to make immediately.[86]

Bushrod Washington was born at Bushfield, the family estate in Westmoreland County, Virginia, on June 5, 1762, with his Uncle George in attendance. Westmoreland County at the time sat between the Chesapeake Bay on the east and swamp land on the west. Today, the Chesapeake Bay still borders on the east, but Washington, D.C., now borders on the west. Bushrod was a colonial by birth at the end of the French and Indian (or Seven Years) War, a conflict in which his Uncle George gained a considerable reputation.

His father was John Augustine Washington, a younger brother of George and a member of the Virginia House of Burgesses. His mother was Hannah Bushrod, a member of a prominent Virginia family.

The Washington and Bushrod families' rise in the colonies were nearly identical.[87] Through hard work, advantageous marriage, and social and political connections, they prospered considerably throughout the eighteenth century. So much so, that even before mid-century, in 1743, the estate named Mount Vernon was created by Lawrence Washington, George's half-brother. It was George's full brother, John Augustine Washington, who married Hannah Bushrod and brought the two families together. John and Hannah lived for several years at Mount Vernon while George was away in the French and Indian War.[88]

Young Bushrod came into a world on the edge of great change brought about by events relating to the imperial policy of a world power. This same power denied his Uncle George a military commission as a colonel in the British Army, despite his contributions during the French and Indian conflict. The year of his birth the British and French signed the Peace of Paris ending the French and Indian War which marked the beginning of the end of Britain's control over her thirteen colonies in North America. Three years after his birth, in 1765, the British imposed the first of a series of Acts designed to generate revenue to offset the high costs incurred during the recently ended war.

Even on their plantation, Bushrod's family would have felt the impact of the new British measures—whether directly by paying the new taxes or indirectly by feeling indignant over them. Certainly through his father's exposure as a delegate, the Washingtons became part of the population in the colonies who were concerned about the new approach to colonial administration. In Leedstown, Virginia, a gathering of protesters in February 1766 included Bushrod's father, John Augustine.[89] They drafted several resolutions to express their displeasure. From 1760 to 1765, George served in the House of Burgesses with John, and the brothers no doubt shared information on the Stamp Act and its fallout.[90]

Bushrod spent his formative years in much the same manner as his peers. He was an introverted and bookish child who was privately tutored in the classics at the home of Richard Henry Lee. This experience provided Bushrod with exposure to the broader world, particularly England. Lee was educated in England and provided Bushrod with the benefits of a more cosmopolitan approach to life. There is no indication that he possessed any greater or lesser talents than others his age, other than his scholarly inclinations. He was known as a small boy, often sickly. Much later in life, he was described as "about common height, of slight figure, sallow complexion, and straight brown hair … one of his eyes apparently sightless, and the other having more than the fire of an ordinary pair."[91] Physically, he clearly did not take after his Uncle George.

Furthermore, Bushrod was described as "easy in manners, and affable, unaffected, unpretending, and as far as possible from stateliness."[92]

Bushrod entered William and Mary College in 1775 and graduated in 1778—the third year of the American Revolution—and returned home. He went back to Williamsburg in 1780 to study law with George Wythe at William and Mary, was elected to Phi Beta Kappa, and met another student who would become a lifelong friend and colleague—John Marshall.[93]

Bushrod appears to have enjoyed his time in Williamsburg. In a letter to his mother in July 1780, he wrote, "My situation here ... is I confess as agreeable as I could wish having my choice in the society of gentlemen whose characters are good and examples edifying."[94] For most of the war, Bushrod seems to have been able to remove himself from the tragedy and hardship taking place around him. This was in part due to the fact that no active theater of war was nearby.

Justice Bushrod Washington of Virginia (**Morristown National Historical Park**).

This changed in early 1781 when General Cornwallis entered Virginia and settled in Petersburg. Bushrod joined the local militia under Col. John Mercer which was part of Lafayette's larger army in Virginia. Bushrod was present at the Battle of Green Spring from which Cornwallis began his march to Yorktown.[95] At Yorktown, Lafayette's army—including the Mercer militia—joined forces with George Washington's Continental Army to defeat Cornwallis and effectively end the Revolution. Bushrod witnessed this event and demobilized shortly afterward and returned home.[96]

RETURN TO THE LAW

After his brief military career, Bushrod furthered his legal studies by gaining admittance to the law office of James Wilson of Philadelphia in 1782 through the financial support of his father and uncle. Uncle George in fact went so far as to recommend Bushrod to Wilson who was cautious about taking on a student. "Permit me to recommend my nephew to you," Uncle George wrote to convince Wilson of the ability of Bushrod.[97]

Uncle George was keen to encourage Bushrod to make the most of his opportunity in Philadelphia. He wrote to Bushrod, "Let the object, which carried you to Philadelphia, be always before your eyes."[98] Bushrod seems to have taken his studies seriously and his uncle's admonition to heart. He wrote his mother that he intended "to devote my whole time to law."[99] Between the time spent with the legal scholar George Wythe in Williamsburg and James Wilson in Philadelphia, Bushrod, by 1785, possessed one of the finest legal educations available in the newly independent United States.

READING LAW

When young Bushrod arrived in Philadelphia to begin his legal studies, Wilson was already an established figure of great stature, highly regarded as a jurist and as a historian. Although Wilson never wrote history for public consumption in book form, he laced his arguments with continual references to English history, principally political history. In his work as a legal historian and scholar, Wilson turned to his history books as often as he turned to his legal books. Wilson's library, from which Bushrod drew instruction, included important names in legal theory, such as Montesquieu, Hobbes, Coke, Blackstone, and Grotius, among many others.[100] While Wilson was capable of preaching a torrent of legal philosophy in an instant, he seems not to have passed this predilection to Bushrod.

This reliance on historical precedent no doubt had its impact on Bushrod. After completing his studies with Wilson, he produced his own historical compilations in the 1790s on Virginia legal cases which required a reliance on historical editing. More importantly, Bushrod was exposed to the possibilities of historical writing through Wilson's extensive inclusion of history in his work. This exposure left an impression on Bushrod in his eventual role as the inheritor and keeper of his uncle's papers. These papers had unquestioned historical importance and the sensitivity Bushrod witnessed in Wilson's office was a part of his desire to see the collection utilized in a historical manner.

STARTING A PRACTICE

After concluding his studies with Wilson in April 1784, Bushrod returned home to Westmoreland County where he married Julia Anne Blackburn and opened a law office. His practice did not thrive, though he did survive by making a respectable living on his own without assistance from his famous family. For the next four years, Bushrod was involved in politics and family matters which kept him confined to the Westmoreland County area. His father's death in 1786 left Bushrod, as the eldest, to run the estate and dispose of the property. He also paid many visits to Mount Vernon where he and his

Uncle George spent considerable time discussing the political events of the day.

In 1787, the year of the Constitutional Convention, Bushrod was elected to the Virginia House of Delegates. The next year he served in the Virginia Constitutional ratifying convention. In this capacity he argued and voted in favor of ratification of the federal constitution drafted in Philadelphia under the watchful eye of his uncle at Independence Hall. James Madison, as a member of the same ratifying convention in Virginia, commented that Bushrod was "a young gentleman of talent."[101]

Following his less-than-anticipated success at a law practice in Alexandria, Bushrod moved to Richmond. This move allowed him to renew his friendship with John Marshall. Due to the frail health of his wife, and his own not-too-robust health, the Washington's rarely socialized. Being industrious though, Bushrod edited, between 1790 and 1796, the Reports of the Virginia Court of Appeals. Bushrod also did legal work for his uncle. Throughout the spring of 1798, George Washington was involved with land purchases in Kentucky from Henry Lee. In a letter dated January 19, 1798, George Washington wrote to Bushrod that he "must request the favor of you to investigate this matter."[102] This work which Bushrod undertook involved not only reviewing the actual deeds, but also researching the exact location, size, tax responsibilities, and so forth.

While still practicing law in Richmond, Bushrod received a letter from President John Adams appointing him to the Supreme Court. With the letter from President Adams of December 20, 1798, Bushrod Washington became one of the youngest appointees to the United States Supreme Court. At 36, Bushrod was picked to replace his old law teacher, James Wilson, who had died. Bushrod's career on the Supreme Court lasted over 30 years, until his death in November of 1829 in Philadelphia.

Alfred Moore

Alfred Moore was born in New Hanover County, near Wilmington, North Carolina, on May 21, 1755. He read law and was admitted to the bar in 1775, after having attended Harvard but leaving without taking a degree. He served as an officer with the First North Carolina Regiment and with the state militia after his return from Boston and before entering private legal practice. He returned to his home in 1777 after the deaths of his father and brother. He remained active in local militia affairs.

In 1782 he was elected to the North Carolina legislature and soon after was appointed the state attorney general, a role he held for eight years. Throughout the 1790s, Moore participated in state politics and ran unsuccessfully for national office. When Justice Iredell of North Carolina died in October 1799, President Adams nominated Moore to the seat on December 4, 1799. He was confirmed by the Senate a week later. He took up his duties with the August 1800 session. Justice Moore resigned on January 26, 1804, having made little impact on the Court.

Oliver Ellsworth

Oliver Ellsworth has already factored in this book as one of the two main movers behind the Judiciary Act of 1789. As a senator from Connecticut and member of the Constitutional Convention, he was uniquely placed to take on the role of leader in moving the act through the Senate.

Oliver Ellsworth was born on April 29, 1745, in Windsor, Connecticut. Ellsworth was born into a lower middle–class family. The Ellsworth family was highly religious (Congregationalist), even for the period, and this left its mark on young Oliver. His early education was a mixture of religion, science, and the liberal arts. For Ellsworth, all learning and effort in life, he was taught, had a moral religious foundation. He entered Yale College in 1762, ostensibly to study for the ministry. Ellsworth's arrival coincided with a period of general upheaval at Yale between the students and the administration of President Thomas Clap. The problems resulted from interpretations of religious obligations and commitments due to aspects of ritualized understandings.

This volatile mixture was not conducive for Ellsworth, who ran afoul of several rules, seemingly steering clear of the religious controversies but impacting the consumption of wine and alcohol. At his parents' recommendation, he left Yale and enrolled at the College of New Jersey at Princeton. The College of New Jersey proved a perfect fit for Ellsworth. The college itself was geographically diverse and the early 1760s saw the student body populated with many future leaders, Founding Fathers, of the American nation. "Notably, no colonial college would train as many future speakers on the floor of the Continental Congress and the Constitutional Convention as Ellsworth's alma mater."[103] These leaders included James Madison, William Paterson, Aaron Burr, Henry Lee, and others.

Upon returning to Connecticut in 1766 after graduation, Ellsworth took up reading law with Jesse Root. In 1771, he was admitted to the Connecticut bar. Two years later, in 1773, Ellsworth, now married, was elected to the Connecticut General Assembly. He served slightly more than one year before devoting all his time to his slowly expanding legal practice. By the end of the decade he was prominent enough to take on legal apprentices of his own, including a young Noah Webster.

In the waning days of his service in the General Assembly, Governor

Jonathan Trumbull convened an emergency session to discuss the events at Lexington and Concord. Ellsworth attended and was appointed to a committee to oversee defense spending. He held this post for three years before being appointed to the Continental Congress, taking his seat in 1779. During his terms in Congress, Ellsworth dealt with judicial issues, currency issues— a particularly thorny subject—and general committee work all members had to deal with. Unlike many other members however, Ellsworth gained a reputation for maturity, wisdom, and dedication to his duties. Ellsworth became convinced of the need for greater taxing power for the national Congress to deal with the significant shortfall in revenue. Ellsworth was mature enough to realize it was one thing to raise the cry of "no taxation without representation" against Britain, but it was quite another to say it against one's own government. Ellsworth's views on taxation and revenue were much in line with other Federalist leaders. Ellsworth wrote to Connecticut Governor Jonathan Trumbull in the early 1780s:

> There <u>must</u>, sir, be a revenue somehow established, that can be relied on, and applied for national purposes as the exigencies arise, independent of the will or views of a single state, or it will be impossible to support national faith or national existence. The power of Congress must be adequate to the purposes of their constitution. It is possible, there may be abuses and misapplication, still it is better to hazard <u>something</u>, than to hazard all [emphasis in original].[104]

After his proposals failed, he was left with the need for a stronger national government capable of dealing with the demands of independence. Ellsworth was not alone in these views, few of his colleagues expressed the American dilemma more succinctly than he did.

Returning to Connecticut in 1784, Ellsworth was appointed to the state's Superior Court. And in 1787, Ellsworth was appointed a delegate to the Constitutional Convention. At the convention, Ellsworth was as studious as ever to his duties as a member and served on numerous committees. He is best remembered for his advocating of the Connecticut Plan, which was presented by his colleague Roger Sherman. Ellsworth's steady application of his talents over the summer would again impress his colleagues, as occurred earlier in the Continental Congress. Unfortunately, Ellsworth left Philadelphia too early to be a signer. Following the convention, Ellsworth would be the prime sponsor of the Constitution at the Connecticut state ratifying convention in January 1788.

Ellsworth's next career posting was as one of the first senator's elected to the new Congress in 1788. As we have seen in Chapter 3, Ellsworth was, along with Senator William Paterson of New Jersey, the prime mover of the Judiciary Act of 1789 in the Senate. This will always be considered his greatest achievement on the national level aside from serving as chief justice.

We have seen in Chapter 3 Ellsworth's strong nationalistic approach to the Constitution and especially Article III, pertaining to the judiciary. We have also seen and commented on Ellsworth's role in the Judiciary Act of 1789. It goes without saying, that the system of jurisprudence, and especially the mechanism of that jurisprudence, was the result most directly of Oliver Ellsworth.

5

The John Jay Court: September 26, 1789– June 29, 1795

As with the Congress and president, everything the Supreme Court did during its first few years was precedent setting; some things lasted, some did not. When approaching the cases that the Court dealt with, the topics they represented were just as precedent setting as anything the Court did in terms of decision making. The cases chosen for review over the next three chapters were picked in part randomly but also for the significant issues they raised and how the Court dealt with them in defining American law. The year 1790 marked the first time in American history that a truly nationwide system of law had come into being. Since independence was declared (1776) and obtained (1783), the states existed in a miasmic arrangement which did more harm than good on a national level. Indeed, the relationship between the states was the main reason for calling the Annapolis Convention of 1786. And when that failed, they called for the Philadelphia Convention of 1787. It is appropriate then that the first case heard before the new Supreme Court on August 2, 1791, dealt with state/federal relations.

The buildup to the meeting of the first term (February 1790) of the Supreme Court occurred over a relatively short period of time. Only six months elapsed between President-elect Washington nominating his picks as justices and the meeting time appointed by the Judiciary Act of 1789. Those six months were filled with planning and preparation for the new justices: for travel, for personal arrangement of business interests, for living arrangements, for placing their affairs into the hands of an overseer, and other issues unique to each individual. It always must be remembered that the infrastructure of the federal government was not in place. There was no permanent civil service to guide new government officials when they arrived to assume their duties. Most did not have office space or staff. Indeed, the pressure was truly upon the first officials to prepare the new government. For the new Supreme Court justices, it was no different. The justices arrived in New York with many different approaches to what could or should occur. There is no evidence that the justices communicated before arriving in New York in an effort to standardize how they would create or establish the new Court. Each justice no doubt arrived with their own ideas and passions, and thus there were six ideas to bring into focus. This had to occur quickly.

Fortunately, New York was the largest city in the country in 1790. Much like today, if one wanted something, or needed something, New York was one place that could guarantee it. Having the new capital in New York made sense. While few if any records exist showing the actual ways in which the new Court settled into their new home, it surely must have been trying at times. Nonetheless, come together it all did.

The Supreme Court first met on Monday, February 1, 1790, at the Royal Exchange Building at the foot of Broad Street. After this first meeting, even without a quorum, the three justices dined with President Washington that

Royal (Merchants) Exchange Building, New York. Site of the first meeting of the Supreme Court, February 1790 (*Harper's Weekly*, Collection of the Supreme Court of the United States).

evening. Chief Justice John Jay and Associate Justices James Wilson and William Cushing were in attendance for the first meeting. They made quite a visual impression at the opening session. Cushing wore a wig similar to the judiciary wigs in English courts, and John Jay wore "an ample robe of black silk with salmon colored facings."[1] On February 2, John Blair arrived and a quorum was achieved. Over the course of ten days, as no cases were to be heard, the Court busied itself with administrative issues: rules and swearing in of lawyers to practice before the Court. The first session of the Supreme Court adjourned on February 10, 1790.

Charles Warren, legal historian, has noted about those first ten days: "That the novel experiment of a national judiciary had awakened great interest throughout the country was significantly shown by the fact that the New York and Philadelphia newspapers described the proceedings of this first session of the Court more fully than any other event connected with the new government."[2] The *Gazette of the United States* commented on these appointments of lawyers and counselors: "Every friend to America must be highly gratified when he pursues the long list of eminent and worthy characters who have come forward as practioners at the federal bar, where the most important rights of man must, in time, be discussed and determined upon, as well those of nations, as of individuals. Happy Country!"[3] The exuberance of the write-up is symptomatic of some of the writing concerning the nascent United States.

Simply because there were no cases to be heard did not mean the Court was not getting work done. "For the first two and a half years after its establishment the Supreme Court's work was confined to reading commissions, formulating rules, admitting lawyers to practice before it, and hearing a few motions."[4] The new Court had even chosen a seal and a coat of arms. With no cases on the docket however, they adjourned until August 1790, in accordance with the Judiciary Act.

The Court reconvened on Monday, August 2, 1790, at the Royal Exchange Building. As with the first term, and with administrative details already concluded, the Court adjourned until February 1791. For the Court's second term, it moved to Philadelphia along with the rest of the federal government. The Court took up the new City Hall building as a meeting space. It was adjacent to the Pennsylvania Statehouse (Independence Hall) and to the home of the American Philosophical Society.

West v. Barnes *(August 3, 1791)*

The reporting and recording of cases in the 1790s was nowhere near as thorough as it is today. In the 1790s "case" was a relative term and was often used rather loosely. As Court historian Julius Goebel has written, "less than half of the dispositions by the Supreme Court were professionally reported so far as the bar at large was concerned, these reports came to be prime sources of information regarding the Court's jurisprudence."[5] For the purposes of this book, the word "case" will simply mean a dispute or problem that found its way before the justices and not always the justices sitting together as the Court. There was plenty of action at the circuit courts when the justices sat during circuit riding duties. In attempting to review the cases and topics dealt with by the Court during the 1790s, this book will primarily follow the list of cases as compiled in *United States Reports*, Volume 2 (often cited as *U.S. Reports*).[6] With all of this being said, the list of cases heard and decided by the early Supreme Court is still a matter of debate among scholars. For our purposes though, we will continue with the historical overview of themes and outcomes without getting too consumed by the minutiae of the record keeping.

West v. Barnes seemed a simple enough case; and in fact, it was. Yet, it also highlighted the newness of the federal judiciary and how the system was intended to operate before actually working out any perceived shortcomings. Nevertheless, problems arose. The issue in *West* hinged on whether a circuit court could issue a writ to itself (a writ simply being an order of a court), in effect being its own keeper separate from the newly established system. The case also tested the access of citizens to the first national judiciary system spread amongst all the states.

West v. Barnes originated in pre–Revolutionary Rhode Island when William West mortgaged his land to Daniel Jenckes and his son John for a mercantile-related debt. West was not able to repay the debt in part due to the tremendous fiscal upsets occasioned by the Revolution. Accordingly, West sought, and received, relief from the state of Rhode Island in 1789 and tried to deal with John Jenckes in September—ironically, the same month that President-elect Washington was sending out letters to his Supreme Court nominees. Rhode Island had anticipated creditors like John Jenckes rejecting the new proposals designed to assist debtors like William West and arranged for debtors to pay their debt in Rhode Island currency to a state court judge who would take over attempting to deal with the creditors. If creditors refused payment in state currency, the state law allowed for the debt to be declared paid in full and the state kept the money.

Through descent within the family, John Jenckes acquired the mortgage (even though the state of Rhode Island declared the debt paid) and decided to take William West back to court. However, this time the family decided to take West to federal court, not state court; the federal court option had never existed in the nearly thirty-year-long contest between West and the Jenckes family. One female member of the Jenckes family married David Barnes of

Massachusetts, who served as Jenckes family attorney and thus gave his name to the case.

The circuit court, sitting with Chief Justice John Jay and Justice William Cushing, ruled against West, finding that he did not, despite following Rhode Island state law, satisfy his debt to the Jenckes family. Appealing to the Supreme Court, Barnes argued that the writ of error obtained by West in Rhode Island was invalid. According to Barnes "it was improper for the Rhode Island circuit court to order itself to remove its proceedings to a higher court for review."[7] This was where the "bugs" in the system became apparent: "if litigants should err on mere matters of form where federal legislation was silent, they should not be penalized unless they" clearly violated the letter of the law.[8] Further, the Judiciary Act allowed ten days for a writ of error to be filed with a clerk of a lower court (not a higher one such as the Supreme Court in this case). This ten day requirement was nearly impossible for those living any appreciable distance from Philadelphia (where the writs were to be issued from). The Supreme Court rejected West's argument and found the writ of error invalid.

Justice Iredell saw *West v. Barnes* from the perspective of two questions. Justice Iredell began his opinion: "There are two questions before the Court. 1st. Whether the transcript of the record be returned here, in consequence of a Writ of Error issued agreeable to law? 2nd. If it be so, whether the return of it be regular?"[9] The Court was clearly looking at the technical aspects of the case. What was completely missing was whether or not West fully discharged his debt as per Rhode Island law (it would later be determined that he discharged per Rhode Island law too late to actually satisfy the law). West's case had moved from one of his financial future (he ended up a broken man in poverty) to one about the literal application of a less than solidly written federal law.

Justice Iredell continued with his opinion:

> The Act of Congress which contains all that concerns Writs of Error, is silent on this point—though it gives other directions, it does not say out of what court the writ is to issue.
>
> We are therefore under the necessity of determining either by *former principles* of law (if such apply) or by *analogy* or *reason* [emphasis in original].[10]

Justice Iredell used his opinion to contrast how England has one central court which issued writs (chancery) and how unintentional inconveniences may attend upon certain untried aspects of new legislation (such as an original case being overlooked by a procedural issue). Justice Iredell concluded: "I am sorry to be under the necessity of voting for a decision which may be attended with the great inconveniences pointed out: but in my opinion, the legislature only can remedy them. It is of infinite moment that courts of justice should keep within their proper bounds."[11]

Justice Blair took a similar approach to Iredell, although he did not see the originating court for the writ as important a feature: "It was not so material from what office it [the writ] had issued, especially as the Judiciary bill was silent as to that."[12] Therefore, for Justice Blair, the question was: Could the Writ of Error obtained by West from the circuit court be valid? As with Iredell, Blair believed the remedy lay with Congress: "[Blair] thought however that this evil, whatever might be its magnitude, required legislative correction rather than the Court should, for the sake of avoiding it, establish an unusual, and very irregular practice."[13]

Justice Wilson also took exception to the idea of a circuit court issuing a writ to itself, even if the law was unclear. Justice Wilson likewise looked at the issue of the inconvenience of the law's ten-day requirement:

> An inconvenience was suggested and pressed with much strength and ingenuity by the counsel for the plaintiff; that at a great distance from the seat of government ... it would be impossible ... in the limited time of ten days ... for rending the Writ of Error a supersedeas [a writ suspending the authority of a trial court to impose a ruling in a case that has been appealed] to an execution. If this inconvenience should submit in all the force which has been stated; it must be removed by *another* power. *We* act in the *judicial*, not in the *legislative* department [emphasis in original].[14]

Similarly, Justice Cushing held a nearly identical view to his colleagues concerning the originating court for the writ: "I cannot believe that Congress designed, [that] a circuit court should have power to remove its own proceeding to this Court.... As the writ before us, therefore, is not from this, but from the circuit court of Rhode Island, I cannot think, that upon its authority, we can proceed to revise the judgment of that court."[15]

Chief Justice Jay provided the most succinct opinion of the justices: "As the reasons already assigned, are fully explanatory of my opinion, it [is] needless to repeat them. I need only, therefore suggest my concurrence with my Brethren."[16]

Barnes and West would continue their case for a few more years while the Congress dealt with the ten-day rule in the revised Judiciary Act of 1792. The Court's first case, which dealt with a technical interpretation of a statute, went well. Their debut showed the Justices to be thoughtful and careful in parsing the meaning of new federal law.

Hayburn's *Case Review*

The Judiciary Act of 1789, which was analyzed in Chapter 3, enabled the Supreme Court to establish itself and begin to adjudicate according to the strictures of the established Constitution. This section will look at how the Court dealt with the first constitutional issue that presented itself, *Hayburn's*

Case. While *Hayburn's* Case is not a traditional case, with a plaintiff and a defendant, it was nonetheless a case which is very instructive in analyzing how the early Court approached its perceived responsibilities under the Constitution.[17]

The essence of American constitutionalism, which was developed primarily through *The Federalist* papers, the Constitution, and the Judiciary Act, was engaged for the first time by the Court in 1792; the previous two years lacked cases, as has been seen.[18] Whether the concept of judicial review was in complete compliance ideologically with the Federalist (whether supporters of the Constitution or the incipient political party) approach to democracy is debatable.[19] Judicial review allowed for the negation of legislation enacted by popularly elected bodies, thus in essence denying the "will of the people." The whole theoretical concept of judicial review is quite undemocratic, in the sense that a court can overrule a legislature. A court, through judicial review, can have considerable claim to being the most powerful branch in a government. The Supreme Court is perhaps the ultimate legacy of the Federalists, both the group that used the title in 1787 to support the proposed Constitution and the political party which adopted the name in the 1790s. In one sense, next to the Electoral College system as a check on possible democratic excess, the Supreme Court serves as a constant check rather than a periodical check through elections.

Writing in the *Harvard Law Review* in 1893, James Thayer theorized that the concept of judicial review of legislation was a

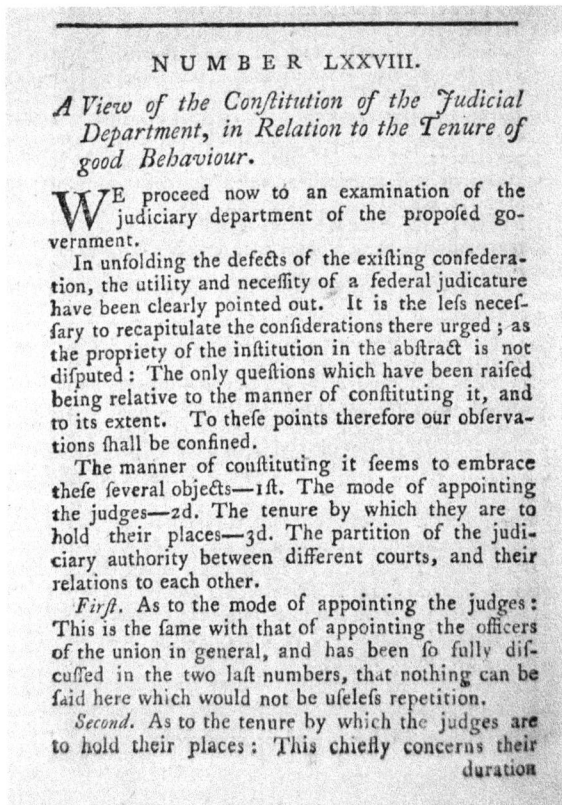

> NUMBER LXXVIII.
>
> *A View of the Constitution of the Judicial Department, in Relation to the Tenure of good Behaviour.*
>
> WE proceed now to an examination of the judiciary department of the proposed government.
>
> In unfolding the defects of the existing confederation, the utility and necessity of a federal judicature have been clearly pointed out. It is the less necessary to recapitulate the considerations there urged; as the propriety of the institution in the abstract is not disputed: The only questions which have been raised being relative to the manner of constituting it, and to its extent. To these points therefore our observations shall be confined.
>
> The manner of constituting it seems to embrace these several objects—1st. The mode of appointing the judges—2d. The tenure by which they are to hold their places—3d. The partition of the judiciary authority between different courts, and their relations to each other.
>
> *First.* As to the mode of appointing the judges: This is the same with that of appointing the officers of the union in general, and has been so fully discussed in the two last numbers, that nothing can be said here which would not be useless repetition.
>
> *Second.* As to the tenure by which the judges are to hold their places: This chiefly concerns their duration

The Federalist papers number 78, the first dealing directly with the Supreme Court. First edition (Morristown National Historical Park).

component of constitutional law and that it sprang from America's colonial past. "How came we then to adopt this remarkable practice? Mainly as a natural result of our political experience before the War of Independence—as being colonists, governed under written charters of government proceeding from the English Crown."[20]

Thayer had an interesting concept, roughly halfway between the Founding generation and our own, concerning a much-debated topic—the appearance of judicial review in the United States. Thayer seemed to argue that Americans came to the concept organically enough through the presence of written governing documents, uniquely unlike Englishmen at home where the unwritten constitution was dominate. Having a written document which outlined governmental functions lent itself to being more easily challenged should the government appear to stray off course. In one sense then, the entire Revolution could be seen as a case of judicial review, with the rebels playing the part of the judiciary holding Parliament accountable for abrogating on established procedures for governing.

The checks and balances exercised among the three branches of government would seem to indicate that the judiciary had some power to act when either the executive or legislative branches overstepped the bounds of constitutional governance. It was a tool the judiciary had to contend with in their delicate balance with the executive and legislative branches. Thayer also contended that part of the reason the concept was never explicitly spelled out was that colliding perspectives on written, constitutional law and natural law kept lawmakers leery of providing an explicit power or tool, given the fluid nature of natural versus manmade law.[21]

According to Thayer, this power of judicial review can only be exercised, by definition, within the scope and boundary of established legal proceedings. Therefore, "It is only as litigation may spring up, and as the course of it may happen to raise the point of constitutionality, that any question for the courts can regularly emerge."[22] Until a particular piece of legislation is brought before the Court, it simply cannot pass judgment on it, regardless of how patently unconstitutional it might be.

One of the earliest known declarative statements on the concept of judicial review occurred in 1610 when Sir Edward Coke is reputed to have commented in a case before the English Court of Common Pleas that "when an act of parliament is against common right or reason, or repugnant, or impossible to be performed, the common law will control it and adjudge such Act to be void."[23] Without going into the specifics of the case, it is enough to acknowledge the importance of Coke's approach and the concept of judicial review his authority carried, and still carries, in Anglo-American approaches to law.[24]

The arguments of Alexander Hamilton in favor of judicial review, as written in *The Federalist*, have already been discussed in an earlier chapter. The arguments of another American jurist who was not yet well known in the early 1790s are instructional too for his support of the concept of judicial review. James Kent, who in 1826 would publish the *Commentaries on American Law*, was a young professor of law in New York City in 1793. Kent's published lectures show a strong advocacy of the concept of judicial review. Kent wrote that "the uncommon efficacy of our Courts of Justice, [is] being authorized to bring the validity of a law to the test of the Constitution."[25] Kent further declared the uniqueness of the concept of judicial review as separate from common law approaches by writing "the doctrine I have suggested, is peculiar to the United States."[26] Kent saw his advocacy in terms of the Constitutional balance of power: "The power in the judicial, of determining the constitutionality of laws, is necessary to preserve the equilibrium of the government."[27] To undertake judicial review, a court would need to rely on a written set of laws, which could be referenced as necessary.

Judicial review as a concept was not codified in any way in the United States (on the national level) until the passage of the Judiciary Act of 1789. Even then, it was not specifically spelled out—similarly, the Constitution seems to imply the concept of judicial review in Article VI.[28] Prior to that, the argument concerning judicial review generally centered on the ability of judges to declare a law void and how this would entail unelected jurists denying the will of the people. If a law passed by a popularly elected legislature could be held to scrutiny by the unelected judiciary, would the democratic process be somehow weakened? The contrary argument of course is: What purpose then is a judicial body if it does not judge on the efficacy of the law?[29]

Under the common law system, judicial review was not as much debated or employed as in a Constitutional system. It therefore emerged as a topic of much debate in America during and immediately after the Constitutional Convention of 1787. In the Convention, the issue of judicial review did not come up as a distinct topic.[30] Instead, the debate over the judiciary involved, beyond the realm of the legal, the extra duties which might be imposed on justices outside the courtroom in service to the nation. The chief justice was someone in a leadership role of a branch of government who could be called upon to undertake various non-judicial roles. It would be in this capacity that the Invalid Act of 1792 was initially questioned by the justices when they first become aware of it.

Hayburn (August 11, 1792)

On March 23, 1792, Congress passed the Invalid Pensions Act, which was designed to provide financial relief for Revolutionary War veterans or for their widows and orphans. Part of the act required potential pensioners to go before federal circuit courts to present their claim. The court would then forward its findings to the secretary of war for final processing before submission to Congress of the claim. Two aspects of the act would immediately draw the attention of the circuit courts (where the Supreme Court justices were sitting on circuit) as being inconsistent with judicial activity as understood through the Constitution, the Judiciary Act, and *The Federalist* papers.

The act required that the judges take the claims of potential pensioners while sitting as a judge, but not in a courtroom scenario. The judges did not find this function to be of a judicial nature. Secondly, the judges were required to submit their findings to the secretary of war for review. This meant their findings (or, official judicial findings) would be liable to review by another branch of the government, thus violating the separation of powers. Therefore, the New York (Northern) circuit, consisting of Chief Justice Jay and Justice Cushing, along with district judge James Duane, sent a letter with their impressions on April 5, 1792, to President Washington concerning the problem presented by the Invalid Pensions Act. This occurred before any claimants presented themselves to the court.

The court, in reading their instructions, clearly felt a constitutional imperative had been breached. The three judges argued that enforcing the rules as written would violate separation of powers and judicial independence.[31] A year later, in 1793, Secretary of State Thomas Jefferson recorded his observations concerning judicial independence. During a cabinet meeting with President Washington and other cabinet secretaries, Jefferson expressed skepticism about placing the judiciary at the behest of the executive. Commenting on a New York state issue involving Governor Clinton and judges in Albany, Jefferson recorded that he "was against writing letters to judiciary officers. I thought them independent of the executive, not subject to its coercion, and therefore not obliged to attend to its admonitions."[32]

When the one claimant whose name has become associated with the trio of cases associated with the 1792 act, William Hayburn, appeared on April 11, 1792, at the Middle circuit in Pennsylvania, Justices Blair, Wilson, and district judge Richard Peters, denied Hayburn a hearing.[33] A week later the Middle circuit sent President Washington their views on the act. The Middle circuit was the only circuit (out of three) to actually have a claimant appear before them prior to drafting their response to the act. "The judges have … called the attention of the Public to Legislative infallibility, by pronouncing a law providing for Invalid Pensioners, unconstitutional and void"[34]

The Southern circuit, with Justice Iredell and district judge John Sitgreaves, felt compelled to issue their impressions of the act even though they had seen no claimants, just as the Northern circuit had done. As with the

Middle and Northern circuits, the Southern circuit judges on June 8, 1792, wrote of the unconstitutionality (they did not use the word) of the portion of the Act requiring circuit courts to hear the petitions of claimants.[35] Justice Johnson, the sixth member of the Supreme Court, did not attend the Southern circuit in the spring of 1792. Johnson did ride the circuit in the fall of 1792 and refused to hear claimants. Although he never formally stated his reasoning, it can be surmised to have been similar to that of his colleagues. Therefore, a unanimous decision attended the Act upon its publication as individually prepared by the circuit courts. That decision was clearly delineated by the Justices using references to the Constitution.

Should the members of the Court not have responded outside of a court case and were they thus merely writing as advisors to the president? Acting outside of a court case in a non-judicial role is one argument the justices felt the act would require, yet that is exactly what they seemed to do to state their objections. It was purely unofficial in that they were not asked to provide opinions; they did so only on their own. Although all the arguments presented by the justices were legitimate, they do seem to miss the point of the humanitarian nature of the act and the need for some expediency for veterans and their families.[36]

The justices, sitting dispersed on circuit separated by hundreds of miles, wrote their opinion in *seriatim* (each Justice giving an opinion rather than one for the entire Court) fashion, unofficially in a court sense, by directly commenting on legislation before it reached the constituted Court as a case. The concept of a test case perhaps had not occurred to anyone.[37] Ideally, the Court could have performed its duty as proscribed in the act and allowed someone to file a case as to the constitutionality of the act.[38] Although it is not simple to explain away the obvious anomalies associated with this course of action, the underlying fact is that the Court collectively made a distinction based on a Constitutional premise. Regardless of whether this was received as a thunderclap in Congress or by President Washington, it nonetheless made a profound statement.[39] The Constitution mattered, and more importantly the Supreme Court mattered.[40] Irrespective of whatever twist and turns the Court would face in the future, the precedent had been established and a course determined. The concept of constitutionality as a means of control in a democratic society was employed, and in this instance, succeeded.[41] The Federalist desire to limit the impact of popular democratic impulses was proven to be a valid strategy. The Supreme Court, consciously or not (and contrary to Hamilton's *Federalist* number 78), became the strongest branch of the Federal system.[42]

In reviewing the *Hayburn* Case, it is first noticed that all the justices drew the same conclusion—all of them, and this was without consulting each other except those who were on circuit together. Apparently, no one in Congress gave any thought to constitutionality while drafting the act. In fact, in a recorded response concerning Congressional reaction to the steps taken by the justices, legislators expressed dismay at the "novelty" of the opinion, as though it were some quaint reflection of law.[43]

In conjunction with the response of Congress, throughout the summer of 1792, Attorney General Edmund Randolph fought with the Court over the legal implications of the Court's actions and his role in them.[44] The attorney general was claiming his Constitutional right, via section thirty-five of the Judiciary Act, to act in an *ex-officio* capacity to ask the Supreme Court to issue a writ of mandamus to the Middle circuit to conduct a review of the claim of William Hayburn through the Act of 1792.[45] On August 11, 1792, the Court split over whether the attorney general could act in an *ex-officio* capacity. Randolph had not consulted with President Washington and when the Court split (meaning Randolph's claim was denied), Randolph returned and claimed to be the personal counsel of William Hayburn. The Court agreed to consider the attorney general's motion to act as William Hayburn's personal counsel in a formal manner in the February 1793 term, but this never occurred.

Although the name of William Hayburn has come to be associated with this episode, two more traditional cases were spawned by the 1792 act: *Ex Parte Chandler* and *United States v. Yale Todd*. Both of these cases were heard and decided by the Supreme Court in 1794. The fact that two traditional cases emerged from the Constitutional crisis of 1792–1793 is startling evidence of the overall patience and commitment to the Constitution that was evolving. While the actual functional process of *Chandler* and *Yale Todd* are not the most important aspects of the February 1794 term, the decisions are instructional for the Court's thinking with regards to Constitutional interpretation. The case of *Yale Todd* is interesting because in the initial confusion of the 1792 act, Justices Jay and Cushing had approved the claim of Mr. Todd as commissioners.

Chief Justice John Jay and Justice Cushing had attempted to compromise in an attempt to avoid disregarding the act entirely. They reasoned that instead of fulfilling the requirements of the act as judges (as provided for), they would constitute themselves as commissioners and on their own time hear the claimants. This would avoid the problem of judges acting outside of the judicial sphere and of another branch of government reviewing their decisions. Todd's legal position had been left in question by the revised 1793 act which did not comment on those veterans who appeared before judges acting as commissioners during the confusion of the 1792 act. On February 17, 1794, Todd's case was decided for the United States, thus invalidating all the claims under the 1792 act.[46]

The issues involved in *Chandler* are more obscure due to the lack of records. However, it can be surmised that Chandler, who was approved by Justice

Iredell also acting on his own as a commissioner during the 1792 confusion, was asking the Court for a mandamus ordering the secretary of war to place him on the pensioners list. The justices refused his request without comment.[47]

On June 9, 1794, the entire matter of invalid pensions was legislatively resolved when Congress complied with the Court's ruling and directed the secretary of war not to accept pensioners who had been certified by circuit court judges in 1792.[48] Federal legislation had been altered to accommodate the rulings of the Court, and a precedent had been established.[49]

The rulings in *Hayburn*, *Chandler*, and *Yale Todd* are all consistent with the first inclinations of the justices concerning the constitutionality of the act.[50] The justices found the act and any actions taken under it unconstitutional. What is probably more important is the fact that the rulings did not declare the act unlawful, but unconstitutional (admittedly the actual words were not used, but in theory). Unlawful would have more appropriately denoted a ruling under common law, whereas unconstitutional denoted something entirely different. A Constitutional ruling implied the reliance upon a more organic, positivist approach to lawmaking.[51]

The case of *Todd* was docketed by consent in the Supreme Court; and the Court appears to have been of the opinion that the Act of Congress of 1793, directing the secretary of war and attorney general to take their opinion upon the question, gave them original jurisdiction. In the early days of the government, the right of Congress to give original jurisdiction to the Supreme Court in cases not enumerated in the Constitution was maintained by many jurists and seems to have been entertained by the learned judges who decided Mr. Todd's case.

> But discussion and more mature examination has settled the question otherwise; and it has long been the established doctrine, and we believe now assented to by all who have examined the subject, that the original jurisdiction of this court is confined to the cases specified in the Constitution, and that Congress cannot enlarge it. In all other cases its power must be appellate.[52]

Congress readjusted the language of the Invalid Pensions Act taking into consideration the challenges by the justices over the winter of 1792–1793. Whether Congress was moved by the Court's challenge (it is hard to see how it was not) or not, the change of wording in fact occurred. The February 1793 Act required circuit judges, or a commission appointed by them, to hear claimants. The revised act left open the status of claimants who received pensions from justices acting as commissioners in 1792. This omission led to the 1794 case of Yale Todd but rendered the case of William Hayburn closed.[53] The Federalists generally were furious with the justices, seeing their behavior as presumptuous. Nevertheless, Congress and the Federalists did concede to the justices concerns.[54]

Several issues seem to be at play to the modern eye. In claiming that the act was unconstitutional the Justices appeared to act in a non-judicial capacity to make their point—there was no case by which to issue an opinion.[55] The Justices were thus actually acting in a non-judicial capacity by advising the other two branches of government. What occurred approached a constitutional crisis carried out in broad daylight without the benefit of a case having been heard.

Overall, the newspaper records which do exist record the use of the phrase "unconstitutionality" in nearly every instance of the story. Fewer than a dozen articles were carried by the Philadelphia press mainly, and nearly all of the stories ran in the spring and early summer of 1792. The reports make clear the concept of unconstitutionality was not something unheard of and was plainly planned as a judicial device.[56]

Throughout the combined *Hayburn* episode, Congress and President Washington seemed willing to accommodate the Court—whether or not this was based on the convincing Constitutional argument. The few remaining references to it tend to show the Court as being somewhat discriminating in its approach, particularly because veterans and their families were involved. The Court was aware of the danger of being seen as unpatriotic, especially in the press.[57]

The result of the opinions expressed by the judges of the Supreme Court in the note to *Hayburn's* Case, and in the case of the *United States v. Todd*, were:

1. That the power proposed to be conferred on the circuit courts of the United States by the act of 1792 was not judicial power within the meaning of the Constitution, and was, therefore, unconstitutional, and could not lawfully be exercised by the courts.

2. That as the act of Congress intended to confer the power on the courts as a judicial function, it could not be construed as an authority to the judges composing the court to exercise the power out of court in the character of commissioners.

3. That money paid under a certificate from persons not authorized by law to give it, might be recovered back by the United States.[58]

No longer in the United States would the general contours of jurisprudence be dictated by a set of loosely conjoined edicts based more on custom and ritual from time immemorial. Rather, the United States would be bound jurisprudentially by a code of positive law. The Hayburn episode represents a major practical shift by the Supreme Court, and also Congress and the president, in the legal approach to governing on two levels. The first represents the presence of the ability to declare legislation unconstitutional, and the second represents the shift from common law to constitutional law.

One of the unique problems in analyzing an event such as the *Hayburn* episode is the challenge of language and meaning.[59] When talking about the Court of 1792 we tend to use the same terms as in the twenty-first century, although they may not necessarily translate exactly and mean the same thing.[60] We think of the Court as the assemblage of justices which meets in Washington at the Supreme Court building behind a large, slightly angular desk in a building which looks like a Greek temple. The Court in 1792 did comprise justices, but not a building. In the *Hayburn* episode they wrote the most meaningful commentary from the vantage of the circuit, not as an assembled group in a formal setting, as occurred with *Chandler* and *Yale Todd*. Aside from the physical and geographical aspects of circuit riding (which no longer exists in the same sense) terms and phrases such as "judicial review," "unconstitutional," "the Court," and "opinion," among others, carry different definitions and shades of meaning in current usage that did not exist in the 1790s.

Chisholm v. Georgia *(February 18, 1793)*

The years between 1791 and 1794 were some of the most profound for the establishment of the authority of the Supreme Court. The nascent structure of judicial review and the supremacy of federal law through the Constitution were established, and the chilling aspect of a Court unwilling to follow political pressure led to a decision which compelled the Congress to propose and pass an amendment to the Constitution. The latter two instances involved the state of Georgia in contemporaneous actions before the Court, the second of which will be the main subject of the current section.[61]

The creation of a powerful Supreme Court in practice began as early as 1791 and continued with the trio of cases spawned by the Invalid Pensions Act of 1792. The outline of the Court's development as the expositor of a nonpolitical interpretation of the Constitution can best be seen through this act. The Court did not naturally stumble upon the course of action they took by accident, nor was it developed in a vacuum. The early 1790s was a period of intense exploration and definition of boundaries for the Court. While not many cases (and cases here means any topic of a judicial nature which the justices decided either formally or informally that impacted constitutional development) numerically came before the Court. Those that did were by default precedent setting and consequently significant.

The case of *Chisholm v. Georgia* represents Congress's acknowledgment of the Court's power relative to the Constitution, in so much as the Congress felt a need to pass an amendment to prevent the Court from deciding other similar cases as they did in *Chisholm*. In deciding *Chisholm*, the Court had an explicit definition in Article III, Section II, regarding the suability of states and of the original jurisdiction of the Supreme Court in cases involving states.[62]

The overall timeframe of *Chisholm* covers nearly eight years from its inception to its conclusion. This section will deal only with the barest elements of the fringe dates and concentrate on the action which occurred in the Supreme Court and the impact it had on Congress. In many ways, this was the first "original intent" case for the Court.

This book lays heavy emphasis on *The Federalist* papers, and although there are instances where the essays are seemingly contradictory, the overall impact of the essays cannot be overlooked for understanding the development of constitutionalism.[63] The case of *Chisholm*, and those of a similar topic, offers one example. The Constitution did appear to permit individuals to sue states without their consent and without regard to sovereignty. However, Alexander Hamilton, in several *Federalist* essays, offered differing viewpoints in relation to the concept of sovereignty and suability.

In number 9, Hamilton wrote that the proposed Constitution "makes [state governments] constituent parts of the national sovereignty."[64] In number 32, Hamilton wrote "the State governments would clearly retain all the rights of sovereignty which they before had, and which were not, by that act, exclusively delegate to the United States."[65] Hamilton appeared to be wanting it both ways in his attempt to persuade passage of the Constitution. In number 30, a sentence itself is contradictory in the sense that, states, according to Hamilton, would "retain all the rights of sovereignty which they before had"; this would be fine if Hamilton stopped here. However, he proceeded on to say that states would retain all prior sovereignty except that "exclusively delegate[ed] to the United States." This could mean anything from the *status quo ante* being maintained to the state effectively losing all sovereignty due to sovereignty being placed with the United States. Hamilton's approach really offers the researcher little to go on, as he clearly was attempting to delicately maneuver around such a difficult topic.

The one overriding issue at stake in the *Chisholm* case and those of similar persuasion dealt with the notion of sovereignty. Who has power, how much do they have, on what level is it a shared sovereignty, at what point can it (sovereignty) be subordinated to another concept—such as constitutionalism? Constitutionalism by definition required a new approach and way of thinking which distinguished it from the recent history of the states. Many associated sovereignty within the context of monarchy, which held various connotations, most of which in some way included an element of the divine rights of sovereigns. To the newly independent Americans, who fought for that freedom within the realm of state sovereignty, the notion of somehow subordinating that sovereignty was antithetical. The idea of a state being sued was in some quarters unfathomable. Particularly to those who favored the concept of state sovereignty in imitation as it existed under the Articles of Confederation. Perhaps this was why Hamilton went to such lengths to assuage concerns in several of his *Federalist* essays.

In addition to Hamilton, James Madison and John Marshall were also two prominent figures who would argue during the ratification process that states would not be compelled to suits without their permission. What is interesting in reading the commentary of Hamilton, Madison, and Marshall is that they were writing for a political audience, whereas the Supreme Court in deciding *Chisholm* and other cases was not. The politics of ratifying the Constitution was in some instances in plain contradiction to the application of the Constitution. Madison stated at the Virginia ratifying convention that "it is not in the power of individuals to call any state into court."[66] It seems somewhat strange that someone who had such a profound position in the drafting of the Constitution would be quoted as saying what would seem on the surface to be patently false. Given Chief Justice Jay's comment of how straightforward the Constitution was in regards to the suability of states by individuals, it is beneficial to speculate on the divergence of their viewpoints and what could perhaps cause such a divergence. The most likely cause was the expedience of politics. Hamilton, Madison, and Marshall all were self-tasked with promoting the new political system.

Although John Jay participated in the *Federalist* project, he withdrew early due to ill health. His view toward the power of the federal government created by the Constitution can be summed up by a statement delivered to the New York state ratifying convention. Jay spoke of the need for the federal government to take the larger viewpoint, as opposed to the more myopic viewpoint of the states. Jay stated that "the objectives of the general government were broad, comprehending the interests of the states in relation to each other, and in relation to foreign powers."[67] Regardless of the motivations, Hamilton, Madison, and Marshall all provided commentary which seemed more designed to mollify than engage. Of the writing analyzed thus far, the commentary dealing with sovereignty was mostly at odds with the language of the Constitution.

The Court, in deciding *Chisholm*, followed the Constitution as written. There really was no interpretation involved. It would seem it was in print for everyone to see.[68] Yet, this case, and the action of the Court in upholding the Constitution as written, caused the Congress to pass what in reality was the first true amendment to the Constitution, although it was placed as number eleven, behind the Bill of Rights.[69] The end result of the case, the Eleventh Amendment, is what sets this case apart from the other contemporaneous cases involving the same issue.

Similar to other cases in the early 1790s, *Chisholm* began in the confusion of war during the Revolution.[70] The confusion necessarily reached to the realm of law and left those conducting business in a unique situation of wondering which law was valid—state law, common law, the laws of war, or perhaps a combination of all available possibilities. Compounding this problem was the issue of loyalist and patriot and who would be protected by law.

In the fall of 1777, the state of Georgia contracted to purchase supplies from Robert Farquhar for the American Army. Farquhar delivered the supplies and sought payment from Georgia through their representatives, Thomas Stone and Edward Davies, but was denied. After years of attempting to gain payment, Farquhar was killed in a boating accident in January 1784, and his executor, Alexander Chisholm, became chiefly involved with pursuing the case.

What propelled this case out of the realm of contract law and into the realm of constitutional law had to do with timing (it came about at the same moment as other high profile British debt cases were in the courts) and an ill-worded response from the Georgia governor over the federal summons of early February 1791 (the governor essentially lectured the Court on the elements of state sovereignty). Georgia would shortly be involved in another similar case, *Georgia v. Brailsford*, which replicated many of the same issues as *Chisholm*. Georgia decided to fight the cases from different angles. Although both approaches would ultimately fail Georgia in the Supreme Court, they were unique for the constitutional questions their strategies raised.

In 1789, Chisholm petitioned the Georgia legislature—now operating as a state under the new Constitution—for payment of the outstanding Farquhar debt. The legislature responded that Stone and Davies, the middleman in the original deal, had already been paid and Chisholm should approach the individuals directly. Probably because Farquhar had originally had a contract with the state and not the middlemen, Chisholm decided to continue pursuing Georgia in court and brought suit in the United States circuit court for the Southern district in early 1791. Why it had taken 12 years for a case involving such a considerable amount of money (over £100,000) to make it this far is not wholly known. Clearly, the circuit courts were not in existence until 1790, but why Farquhar's executor did not pursue it earlier is a mystery.

In their reply to Governor Telfair's request for information, Georgia Attorney General Thomas Carnes and Solicitor General John Noel seemed to question the summons in a practical sense. They wrote:

> The General Assembly of the state at the late session, passed a law for the express purpose of giving individuals the power of instituting suits or actions for such claims as they might have against the state and the mode which the citizen is to pursue is therein particularly pointed out, if therefore that mode is not pursued, the individual is without remedy.[71]

It would seem clear from this comment that, from Georgia's standpoint, they had already provided a remedy for citizens while not specifically stating which citizens. In Georgia's view, Chisholm was in some respects casting dispersions on the state and the state judiciary (if he had been a state citizen he would probably have been viewed in some light as a traitor for going outside the state).[72]

Carnes and Noel represented Georgia on October 17, 1791, in the federal district court in Augusta. They denied the court's jurisdiction by saying that Georgia "was a free, sovereign, and independent state" and that "Georgia cannot be drawn or compelled" against its will to answer before a federal court.[73] Leaving aside the meaning of the word "independent" as applied to a state in a federal system, Georgia was not arguing from a direct constitutional standpoint. In fact, Georgia did not even mention the Constitution. They argued strictly from the ancient concept of sovereignty and the power inherent in that sovereignty. They did not need to explain what that meant, as it was difficult, if not impossible, to explain what that meant. Even in eighteenth-century terminology, "sovereign" was at best an ambiguous term, but nonetheless, one that everyone thought they knew the meaning of. As far as Georgia was concerned, the Constitution was irrelevant.[74] Justice Wilson, in his Court opinion on *Chisholm*, dismissed Georgia's claim, indeed any states claim, to sovereignty by stating, "To the Constitution of the United States the term sovereign, is totally unknown."[75]

Once the suit was filed, the governor of Georgia, Edward Telfair, made an inopportune comment on the case through his attorney general and solicitor—already mentioned. Governor Telfair had set in motion a virtually certain constitutional showdown a little over three years after the Constitution was adopted. The governor, no doubt attempting to show his state's sovereignty within the new federal system, proudly proclaimed that Georgia was not in any way under the suzerainty of the United States.[76] The governor seemed to be saying that the debt issue was irrelevant, the true issue or principle involved state sovereignty. Further adding to the combustible verbal atmosphere, the Georgia Attorney General Thomas Carnes engaged in an early form of original intent argument when he wrote that "those persons delegated from the different states" to form the new union did not mean to subject states to federal law.[77]

With these incendiary words, the governor moved from a case concerning non-payment of debt (like its sister case *Brailsford*) to a case involving the highest principle of constitutional law. Not only did the Constitution in 1789 explicitly (some would say implicitly) give individuals the right to sue a state through Article III, Section II, but the Constitution also made itself the supreme law through Article VI.

Farquhar v. Georgia was argued during the October circuit court term of 1791 before Justice Iredell and Circuit Judge Nathan Pendleton. Both judges sided with Georgia due to the reasoning that the state could not be sued by an individual or be a party to any suit without its consent. Justice Iredell felt that finding for Farquhar would only create undue hardship for Georgia, and indeed any state which was sued.[78]

Justice Iredell argued from the standpoint of a combination of the Judiciary Act of 1789 and the Constitution. His opinion focused solely on whether the federal circuit court had original jurisdiction in the case. The idea of original jurisdiction was intimately connected with the idea of state sovereignty. As historian Kemp Yarborough points out, "Iredell's opinion ... simply expressed the divided sovereignty concept of his generation."[79] In other words, Justice Iredell should not be seen in the light of later nineteenth-century states' rights advocates but rather within the context of his time.[80] This however may be a too generous view of Iredell's opinion, which he was alone in rendering in the South Carolina version of the case.[81]

Justice Iredell admitted when he pointed out that "whereas by the Constitution of the U.S. it is declared that the judicial power shall extend to controversies between a state & citizens of another state" the current case does indeed fall within that definition and is thus within constitutional definitions.[82] For Iredell therefore, it was a straight textual reading which was not difficult to fathom.

Section eleven of the Judiciary Act of 1789 stipulated that the federal circuit courts would have "original cognizance, concurrent with the courts of the several States, of all suits of a civil nature at common law [where] the suit is between a citizen of the State where the suit is brought, and a citizen of another State."[83] Section thirteen noted that the "Supreme Court shall have exclusive jurisdiction of all controversies of a civil nature, where a state is a party, except between a state and its citizens; and except also between a state and citizens of other states."[84] This would seem to exclude the Supreme Court, and indeed be contradictory to the Constitution. Using these two sections of the 1789 act, and Article III Section II of the Constitution, he constructed an argument whereby the Supreme Court would end up being the inferior court relative to the circuit court, if in fact the case was appealed because the Constitution accepts appellate jurisdiction in cases involving states.[85] Justice Iredell felt "that the Constitution, so far as it respects the judicial authority, can only be carried into effect, by acts of the legislature, appointing courts, and prescribing their methods of proceeding."[86] While this quote is chronologically from the case once it arrives at the Supreme Court, it nonetheless portrays Iredell's opinion concerning the circuit court case.

Iredell would seem to be far too generous in granting sole power to the Congress in developing the legal system of the United States. The Constitution created the Supreme Court, not the Congress. If nothing else, the Supreme

Court must exist unless Congress passed an amendment (the most utilized method) to abolish it. Congress did not, nor did the Constitution, "create" law in the sense that Iredell was using it. Given Iredell's definition, law cannot exist as a concept or theoretical embodiment.[87]

Chisholm appealed to the Supreme Court and in August 1792, the case, renamed *Chisholm v. Georgia*, was heard. By a political decision of the governor, no one represented the state of Georgia, as they felt the case violated their dignity and sovereignty as a state. The justices postponed the case until the February 1793 term. If Georgia was not represented by this time, the case by default would be decided for Chisholm.[88] Although the case was postponed, Justices Jay, Blair, Cushing, and Wilson indicated a favorable opinion for Chisholm's argument. Justice Iredell, who was already on record indicating he was unfavorable to the case on principle, maintained his views.[89]

Why Georgia choose to argue this case as an issue of state sovereignty as opposed to an issue of debt payment is not absolutely clear. Under Georgia law, claims of loyalists were "sequestered or extinguished" by the state—but Farquhar was not a loyalist.[90] Given that they were simultaneously involved with the *Brailsford* case may have played a role too. Even though in *Brailsford* Georgia was engaged in what was essentially a federal supremacy issue, in *Chisholm* they opted for what would seem again a federal supremacy issue. It is interesting how two cases which had roots in a conflict which heralded itself as throwing off the heavy hand of a central government (Britain) ended up facing a central government. However, in the follow up of both cases in the Supreme Court, the Court (representing the central—federal—government) had a Constitution, something the central government (the British government) in the beginning of both cases did not have.[91]

As Justice Iredell can easily be said to speak for the minority opinion, Chief Justice Jay can be said to speak for the majority opinion. Jay argued chiefly from a strong, national view of the Constitution. Jay reasoned that "one state may sue another state in this court, it is plain no degradation to a state is thought to accompany her appearance in this court."[92] Jay was basing his argument on the essence that a state is composed of individuals, similar to the "We the People" opening to the preamble to the Constitution.[93] If a group of people can sue another group of people, what is the difference if a singular person sues a group of people, or vice versa?

Jay was also concerned with the signal that the *Chisholm* case could send to other nations, if in fact Georgia succeeded in obtaining its immunity in contradiction to the Constitution. The United States had an obligation in the community of nations to be "responsible to foreign nations for the conduct of each State."[94] Jay was making the Constitution, and the enforcement of it, an issue of foreign policy in the sense that the United States could not be seen as having allowed a direct violation to the new Constitution.[95] Jay believed the extension of "the judiciary power of the United States to such controversies, appears to me to be wise, because it is honest, and because it is useful."[96]

Newspaper coverage of the case was surprisingly attentive and intuitive to the magnitude of the issues involved. Considering that *Chisholm* represented one of the earliest cases the Court dealt with, the press appeared well versed in developing Court procedure. The earliest known reference is from August 1792 in the *General Advertiser* in Philadelphia. The paper read simply, "It is expected that some questions of magnitude will be agitated at this session—questions that may affect the interest of states and individuals."[97]

Somewhat predictably, the Georgia papers generally followed the lead of Governor Telfair in disclaiming federal jurisdiction on the basis of state sovereignty. Also, the Georgia papers tended to carry in full the proceedings of the legislature where the strategy sessions were played out in debate, although little debate occurred.[98] Shearjashub Bourne referred to this situation in a letter to Robert Treat Paine in February 1793. Bourne wrote, "Doubtless you have seen, by their resolutions published in the papers" that Georgia objects to the Court's jurisdiction. Bourne also commented on the *Van Ataphorst* case, in which the state of Maryland agreed to pay a considerable amount in a judgment against them.[99]

As early as the week of the decision in February 1793, John Wereat wrote to Governor Telfair in Georgia that "I was in company with some of the New-England Delegates who were unanimously of opinion that an explanation of that part of the Constitution should be made."[100] It would not take long for the shock effect of the opinion to generate talk of an amendment to rectify what many saw as a poorly worded clause in the Constitution.[101] Therefore, the concept as expressed in the original pre–Eleventh Amendment Constitution was indeed a straightforward expression of an idea. The idea however was what was incorrect according to the states. The easiest remedy would be to simply amend the language and excise the original sentence.

This section focused on one of two similar cases involving the state of Georgia resulting from debt incurred during the Revolutionary War. As mentioned, Georgia was not the only state facing similar suits dating from the War period involving American or British citizens. The magnitude of the problem and the awareness of the potential impact this issue could have was evident in the Paris Peace Treaty of 1783 ending the Revolution. Naturally, the Treaty pertained only to the repayment of foreign creditors, mostly British citizens, while other avenues allowed for the repayment of American citizens, such as occurred in *Chisholm*.[102] This case, which seemed so simple on the surface, eventually became the symbol of unintended power placed with the federal government to the detriment of the states. The ultimate symbol of this case and indeed the end result, the passage of the Eleventh Amendment, seemed unquestionably to overturn the ruling of the Court.

Congress has every right to propose and pass amendments consistent with constitutional procedure. While this would by some be seen as a failure for the Court, others might see it as yet another example of the increasing power of the Court in the realm of constitutional jurisprudence and in the continuing development of the federal system.

Georgia v. Brailsford *(February 7, 1794)*

As the state of Georgia was the most litigious of the states on the federal level during the opening years of the new nation under the Constitution, and as *Chisholm v. Georgia* has been discussed at length, a brief overview of *Georgia v. Brailsford* is in order.[103]

Even without drama attending the end of the *Brailsford* case, such as an amendment to the Constitution as in *Chisholm*, the fact remains that a state (Georgia) in the new federal system attempted to abrogate the requirements of the Constitution to which it was a signatory, thus ensuring a constitutional debate before the Supreme Court.

The developing patterns of the Supreme Court's constitutional awareness were more fully engaged in *Brailsford*. Although *Chisholm* dealt specifically with explicit language in the Constitution, *Brailsford* challenged the Constitution in terms of commitments made prior to the Constitution (the Treaty of Paris), yet accepted by the Constitution. Further, these commitments impacted not only federal and state relations; they more importantly impacted international relations. The stakes in *Brailsford* were very high.

The complex issue of debt payment was bound in issues of international law, common law, admiralty law, state law, and untold numbers of customs and theoretical machinations concerning mercantile transactions. The overwhelming nature of attempting to sort through the impenetrable interconnecting problems was deftly handled in three sentences in the Treaty of Paris. The willingness of the United States to agree to the validity of the contracts and the willingness of the British to accept the commitment was quite remarkable. The British could just as easily not recognized the contracted debt or the confiscated property and thus by implication not recognized the United States by denying it the opportunity of ensuring repayment.

The aspect which seemed most problematic for the United States was enforcement of the Treaty. The Continental Congress was not able to force states to follow the Treaty, much less force individual debtors to abide by it. The United States was at a distinct disadvantage. The new nation had no national tribunal and no national system to adjudicate claims.[104]

The case did not originally begin as a British creditor case. Samuel Brailsford and several associates filed suit against James Spalding and his several associates. In November 1790, Brailsford had brought suit in the Georgia federal district court where Judge Nathaniel Pendleton dismissed the case due to the failure of the defendant James Spalding to present himself at the trial. At the April 1791 term, Brailsford again filed suit and this time labeled himself a "merchant" and a British subject.[105] This admission changed the entire tenor of the case. The case became more than a simple debt collection issue between two parties; it became a debt collection issue between an American and an Englishman and it immediately fell under the Treaty of Paris.[106]

While there was some debate as to Brailsford's actual status as a British subject (his son disputed the claim), he was regarded as such "in the eyes of the law."[107] By April 1792, when the case finally arrived before the Supreme Court, the state of Georgia had maneuvered to the point whereby Georgia maintained it had a right to recover the debts of all creditor (much like Virginia) cases originating in Georgia based on legislation passed prior to the Treaty of Paris in 1783.[108] This case now pitted state law versus federal law in the context of a private debt between parties of different nationalities.[109]

By inserting itself into the case on such a large scale (claiming the state could override all British creditor claims against Georgia's citizens), Georgia placed the issue of federal supremacy squarely on notice.[110] The case had now arrived at the point where Georgia, once again (as in *Chisholm*), forced the hand of the federal government by testing the limits of the new Constitution.[111] Georgia, and several other states, simply could not fundamentally accept the contours of a system of government that in certain instances held more authority than the state itself.

It seems strange that Georgia would find itself a party to a constitutional case so soon after the federal government began operation. Georgia was one of three states (Delaware and New Hampshire the others) that ratified the Constitution at its state convention without a single dissenting vote. Rather than challenging basic elements of the Constitution, it was thought that Georgia would actually have been more supportive of it rather than challenging it.[112] As a small state, Georgia no doubt saw the advantages of joining the union, especially when it needed military assistance.[113]

In his opinion, Judge Pendleton looked at the specifics of the Georgia law in relation to whether this case hinged on British creditor claims or British or loyalist property, and he sought to distinguish precisely what the Georgia law stated and implied in relation to either creditor or property claims.[114] Judge Pendleton ultimately ruled for Brailsford in major part because he saw the Constitution and treaties under it as the supreme law, unlike his ruling in *Chisholm*.[115] His closing remarks were indicative of his views on federal power (again with the exception of his view of *Chisholm*): "Where the law is clear it doth not belong to us to consider what may be its consequences. I believe we shall always find the real good of our country to consist in a cheerful obedience to the established laws and a faithful and honorable compliance with all national engagements."[116]

Justice Iredell, riding on circuit in Georgia, was the first Supreme Court justice to hear *Brailsford v. Spalding*.[117] It is clear both Judge Pendleton and Justice Iredell saw this case in terms of two conflicting laws, where one would have to give way to another. This is precisely the type of scenario the Anti-Federalists feared when they discussed issues involving the federal judiciary. To both Federalists and Anti-Federalists, a case such as this was bound to come up eventually. Squarely facing off federal versus state law in an argument where one would need to be inferior and one superior. It was the ultimate nightmare for the Anti-Federalist and the perfect opportunity for the Federalists.

Justice Iredell approached the legal issues of *Brailsford* much as Judge Pendleton did. He anticipated a thorough review of both federal and state law, impacting not only the relationship between federal and state law, but also what was meant by citizen and residence. Justice Iredell minutely examined the various intersections of the case.[118] His finding rested squarely on the fourth article of the Treaty of Paris, which stated that creditors would "meet with no lawful impediments to the recovery of … debts."[119] To Justice Iredell, the obligation was evident in the statement. Both Judge Pendleton and Justice Iredell spoke unequivocally for the supremacy of federal law as delineated in the Constitution regarding treaties.[120]

The case that appeared before the Supreme Court had magnified out of all proportion from how it originally started. In fact, two unique cases would evolve from the original 1792 case[121]: the first case an appeal heard in 1793, and the second, which became a rare trial case in the Supreme Court in 1794. The first case, in 1793, was not so much an appeal of the district court ruling as an attempt to approach the issue from another vantage point.

In an effort to allow all parties to come before the Court and be heard in this matter, the Court decided to grant an injunction to temporarily delay payment to Brailsford (the Court did not accept the bill of equity argument).[122] Justices Iredell, Blair, Wilson, and Jay believed Georgia could "not be defeated by a judgment upon a trial at which she had not been heard," (unlike *Chisholm* where Georgia was threatened with a default judgment).[123] The "peculiar circumstances," not to mention the novelty by default of the case, likewise persuaded the four justices to grant Georgia's petition.[124]

In Philadelphia, the *American Minerva* on February 7, 1794, reported, "The case which has been for several days before the *Supreme Court of The United States*, in which the *State of Georgia* was petitioner in Chancery, and [Brailsford] and other Respondents, was this day decided by a Special Jury in favor of the Respondents [emphasis in original]."[125]

The *Connecticut Journal* of September 29, 1794, editorialized on the perceived indelicacies of placing creditor and loyalist cases within the federal system: "As late as last month, the Grand Jury of the Federal Circuit court in Virginia presented as a *national* grievance the recovery of debts due to British subjects [emphasis in original]."[126] This type of editorial clearly demonstrated how the debtors had taken what was mandated as a national issue, through the Treaty of Paris, with national consequences, and compressed it into a series of individual local issues (through their insistence on state sovereignty—much like in *Chisholm*), thus potentially weakening further the new government.

As noted, this case combined the elements of multiple systems and theories of law. The intricacy of the interlocking jurisprudential systems is somewhat difficult to follow due to an absence of some of the documentation. What is clear is that the Supreme Court found for Brailsford individually through a common law application but not necessarily for the unquestioned supremacy of constitutional law—as opposed to the decision in *Chisholm*. This could perhaps mean that those Justices agreeing with Brailsford (Jay, Blair, Wilson, and Iredell) sought to ensure Brailsford victory by some measure other than a constitutional pronouncement solely. Perhaps too the justices wanted to allow Georgia some dignity (given the defeat in *Chisholm*) as a state and therefore pursued a more common law remedy. Whatever the real reason, *Brailsford* did in effect (regardless to what degree) establish the precedent concerning British creditors, the Constitution, and the Treaty of Peace of 1783.[127]

Glass v. Sloop Betsey *and France (February 18, 1794)*

The four cases reviewed thus far under the Jay Court involved topics related to a technicality in *West v. Barnes*; the extra-constitutional role of justices in *Hayburn*; and the supremacy of federal law over state law in *Chisholm v. Georgia* and in *Georgia v. Brailsford*. With *Glass v. Sloop Betsey,* the Court took on a case with international ramifications, thus securing a unique place for the Court within the new framework of American government. It should also be noted that *Glass* was just one of many admiralty cases which came before the Court in the 1790s.

The case began in June 1793 when the sloop (a type of ship) *Betsey* was forced into Baltimore harbor, the prize of a French privateer operating under the direction of the French minister to the United States, Edmond Charles Genêt, better known as Citizen Genêt. Genêt ran this venture out of Charleston, South Carolina, in direct contradiction of President Washington's official policy of neutrality (Neutrality Proclamation of April 22, 1793) in the European wars raging at that point. What was most distressing was that the *Betsey* was owned by a Swedish concern when Sweden was not a combatant to any aspect of the war in Europe. Genêt however felt he had the authority to prepare and launch his ships from Charleston due to a 1778 treaty between France and the then struggling United States in which both sides agreed to come to the aid of the other if attacked, among other promises. The issue was of course that both France and the United States had evolved from what they were in 1778 into something unimaginable by 1793. Before continuing with a review of the case, it would be useful to review the world situation as it stood for American leaders when the *Betsey* came before the Court.

Citizen Genêt

Aside from creating the Supreme Court and laying the foundations of American law, the first few years of the Jay Court were inextricably linked to the developing Revolution occurring in America's ally France. What began physically on the streets of Paris would soon ricochet across the English Channel and not long afterward across the Atlantic. Dealing with the aftereffects of the French Revolution would plague Presidents Washington and Adams (and Jefferson), and impact the Jay, Rutledge, and Ellsworth Courts. The first hints of trouble came ashore in Charleston, South Carolina, in the person of Edmond Charles Genêt, known simply by his Revolutionary moniker, Citizen Genêt.

Genêt was the first "in person" experience of the French Revolution that nearly every American could claim to have had when he arrived in April 1793. Before the end of the summer, Genêt had managed to make himself intolerable by having "done one foolish thing after another to muddle the relations of the two countries."[128] This was not an easy task to accomplish, given the close relationship between France and the United States and the treaties the two shared. Genêt had a revolutionary spirit that far outpaced anything the Americans would have advocated at the time. He had utterly misunderstood the American Revolution. In fact, in Genêt's thinking after his time spent in America that first summer, the Revolution that France had funded and made possible in 1780 was anything but revolutionary by 1793. Still, during his brief time as ambassador, he organized such ventures as the privateer business out of Charleston, an activity that did not meet with the approval of President Washington and most of his cabinet.

Neutrality

France declared war on Great Britain and Holland on February 1, 1793. President George Washington was a month away from officially starting his second term. Thomas Jefferson was still secretary of state and Alexander Hamilton was still secretary of the treasury. Relationships within the cabinet however, were tense, and staffing would change within the year. President Washington struggled to find a neutral path between the warring countries and his warring advisors. No one in the administration felt America should risk war. The country was far too weak—financially, politically, and emotionally—to risk another conflict. This was an especially acute observation given that America's greatest benefactor, France, was at war with another one of America's great benefactors, Holland. Furthermore, the United States was interested in renewing relations with Britain, especially economically, and President Washington would send Chief Justice John Jay to Britain in 1794 to negotiate a new treaty. Domestic issues lent to the general angst felt during the year from 1793 to 1794 as well. The Whiskey Rebellion, combined with France and Britain, seemed to send a message that the United States was finding independence too much to cope with. Additionally, personnel changes on the Supreme Court added more components to the president's constantly shifting troubles.

After the president learned of the new European war, he asked his cabinet secretaries to respond to a series of questions about how the United States should proceed. Into this policy formulation strode Genêt, someone who would have been difficult to deal with even had a fully articulated policy been in place. President Washington's deliberative pace over the meaning of a Neutrality Act which he issued in late April 1793, without it being fully formed, lasted throughout the spring of 1793 into the fall. His decisions would in part lead to the resignation of Secretary of State Thomas Jefferson on December 31, 1793. The debates also caused the ideological fault lines in the cabinet to heave beyond the point of return. A major part of the president's questions about neutrality dealt with the role of the United States towards France. The summer of 1793 contributed greatly to the rise of political parties generally during the early 1790s and would solidify by the end of Washington's second term. A Treaty of Alliance and a Treaty of Amity and Commerce existed between the countries, but the France of 1793 was certainly not the France which originally signed the treaties under King Louis XVI. For that matter, the United States of 1793 was certainly not the United States that negotiated the treaties with King Louis XVI either.

The France that America encountered in 1793 was represented by the unstable Citizen Genêt. His mission nearly derailed American/French relations that had been over a decade in development. More importantly, his presence amplified the divisions already forming among America's political elite, and especially within the president's cabinet. Yet, France held a special place in the imagination of the "average" American. Americans largely identified with "the efforts of the French people to establish republican liberty,

France's challenge to the menace of England, her struggle against the ancient forces of monarchy, aristocracy, and European despotism....”[129] This bond was felt at a visceral level, much like the opposite feeling was held for the British.

Incensed by Genêt's actions, President Washington ordered an immediate end to the French activities in Charleston. Secretary of State Thomas Jefferson was the president's point of contact in the matter, whom Genêt ignored, and Jefferson warned him (Genêt) against such a course. It must be recalled that the United States at this point (1793) had only been in operation as a government for fewer than four years. As such, the country had difficulty dealing with domestic issues much less international ones. Adrian Koch has written concerning Genêt: “Genêt's diplomatic impudence in the realm of propaganda came on top of his unprecedented violations of this country's sovereignty, including fitting out ships of war in American ports and capturing British vessels in American waters.”[130]

The principle actors in the escalating political confrontation were names well known to most observers: for the Republicans, Thomas Jefferson, James Madison, and James Monroe; for the Federalists, Alexander Hamilton, John Jay, and Rufus King. Knowing as we do now that Jefferson, Madison, and Monroe were combined to be presidents of the United States from 1800 to 1825 clearly indicates which party won the long term contest. However, in 1793, this was all in the future. In 1793, and indeed for the next two years or more, the political fortunes of Jefferson and his followers were low.

The Whiskey Rebellion was still raging in Pennsylvania at this point. Therefore, it was not surprising that the president and his cabinet were confused as to how best to deal with the thorny issues posed by Genêt and his “enterprise” which he operated out of the neutral American port of Charleston. Under the circumstances, the president sent letters to the justices seeking their advice. He hoped that at least three justices could come to Philadelphia in July (during their recess) to meet the president and his cabinet to determine the best approach to the French (and Genêt) problem.

Secretary Jefferson wrote a brief letter for the president to the justices outlining the problem and issues at stake to provide some context as to what the president was asking of them. Jefferson wrote (for Washington):

> The war has taken place among the powers of Europe produces frequent transactions within our ports and limits, on which questions arise of considerable difficulty, and of greater importance to the peace of the United States. These questions depend for their solution on the construction of our treaties, on the laws of nature and nations, and on the laws of the law....[131]

President Washington asked Jefferson to write the letter because he was secretary of state and highly knowledgeable in the law. Yet, his letter to the justices was about as unclear as one could be. He seemed himself to be unsure what he was asking and threw in a hodge-podge of possible law which the justices could consider. The one item Jefferson left out was the Constitution.

Jefferson however quickly got to the point, which was how to interpret the multiple laws in force and apply that reasoning to the issue at hand. Furthermore, Jefferson had a simple request on behalf of the president: "The President would therefore be much relieved if he found himself free to refer questions of this description to the opinions of the judges of the Supreme Court...."[132] President Washington wrote to Jefferson later in the day on July 18 and said that Chief Justice Jay and Justice Paterson were in town and asked Jefferson to expedite matters at the meeting the next day "to draft something (before you come) that will bring the question properly before them."[133] Finally, Secretary of Treasury Alexander Hamilton assisted in drafting a list of questions for the justices to consider. After two days, the four justices in Philadelphia asked if they could delay their reply until the two other justices could be consulted. The president granted the delay.

The Court would not formally respond to the president until August 8, nearly a week after their August term began. By this point however the president had moved on to consultations with the Congress over the issue. The president may have had an inclination that the Supreme Court would be disinclined to give advice on matters that might come before them as a court; and even if it did not come before them as a case, the justices were not inclined to give advice outside the formal judicial process. The new country and its leaders were quickly evolving into statesmen employing the branches of government in what was at the time precedent-setting ways—ways which would in some instances be quite familiar to us today. Finally, it was also known certainly by Jefferson and Hamilton that several cases in the lower courts impacting the *Betsey* and neutrality issues were being heard. Without question, there was a near guarantee one or more of these cases would wind up before the Supreme Court.

For Jefferson and his colleagues, Citizen Genêt was a problem of epic proportions. The sooner he left the better in Jefferson's mind. As the historian Gordon Wood has pointed out, "No one could have been more ill-suited for his diplomatic mission."[134] The residual effect of the American Revolution mingled in the minds of many Americans when Genêt arrived and at first impression they conflated the two events. It would take Genêt's bungled diplomacy, the president's good office, and a few Supreme Court cases involving privateers, to break the spell Genêt and the French Revolution initially cast over the American political scene.

Within a few months of Genêt's arrival, Secretary of State Jefferson was becoming alarmed at how thoroughly Genêt was becoming a liability to the nascent Republican cause. Genêt, Jefferson felt "was working not only against himself but against the republican interest. Because of his outrageous conduct, a popular swing to the support of the President's neutrality policy, and to the President personally, was in progress."[135]

The years from 1793 to 1795 would see the triumph of a more pro–British approach to foreign policy, especially after President Washington sent Chief Justice John Jay to England to negotiate a new treaty. The other aspect which made America's leaders less inclined to favor the French with their new terrifying revolution was the Whiskey Rebellion—similar to Shays' Rebellion of 1786. The specter of domestic insurrection, like in France, was too great a risk for America.

Genêt's time in America included planning to raise an army in Kentucky to attack Spanish Louisiana and Florida and to work to agitate Canada to free herself from British rule. The French, especially Genêt, completely misread the American appetite for war in the name of liberty. It was totally inconceivable that Americans would depose President Washington and behead him and Lady Washington in front of the Pennsylvania Statehouse in Philadelphia (as was the fate of Louis XVI and Marie Antoinette in Paris). Furthermore, Americans had endured by 1793 nearly a quarter-century of social, economic, and political upheaval. Genêt's mission to the United States was one of the greatest diplomatic miscalculations in history. Genêt's threats to go over the president's head and appeal directly to the American people, whom he felt supported his cause more than the president, nearly unhinged the president with anger. It was not long before Genêt's recall by the French government was demanded by the president. As events dragged on through 1793, with Jefferson's resignation on December 31, 1793, Genêt lingered and was eventually granted asylum in the United States due to the rise of an even more radical element in France who would have killed him had he returned.

Thomas Jefferson and Citizen Genêt

Secretary Jefferson's enthusiasm for France was founded upon more than the time he spent in France during the 1780s as the American minister. The refinement, culture, art, and learning of pre–Revolution France dazzled him. After his return to America and appointment as secretary of state by President Washington, he had to deal with not only the horrors of the French Revolution but with the much larger geopolitical issues occasioned by near-constant warfare at any given time somewhere on the European continent. In the end, though, Jefferson was still captivated by the splendor of the French mystique. His effusive embrace of Citizen Genêt when he first arrived in the United States is seen in a letter Jefferson wrote to Congressman James Madison on May 19, 1793. Jefferson wrote:

It is impossible for anything to be more affectionate, more magnanimous than the purport of his mission.... In short he offers everything and asks nothing. Yet I know the offers will be opposed, and suspect they will not be accepted. In short, my dear sir, it is impossible for you to conceive what is passing in our conclave [cabinet meetings]...[136]

As effusive as Jefferson was, Secretary of the Treasury Alexander Hamilton was critical. In a letter of 1800, seven years after the Genêt affair, Hamilton reflected on that troubled summer of 1793: "The intrigues of Genêt and his successors were perplexing to the government, chiefly because they were too well seconded by the prepossessions of the people. The great alteration in public opinion, had put it completely in the power of our executive to control the machinations of any future public agent of France."[137] Hamilton saw the greatest threat from Genêt to be the public at large. Jefferson and his Republicans were bad enough for Hamilton, but the public could be easily swayed in Hamilton's view. Someone like Genêt stoking the past glories of the American Revolution to curry favor for the French Revolution was about as dangerous as it could get. The public was fickle and frankly still trying to understand what it meant to be a citizen of an independent country like the United States. In fact, the United States, through the federal government, was still trying to figure out what it meant to be an independent country. The last thing America needed in 1793 was agitation from France. Hamilton's assessment, with the benefit of hindsight, was in stark contrast to Jefferson's initial passion for Genêt in 1793.

In a private letter of August 26, 1794 (nearly a year after the Genêt affair), President Washington, writing to Henry Lee, opined:

> I early gave it as my opinion to the confidential characters around me, that, if these societies [liberty groups supporting Genêt] were not counteracted or did not fall into disesteem from the knowledge of their origin, and the views with which they had been instituted by their father, Genêt, for purposes well known to the government; that they would shake the government to its foundation.[138]

Washington saw nothing but ill from Genêt and his supporters: "I see, under a display of popular and fascinating guises, the most diabolical attempts to destroy the best fabric of human government and happiness, that has ever been presented for the acceptance of mankind."[139]

The president provided one final observation on the Genêt affair. Writing to Burges Ball on September 25, 1794, the president expressed his anger over the liberty of democratic societies that sprang into existence the preceding year in the momentary euphoria surrounding Genêt's mission. Washington wrote that these societies, inspired by Genêt, sought "the express purpose of dissention, and to draw a line between the people and the government, after he found the officers of the latter would not yield to the hostile measures in which he wanted to embroil the country."[140]

Washington also alluded to an event which must now be acknowledged—the Whiskey Rebellion. In the same letter to Burges Bull, the president mentioned "the insurrection in the Western counties of this state [Pennsylvania]" as evidence of the machinations of Genêt and his followers.[141] The president expressed his dismay that he "did not, I must confess, expect their labors would come to maturity so soon; though I never had a doubt, that such conduct would produce some such issue; if it did not meet the frown of those who were well disposed to order and good government...."[142]

The Whiskey Rebellion

The Whiskey Rebellion of 1794, much like Shays' Rebellion of 1786, ignited intense internal debates among America's elite Founders. Once again, the question of how to deal with an insurrection founded on similar principles as the founding of the new nation (taxation) should be dealt with. It was not an easy question to answer.

Shays' Rebellion and the Whiskey Rebellion had many parallels. Both erupted over taxation; both were headed by non-coastal residents (interior farmers); both threatened to disrupt the established pattern of life; both threatened federal armories; yet, there was one major difference. Shays' concerned a state tax while the Whiskey Rebellion concerned a federal tax. This was no minor difference. Shays' rebels had to only be concerned with the reaction of the state, not so with the Whiskey Rebellion. Shays' had to contend with a governor, Whiskey rebels with a president. With Shays', no federal government existed. With the Whiskey Rebellion, a federal government (although weak) existed. The dispute arose over points of contention as old as human society. The government (federal) needed money; and the back-country farmers did not want to pay to a remote government from their hard earned and limited income. Some farmers even compared the excise tax to the Stamp Tax of 1765—and everyone knew how that episode ended.[143]

Violence flared throughout 1792 and 1793 against the president's 1791 law, especially in western Pennsylvania. President Washington threatened militia action to quell the violence but did not act. Secretary of the Treasury Alexander Hamilton was incensed that the president was allowing these challenges to national authority to go unchecked. At worst, some felt the British were behind the uprisings while others saw the influence of the French Revolution and the feelings it stirred against central government. Either way, it was not a good situation for the president. The Whiskey Rebellion smoldered long enough to become "the largest incident of armed resistance to federal authority between the adoption of the Constitution and the Civil War."[144]

President Washington sent a negotiation team to the affected part of

Pennsylvania to try and talk through differences. When that failed in late September 1794, the President ordered the raising of a 15,000-member force (under the Militia Act of 1792) to head to the afflicted area. Supreme Court Justice James Wilson had notified the president in August that civil disorder was beyond what the courts and local law enforcement could deal with peacefully.[145] The arrival of troops and the overwhelming threat of force caused the rebels to collapse and the rebellion died a quick, mostly peaceful, death. It is just as well that the threat of force did not descend into actual use of force. The militia was in no shape to be an effective fighting or law enforcement tool. Their supplies were rotten, food was rotten, leadership was rotten, and the commitment of the soldiers was rotten. By some quirk of fate, the loose organization of Rebellion leaders melted away without confronting the militia. It was something the unusually fortunate President Washington could count among his long list of lucky breaks.

To the extent that President Washington excoriated the democratic societies that he felt generated feelings such as led to the Whiskey Rebellion, it is safe to say that Thomas Jefferson, in retirement at Monticello, had a slightly different view. In a letter to James Madison on December 28, 1794, Jefferson wrote:

> The denunciation of the democratic societies is one of the extraordinary acts of boldness of which we have seen so many from the faction of monocrats [Federalists]. It is wonderful indeed, that the President should have permitted himself to be the organ of such an attack on the freedom of discussion, the freedom of writing, printing and publishing.[146]

From the very beginning, Jefferson saw this rebellion in terms of personal freedom, not as a threat to orderly government. While Jefferson acknowledged some imprudent behavior, he felt this more the actions of ruffians who took advantage of the situation to cover their digressions. He continued: "The excise law is an infernal one. The first error was to admit it by the Constitution; the 2nd, to act on that admission; the 3rd and last will be, to make it the instrument of dismembering the union, and setting us all afloat to choose which part of it we will adhere to."[147] Jefferson also belittled the sorry state of the militia the president sent to western Pennsylvania. He correctly pointed out that many of the militia felt the same way about the tax as the rebels they were sent to confront.

Much like President Washington, Secretary of the Treasury Alexander Hamilton saw the Whiskey Rebellion as an affront to the Constitution. Unlike the president, Hamilton wanted stronger action against the rebels from the start. In a response to President Washington on August 2, 1794, Hamilton began his overview by pointing out that the western counties of Pennsylvania, since the inception of the law, "have been in steady and violent opposition to them."[148]

Hamilton's letter to Washington occurred right as events were coming to a point of no return. The peace commission was working to defuse the standoff, with little success, and the president was being advised to take stronger measures, as any continued opposition was weakening the image of the United States in the world of nations. Hamilton observed this in his letter: "Neither the legislative nor the executive accommodations have had any effect in producing compliance with the laws. The opposition has continued and matured, till it has at length broke out in acts which are presumed to amount to treason."[149] Hamilton, ever the military prognosticator, advised the president "to be prepared for the worst ... twelve thousand militia ought to be ordered to assemble."[150]

President Washington wound up taking much of Hamilton's advice as to militia size. In his proclamation calling forth the militia, dated September 25, 1794, the president stated he took the action only after exhausting other options: "I thought it sufficient, in the first instance, rather to take measures for calling forth the militia than immediately to embody them, but the moment is now come, when the overtures of forgiveness, with no other condition than a submission to law, have been only partially accepted."[151] In fact, Washington did go to great lengths, for the time, to accommodate the protesters' grievances. Most world leaders in the late 1790s would not have thought twice about sending the army to subdue any sign of dissent or disobedience to a government. Washington wrote that he deplored "that the American name should be sullied by the outrages of citizens on their own government."[152] The President left no question as to the authority of the federal government and ultimately the Constitution in these matters. The Whiskey Rebellion, along with the Citizen Genêt affair, represented the first two trials the young government had to face between 1793 and 1795. The final test involved the Supreme Court directly—the Jay Treaty with Britain.

The Jay Treaty was not only a low point for the Federalist party and their approach to foreign policy, but it marked a low point in the career of Chief Justice John Jay. For a sitting Chief Justice to undertake such a mission was fraught with problems from multiple perspectives, not the least of which was Jay's impartiality as a judge. It was just as well that he resigned to be the governor of New York after his mission to Britain ended as he would have no doubt faced stiff scrutiny had he returned to the Court. Indicative of the opposition feeling about Jay was a letter Madison wrote to Robert Livingston on August 10, 1795. Madison charged that Jay was the head of an American British party (Federalists) that was "systematically aiming at an exclusive connection with the British government and ready to sacrifice to that object as well the dearest interests of our commerce as the most sacred dictates of national honor."[153] It was clear, if more evidence was needed, that the political party system was well underway in the United States. Madison did, however, offer some words of sympathy for President Washington: "With respect to the President, his situation must be a most delicate one for himself as well as for his country; and there never was, as you observe, a crisis where the friends of both ought to feel more solicitude, or less reserve."[154] Jefferson himself was positively apoplectic over the Jay Treaty, further pushing him into the political party frame of mind. We have seen too that the Jay Treaty, along with manifested mental illness, ended the judicial career of Chief Justice John Rutledge in December 1795. The Treaty took its toll on all three branches of government, the country at large, and the American political party process.

Perhaps the most unusual development in the events surrounding Washington's Neutrality Proclamation, was the reemergence of *The Federalist* papers authors, Hamilton and Madison. Unlike their collaboration during *The Federalist* papers project, the two men found themselves, anonymously, attacking each other and the ideas they were promoting relative to the English and French war. This was a topic which would dominate American foreign and domestic policy well into the first decade of the nineteenth century. In their new essays, Hamilton (writing as "Pacificus") and Madison (writing as "Helvidius") struck out against the tendency to support the British or French cause to the detriment of the United States' interest. Madison attacked those who supported the British (and by extension President Washington) while Hamilton attacked those who supported the French. The essays did little except to highlight further the growing factions which would soon blossom into political parties.

Betsey

Returning to the Supreme Court, the cases in the lower courts centered around whether the *Betsey* and her cargo were a legal (from a law of nations perspective) prize taken by the French. The French consul in the United States, Citizen Moissonnier, unilaterally declared it a legal prize in July 1793. His proclamation essentially ensured a legal approach to end the stalemate rather than a diplomatic one. The Swedish consul had sought a quick diplomatic solution through Secretary of State Jefferson, but the action of the French ensured this would not occur. The first case was filed by the owners of the *Betsey* for her return with the United States district court in Maryland, where the *Betsey* had been taken after her capture. In Baltimore, District Judge William Paca, who ordered the *Betsey* impounded, faced a skeptical attorney in James Winchester, representing the captain of the *Citizen Genêt*, which took the *Betsey* off the coast of Charleston. At the trial, the French captain argued that the *Betsey* was British, not Swedish, that it was taken fifteen miles off the American coast (outside of territorial waters), and that treaties bound the United States to assist the French when at war. Naturally, the team fighting for the return of the *Betsey* challenged every point made by the French. The issue which really rankled Judge Paca, and other American officials, was the claim that the French could set up courts (even on foreign soil) to adjudicate prize trials during times of war under the laws of nations. Paca ruled that given the evidence, the United States, as a neutral party, could not rule on the legality of the seizure of the *Betsey*. Paca's ruling essentially allowed the French to sell the *Betsey* and her cargo as a war prize. The owners immediately filed an appeal with the circuit court. The owners continued to take every conceivable action, including petitioning the Washington administration under the terms of the Neutrality Act.

With little help coming from the administration, the owners waited for the circuit court session on November 7 in Easton, Maryland. Justice William Paterson was sitting at the time and ruled in concurrence with District Judge William Paca. Essentially, the circuit court upheld the decision of the district court. The owners of the *Betsey* immediately moved to appeal to the Supreme Court. Again, this in itself was indicative of the new America—being able to appeal to a Supreme Court. An America with a national judiciary capable of hearing cases with national, and in fact international, implications was a far cry from what existed before the Constitution.

On February 8, 1794, the case was first heard by the Court. It was clear from the beginning that this was an important case which would have far-reaching consequences. In a decision that would help to firmly establish the sovereignty of the United States, the Supreme Court by-passed many of the arguments presented. Both sides brought cases which were carried over from the district and circuit courts. The Supreme Court however saw another more critical issue: American sovereignty.

One of the reasons behind the Constitutional Convention of 1787 was to create a more stable, defined country that could function on the world stage with the appropriate respect due to a nation acknowledged and respected by other established powers. One element of a nation's integrity involved the inviolability of its territory. The right of every nation to be secure in its own boundaries. As a new nation, the United States had more than enough to prove on the world stage. Maintaining the sanctity of its borders was high on the list.

The Supreme Court found, absent any treaty, that foreign governments could not establish prize courts, or any courts, on American soil. This rendered the French court, which ruled the taking of the *Betsey* legal, irrelevant. Therefore, the case hinged on what it did from the beginning, whether or not France had in fact stolen the *Betsey* from its owners. And this question the Supreme Court sent back to the district court in Maryland. The significance of the case, aside from the injustice suffered by the owners of the *Betsey*, was the decision by the Supreme Court to approach the case as they did. In reality, the Court made two momentous decisions. The first one was the decision to look at the issues involved from a new perspective; the second was to decide the case in a way that would empower the new American system. The Court established itself as a significant force in American government, and it established America as a country with all the rights and prerogatives as any other country. It was a brilliant solution to a thorny diplomatic problem, and the Court and the country were made stronger by the decision.

Penhallow v. Doane's Administrators
(February 24, 1795)

As commented on already, nearly every case (whether a "case" was what we recognize today is not relevant here) that came before the Court was precedent setting. That was truly the issue at hand in *Penhallow v. Doane's Administrators*. This was a sweeping case which lingered through war, peace, political turmoil, political stability, and finally disappearing without a trace nearly thirty-five years after it began. The topic at stake was state versus federal rights, a topic of constant interest and debate. *Penhallow* also involved a review of the status of the Continental Congress by the Court as the case originated in pre–Constitution days. The Court was often called upon during the early years to adjudicate cases which had their beginnings in the pre–Constitution period of American history. In that sense, the justices were being asked to be historians as well as jurists; in effect, they were writing an official or sanctioned version of events conformable with American law during the 1790s. As with *Glass v. Sloop Betsey*, *Penhallow* originated in 1777 as a case involving ships and the taking of ships as a prize. The case sprang from a dispute between John Penhallow of New Hampshire and Elisha Doane of Massachusetts. The case was prominent enough in 1777 to attract the services of one of the country's most capable, and famous, lawyers: John Adams.

JOHN ADAMS FOR THE PLAINTIFFS

During the second year of the American Revolution, and a year after the signing of the Declaration of Independence, a private ship fitted out for military service in aid to the American cause, the *McClary* owned by John Penhallow of New Hampshire, captured the vessel *Lusanna*, owned by Elisha Doane of Massachusetts. The case was actually quite complicated due to the escalating war between America and Britain.

The *Lusanna* left Cape Cod bound for London in September 1775 just as the American War had ignited beyond the point of no return and before an export ban went into effect. Elisha Doane's son-in-law Shearjashub Bourne was in overall command of the trip. Bourne was forced to stop in Halifax, Nova Scotia, for repairs after the ship was damaged in a storm; in Halifax, Bourne was detained for several months by the British while they tried to determine if the ship was American contraband. Released, Bourne and the *Lusanna* proceeded to London to carry out its business of trade. Fearing more problems if he returned immediately to America, Bourne registered the *Lusanna* with the British authorities (to prevent any possible problems over perceived loyalties) and completed a trip to Gibraltar. In the summer of 1777, Bourne sailed for America with a scheduled stop in Halifax to conduct more trade. After leaving Halifax, the *Lusanna* was intercepted by the *McClary* and taken as a war prize due to her involvement with British trade, regardless of whether the owners were American. But the owners, Elisha Doane and his son-in-law, were not just any Americans; Elisha Doane was one of the wealthiest men in New England and a major figure in trans–Atlantic trade. He was also a long-term client of John Adams. Adams had recently retired (November 1777) from active work in the Continental Congress and had resumed his private practice when the case of his friend came before him. This case would mark the last recorded time that Adams appeared as a private attorney (he would soon be posted to Europe to represent the American cause).[155]

The *Penhallow* case was indicative of the fluid nature of the escalating crisis between America and Britain. As much was at stake beyond the justice or legality (not always the same) of what occurred off of the coast of New Hampshire, it was imperative for Doane to proceed cautiously so as not to inflame passions unduly. Beyond the financial stake were questions of identity and loyalty. Commerce and fidelity were twisted and morphed by Doane to appeal to the sentiments most favorable depending on which tribunal he was addressing. That was why, even in the political powder keg that was Massachusetts in late 1777, Doane sought out his good friend John Adams. It was symptomatic of the American conflict that the dispute was far beyond what we like to recall today. Concepts of liberty, or freedom, fuel our minds with patriotic nostalgia for the American founding. Yet, for those who lived it and had to navigate the intricate competing demands the period was far from simply heroic.

Many American leaders were engaged in organized trade before and during the American War, thus straining allegiances. Trade as a policy may even be older than war as a policy. Nevertheless, trade in ideas, commerce, and people through immigration brought the world together. The same was true for our immediate ancestors during the Founding Era. Elisha Doane, and hundreds, perhaps thousands, of his fellow Americans had interest in trans–Atlantic trade. It fell to John Adams to straddle the interests of an America which by late 1777 had declared itself independent and with the mercantile concerns (which had made the colonies rich) of hundreds of interested parties whose livelihood was impacted by that trade. Furthermore, Adams had to think about the future, to a point when the conflict would be over and the economy of the new nation would be in shambles, presuming independence was achieved. The trade routes had to be maintained as viable, regardless of personal feelings.

On December 15, 1777, the night before the trial, John Adams wrote to his wife Abigail:

> The cause comes on tomorrow, before my old friend Dr. Joshua Brackett, as judge of admiralty. How it will go I know not. The captors are a numerous company, and are said to be very tenacious, and have many connections; so, that we have prejudice, and influence to fear: justice, policy, and law, I am very sure, are on our side.[156]

John Penhallow, represented by Oliver Whipple, attempted to base his case on three facts:

> 1st. That the property of [the ship] and cargo belonged to some inhabitant or inhabitants of Great Britain.
> 2nd. That at the time of capture she was carrying supplies to the enemy.
> 3rd. That the property on board was British manufacture.[157]

Whipple was clearly attempting to establish that rules of war were in effect in this case which would mean an easier burden of proof for him to establish. Rules of war are much more lenient to cases of piracy, or privateering, as it was called during war.

John Adams essentially argued that Elisha Doane was a victim or casualty of war. Adams acknowledged the war, and agreed it played a major role in the case. Adams noted that Doane had transferred control on paper to his son-in-law Bourne to protect his investment from British naval ships; Doane never imagined he would have to protect himself from his fellow Americans. Penhallow and his private American naval ship, with their attorney Whipple, argued it was simply too bad that this occurred, but it was simply the vagaries of war. Doane's actions of putting in place a cover story via paperwork showed that his actions were those of a Loyalist from Whipple's perspective. Doane was caught in the middle with no easy way out, especially in late 1777 when the case was first tried, and John Adams knew this. Adams's best argument was the time the *Lusanna* and its crew were detained in Halifax by the British on fears that the cargo would be used to fund the American rebellion. In fact, Adams even tried to argue a technical point that Britain was not an enemy in the sense of existing statutes that Whipple and Penhallow were relying on to press their cause. Adams would argue throughout that any perceived links between Britain and Doane were all part of Whipple's subterfuge.[158]

The case in New Hampshire relied on New Hampshire law. And the jury found for Penhallow, thus condemning the *Lusanna* to be sold as a war prize.

Naturally, Doane appealed the case, but to the Continental Congress, as they ostensibly sanctioned privateering and were the ersatz highest appeal court in the country. New Hampshire law recognized an appeal only to the New Hampshire Superior Court. For our purposes, this is where the pre–Supreme Court activity will cease. As the editors of the *Legal Papers of John Adams* state: after the case was decided in the New Hampshire court, "the subsequent history of the *Lusanna* is of great complexity."[159]

The case dragged on for nearly twenty more years before arriving at the United States Supreme Court on February 6, 1795. By this time, Doane's original attorney, John Adams, had left the case before it was decided in December 1777 and was Vice President of the United States; although Adams would have no role in the case when it came before the Supreme Court.

Losing on appeal in New Hampshire, the cargo of the *Lusanna* was sold in September 1778 for nearly £34,000, an immense sum. It was a case of lawful piracy to enrich Penhallow, his colleagues, attorney, and the state of New Hampshire. As the case permutated throughout the 1780s, the country did as well. Within those changes were new courts of law and new systems of law. This was especially true concerning the national law as the country moved to a more responsible government capable of maintaining a new country at peace. By the time the case reached the Supreme Court in 1795, it looked at the question of federal power versus state power, which entity controlled profiteering during wartime?

Doane's administrators (Elisha Doane died in 1783) won their first victory with the new federal system (having already proved victorious in Articles of Confederation–era courts) in the circuit court in October 1793, when Justice Blair ruled in favor of the Administrators. In reporting the first circuit court case in Exeter with Justice John Blair, the *Columbian Centinel* reported: "At the circuit court, held at Exeter for the district of New Hampshire, in October last, in which the Hon. Judge Blair, sat, *solely*—a question of great importance, not only to those immediately concerned, but probably to the United States in general, was decided [emphasis in original]."[160] The newspaper clearly saw the significance of this case to the nation at large. They were somewhat dismayed however that only one judge was sitting.

A year later, on October 24, 1794, Justice Cushing sitting as a circuit court judge ruled that Penhallow and his colleagues owed Doane's descendants £38,500, which included interest. On appeal, the full Supreme Court considered the following points, among others:

1st. That the decree was void because the court of appeals lacked jurisdiction (which overturned the New Hampshire verdict).

2nd. That it was a matter of record that Elisha Doane was dead when the decree was issued in his name.

3rd. The libel sought performance of the court of appeals' decree of restitution, rather than damages for nonperformance.

4th. That the decree of the circuit court held the owners' agents and the captors' agents each in full damage, although the proceeds had originally been divided equally between them.

5th. That there was no jurisdiction in Admiralty of the libel filed in the district court.[161]

This was a knot of issues the justices distilled to one: the power of the federal government over wartime activities. Justices Cushing, Iredell, Blair, and Paterson all found for the right of the national (Articles of Confederation) and federal (Constitution) government. It was a muscular defense of American power and a defining moment in Supreme Court history. Indeed, it was a muscular defense of the Continental Congress under the Articles of Confederation. It was one of the few times the pre–Constitution Congress was seen in such a positive light. As to be expected, "the decision brought a flurry of newspaper and pamphlet criticism of the court for this blow to the sovereignty of the states...."[162] In fact, the state of New Hampshire sent a remonstrance to the Congress on January 16, 1795. The state leaders, not amused that the Supreme Court overturned the initial ruling of 1777, felt the decision had in their view, diminished state sovereignty. They wrote to the Congress: "That impelled by a firm attachment to the first principles of a free government, and the accumulated distresses of a number of their citizens; they again remonstrate to Congress against a violation of state independence, and an unwarrantable encroachment in the courts of the United States."[163] The state of New Hampshire was upset. After nearly twenty years the struggle between state and federal power was still being played out. New Hampshire was allowed to grouse; both the Senate and House of Representatives tabled the remonstrance.

Personnel Changes

After the August 1791 term Justice John Rutledge, who never sat with his colleagues as a justice, resigned. In his place, President Washington appointed Thomas Johnson of Maryland. Johnson was lured to the Court with the expectation that Congress would lessen the burden of circuit riding required of the justices during the next session of Congress.

Throughout the first few years of the Court's existence they kept busy with administrative matters as we have seen; the Justices also were occupied with other aspects of the Judiciary Act than sitting as the Supreme Court. Their duties under the act included sitting as judges on circuit court—a detested task due to the travel involved. Charles Warren has written: "By the provisions of the statute [Judiciary Act], the country had been divided into three circuits (the Eastern, Middle, and Southern), to each of which two Supreme Court Justices were permanently assigned and directed to hold Court twice a year in each district, in company with the District Judges."[164] It seems a simple enough duty, and in some measure it was. What made circuit-duty so onerous was travel. It goes without saying that travel today is much easier and a non-issue when compared with eighteenth-century travel. There was no first class—everyone, high or low, had to travel the same roads, stay in the same taverns, and eat the same food. Travel was a democratic (with a lowercase "d") undertaking during the 1790s. For some, it was a grim prospect from a personal perspective.

From a national perspective, however, the circuit courts allowed for two important aspects to occur. First, it brought the new, still somewhat controversial, federal judiciary to the "average" American. Second, it allowed for the justices to deliver jury instructions which contained their early views and understandings of the Supreme Court and federal judiciary.

Few Americans had an opportunity to travel to the nation's capital—whether in New York, Philadelphia, or later, Washington, D.C. Circuit travel, regardless of how odious, brought the capital to Americans in the physical presence of the justices. The justices also brought the most current thinking and understanding of the role of the Supreme Court to Americans through jury instructions. These two developments proved to humanize the federal government in the days before instant travel and communication. It also made the Supreme Court justices into something of celebrities. Attending sessions of the court quickly became an event on the social calendar. The activities of the Supreme Court and circuit courts were also closely followed by the newspapers of the period.

Observations During the Jay Court on the Federal Judiciary

During the Jay Court (September 26, 1789, to June 29, 1795), topics included observations on how the Court adapted to uncharted areas which were left undefined by the Judiciary Act. This made the Jay Court the precedent-setting Court, much like the first Congress and President Washington, each in their own branch and by default of being the first, were setting a course that others would follow. It is therefore useful to review how those observing this Supreme Court saw events unfolding as they occurred in "real time."

John Lowell, in a January 10, 1791, letter to Fisher Ames, concluded that the time to move forward with the judiciary was at hand. "Everything that relates to the judicial system appears to me to be extremely important and that the present crisis is such respecting it that if it is altered at all it may be essentially mended or fatally injured."[165] Lowell was not naïve enough to think that nothing would be challenged in the Judiciary Act. What was more important however was that the federal court system be up and operating. The Congress and the president did not need an act as such to get them started and going as the judiciary did. Lowell acknowledged that the time for the judiciary to work out its own problems had arrived. The legislative process can only do so much, solutions would have to be primarily found organically.

Once the Supreme Court began to actually adjudicate cases, some of the concerns about the Judiciary Act became less of an issue as the Court, and the legal system in general, began to function. While problems manifested themselves, solutions were found within the system as it too expanded and developed. Some of the issues that never seemed to find resolution were circuit riding and the proper balance of state versus federal court power. These issues would linger for decades, even a century, before modern transportation and modifications made the circuit less arduous. Federal and state power has never truly been settled. The new issues which occupied the minds of Court watchers began to settle upon the topics and decisions the Court would face during the 1790s.

The Court endured the first bumpy months without any cases, which meant that some of the concerns raised during the debates over the Judiciary Act would have to wait to see how certain topics progressed. Writing on February 23, 1791, future Supreme Court justice Alfred Moore, in a letter to Samuel Johnston, expressed, with some doubts, his faith in the Judiciary Act and the need for it to move into operation. He wrote, "[I] am not yet able to approve or to offer satisfactory reasons against the most important parts of it, I am as yet checked by the great character of its author [Senator Oliver Ellsworth]...."[166]

On March 2, 1791, an editorial appeared in the *Gazette of the United States* which reviewed the work of the first federal Congress. The anonymous writer captured the essence of the Judiciary Act: "In the judicial department, as much has been done, as circumstances would admit. Judges of eminent virtue and learning preside in the federal courts."[167] The editorial summarized that the Act was the best that could be had. Legislation is (usually) an act of compromise. It is seldom perfect. However, at some point the legislation has to go into effect and those who implement it have to do their best to work within the proscribed boundaries. It cannot be overstated that within the new Constitution, only the Supreme Court had to be created from nothingness. The Congress and president existed in a sense the Supreme Court, and federal judiciary, did not.

Nearly two years after the president signed the Judiciary Act into law, some were still complaining as though they had read it for the first time. William Richardson, writing to Supreme Court Associate Justice James Iredell, expressed, "I sincerely hope something will be done at the next session of Congress with the judicial law, it is so defective in point of arrangement and so obscurely drawn or expressed, that in my opinion it would disgrace the composition of the meanest legislature of the states."[168] Richardson, clearly no fan of the Judiciary Act, also overstated his opposition. His over-critical language was not accurate in the sense that he compared the act, drawn by the Senate, to some small-state legislature without meaning. Yet, criticism existed. Even Chief Justice John Jay, responding to President Washington's request for legislative suggestions, wrote: "The judicial system undoubtedly calls for revision...," without offering specifics and without resorting to the somewhat childish language other writers chose.[169] Jay continued, "all things have their order. All that ought to be done cannot be done at once."[170]

An entertaining, if spirited, response to the failure to make changes to the Judiciary Act is found in a letter of Henry Van Schaak to Theodore Sedgwick. Writing on December 18, 1791, Van Schaak vented:

> What in the name of common sense is the reason that the judiciary business has been dismissed so abruptly? Is a certain attorney inadequate to the task or is Congress incompetent to the business? As the matter now stands it is wholly mysterious to me. Without a good system of judicial proceedings it would seem to me that the fabric will be incomplete.[171]

This rather un-varnished assessment may have represented a moment of frustration, but by this date there had already been two cases before the Supreme Court with more to arrive in 1792.

Henry Marchant, writing three days later in Rhode Island, expressed similar frustration in a letter to Benjamin Bourne. Marchant wrote, "I mention the judicial system. It has been hinted that no great alteration is like to take place. But a continuance of the present system with addition, and amendments. And it may be most wise to try thoroughly one first."[172] Marchant, while expressing dismay with the process, although not as expressively as Van Schaak in neighboring Massachusetts, also felt it best to let the act work (which it was already for over two years) and make adjustments as necessary.

Attorney General Edmund Randolph wrote to President Washington on December 26, 1791. He too expressed some pointed issues with the operation of the now two-year-old Judiciary Act. Randolph assured the president that he would not bother him personally if the operational issues "were only personally inconvenient...," however, "while I consider them as injurious to the public service, I cannot satisfy myself of the propriety of withholding them from you."[173] Randolph was chiefly concerned with the relationship between the attorney general and the district attorneys.

As 1792 began it was clear that only minor adjustments were in the offing for the Judiciary Act. The large-scale changes, or even full-scale replacement, some envisioned were not going to occur. Roger Sherman wrote that "I believe that no radical reform of the judiciary law will be made."[174] The year 1792 saw the Supreme Court take its first significant case which would have lasting influence and generate intense controversy at the time. *Hayburn's* Case, as previously discussed, involved the Court in unanimously asserting its prerogative as the nation's legal arbiter. Attorney General Randolph, writing to the president, voiced this role the Court assumed and drifted into further observations on the American legal system:

> It is much to be regretted, that the judiciary, in spite of their apparent firmness in annulling the pension law, are not, what sometime hence they will be, a recourse against the infractions of the constitution, on the one hand, and a steady asserter of the federal rights, on the other. So crude is our judiciary system, so jealous are state judges of their authority, so ambiguous is the language of the constitution....[175]

The *National Gazette* criticized Congress, "notwithstanding the number of professional gentlemen in both houses...," for leaving the alterations to be undertaken by Attorney General Randolph.[176] Even with plenty of legal-minded members, Congress decided to let the attorney general, through the president, determine which aspects of the act would be adjusted. The *Gazette* could only speculate that Congress saw the revisions as "a task beyond their strength."[177]

"Timolean," writing in the *Independent Chronicle* on June 5, 1794, noted, "The court of the United States of America, is founded in the humble imitation of the English judiciary."[178] Timolean went so far as to suggest that it was understood among the Justices *"that in all cases where statutes did not make other provisions, their procedures should be according to the rules established in Westminster Hall, England* [emphasis in original]."[179] Timolean was clearly an acute observer and commented further: "The judiciary system of the United States has already become irksome and unwieldly to the officers who are appointed to execute it; and no body appears to be satisfied with it."[180] This was certainly not the situation, as the system was working and, as with anything, there was a learning period which had to be accommodated. Especially when considering the judiciary, allowances had to be made. No such entity had existed in America—ever. A national system of law and courts was not going to satisfy everyone from the start. Most knew that and resorted to letters and articles to express frustration. The gears of justice may move slowly, but legislation is not much faster.

"A Citizen," writing in *Claypoole's American Daily Advertiser* on November 1, 1795, asked readers to go back to the period when no national judiciary existed. It was a time of bleak prospects for uniting the nation, and now, in

1795, that it has been united with a national law complaints seem more numerous than supports of the system. A Citizen wrote:

> Look back to the period preceding the formation of the constitution of the United States, when the inconveniences of the former system were felt and exposed, and say, was a judiciary to such extent then supposed necessary? Look back to the period when the constitution was under discussion, when all its virtues and faults were examined and displayed; and say, was a practical judiciary to such extent either feared by its enemies, or justified by its friends?[181]

During the 1790s, salaries were a constant item of debate for justices and other officers of the federal judiciary. Then, as now, talented attorneys could earn much more in private practice as opposed to working as a judge or justice, or other official, in the federal judicial establishment.

Justice James Iredell was acutely aware of this and wrote to his wife Hannah on February 9, 1797: "We shall get no addition to our salary. It has not even been proposed that I have heard. The Senate, I believe, were well inclined, but feared the proposition might defeat a measure of great moment to take place immediately—raising the salaries of the President and Vice-President."[182] Chief Justice Oliver Ellsworth wrote to fellow Justice William Cushing on April 15, 1798, that: "I left [the capital] pending before the senate, on the 23rd of March, a judiciary bill with a prospect of its making some progress this session and being an early subject for the next. It goes to relieve us from circuit riding, to form five new districts and two associate district judges for the circuit courts."[183] Ellsworth alluded to proposals that eventually became the Judiciary Act of 1801. The addition of new states to the union required new districts to be created and states to be added to an already busy circuit court schedule. Ellsworth and Cushing, like the other justices, were never satisfied with the rigors of circuit riding.

Not everyone was pleased with President Washington or the Supreme Court. At times, the president and the Court would come in for criticism. As an example, writing to his mother Abigail, Thomas Boylston Adams, on August 10, 1793, reported that both President Washington and Justice James Wilson had been attacked by anonymous hacks in the press who sought to ridicule the men for their handling of an international incident related to France. Thomas Adams wrote that "handbills have been distributed representing the President and Judge Wilson with their heads under the guillotine, and proclaiming their death to the citizens of Philadelphia on account of the acquittal of Henfield lately tried for entering into the service of France."[184] While the Adamses were aware of events and followed developments more than most, the episode clearly signifies how much of an impact the Supreme Court had on American life in the 1790s.

Based on all available evidence, the justices and circuit judges acted in what they considered an appropriate manner. Appropriate from the standpoint of the Constitution, jurisprudence, politics, and the sphere of judicial integrity. In a generous approach to their actions, they spared Congress the embarrassment (in their eyes) of formally finding one of their legislative actions unconstitutional.[185] The justices genuinely wanted to avoid what they saw as a potentially embarrassing situation for the Congress. While acknowledging their turmoil over how Congress would be perceived, it is not lost in the analysis that the Court had the upper hand. The power to pass judgment is the most powerful element of a Constitutional system. On balance, even though they challenged the constitutionality of advising Congress by advising Congress, their action would seem in accordance with an as yet untried system. Within that system, they had established a precedent and further defined that system.

The establishment of the most critical element of Constitutional jurisprudence, judicial review, was accomplished through *Hayburn*. The Supreme Court of the 1790s however decided multiple cases which determined aspects of Constitutional supremacy. While promoting the supremacy of Constitutional law, the Court's actions also served to create the international recognition so vital to the expanding Republic created through the Constitution.[186]

To a certain extent, the arguments over the development of Constitutional concepts in an ancient court over two hundred years ago are a moot point. It is just as easy to prove that they were not visionary as it is to prove that they were, thereby rendering the argument a draw and not worthy of analysis. This would seem though a too easy explanation for why the Court of the 1790s is overlooked.

6

The John Rutledge Court: June 30, 1795– December 28, 1795

The Rutledge Court was a bit of an anomaly. As we have seen, Rutledge had a long history of suspected mental illness by the time he was appointed by President Washington to be chief justice. Rutledge had already served as an associate justice but had resigned to serve in the judiciary of his home state of South Carolina. President Washington, as previously mentioned, was somewhat humiliated at the rising numbers of justices leaving their posts and the difficulty he was having of finding replacements. This all occurred against the backdrop of foreign and domestic intrigues including the Citizen Genêt affair, the Whiskey Rebellion, and the Jay Treaty. John Rutledge's recess appointment was completed against this backdrop of uncertainty in staffing the Court and the multiple foreign and domestic crises.

Given that the Court met just a few months during Rutledge's time as chief, the number of cases heard or decided were small. There was one however which fell within the period covered by the Rutledge tenure which had significant ramifications that reach into our current world.

Talbot v. Jansen *(August 22, 1795)*

Many of the cases heard by the Supreme Court during the 1790s had originated as admiralty cases involving privateering. Among these many cases most dealt with French privateers operating out of American ports. After the establishment of the new American government under the Constitution in 1789, the French had their own encounter with a new government, one that was decidedly less organized than the new American version. The outright terror and anarchy of the early years of the French Revolution shocked even committed Francophiles like Thomas Jefferson. The renegade spirit unleashed by the Revolution manifested itself in multiple ways. One of the most egregious for the United States was the effort by France to outfit and deploy privateers (private vessels outfitted with weapons and given a warrant from the government to be a military vessel) from American ports to prey on shipping. As we saw in *Glass v. Sloop Betsey*, this issue had already come before the Court (and would many more times), just in a slightly different guise and seeking a different result from *Talbot*. With *Talbot v. Jansen* the Court once again made a forceful declaration of American sovereignty and set a precedent that has endured to our day. *Talbot* was clearly important. As Justice Iredell wrote in the opening to his opinion:

> The present case is undoubtedly of the highest importance, and has been argued with extraordinary ability on both sides. It involves some points new, as well as interesting, and upon which therefore reason, unaided by authority, must necessarily be exercised. It contains a greater variety of questions than often arise in the course of any cause, to all of which, so far as they concern the principles of our decision, a careful and strict attention is due.[1]

Once again, as with *Glass,* the action in *Talbot v. Jansen* occurred in Charleston, South Carolina, or the end of the action played out in Charleston. On May 16, 1794, the Dutch ship *De Vrouw Christina Magdalena*, northwest of Cuba, was taken by the French privateer *L'Ami de la Liberti*. It was escorted as a prize to the port of Charleston as per the 1778 Treaty of Amity and Commerce between France and America.[2] The difference from 1778 was that the French were trying to conduct their own courts on American soil to sanction the privateering. With the outlawing of such courts, the French would often simply sell their capture without a formal inquest and be done with it. This time, the captain of the *Magdalena*, Joost Jansen, filed suit against the privateers. In the United States district court for South Carolina, Jacob Read, attorney for the *Magdalena*, presented his case. Read pointed out that Edward Ballard, captain of the *Liberti*, and William Talbot, captain of the accomplice vessel the *Point-a-Petre*, were both American, and:

> Therefore, even if Ballard could lay before the court the French commission he allegedly possessed, that commission would be invalid. As an American commanding an American ship, Ballard had illegally seized a Dutch vessel in violation not only of the administrations neutrality policy but of the Treaty of Amity and Commerce signed by the United States and the Netherlands in 1782.[3]

Edward Ballard, captain of the *Liberti* receded from his claims when the district court requested claimants on the *Magdalena* to come forth. Captain Talbot of the *Point-a-Petre* however did come forward with a compelling argument. Talbot was able to show that he was a naturalized French citizen and that his vessel had a French commission as a privateer. Attorney Read showed that Talbot and Ballard were both Virginians, that their vessels were fitted out only recently as privateers and that in fact Talbot and Ballard were only recently made French citizens for the express purpose of trying to profit off the European war.

District Court Judge Thomas Bee delivered his opinion on August 6, 1794. Bee immediately dismissed concerns over jurisdiction by in part pointing to the recent *Glass v. Sloop Betsey* case. Bee also made clear that while becoming a naturalized citizen of France was legal, the manner and timing of his action marked him as nothing more than a base opportunist.[4] Judge Bee quickly concluded the case and ruled for Jansen and the *Magdalena*. Talbot and Ballard were little better than pirates. (In fact, both Talbot and Ballard were charged by the federal government as pirates but were acquitted.) Talbot appealed to the United States circuit court where Judge Bee and Justice Wilson sat. On November 5, 1794, the circuit court ruled in favor of Jansen and the *Magdalena*. Talbot and Ballard lost again. Talbot, rather foolishly, appealed to the Supreme Court which did not hear the case until August 1795, a year after it was first decided in the district court. At the Supreme Court, Talbot's team again raised the issue of jurisdiction and, cleared of piracy charges, admitted that they were out to make a quick return on the European war.[5]

Jansen and his legal team argued that Talbot, far from being French, was simply pretending to profit off of the worse kind of commerce and human misery. The full Court, including Chief Justice John Rutledge (in the only case he would oversee as chief during his tenure) ruled in favor of Jansen, the *Magdalena*, and the original decision of the South Carolina district court. Justices Cushing, Paterson, and Rutledge all saw the case as one of fraud on the part of Talbot and to an extent Ballard. None of the justices saw the naturalized French citizenship as an issue. Justice Iredell, while acknowledging the fraud of Talbot, delved more closely into the citizenship issue. Citizenship was not intended as a way to earn a quick profit. If that were the case, a person could flip on or off citizenship as the money dictated. Justice Iredell found accepting citizenship under such pretenses as "an act of expatriation was only partial if a person was admitted to citizenship in another but then did not emigrate to and reside in that country."[6] The final decision was delivered on August 22, 1795.

Ware v. Hylton

The Supreme Court Establishes a Treaty as Law
(Ware *actually occurred during a period between
the Rutledge and Ellsworth Courts*)
March 7, 1796

In the preceding cases presented, the developing awareness of constitutional jurisprudence became more defined through the coalescing efforts of the Supreme Court. While many of the cases analyzed often were running contemporaneously, a single effort on the part of the justices is discernable. This effort involved the Court in ensuring the constitutional mandates of Article III were fulfilled. It has been discussed that this mandate established by a Constitution represented a new approach to governing and more importantly an untried approach to jurisprudence.

By the mid–1790s, the justices had successfully handled a host of cases, all of which through their opinions firmly established the Court as the interpreter of the Constitution and the expositor of constitutional jurisprudence. While this occurred in a demonstrable way, it is also clear that the Court suffered from personnel changes (on an almost annual basis), lack of respect from the legislature and executive, and the onerous duties of circuit riding.

Perhaps the most significant personnel change occurred when Chief Justice Jay left the Court to resume his diplomatic career. In 1794, Chief Justice Jay accepted a diplomatic assignment which ultimately led to what became known as Jay's Treaty. Jay was still formally chief justice when he accepted the post and seems to have overcome some of his earlier doubts of engaging in non-judicial activities which he exhibited in the *Hayburn* case. Without going into the details of the Jay Treaty, it will only need to be said that upon his return from Great Britain in late 1794, Jay resigned as chief justice to accept the governorship of New York. With Jay's resignation, the first transfer of power concerning the head of one of the branches of government occurred.

One of the reasons Jay had accepted the diplomatic mission to Great Britain was his concern over the disregard of key provisions of the 1783 Peace Treaty which he helped to negotiate. Specifically, Jay was concerned about repayment of British debt contracted before the Revolution and the ways states were ignoring the provisions of the Treaty calling for repayment of contracted debt. Jay was intimately aware of the issue not just from the standpoint of his work on the Treaty as a negotiator but also through Supreme Court cases such as *Georgia v. Brailsford*. Not only did these cases highlight the extent to which states were going to ignore the Treaty, it also illustrated the level of animosity which some states displayed concerning the supremacy of federal law as established through the Constitution.[7] The international implications were obvious and Jay felt compelled to go over the discussions with grand juries.[8]

As Jay was on his diplomatic mission, a case first came before the Court (without a chief) which once again tested the boundaries of federal authority. *Ware v. Hylton* dealt like *Brailsford* and *Chisholm* before it with the issue of British debt.[9] Indeed, *Ware* was seen as a case which would decide unequivocally the issue of British debt.

John Ware was administrator of the estate of William Jones, under whose name the case originally began in the circuit court in Virginia. The debtor, Daniel Hylton, appeared the classic non-payer who took every advantage to avoid responsibility and delay review of the facts in the case. Hylton was not alone among his fellow debtors in claiming money already paid to the Virginia loan office (as per a Virginia law confiscating British debt) as absolving them from their liability.[10] Nearly every state had some law comparable to Virginia's whereby debts were confiscated or sequestered in an effort to raise revenue for the state. This practice, which factored into the *Brailsford* case, was a common defense raised by debtors. The Treaty of Paris recognized the potential of such an issue when the broadly encompassed article four was written.[11] As with *Brailsford*, the underlying friction was not necessarily about money and who owed what to whom. Rather, for the purposes of constitutional development, the issue dealt with power, and which entity was sovereign, and who would judge who was sovereign.[12]

Article XII of the Articles of Confederation approached the issue in a similar manner as did the Constitution. Article XII, dated March 1, 1781, clearly determined that debts incurred "before the assembling of the united states ... shall be deemed and considered as a charge against the united states."[13] Although Article VI of the Constitution would stress much the same sentiment, the Articles of Confederation gave the reason why the government should guarantee individual debt: the public faith. Previous chapters have argued that the Treaty of Paris in part mandated payment of British debt to establish the credibility of the government. Cases such as *Brailsford*, *Chisholm*, and *Ware*, all have an element in which the debtor attempted to prevent the establishment of that credibility through non-payment. Whether this was consciously or not, the result would have been the same had the Court not followed the Constitution and furthered the foundation of constitutionalism.[14] In both instances, Chief Justice Jay was instrumental in defining the power of the United States, but more importantly the power of the Constitution.[15] In the *Ware* case however, Chief Justice Jay would not sit. As mentioned, he had resigned after his diplomatic mission to Britain to become the governor of New York.

The Supreme Court did not have a chief when *Ware* finally came before the Court in February 1796. Two new justices, William Paterson and Samuel Chase, joined the three remaining original Washington appointees—Cushing, Wilson, and Iredell.[16] The case reached the Court on appeal from the circuit court, where judgment was decided for Hylton. Justice Iredell, sitting on circuit, wrote an opinion in favor of Hylton, and therefore did not sit in an official capacity in the Supreme Court session.

Six years before the case actually came before the Court, an editorial under the name of "Judex" appeared in the *New York Journal* on May 4, 1790. This was barely three months after the Court officially began operations, but

Chief Justice Jay was already being attacked for having pro–British sympathies.[17]

Judex seemed to be out in front of a major issue in constitutional interpretation before it even started. The conflicts over Article VI, Section I, were already brewing in state courts and would soon enter the circuit court system. The evolving argument centered around whether a treaty, in this instance the Paris Treaty of 1783, with a provision for repayment of debt was valid over state law by constitutional promulgation. On the lowest level, the debate centered around state versus federal law. Did the federal government have the right and power to render irrelevant state law in a given situation? It has been shown that not only the Constitution and the 1783 Treaty called for repayment of British debt, the Articles of Confederation did also. It has been discussed that these issues were more than just a matter of fiscal propriety. National standing was also, and probably more importantly, involved.[18] The United States needed recognition and acceptance in the community of nations and they needed it quickly. Nearly ten years after the Treaty, the states were still bickering along sectional lines about who should or should not pay and who has and does not have political power.[19]

The sectional rivalries of *Ware* became clear during the circuit court phase of the case. Daniel Hylton, the defendant in the case, wrote to Thomas Jefferson on May 29, 1791. Hylton was "much alarmed at the decision of Northern judges respecting the payment of the British debts, without any provision for the payment of the negroes under the treaty."[20] Hylton was exhibiting the latent sectionalism that the Court sought in part to quell through cases such as *Ware*.[21] The parameters evolving around the British debt cases magnified the already well-developed political party consensus taking hold in the government. This was not to suggest that the Supreme Court was consciously taking sides in the party alignment or that they hoped to steer a neutral path with decisions in these cases. The Court held to the principles of constitutional interpretation generally without the pressure of political allegiance.[22] However, it can be adequately argued that the Court's decisions inflamed those with more sectional or political allegiance and contributed to the breakdown of judicial review during the soon to occur Alien and Sedition Acts crisis.

In his circuit court opinion in Richmond of June 7, 1793, Justice Iredell essentially sided with Hylton in that he agreed with Hylton's argument that money already paid into the Virginia loan office should absolve him from further payment to Ware.[23] What was interesting in the opinion was Justice Iredell's statement concerning the often-attempted defense that the change in government during the Revolution somehow negated the original debt. Justice Iredell positively conferred that this line of argument was "not tenable."[24] Chief Justice Jay, also sitting in Richmond at the circuit court before his departure for England, saw the argument of a dissolving responsibility due to a change in government as "unsupported by any principle recognized by the laws of nature or nations."[25] In terms of payments made to the Virginia loan office, Chief Justice Jay differed with Justice Iredell. Chief Justice Jay saw those payments and the Virginia sequestration law as being grown "out of the war."[26]

Upon a writ of error the case moved to the Supreme Court in June of 1794. The case was scheduled to be heard at the February term of 1795. The writ dealt with the payment that Hylton had already made to the Virginia loan office and his contention that he was absolved from his debt by that action. The split between Justice Iredell and Chief Justice Jay over the issue of payments to the Virginia loan office was neutralized in the Supreme Court by Chief Justice Jay's resignation, as discussed. In theory the circuit court upheld the Constitution and the Treaty of Paris by affirming that Hylton was required to pay his debt.[27] What the Court disagreed on was whether or not Hylton had discharged his debt through payments he made to the Virginia loan office under the Virginia Sequestration Act.[28]

As with cases in the 1790s, the Court delivered their opinion in the *seriatim* manner, meaning each Justice read his opinion and the Court itself did not enter an opinion.[29] By most accounts, Justice Chase offered the most original argument while the other justices relied on what today is referred to as a textual opinion in that they simply quoted the language of the Constitution and did not engage in legal reasoning.[30] Justice Chase's opinion seemed very straightforward. He wrote that: "It seems to me that treaties made by Congress, according to the confederation, were superior to the laws of the states, because the confederation made them obligatory on all the states."[31] Justice Chase continued: "If doubts could exist before the establishment of the present national government, they must be entirely removed by the sixth article of the Constitution."[32]

This book is not arguing from a specific legal perspective, but rather it argues from a causal perspective in the sense that the opinions (events) of the Supreme Court impacted the actions of other branches of the government which further impacted constitutional development. Therefore, whether a justice had profound legal insight or took the rather narrow textual approach, the fact remains that the Court impacted significantly the development of American national government in the 1790s.[33]

Although the Supreme Court in *Ware v. Hylton* was called upon to answer a relatively narrow question, it nonetheless also established yet again the constitutional prerogatives of the Court to interpret the Constitution. Given the lack of a chief (Chief Justice Oliver Ellsworth joined the Court immediately after the arguments in *Ware*) and the addition of two new members, the Court maintained the foundations established in earlier cases such as *Brailsford*, where the Court found the requirements of Article VI, Section I, concerning Treaties to be valid and actionable relative to state law.[34] The most significant sentence to come out of *Ware* was: "Treaties as I understand the Constitution are made *supreme* over the constitutions and laws of the particular states [emphasis in original]."[35]

7

The Oliver Ellsworth Court: March 8, 1796– September 30, 1800

The arrival of former Senator Oliver Ellsworth as chief justice signaled the start of the second of the two main drafters of the Judiciary Act of 1789 to the Supreme Court. Former Senator William Paterson had already been seated as a justice on March 4, 1793. With these two men, who literally created the outline of the federal judiciary with the Supreme Court at the apex, the Court could certainly be said to be in good hands.

Wiscart v. Dauchy *(August 1, 1796)*

The case *Wiscart v. Dauchy* occurred against the backdrop of further personnel disruption on the Court. Justice Wilson was near the end of his rope financially and in fact *Wiscart* would be the last case he would hear as a justice before going into hiding from his creditors.

Wiscart lacked the drama of some cases but involved issues which confirmed the Court's maturation as the legal arbiter of the American system under the Constitution. Having been tried in the Virginia circuit court, the case was appealed to the Supreme Court "to review only the points of law involved rather than law and fact."[1] The case looked at the rather narrow issue of interpreting a clause in the Judiciary Act "that provided for the removal of civil cases from the circuit court to the Supreme Court on writs of error."[2]

Section 22 of the 1789 Judiciary Act prohibited the Supreme Court from reviewing a circuit court decision upon a writ of error based on an error of fact. This limited the Supreme Court review to errors of law. This prohibition became entwined with the numerous admiralty cases which came before the Court. "These cases raised the related problem of what procedure—error or appeal—was the correct method for obtaining Supreme Court review of circuit court rulings in admiralty proceedings."[3] The Court did not settle this issue with an admiralty case however. It was through an equity case, *Wiscart v. Dauchy*, that the Court provided guidance concerning the extent of a writ of error for both admiralty and equity cases. The Justices took pains to distinguish in their opinions the differences.

The case of *Wiscart v. Dauchy* began simply enough. Alexis Dauchy consigned a cargo of merchandise to Adrian Wiscart and Augustin Deneufville in August 1784. The voyage with the merchandise went from France to the United States. Two years later, Dauchy, in France, and not having heard from Wiscart and Deneufville, sent his brother to Virginia to investigate. Virginia was the presumed location of Dauchy's cargo. Two more years passed, and by the summer 1788, Dauchy sought the assistance of the French representative in Richmond, Virginia. It would be another two years, until May 1790, that Wiscart and Deneufville were in custody and charging Dauchy with a claim for reimbursement. In what some saw as an attempt to evade prosecution, and an attempt to change the tenor of the charges, Adrian Wiscart and Augustin Deneufville became American citizens. The six years it took to get to this point are somewhat of a mystery. It seems an exceptionally long time. Nonetheless, the case was heard by the circuit court in Virginia on December 4, 1792. Justice Cushing was then sitting on circuit duty.

The court created a commission of three members to study the complaint and on May 22, 1793, they reached their conclusions. The commission found for Dauchy, but on review they were ordered to reconsider their findings to take account of other pieces of evidence. The commission again found in Dauchy's favor and Justice Paterson affirmed the conclusion in the hopes of closing the case once and for all. Augustin Deneufville however, before Paterson's actions, had sold all of his property to his brother in an attempt (he disavowed this) to avoid having to pay Dauchy by claiming poverty. The circuit court took up this twist to the case in June 1795, only to postpone a decision until December. At the December term, Justice Cushing was replaced by Justice Iredell and the case was heard once again. On December 12, 1795, the circuit court found for Dauchy. Wiscart and Deneufville decided to ask the Supreme Court for a review of the case. This was where the case got tricky, as if it was not already quite complex. "Instead of taking out a writ of error and then obtaining judicial allowance of it—the typical route—they [Wiscart and Deneufville] sought allowance of the writ first."[4] The writ of error was granted on December 21, 1795. The Court did not hear the case until August 10, 1796. By this time, Dauchy had acquired what today we might term a celebrity defense team—Charles Lee, attorney general of the United States; Jared Ingersoll, attorney general of Pennsylvania; and Edward Tilghman, a noted attorney in Philadelphia.

In the arguments, the topic quickly went from the fast-dealing Deneuf-ville brothers to "the conclusiveness of the circuit court decree."[5] Dauchy's celebrity defense team argued that the case centered on a matter of law; Wis-cart's attorney, Peter S. Du Ponceau, argued the opposite, namely, that the case was centered on a matter of fact, not law, and therefore outside the area of review for the Supreme Court.

The court quickly determined a part of the case on August 10, by ruling that a circuit court opinion on facts, in equity or admiralty, was conclusive in the Supreme Court. Justices Wilson and Paterson dissented that a circuit court decision of fact had to be preserved when appealed to the Supreme Court. With that, the Court found that the Deneufville brothers and Wiscart were fraudulent and were ordered to pay Dauchy his due, in accord with the circuit court ruling. The Deneufville's went into hiding and refused to comply with the ruling. Dauchy filed new suits in the circuit court but eventually gave up without ever having collected.

All six justices had opinions in this case that was decided by a four-to-two split. Chief Justice Ellsworth was in the majority, with Justice Wilson in the minority. Chief Justice Ellsworth and his colleagues in the majority rea-soned that the Court should follow the Judiciary Act as written, limiting the Court to appeals of law and fact rather than only points of law. Justice Wilson, who dissented with Justice Paterson, argued that the Constitution allowed appeals of law over and above the Judiciary Act and wrote in his dissent:

> I consider the rule established ... to be of such magnitude, that being in the minority on the decision, I am desirous of stating ... the principles of my dissent. The decision must, indeed, very materially affect the jurisdiction of all the courts of the United States, particularly of the Supreme Court, as well as the general administration of justice.[6]

After making clear his high appreciation for the case, Justice Wilson contin-ued:

> I concur in the opinion, that, notwithstanding the provisions of the judicial act, an appeal is the natural and proper mode of removing an admiralty cause [appeal a case], and, in that case, there can be no doubt, that all the testimony which was produced in the court below, should also be produced in this court. Such an appeal is expressly sanctioned by the Constitution, it may, therefore, clearly in the first view of the subject be considered as the most regular process; ... even, indeed, if a positive restriction existed by law, it would ... be superseded by the superior authority of the constitutional provision."[7]

For his part, Chief Justice Ellsworth saw no such authority in the Con-stitution:

> Only an appellate jurisdiction is given to the court; and even the appellate jurisdiction is, likewise, qualified; ... Here then, is the ground, and the only ground, on which we can sustain an appeal. If Congress has provided no rule to regulate our proceedings, we cannot exercise an appellate jurisdiction; and if the rule is provided, we cannot

depart from it. The question, therefore, ... is simply, whether Congress has established any rule for regulating its exercise.[8]

Justice Wilson saw a constitutional prerogative, and Chief Justice Ellsworth did not. The chief justice saw it as a qualified prerogative needing Congressional structuring.

Moodie v. The Ship *Phoebe Anne* *(August 9, 1796)*

In the second term of new Chief Justice Oliver Ellsworth's first year, the Supreme Court heard a case surrounding the continuing saga of shipping on the high seas during a period of war when the United States was desperately trying to stay neutral. The ship *Phoebe Anne* was a British vessel that had been captured by a French privateer and taken to the port at Charleston, South Carolina (the port of Charleston was a den of French smuggling and privateering due to its proximity to the Caribbean). The British quickly filed a suit claiming the seizure unlawful due to the fact that the French privateer had been given sanctuary previously in the Charleston port after having been damaged in a storm. The British claimed this violated American neutrality. The American's responded that the ship was in distress and stayed just long enough to repair the damage. She did not acquire new armament while in Charleston. The British felt the aid given to the French (although non-military aid) rendered the French privateer a neutral. The British immediately presented a lawsuit in district court, in South Carolina, where they lost. Again, on appeal to the circuit court in South Carolina, the British lost. On appeal to the Supreme Court, Chief Justice Ellsworth noted that America's treaty with France (specifically the nineteenth article) allowed that "French vessels, whether public and of war, or private and or merchants, may, on any urgent necessity, enter our ports, and be supplied with all things needful for repairs."[9] The Supreme Court affirmed the circuit court findings against the British.

Calder v. Bull *(August 8, 1798)*

The case of *Calder v. Bull* highlights an aspect of eighteenth-century life not given much attention when the role of the Supreme Court is considered at that time: women. It is well known that women lacked many rights we take for granted today and that men took for granted in the eighteenth century. The *Calder* case, like so many cases before the Supreme Court in the 1790s and now, began years before it ever reached the Court. In fact, many cases began in the years when the Revolutionary War was still raging. Such were the beginnings of the *Calder* case.

In 1779 Norman Morison of Connecticut drafted a will that left his wife Abigail principle heir and executrix. Upon his death in 1783, Mrs. Morison set out to undertake the settling of Norman Morison's estates. A son had been born to the Morison's and the young child, unbeknownst to him or his parents, caused an issue with the probate judge who did not settle Mr. Morison's will immediately because he wanted to consider the child since the will made no mention of a child, even though the child was born between the writing of the will in 1779 and Mr. Morison's death in 1783. The judge assumed that if Mr. Morison had known of a son, Mrs. Morison would not have been the primary heir. The judge did honor Mr. Morison's request that his wife act as executrix, a relatively rare occurrence, and her role as heir without being the primary heir. What he did, without notifying Mrs. Morison (she did not find out until 1790), was to not probate the will, thinking that Mr. Morison would certainly have updated his will to reflect the presence of a male heir had he not died so young. The judge was clearly making assumptions based upon the patriarchal society in effect at the time. While this provides an explanation as to why the judge acted as he did, his actions, based on male assumptions, started a cascade of events that ended up before the Supreme Court of the United States.

Mrs. Morison remarried before the death of her son in 1790. Her new husband, Caleb Bull, sought with his wife to ensure the will of her first husband, Norman Morison, was probated. They learned of what occurred seven years before and in quick order learned that absent a probated will, Mrs. Bull, by the terms of a 1784 state law, was no longer the heir of her late husband's estate. The judge's actions in 1783, based on vestiges of male inheritance, had resulted in the loss, coupled with the new 1784 law, of the property provided her by her late husband. The Bulls immediately sought legal advice.

Since the 1784 law was the immediate concern for the Bulls, they petitioned the Connecticut General Assembly to allow an appeal of the probate court's ruling to the state Superior Court. The Bulls received no remedy from the General Assembly for several years. Finally, in 1794, they filed a new petition and took a different approach. The Bulls:

> Pointed to the fact that they had hard evidence to disprove some of the assumptions the probate court made in 1783 and noted that if the court had decided the case correctly, Abigail would have been lawfully in possession of her husband's property before the Connecticut legislature passed a new statute changing the law on the descent of property.[10]

In essence, the Bulls were asking for a trip back in time to reorient events to more equitably impact them in the present. In their hearing, the Bulls showed that Norman Morison would not have changed his will after the birth of his son, and therefore the original probate judge was wrong in making his assumption about the will.

The new court of probate session approved Norman Morison's will on July 27, 1795. This meant that the new claimant on Morison's will, his aunt Jennet Knox Calder, now out of line of inheritance, immediately sued to appeal the ruling.

Jennet Calder and her husband, through their attorneys, argued in superior court that the new ruling violated the Constitution's ban on *ex post facto* laws (laws which go back in time to alter the course of current rulings). The Calder's lost in every appeal they initiated in the state courts. This type of lawmaking, known as *ex post facto* (after the fact) law, was prohibited by the Constitution in criminal cases but not explicitly in civil cases. It was presumed to apply to civil cases, and the Supreme Court, when they heard the case, set a precedent with their opinion that *ex post facto* prohibitions in the Constitution do not apply to civil cases. It was not until February 1798 that the Supreme Court heard the case but decided to delay its ruling.

When the Court delivered its opinion on August 8, 1798, it was Justice Chase who took the lead with his opinion. Justice Chase succinctly stated the matter in the opening of his argument: "The sole inquiry is, whether this resolution or law of Connecticut, having such operation, is an *ex post facto* law, within the prohibition of the federal constitution."[11] Chase continued to argue his point that Connecticut was free under the federal Constitution to protect private property as it saw fit:

> The legislature may enjoin, permit, forbid, and punish; they may declare new crimes, and establish rules of conduct for all its citizens in future cases; they may command what is right, and prohibit what is wrong; but they cannot change innocence into guilt; or punish innocence as a crime; or violate the right of an antecedent lawful private contract; or the right of private property.[12]

Perhaps though, Justice Cushing had the most succinct statement when he wrote in his opinion: "The case appears to me to be clear of all difficulty, taken either way. If the act is a judicial act, it is not touched by the federal constitution; and if it is a legislative act, it is maintained and justified by the ancient and uniform practice of the state of Connecticut."[13] He argued that states, through their legislatures, were free to make those laws peculiar to that state which do not directly violate the Constitution. Still, "Chase announced that he did not believe in the 'omnipotence' of state legislatures..." but nonetheless it was not the job of the Supreme Court to adjudicate on a state legislature following the state constitution that did not violate the federal Constitution.[14] Finally, as to the *ex post facto* controversy, Chase was adamant that the constitutional prohibition against such laws dealt with criminal cases, not cases involving private rights or property. Justice Iredell began his opinion by noting the practice of the Connecticut legislature to be favorable to restructuring cases to create more balanced outcomes in their view. Justice Iredell began: "From the best information to be collected, relative to the Constitution of Connecticut, it appears, that the legislature of the state has been in the uniform, uninterrupted, habit of exercising a general superintending power over its courts of law, by granting new trials."[15] Iredell gave an overview of the theory of separate powers in a state or national government and how each is separate in its field. He concluded:

> In order, therefore, to guard against so great an evil, it has been the policy of all the American states, which have, individually, framed their state constitutions since the revolution, and of the people of the United States, when they framed the federal constitution, to define with precision the objects of the legislative power, and to restrain its exercise within marked and settled boundaries.[16]

Iredell carefully laid out his argument concerning the separation of power and how carefully that had to be maintained. His most interesting point dealt with the authority of the Court to declare acts of Congress unconstitutional. While not called for in the Constitution, it was a concept widely accepted and understood to exist. Iredell wrote that it was a great power of the court and should be used infrequently: "If any act of Congress, or of the legislature of a state, violates those constitutional provisions, it is unquestionably void; though, I admit, that as the authority to declare it void is of a delicate and awful nature, the court will never resort to that authority, but in a clear and urgent case."[17] Iredell concluded the *ex post facto* law review by stating laws "do not ... extend to civil cases, to cases that merely affect the private property of citizens."[18] The remaining justices, Paterson, Iredell, and Cushing, all came to similar conclusions though via different paths.

Irvine v. Simms Lessee *(February 19, 1799)*

Of the sixty-odd cases that came before the Supreme Court during the 1790s, many dealt with the ongoing European war and the role of the United States as a neutral. Few cases dealt directly with the topic presented in *Irvine*: the vast expanse of western land where fortunes were made and lost and nearly every American leader from President Washington to Justice James Wilson had money invested. Land speculation had a long pedigree in America, stretching back to the founding settlement at Jamestown in 1607. By the 1790s, the practice was much more sophisticated and concentrated. By that point it also involved the states, which jealously claimed what title they could to western lands. (In fact, it was a land dispute that delayed ratification of the Articles of Confederation, although written in 1776, until 1781, much to the detriment of the fledgling United States.) *Irvine* dealt with a strip of land (an

Promissory note by Justice James Wilson to William Bingham, 1793, for five-thousand pounds (Morristown National Historical Park).

island) in the Ohio River near Pittsburgh that was claimed by both Virginia and Pennsylvania.

The case began on May 30, 1780 (before the Articles of Confederation were adopted), when Charles Simms formally located the island of Montour with a local surveyor for his own personal property. The claim for the land was acquired by Simms from a French and Indian War veteran who sold the land to him. Later, in the fall of 1780, Virginia and Pennsylvania settled their boundary dispute and Montour Island came to be within the State of Pennsylvania, not Virginia, as Simms had registered his claim (Simms could claim title once an official survey was filed). There the matter rested for three years until Pennsylvania granted General William Irvine land for his Revolutionary War service. Irvine requested Montour Island, not knowing of the Simms claim, and the state agreed providing that Irvine conduct a survey and that no one could claim prior ownership.

Charles Simms by this point was practicing law in Alexandria, Virginia. He learned of this encroachment on his property and immediately contacted Irvine and informed him of his ownership and of his desire to amicably settle the matter. General Irvine, perhaps reverting to his military approach to life, ordered a survey in his own name and recorded it in Pennsylvania, similar to Irvine having filed his surveyor's claim in Virginia three years earlier. Simms seemed unconcerned about Irvine's tactics and calmly waited until April 1787 to commission another survey, this time in Pennsylvania, to prove his ownership. At the same time, Irvine obtained further legal protection by the purchase of a patent on the island. Still, it was not until 1791 that Simms and his associates filed legal action against Irvine in the United States circuit court for Pennsylvania.

Irvine naturally raised several procedural issues, one of which was that one of Simms's associates was a resident of Pennsylvania and therefore the case should be heard in state court, not the federal circuit courts—a technical matter addressed in the Judiciary Act of 1789. The case faltered and reappeared three years later in 1794 but again waivered and delayed until 1797. Simms had a superlative legal team in Charles Lee, Jared Ingersoll, and William Rawle. In the October 1797 term, the circuit court recessed due to an outbreak of yellow fever in Philadelphia.

On April 20, 1798, after a jury trial, with Justice Chase and District Judge Richard Peters presiding, a finding for Simms was recorded. An appeal to the Supreme Court by Irvine was postponed again because of a yellow fever outbreak. The case was finally heard in February 1799, nearly twenty years after Simms first acquired the property. The case drew great attention due to the presence of the high profile attorneys for both Simms and Irvine. Procedural and technical matters formed the bulk of Irvine's defense under the Judiciary Act of 1789. Parsing the meaning of the act was more than a sport for famous lawyers. They sought to sway interpretation of the act's many undefined sections along certain political and ideological lines. This opportunity to impact law interpretation for decades to come was an almost overwhelming lure for many lawyers and some took on cases gratis for the chance. Simms's attorneys had an easier argument, Simms was there first on Montour Island; and regardless of technical issues, that meant something. They also argued that given the land in question was an island, a survey, which Irvine had argued was not completed by Simms, was irrelevant. The boundaries could not be open to debate. It was surrounded by water and no further delineation was necessary. At the end of the August session of 1799, the Court found for Simms. Irvine immediately petitioned the Pennsylvania legislature for a new grant of land based on his Revolutionary War service and was granted a new tract on March 28, 1799.

Priestman v. United States *(August 13, 1800)*

The issue involved in *Priestman v. United States* centered on the movement of foreign commerce (in this case watches) between states in possible violation of a coastal trading law. The watches were seized in Pennsylvania and were subject to forfeiture if no owner claimed them. William Priestman claimed ownership and furthermore claimed to have paid all import duties and denied transporting the watches through Maryland, Delaware, and Pennsylvania. In district court in Philadelphia Priestman's claim was accepted; he also petitioned the district judge to approach the secretary of the treasury to forfeit any penalty should he (Priestman) be found guilty.

Priestman's defense was simple, he claimed ignorance of the law concerning transporting the merchandise across state boundaries without proper authorization. Priestman was found not guilty in July 1798. In November 1798, Secretary of the Treasury Oliver Wolcott rejected Priestman's request to forego any penalties even though he had been acquitted. Wolcott's decision forced the case back to court where both sides agreed to an expedited format which provided for "a statement of facts which would allow counsel to make purely legal arguments before Judge Peters, who would then come to a decision on the law."[19] After hearing both sides, especially provisions of the 1793 law, Judge Peters ruled against Priestman on December 11, 1798, and ordered the watches confiscated.

Priestman immediately appealed to the United States circuit court where Justice Iredell and Judge Peters heard the case in April 1799. The case lingered a year without a decision and with the arrival of Justice Chase on the circuit court it had to be reargued. The decision, announced April 17, 1800, upheld the decision of the district court. Even with two loses at the federal level,

Priestman appealed to the Supreme Court, which in August 1800 consisted of William Paterson, Samuel Chase, Bushrod Washington, and Alfred Moore. Justice William Cushing was indisposed, and Chief Justice Oliver Ellsworth was in France. The third time in the federal courts was not a charm for Priestman, who lost his bid before the justices in an opinion of August 15, 1800. Their decision, like the district and circuit courts before them, relied on the 1793 coastal trade law. Undeterred, Priestman made one more stop in the federal government: President of the United States Thomas Jefferson. Priestman requested a pardon, and on June 7, 1801, on the advice of his Attorney General Levi Lincoln, the president granted the pardon. President Jefferson, through Attorney General Lincoln, saw Priestman's "crime" as a mistake; furthermore, the law was ambiguous even if he had known of its existence.[20]

Bas v. Tingy *(August 14, 1800)*

The last case to be considered by the Court in Philadelphia before they moved to the new capital city of Washington, D.C., was also the last case to be heard by the pre–John Marshall court. As such, it is also the last case to be considered in this book. This case, as we have seen in other cases before, dealt with another instance of privateer prize taking. However, rather than the traditional argument over rights of the owners of the purloined vessel versus those of the privateers, *Bas v. Tingy* saw the Court wade into the growing political party debate that had been escalating throughout the 1790s in the other two branches of government. It has often been written that the Founders created the Constitution without thought given to political parties. While that assessment is no doubt partially true, it is hard to imagine the Founders not foreseeing leaders congregating around certain principles and thus forming parties. The political caldron was boiling by 1800. Federalists and Democratic-Republicans (Republicans) had settled their perspectives around foreign affairs as much as domestic concerns. The Federalists generally favored England while the Republicans France. Federalist favored the Jay Treaty, Republicans not so much. This cleft would spill over into the presidential election of 1800, pitting Federalist incumbent John Adams against Republican Thomas Jefferson. Similarly, in the Supreme Court, the justices experienced significant criticism for their opinion in *Bas v. Tingy*; the criticism fell along party loyalties over the quasi-war America was engaged in with France. Some legislators came to feel the Court had overreached in its opinion.

As domestic (Whiskey Rebellion) and foreign (Citizen Genêt, Jay Treaty) concerns cast a spell over the American government and the Supreme Court during the early 1790s, so too did foreign matters impact the later 1790s

Supreme Court. The case *Bas v. Tingy* was set against the backdrop of the so-called Quasi-War with France and more specifically the infamous XYZ Affair. In fact, the ship involved in *Bas*, the *Eliza*, left Charleston, South Carolina, exactly a year after the XYZ Affair broke in America. The *Eliza* was headed for Havana and carried extensive paperwork to indicate that the vessel was American and under command of an American (John Bas) and was carrying American commerce. The *Eliza* was captured by a French privateer off of Cuba. About a week later, the American warship *Ganges* caught up with the pirated *Eliza*, reclaimed her for America, and escorted her back to Philadelphia, arriving May 15, 1799. The captain of the *Ganges*, Thomas Tingy, immediately sought more than his country's thanks from Captain Bas and the American Navy and nation. In fact, he sought a part of the spoils from the cargo aboard the *Eliza* as reward for his salvage. There actually existed two laws, both meant to encourage the American Navy to undertake the recapture, or salvage, of pirated American vessels, that had recently been passed by Congress. One, called for less than one-half the value of the cargo as recompense; the second law called for half, but it included the word "enemy" in the language used. In other words, the ship rescued by the Navy had to be retaken from enemy hands to claim half the value of the cargo. In the case of the *Eliza*, was France an enemy, or merely a nuisance? An enemy generally implied war, and war, according to the Constitution had to be declared by Congress and signed by the president, something which had not happened in the *Eliza* situation with France. If France was an enemy, Tingy stood to gain much more than if France was merely a nuisance.

Bas v. Tingy revolved around whether an undeclared war was actually a war from a constitutional standpoint. On this answer hinged the solution to the case. Justice Washington stated this at the beginning of his opinion, "The decision of this question must depend upon ... [whether] there subsisted a state of war between the two nations [France and the United States]."[21] Justice Washington provided his view "that every contention by force between two nations, in external matters, under the authority of their respective governments, is not only war, but public war."[22] Justice Washington saw an undeclared war as an "imperfect war," but war nonetheless, having all the attributes of a declared conflict.[23] One of the issues giving rise to the *Bas* case was the action of Congress on March 2, 1799 (the formal professionalization of the United States Navy in preparation for possible war), when they took steps that would have been taken in a declared war without actually declaring war as provided by the Constitution.

The semantics over what "enemy" meant served as the summation of the entire case. For Tingy, enemy meant more money in the form of a greater share of the value of the cargo. For Bas, enemy meant less money, in the form of a lesser share of the value of the cargo of the vessel he was in command of. Both the superior and circuit courts found for Tingy. France, they ruled, was an enemy, with or without a declaration of war. While not declared by constitutional means, the laws against the French were every bit as militarily significant if viewed in the larger picture. When the case arrived at the Supreme Court, the issue was entirely the same as in the lower courts: what does enemy mean? Justice Chase, who sat on the circuit court trial for *Bas*, wrote that "Congress has authorized hostilities on the high seas by certain persons in certain cases. There is no authority given to commit hostilities on land; to capture unarmed French vessels, nor even to capture French armed vessels, lying in a French port."[24] Justice Paterson also saw the issue in terms of a limited war based on the action of Congress on March 2, 1799, to allow American naval vessels (public and private) to defend themselves and American shipping from French attacks. Justice Paterson stated unequivocally that "the United States and the French republic are in a qualified state of hostilities."[25] The Court unanimously ruled that the taking of the ship was lawful and that war, declared or not, existed.

To complicate matters, Chief Justice Oliver Ellsworth was in France at the time *Bas* was argued. He was sent by President Adams as one of three diplomats to try and ease tensions between the two countries. For Ellsworth and his colleagues, there was not a war raging between America and France, and consequently they were not enemies. In fact, they were sent to France by President Adams to avoid a war from occurring.

While Ellsworth was working diplomatically to prevent the term "enemy" from becoming a constitutionally recognized reality, his colleagues on the Supreme Court found that indeed, France was an enemy of the United States.

Chief Justice Oliver Ellsworth in France

Much like Chief Justice John Jay in 1794 with England, Chief Justice Oliver Ellsworth was asked to try and subdue the rising tensions between America and France in the late 1790s—the so-called Quasi-War. Specifically, President Adams asked him to be part of a delegation to work out the differences between the two one-time allies. Adams's term as president was dominated by French foreign relations. As we saw in *Bas v. Tingy*, French predation on American commercial shipping was ruinous. "Over a twelve-month period beginning in 1796, French vessels seized more than three hundred American ships."[26]

Adams was risking a great deal with the Ellsworth mission. Adams's first diplomatic mission, sent in the summer of 1797, ended up resulting in the infamous XYZ Affair (XYZ were monikers given by President Adams to mask the identity of the three French diplomats trying to obtain a bribe from the

Americans). The three American representatives were Elbridge Gerry, Charles Cotesworth Pickney, and future Supreme Court chief justice John Marshall. The three American ministers were harassed by the French before being told that a bribe was the price for dealing with them. The American ministers rejected this and exposed the whole affair much to the amazement of their fellow Americans, who saw the men as heroes for resisting the dishonorable approach of the French. Still, President Adams had hope. He wanted to avoid the European war at nearly any cost. Therefore, he tried again, with a second delegation in 1800.

Vice President Thomas Jefferson, the supreme Francophile among America's political elite, was dumbstruck. He did not try to defend France over the XYZ Affair, and even tried to insinuate that it did not happen the way it was reported. The public relations fiasco resulting from the XYZ Affair was difficult to manage for Jefferson and his Republicans. Yet, the Federalists made their own miscalculations with the Alien and Sedition Acts (see Chapter 8). In the fluid and fast paced movement of events (by eighteenth-century standards) President Adams surprised nearly everyone by appointing another delegation.

Adams turned to Chief Justice Oliver Ellsworth, who helped to ease tensions within Adams's own Federalist party which was dominated more by the Alexander Hamilton (confrontation) approach than President Adams's (conciliatory) approach to France. The peace commission decided upon by President Adams and the Federalist Senate included Ellsworth, Maryland Representative William Vans Murray, and North Carolina Governor William Davie. Ellsworth's pick to lead the delegation to France was not a surprise. Many already considered Ellsworth an unofficial member of President Adams's cabinet. He often served as a counselor to the president on a wide array of issues. Ellsworth and his colleagues arrived in Paris in March 1800. By this point, President Adams was doubting his re-election chances for the November election, but he was determined to have peace with France and there was no turning back.

The negotiations with the French were relatively quick. The American team had two objectives:

> To secure reparations for American cargo seized by French vessels since the beginning of hostilities, and to reach a new treaty with France that abrogated the terms of the 1778 alliance. In reply, the French negotiators offered a choice: either France would reimburse the damages sought by the United States on the condition that terms of the earlier alliance were renewed, or it would consent to undo the earlier alliance without guaranteeing the payment of damages.[27]

The 1778 Alliance has been referred to previously. The problem was, neither France nor America were, in 1800, what they were in 1778. Returning to the 1778 Alliance would have greatly benefited France as opposed to America. In 1778, America, politically, economically, and socially, was in shambles. The American Revolution hung by the slightest thread and any agitation could have snapped it in Britain's favor. France, on the other hand, in 1778, was one of the most powerful countries in Europe. It had a long and enviable history of law, government, society, and above all, culture. For Ellsworth and his fellow negotiators to return to this point, would have been to reject everything that had transpired in America since 1778—independence, the new Constitution, and a decade under a new federal government.

The American ministers agreed to compromise and dropped "their demand that France reimburse the United States for the entirety of the property it had seized."[28] Concerning the 1778 Alliance, both sides agreed to respect current realities by "lifting the obligations that the United States owed France under their earlier agreements...."[29] It was an acknowledgment that, unlike 1778, the United States had a much stronger point from which to bargain. Even though the United States was far too weak militarily to engage France in war, it was already proving itself to be a significant economic force in the community of nations. Additionally, should the United States side with Britain against France, the latter would have almost certainly suffered serious setbacks—perhaps even to the point of Napoleon never having been able to gather the type of power he did between 1801 and his final defeat at Waterloo in 1815.

The Senate approved the Treaty on February 3, 1801, during the interregnum between presidential administrations; President Adams having been defeated the previous November for re-election. The Senate had initially not approved the treaty on January 23, 1801, by the Constitutional mandate of two-thirds majority due to in-fighting by the Federalists. The treaty went a long way in stabilizing relations between France and the United States. The atmosphere allowed for Napoleon to consolidate his power, focus on European relations, wage endless war for over a decade, and sell President Jefferson the Louisiana Territory in 1803 by the Treaty of Mortefontaine on October 3. Napoleon at the time was not yet emperor of France (that occurred in December 1804).

8

The Supreme Court and the
Alien and Sedition Acts Cases

The Alien and Sedition Acts cases represent a problem for anyone study-ing the first decade of the Supreme Court due to the drastic change of course these cases caused. By and large, the Court kept to what can arguably be iden-tified as a non-political approach to adjudication during the 1790s. The Court kept to the realm of constitutional development and jealously guarded the prerogatives of the separation of powers principle. This book has analyzed in the previous chapters the phenomena associated with the Court's dedica-tion to the concept of constitutional development without regard for the political imperatives of their decisions.

With the Alien and Sedition Acts cases however, the Court appeared to lose its direction and focus and surrendered to the specter of political party machinations. The rise of the political party structure, while alluded to pre-viously, was for all intents and purposes complete by the administration of John Adams, 1797–1801. This is a significant development for the Court as they could not help being impacted, although they were not as intimately involved as the other two branches of government.

This chapter will only provide the most basic references pertaining to the political party creations, and it will be understood that the creation of the political party process in fact did occur by the time of the Adams admin-istration.[1] The focus of this chapter will be to analyze the impact this creation of the political process had on the Court and in particular the response of the Court through the Alien and Sedition Acts cases. These cases on first appearance do not necessarily seem to fit the goal as stated in the introduction to this book. However, while the Court did not undertake to challenge the constitutionality of the Acts, the concept of judicial review was a relevant constitutional procedure which this book has placed much positive emphasis on. Therefore it is more that the Court in the Alien and Sedition Acts cases abdicated its role as the interpreter of the Constitution in favor of adhering to political party policy. This tension, as mentioned, will form the basis for this chapter.

John Adams served as president of the United States from March 4, 1797, to March 4, 1801. During that time the United States, barely a decade old under the Constitution, had survived amidst the imperial struggles of Continental Europe occasioned by the collapse of the Bourbon dynasty in France. President Adams considered it among his chief goals to keep the United States out of the wars which the country could in no manner expect to survive if it became a belligerent. President Washington too, in his farewell address in 1797, had cautioned against entanglement in foreign affairs for the same reason.

President Adams had the delicate task of attempting to maintain neutrality with both combatants for the simple reason that the United States was far too weak economically, politically, and militarily, to engage either of the highly experienced war machines of Europe, especially on the high seas. To add to Adams's plight, the ever-tightening development of political party factions ensured at any given time he was being counseled to be more forceful with either one of the two belligerents. In a sense, not only was Adams attempting to keep peace abroad (by maintaining Washington's precepts as he stated in his Proclamation of Neutrality of 1793 and his Farewell Address), he was also attempting to keep peace at home.

The better part of the John Adams administration was consumed with the shifting elements of foreign affairs.[2] England and France were the principle antagonists. Adams was not unfamiliar with either nation, having spent time in both countries in various diplomatic capacities in the ten years leading up to his election as vice president in 1788. By 1797, the perennial foes were in the midst of a war that began in 1793, occasioned by the fallout of the French Revolution. They were about to enter into an even more terrible period of war, with even higher stakes, occasioned by the rise of Napoleon.

What exactly was the crisis which Adams found himself facing at the beginning of his term? The crisis was a holdover from the Washington administration and was precipitated by America's attempt to keep the peace with both belligerents, France and England. The Jay Treaty, negotiated by Chief Justice John Jay in 1794, seemed to settle the crisis for the moment with England, but conditions with France continued to deteriorate over numerous issues such as trade and neutrality. President Adams sent a delegation to France in an attempt to negotiate. The delegation was composed of Elbridge Gerry, Charles Cotesworth Pickney (already the American ambassador to France, although not recognized by France), and John Marshall, future Supreme Court chief justice. The result of this mission was the famous XYZ Affair.[3] Due to the failure of the mission, Congress began to appropriate military hardware and sought new power to secure the United States from domestic threat. One of the measures designed to ensure domestic peace included what are known as the Alien and Sedition Acts of 1798.[4]

John Marshall, standing for Congress in 1798, responded to a question concerning his views of the Acts in the following manner:

> I am not an advocate for the alien and sedition bills; had I been in Congress when they passed, I should, unless my judgment could have been changed, certainly have opposed them. Yet, I do not think them fraught with all those mischiefs which many gentlemen ascribe to them. I should have opposed them because I think them useless; and because they are calculated to create unnecessary discontents and jealousies at a time our very existence, as a nation, may depend on our union.[5]

Curiously, Marshall did not comment on the constitutionality of the Acts (he was still three years away from the Supreme Court). Rather, he focused on the fact, in his view, that they were inherently divisive presumably because they mandated the questioning of one's loyalty.

The trend throughout the 1790s was towards the centralization of political power wielded between two opposing parties. Unlike the British Parliamentary common law system, which thrived on a multitude of interpretations and hence parties, the American version of a constitutional system lent itself well to the establishment of two major parties, each with contrasting views of the central founding document. The climax of the creation of the two-party system as mentioned reached fruition during the Adams administration and impacted every branch of government. This was convenient in that one party, the Federalists, dominated every branch, including the Supreme Court. It would be Adams's inability as a politician, and the desire of the Court to play a more strident role in internal security affairs, which would lead to what is mostly seen as the debacle of the Alien and Sedition Acts cases.[6]

While Adams worked to maintain some level of operational neutrality, the pro–English Federalist which dominated Congress (Adams himself was a Federalist, although not necessarily a party operative) decided to take full advantage of the situation.[7] The most egregious of all Federalist measures taken were the Alien and Sedition Acts.[8] These collective measures, under the thin veil of patriotism or nationalism, sought to curb the power of the opposition Republican party by turning their operatives into enemies of the state.[9] The Acts in total would eventually result in fifteen to twenty-five indictments (the sources vary), including those prosecuted under the common law, producing ten convictions.[10]

The acts were composed of four individual acts. Passed in quick succession were the Naturalization Act (June 18, 1798), which required immigrants to register with a federal officer and to pass fourteen years in a probationary status before citizenship; the Act Concerning Aliens (June 27, 1798) and the Act Respecting Alien Enemies (July 6, 1798) both of which allowed the president to deport aliens, the first act in times of peace, and the second act in times of war; and the Act for the Punishment of Certain Crimes (July 14, 1798), which made it a crime to "write, print, utter, or publish ... any false, scandalous and malicious writing or writings against the government of the United States."[11] Federalists argued in attempting to counter opposition to the acts on constitutional grounds that the first amendment meant freedom from prior restraint, not from subsequent punishment. The debate on the constitutionality of the acts in Congress prior to passage was not as profound or nearly as long as might seem necessary, even though under modern precedents, the acts would most certainly be unconstitutional.[12] The issue of free speech was unique in the sense that the first amendment guarantor of this right had never before been challenged (and would not be at this time either), whether directly as a free speech case, or indirectly as a sidebar in some other constitutional case.

Two of the seminal eighteenth-century works (both of which influenced the Founder's in one way or another) on the topic of free speech are Montesquieu's *Spirit of the Laws*, and Blackstone's *Commentaries on the Laws of England*. Montesquieu maintained, "Speech is so subject to interpretation; there is so great a difference between indiscretion and malice; ... that the law can hardly subject people [to punishment] for words unless it expressly declares what words they are."[13] This argument was nearly followed by Madison in *Federalist* 44 to support the necessary and proper clause.[14] Montesquieu further stated simply the "words do not constitute an overt act; they remain only an idea."[15] Attempting to achieve total enumeration of offenses or probable conditions is impossible given the infinite combinations possible in human affairs.

Much nearer to the Federalist conception of the acts was the passage in Blackstone's *Commentaries* in which he discussed libel. He wrote, "Taken in their [aspects of libel] largest and most extensive sense, signify any writing ... of an immoral or illegal tendency" and further, "are malicious defamations of any person ... in order to provoke him to wrath, or expose him to public hatred, contempt, and ridicule."[16] Blackstone continued, "the direct tendency of these libels is the breach of the peace, by stirring up the objects of them to revenge, and perhaps to bloodshed."[17] Blackstone was naturally writing in the common law tradition, whereas the Federalists in 1798, while in theory freed of the common law through the Constitution, nevertheless saw fit to invoke the practical aspects of common law libel under the acts. What the Federalists attempted to do was invoke a creation found on natural law theory, conjoined with a common law precedent, to produce a statutory law which they pronounced as constitutional. "The stage of equity and natural law..., a stage which involved an infusion of morality—an infusion of purely moral ideas developed outside the legal system."[18] This pronouncement included members of the Court who had yet to hear any arguments in a case. In fact, they saw little need to try cases, as the matter was self-evident under natural law. It could be argued that this attempt to resurrect natural law doomed the acts to failure, and ultimately the Federalist Party too.

John Adams, as president, naturally had to sign the bills to make them law. However, the individual acts were not promoted by, nor did they represent, Adams administration policy.[19] Abigail Adams, an acknowledged keen observer of the political scene, had perhaps more inflammatory feelings in favor of the acts. She apparently urged her husband to not only encourage the publishing of the acts, she saw it as advantageous to include a copy of Justice William Cushing's charge to a grand jury in 1794 (albeit prior to the actual acts themselves) on the nature of republican government and the role each citizen plays.[20] It can certainly be argued that Abigail Adams might not have been the best exponent of constitutional law. However, she had an independent ability and more importantly access to more information than the average citizen. Her desire to use a four-year-old grand jury charge to bolster a new law (one which had not been tested by the Court) can serve to indicate how seamlessly some of the Federalists viewed the three branches of government whether or not it created a conflict of interest as we know it.

The highest officers of the government which the Congress was ostensibly trying to shield were naturally the president and certain members of his cabinet, as well as certain members of Congress.[21] The one branch of government (really, the only one left) which Congress seemingly failed to "protect" from obloquy and contempt was the Supreme Court.

By 1798, the Supreme Court was working under its third chief justice in less than ten years and had gone through five personnel changes from the original six justices appointed by President Washington in 1789. In political makeup, the Court, as well as the executive and legislature, was Federalist to the core. This ensured an easy political victory for the party in the Alien and Sedition Acts cases and with the clarity of two centuries through which to gaze, it also marked the limit of Federalist power and the beginning of their eventual extinction as a political party and philosophy.[22]

From a structural legal standpoint, the Sedition Act (ironically passed on Bastille Day) codified the English common law of seditious libel.[23] Seditious libel was the crime of political criticism that threatened to diminish respect for the government.[24] It combined the two separate laws of sedition and libel in an omnibus, or all encompassing, law. At common law, truth was not a defense in libel cases until 1843, with the passage of Campbell's Libel Act in England.[25] One other aspect of the eighteenth-century common law conception of seditious libel was that of general verdicts.[26]

Chief Justice Ellsworth seemed to concur with this reasoning by allowing truth as a defense and thus perhaps limiting the actual number of convictions.[27] Ellsworth saw the acts as a positive codification of law (positive in the sense of protecting the country, not necessarily in the philosophical sense of positivism).[28] In doing so, Ellsworth seemed to be acting more as the Senator he once was rather than an impartial justice who decided cases on the merits of individual arguments. It would not have been a comforting thought to have faced Ellsworth as an accused knowing that he lobbied in favor of the acts.

One case, that of William Durrell (who has the distinction of being the first editor arrested and who Adams eventually partially pardoned in 1800), was actually tried under the common law doctrine of seditious libel rather than the Sedition Law of 1798.[29] The Durrell case was handled by the most recent appointment to the Court, Bushrod Washington, who was a nephew of the former president. This case serves to highlight the disjunction between statutory and common law which still pervaded the highest levels of American legal practice. The specter of William Blackstone and common law was still a very powerful influence a dozen years after the Constitution was passed.[30] This combination of two legal systems in the defense of the authorities allowed elected officials protection while not protecting individual citizens from the same types of attacks.[31]

The debate over the definition of the necessary and proper clause (which the Federalists advanced to support the Alien and Sedition Acts) in 1798 was of course nothing new. During the ratification process a decade earlier, the last clause of Article 1, Section 8, occasioned plenty of disputatious editorials. As an example, in the fall of 1787, pseudonymous writers Centinel, Brutus, Old Whig, and Federal Farmer all argued against the then-proposed Constitution in part because of the expansive language of the necessary and proper clause. Centinel felt "whatever law congress may deem necessary and proper for carrying into execution any of the powers vested in them, may be enacted: and by virtue of this clause, they may control and abrogate any and every of the laws of the state governments."[32] The Old Whig writer summed up the tone for most of the opponents of this clause: "Under such a clause as this [necessary and proper] can any thing be said to be reserved and kept back from congress?"[33] It is interesting that virtually all opposition to this clause rebounds against the states rather than individuals (the primary focus of the acts). Although the First Amendment had not yet been ratified respecting individual liberties, the opponents of the Constitution saw only the states' rights issue in ratification. The Federal Farmer—who wrote, "It is almost impossible to have a just conception of these [necessary and proper] powers"—can actually be seen as one writer who imaginatively thought beyond the state issue to envision the clause being used in some other way.[34] And, in fact, in 1798, the clause was used to invoke the acts primarily against individuals rather than the states.

Arguing in favor of the expansive nature of the necessary and proper clause were Alexander Hamilton and James Madison. In *Federalist* 33, Hamilton wrote for the clause as a mechanism to ensure Congress had the ability to respond as needed to as yet unforeseen circumstances. Hamilton inveighed against those who "have been the sources of much virulent invective and petulant declamation against the proposed constitution."[35] Madison argued in a similar manner in *Federalist* 44. Madison maintained that to have attempted to enumerate every necessary and proper law would have been "chimerical," and further would have given the inevitable omission(s) the "equivalent to a positive grant of authority."[36] Thus, only a generalized, broad compilation could realistically serve the needs of Congress and of the legal system. Hamilton and Madison agreed that only a positive statement of power could encompass all the various manifestations this clause could come into contact with.

Writing after the turn of the nineteenth century, in 1803, St. George Tucker, a prominent jurist, professor, and editor of Blackstone's *Commentaries* for an American audience, expanded on the nature and role of the necessary and proper clause. Tucker stated, "It neither enlarges any power specifically granted, nor is it a grant of new power to congress, but merely a declaration, for the removal of all uncertainty, that the means of carrying into execution those otherwise granted, are included in the grant."[37] Tucker, with the hindsight of fifteen years of constitutional operation, clearly sided with the Hamilton/Madison argument without necessarily invoking the issue of individual liberty or states' rights as a possible negative consequence of the clause.

No branch of the government fully explored the status of the acts from a constitutional standpoint. This is a far different situation which attended to the issue involving the Invalids Pension Act in the *Hayburn* case. First, the full Supreme Court never heard a case involving the acts. The justices heard cases in circuit court while on their circuit, but never assembled as the Supreme Court. Secondly, with all the branches of the government run by adherents to a particular political philosophy, the genuineness of any trial at the Supreme Court would be highly suspect to say the least.[38] The nature of this relationship (where leaders "partook of the majesty of the whole people") had been defined by William Blackstone in 1765 in his *Commentaries on the Laws of England*.[39] Thirdly, the Sedition Act was designed to expire in March of 1801, after the 1800 presidential election, thus pointing to a further political motive.[40] In 1802, the Alien Act expired and Congress returned the Naturalization Law to its pre–1798 language. The Alien Enemies Act however remained in effect. Fourth, the main Republican opponents of the acts, Thomas Jefferson and James Madison, fought the premise and rationale of the acts through the states and sought to draw a distinction between federal power and state acceptance of that power (another very common theme during the 1790s Court).

Madison and Jefferson realized a fight on the federal level was pointless and took their argument directly to the states in the form of resolutions. This acknowledgment of hopelessness stemmed from not only the Federalist control of the federal government, but also from a realization that the common law argument for seditious liable was won by the Federalists concerning their efforts to keep the trials out of state court. The essence of the Federalists' argument for constitutionality was that the federal courts had already been granted common law authority and thus the acts were legal and proper to try in federal court, as seditious liable was a common law recognized crime and thus capable of being codified by statute.[41]

Two resolutions (one adopted by the Kentucky Legislature—written by Jefferson—and one by the Virginia Legislature—written by Madison) sought to strike a defiant tone for states' rights. The resolutions argued the states had the ultimate power of deciding the constitutionality of federal legislation, not the Supreme Court. The resolutions did not cause the Federalists to have a change of heart, and the resolutions faded until they were resurrected in part by John C. Calhoun in the 1830s to support his strident states' rights theories. In a sense, the whole states' rights theory, as it evolved in the United States, pitted the natural law concepts adopted by the Federalists in 1798 (the federal courts, and hence, the federal government, as inheritors of the common law mantle), against the quasi-statutory argument adopted by Jefferson and Madison (arguing the states were the source of law, not the natural law). It is not a far stretch to say this reasoning led in a straight line to the Civil War and beyond.[42] In fact, it was roughly halfway between these two periods, when the Supreme Court ruled in *U.S. v. Hudson and Goodwin* (1812), that "the United States did not possess common-law jurisdiction over the crimes of seditious libel."[43] The notion of natural law versus statutory law seems not to have really ever been settled.

The Supreme Court justices, through their circuit-riding-duty role, dispensed with numerous cases working through the system in favor of the federal government and against the defendants. These decisions surprised no one, although the ferocity with which one justice in particular, Samuel Chase, pursued the prosecution would eventually lead to his impeachment, but not conviction, in 1805. Chase's behavior had particularly raised concern, even among Federalists, when he sentenced John Fries to death for treason under the Sedition Act after Fries's defense counsel resigned in outrage, leaving Fries defenseless.[44]

Justice William Paterson of New Jersey, sitting on circuit court duty in Rutland, Vermont, was credited with achieving the first successful judgment on October 5, 1798.[45] Paterson secured a guilty verdict not just against an ordinary citizen, but against United States Representative Matthew Lyon. Lyon was indicted on three counts: publishing a seditious letter in the *Vermont Journal*; libeling the president and Senate; and aiding and abetting the publication of his letter.[46] After his imprisonment, Lyon would be re-elected in a campaign he managed from prison.[47]

In a charge to the grand jury on October 3, 1798, Paterson spoke in laudatory tones on the nature and purpose of law and the roles the grand jury played. Paterson also informed the grand jury of "two species of offences, which, under the existing circumstances of the United States, merit your particular attention."[48] The first offense was forgery of notes issued by the Bank of the United States. The second was "unlawful combinations and conspiracies, seditious practices, and false, scandalous, and malicious writings, publications, and libels against the government of the United States."[49] Paterson continued with a description of the Sedition Act which strained the credulity of modern judicial impartiality. Paterson used descriptive language which left no question as to his view: "odious," "destructive," "wound," "injury," "sins." "No government, indeed, can long subsist, where offenders of this kind are suffered to spread their poison with impunity."[50] Paterson reminded the jury that power resided with the people, and every citizen, as part of "the people," has the duty to support the people.[51] Paterson ended with, "libelous publications and seditious practices are inconsistent with genuine freedom."[52]

Justice Paterson's charge to the grand jury can be seen as representative of the charges delivered by the other justices (James Wilson died in August of 1798 and was not a major participant in the Alien and Sedition Acts trials; his successor, Bushrod Washington, was, as mentioned, an active participant) in their impaneling of a grand jury on their respective circuits. Although the style and magnitude no doubt differed to accommodate individual personalities, the general outlines pertaining to the need to protect the government and the country are clearly similar. What would today be seen as a violation of judicial neutrality was seen as forceful advocacy in 1798. Federalist Congressman James Bayard commented on this practice of judges expounding theory or invective language before a trial.[53] Thomas Jefferson saw the biased charges to grand juries as, "a perversion of the institution of the grand jury from a legal to a political engine."[54]

In pursuit of those who would threaten the American government, the justices, between 1798 and 1800, displayed perhaps their most partisan feelings. In Federalist thinking, when American security was threatened, the American legal system needed to respond. The Federalist envisioned a threat which in reality was not only from France (the weak threat), but from the Jeffersonians (the strong threat) as well. The Supreme Court in some measure could be seen as contributing to the Jeffersonian victory in 1800. What appeared to many as the Court's blatant insertion into politics caused a crisis of confidence in the way the country viewed the Federalists commitment to republican principles. A major component of republican principles with which the Federalists now found themselves at odds was the notion of where governmental power ultimately resides?

One aspect that could be seen as hindering the alien and sedition laws from full operation were the relatively small number of federal judges available to handle the cases. The laws were designed to ensnare a large number of people. William Cooper, in a letter to Oliver Wolcott, Jr., on August 20, 1799, wrote, "Many evils that exist in the United States might be remedied or cured by altering the law for establishing judicial courts in the United States. I mean that of having more judges in each state ... with power to take up and try seditious persons...."[55] The idea that a law, Alien and Sedition, generated so many violations within a year of being enacted seems absurd. So many violations were generated that additional courts and judges were deemed necessary, although not hired, to deal with the number of offenders apprehended. This is one aspect of the laws which the Republicans heavily criticized.

A civil war over constitutional issues had been fought among Englishmen from 1775 to 1783. The war ostensibly was fought to reverse the common law dictum maintaining that the governed were inferior to the governors. The Constitution, in the preamble, unequivocally declared that "We the People" formed the government and breathed life into it. Quite the contrary by 1798, the Federalists sought to not only subvert constitutional law with common law, they sought to regain the exalted position of the governors relative to the governed.[56] Perhaps it can be said that the Federalist took a queue from King George III who proclaimed in his war message of 1775 that he was taking action for "suppressing rebellion and *sedition* [emphasis added]."[57]

Virginia and Kentucky Resolutions

The Virginians James Madison and Thomas Jefferson, through their Virginia and Kentucky Resolutions in response to the Alien and Sedition Acts of 1798, charged that the acts inferred a federal common law within the Constitution while the Congress, dominated by Federalists who supported the acts, argued the resolutions were wrong.

The acts were one of the first great political fights in the young country. The Federalists, who controlled the presidency, Congress, and the judiciary, sought the legislation to prevent libelous commentary about the government from being printed. They also sought to prevent non-citizens from entering the country to prevent threats of foreign intervention. Ostensibly, the Federalists grouped multiple laws together during the height of the Quasi-War with France. They were designed to limit immigration, prevent written or spoken criticism of the government, and to antagonize Jefferson's Republicans. The Federalists did not view the First Amendment as giving protection against libelous attacks against the government. Federalists also argued that "the federal courts could punish sedition under common law."[58] The Republicans countered that if the charge be true concerning common law, why did a new statute need to be written? The Federalists countered they wanted to clarify beyond the common law definition and relied heavily on British Parliamentarian Charles James Fox's Libel Act of 1792. The one important aspect of the Federalists' acts was that it allowed for truth as a defense, unlike the British Act of 1792. As Jefferson scholar Merrill Peterson has written, the Alien and Sedition Acts were designed "to cripple and destroy the Republican opposition under the pretense of saving the country from anarchists, demagogues, and incendiaries…. And in the climate of fear and suspicion the Federalists had created, what would be the benefit of the boasted safeguards."[59]

James Madison, writing anonymously in the Virginia Resolutions, approached the common law idea in classic Madison fashion—detailed, long, and laborious. Madison wrote that the Federalists sought to build the foundation of the acts upon common law, "a law of vast extent of complexity, and embracing almost every possible subject of legislation, both civil and criminal…."[60] Madison, as he often did, offered a historical lesson concerning the common law in the colonies:

> In the state prior to the revolution, it is certain that the common law under different limitations, made a part of the colonial codes. But whether it be understood that the original colonists brought the law with them, or made it their law by adoption; it is equally certain that it was the separate law of each colony within its respective limits, and was unknown to them, as a law pervading and operating through the whole, as one society.[61]

Madison was very careful not to insinuate that the common law was a national law when he wrote: "It is equally certain that it was the separate law of each colony within its respective limits, and was unknown to them, as a law pervading and operating through the whole, as one society."[62] This was a crucial point as the Federalists claimed the Alien and Sedition Acts, in part, were viable based upon an understanding that a national common law existed. Madison continued: "The common law was not the same in any two of the colonies; in some, the modifications were materially and extensively different. There was no common legislature, by which a common will, could be expressed in the form of a law; nor any common magistracy, by which such a law could be carried into practice."[63]

As the Federalists also claimed that the Constitution established a federal common law, Madison acknowledged "that particular parts of the common law, may have a sanction from the constitution."[64] After pages of examples and argument, Madison concluded "that the common law never was, nor by any fair construction, ever can be, deemed a law for the American people as one community."[65] In fact, Madison saw nothing but danger in viewing a national common law in the Constitution: "A law filling so many ample volumes; a law overspreading the entire field of legislation; and a law that would sap the foundation of the constitution as a system of limited and specified powers."[66]

Julius Goebel, in his massive study of the early Supreme Court, saw the common law issue as a distraction raised by the Federalists during the Alien and Sedition Acts fight. Goebel wrote, "The common law was plainly a contrived issue, for the conflict was essentially one over opposing political philosophies."[67] No thorough discussion, aside from Madison's lengthy missive known as the Virginia Resolutions, were held. No great debate occurred in Congress. As Goebel pointed out, "The problem was never adequately considered on the level it deserved."[68] Yet, as he wrote, in the first year or two of the federal Congress, Madison voted for several measures which seemed to indicate an understanding of a functioning federal common law. Goebel wrote, "Demonstrably sections of these were either direct borrowings from the common law or were premised upon a belief that recourse to the common law was warranted by the Constitution."[69]

What Goebel, and others, were pointing out was that the American legal system was not as organic as many at the time, and many even today, liked to think. The concept or idea of law and legal systems was not far removed from the Founders, and it was impossible for the Founders to have not been influenced by foreign systems, especially Britain's. It was a common practice at the time not to preface common law with the word English; in other words, if not English common law, then which common law?[70] It only shows how complicated it was in the 1790s to follow and participate in the process. Goebel continued:

> But there were some who used the term in the sense of legal institutions common to all states, and others who spoke of it in the sense of a law reduced to possession and altered by the several states. The lack of consensus on the meaning of what had become fighting words seems to have blocked consideration of the extent to which the Constitution as amended was an instrument of reception.[71]

It should be remembered that the argument over a federal common law dealt with criminal, not civil, common law. In the end, neither the Federalists nor the Republicans pushed the common law issue to the point of no return. It was too complicated and complex (and expensive) to revisit the decisions of the Constitutional Convention of 1787.

Updating the Judiciary Act

By 1800, as the United States continued to press westward, the tribulation of circuit riding became more pronounced—not just the distance involved, but the immensely difficult terrain between the Mississippi and Ohio River Valleys region. In most instances, only one or two roads had been hacked through the wilderness to Kentucky, Tennessee, Indiana, Ohio, and other states west of the Appalachia mountains. Henry Innes, writing to John Brown, on March 5, 1800, sounded these themes when he wrote:

> If the circuit is established [Western] one idea has often occurred in the course of my reflections, ... that no particular advantage can be denied by compelling the judges who may ride circuit here, to attend the supreme court. The distance to the federal city is great—the road uncomfortable. The judges will be men advancing in years, ... The courts of this [Kentucky] and the Tennessee district are now in that situation.[72]

Eighteen hundred was a busy year for Congress concerning the judiciary, when yet another bill was offered to amend the original 1789 Act to account not just for the by now decade-old complaints about the 1789 Act, but also to account for the increase in population and the addition of new states (Kentucky, Tennessee, and Ohio). Elizur Goodrich, in a letter to David Daggett on March 27, 1800, wrote: "We are employed on the judiciary bill [the Harper Judiciary Bill of 1800 which became the Judiciary Act of 1801] which I don't think will pass this session in its present shape. It contemplates a supreme court *stationary* at the seat of government; twenty nine districts, divided into nine circuits [emphasis in original]...."[73]

Thomas Boylston Adams, in a letter to his brother John Quincy Adams, wrote on April 1, 1800, that: "The bill reported to Congress for improving the judiciary system, has met with great opposition. It will not pass as reported, though a modification of it may. Consolidation of the states is the bugbear so much dreaded, and private views in some instances get the better of devotion to the public cause."[74] Adams brought to light the continuing issues involved with administering a national legal system: sovereign states. In the balance of federalism, where did states' rights end and national rights begin? This was what nearly wrecked the country immediately after the Revolution and it was still an issue in 1800. It would be a topic that would only continue to grow in complexity.

Andrew Gregg voiced this concern over states' rights in an April 18, 1800, letter to William Irvine. Gregg noted:

> A few days ago we rejected the judiciary bill by a majority of two. As this bill pointed more openly at a consolidation of the government, than any one measure that has ever been before congress, its rejection has afforded no small pleasure to those, who are anxious for preserving the sovereignty and independence of the state governments....[75]

The difficulty of the 1800 Judiciary Bill can best be summarized in an April 15, 1800, letter from Benjamin Bourne to Ray Greene: "The Judiciary Bill appears to have a very hard time in its gestation insomuch that I think it questionable if it does not perish before its birth."[76]

One of the recurring complaints about the original Judiciary Act of 1789 were the hardships imposed by the Act on the administration of justice due to the geographic distance involved. This argument harkens back to similar arguments about the proper size of a republic. These debates, especially during the Constitutional Convention of 1787, centered on whether the United States was too large a territory to efficiently administer. In many ways, this argument had its greatest impact in the realm of the national judiciary.

By 1801, the Federalists, knowing that their candidate, President John Adams had lost to Republican Thomas Jefferson, pressed ardently for the passage of the new Judiciary Act, making it one of their top priorities. In its basic outline, it strengthened the federal legal system much to the dismay of the states. The Republican newspaper the *Aurora* offered this assessment of the 1801 Judiciary Act:

> The judiciary bill merits public regard from the time and intention of it. That there are defects in our federal judiciary system is true, but that the present bill is calculated to cure them, is not true; it is rather calculated to increase the public expense, the quantity of litigation, and to enfeeble and impair the course of justice in the state courts.[77]

Robert Goodloe Harper, the main force behind the new act, wrote to his constituents on February 26, 1801:

> The most important act of Congress which has passed in the present session, is that for regulating the courts of the United States....
>
> The new system relieves the judges from this intolerable labor [circuit riding], reduces their number to five, and assigns them no other duty but that of holding the supreme court at the seat of government....
>
> There are two states, Tennessee and Kentucky, in which, on account of their very remote situation, no circuit courts could be held....[78]

Many states' rights advocates (Jefferson and his Republicans) saw the 1801 Judiciary Act as an attempt to further weaken the power of the states in the federal system through siphoning power away from their courts. It was widely seen as a partisan act and it did not stand. A year after its passage the Republicans repealed it and reverted to the standards of the previous 1789 Act.

John Marshall, newly minted chief justice of the United States, and a Federalist of moderate leanings, found the new act to be beneficial for the Court. Writing to fellow Justice William Paterson, Marshall, on February 2, 1801, reported that he saw the main benefit of the new act to be "the separation of the judges of the supreme from those of the circuit courts."[79] This was to be effected by removing justices from the circuit court system. This was a benefit for all the justices, not just Marshall. Not having to ride circuit was something the justices had been wishing for since 1789. The arduous duty of traveling America's less than functional road system and lodging in less than congenial boarding houses was not going to be missed by the justices. However, it was not to be.

9

Presidents Washington and Adams and the Law

It has already been pointed out numerous times in this book that George Washington, upon his election as president, wrote eloquently about the role of the judiciary in the new government under the Constitution. Washington's approach to the third branch of government was one that worked in seamless harmony both independently and in conjunction with the other two branches. Naturally, this observation was in part created by the exuberant expectations of a new government. In practice, there was a tremendous amount of work that needed to be done. This was work both required of all these branches of government individually and combined. Washington, with other members, was no doubt aware of this.

In the choice of his first six nominees to the Supreme Court (Wilson, Jay, Rutledge, Cushing, Harrison/Iredell, and Blair), Washington choose accomplished jurists; all of them capable of performing their duties. As a whole, they were not deep legal thinkers (with the exception of Wilson and Jay) but more assembly-line workers in the field of law. This is not to in any way demean the justices; rather, it highlights the fact that none, with the exceptions of Jay and Wilson, were the types of expansive thinkers necessary to create and frame a new branch of government. While they were not visionaries, they were however capable and committed to the role of the judiciary in the new government.

Politics

President George Washington is often portrayed as being above the political fray on most issues, and in many he was. However, he could not avoid the swirling vortex enveloping his first administration, no matter how hard he tried. It was a vortex which was soon to collide with the naive hopes of a unified government free from faction. President Washington, who genuinely sought consensus, rarely found it. In his view, the economic approaches of his secretary of the treasury Alexander Hamilton were truly inspired to benefit all of America. In creating a strong national government, Hamilton and the president sought to strengthen the ties between the states: "The means to accomplish this alliance were the establishment of a national bank, the funding by the national government of the confederate and state debts at their face value, and the adoption of a protective tariff with a comprehensive system of protection or bounties to aid industrial development in the United States."[1] President Washington watched with dismay as his secretary of state Thomas Jefferson reacted negatively to such ventures. From these humble beginnings, the political party system quickly gained momentum. This momentum would not take long to reach the Supreme Court. By the end of the 1790s, the Court was seen as overtly political. Even early on in the 1790s, Secretary of the Treasury Alexander Hamilton sought to have Chief Justice John Jay weigh in on the appropriateness of his funding strategy. Jay would not take the offer, calling for the Court to remain silent unless or until the issue came before it as a case.[2]

John Adams

Unlike George Washington, who had to consider multiple factors and ask for direction due to his lack of legal training, John Adams had no such handicap. Adams could intuitively know who was and was not legal material for the Supreme Court, or any other court position. "Adams did not consult with advisers, communicate with individuals knowledgeable about proposed candidates, or contact the candidates themselves."[3] Interestingly, Adams felt the "Constitution was flawed in mixing the executive and legislative branches in the appointment process."[4] Adams saw, as this book has pointed out, that the Supreme Court was a hybrid of the other two branches and as such was, and is, forever being toyed and tinkered with. The Constitution framers could have made a much easier system by simply creating a judiciary branch, like the legislative or executive, that would simply operate as the legislative or executive did, rather than waiting to be created by the will of the other two branches.

Adams himself, aside from his personality, would have been an excellent Supreme Court Justice. So, he knew, unlike Washington, about legal ability and training. Washington also added factors such as the level a nominee contributed to the Revolution whereas Adams did not.[5] Sadly, this trait soon gave way to political factors by the Adams administration.

Another difference in how the two presidents approached the picking of justices was that Washington, again partly due to his lack of legal training, would enquire about possible nominees and would generally ensure that they would consent to the nomination if chosen. Washington, always concerned for the appearance of situations, did not want a scenario where he offered a position only to have it rejected. He felt this was not only bad form personally, but bad optics for the young country. "He inquired freely of senators and congressmen as to qualified individuals in their states."[6] Washington mulled over nominations and rarely acted in haste, a trait that applied to nearly every aspect of his life. The fiasco over the nomination of John Rutledge to the position of chief justice caused Washington much distress and angst: not only because Rutledge was a friend and colleague, but because it was the first replacement of a chief justice on the Court—a significant role seemingly brought low by the antics of Rutledge (although to be fair he did suffer from mental illness).

Finally, Adams had to deal with the very real prospect of a new Judiciary Act (passed in 1801) reducing the number of justices from six to five. Adams was determined not to let the Court lose a seat and hurriedly appointed John Marshall as chief, which led to the stories of the appointment of "midnight judges" to fill other federal vacancies. That is an entirely separate story that goes beyond the reach of this book.

A Federal Common Law

The eighteenth century marked a watershed moment in the way law was grounded in the English-speaking world. In Great Britain, the common law (alluded to multiple times already) was an established fact. In the colonies, it was practiced with great regularity.

In its simplest form, the common law is exactly as what it sounds to be: common. It was, and is, a law system applicable to all; a law in its most common construction which can be applied to most common types of cases. In Britain, the common law, by the eighteenth century, had a long pedigree which in some instances was lost to the mists of time. It was an approach to law that was enshrined in a constitution that did not exist in written form. Britain did not, and to this day does not, have a written constitution. Yet, it was this unwritten constitution that so many of the Founders saw themselves being deprived of by Britain during the years leading to the Revolution, even though the colonies generally followed this system from 1607 to 1776, when most states wrote their own constitutions. Furthermore, the colonies, soon to be states, abandoned this free-form approach to law and opted for written constitutions. It would be another ten years after 1776 before the entire country would take such a collective approach to a legal and governmental system. The Constitution of 1787 was in many respects just as revolutionary as the actions of the military struggle for independence during the late 1770s. Even with this new reliance on a written system of law and government, the idea of a common law was still prevalent in American legal thinking and would resurface before the end of the eighteenth century in the Supreme Court.

The common law approach was invoked in the early 1790s in part due to an absence of precedent especially within the Supreme Court. Nearly all the justices referred to the common law in their writings and opinions in some manner. The Supreme Court was considered a common law court in that it placed great merit on the concept of judicial precedent. Naturally, one glaring problem with this is that relying on precedent without factoring in new contingencies created a situation of seeing the law of the past ascribed to the present. Again, while not in and of itself inaccurate, it is nonetheless a narrow and myopic approach to life and shows why each case must be handled on its own unique circumstance and within its own period. Scores of later nineteenth-century writers observed that the fast-expanding America of 1850 could hardly be held in place by precedents of 1800. "Beginning sometime in the 1780s and reaching a high point in the first decade of the nineteenth century, American jurists succeeded in dethroning the common law from the unchallenged place it had occupied in the jurisprudence of the revolutionary generation."[7] In fact, these concepts are debated to this very day, especially when a vacancy occurs on the Supreme Court.

The Constitutional Convention did not think it wise to limit the Supreme Court to issues of congressional lawmaking.[8] This proscription would have dramatically limited the role of the Court and would have greatly reduced its impact on American life—much to the detriment of American life. The bulk of the developments concerning common law in the Supreme Court postdate the period covered by this book and will not be reviewed. In fact, one of the most important books on American law, simply titled *The Common Law*, by Oliver Wendell Holmes, Jr., was published in 1881. In the twentieth century, the Court ruled in *Erie Railroad v. Tompkins* that "there is no federal general common law."[9] This aside, the issue is far from resolved: "Federal common law is an important part of our tradition of case-by-case adjudication, allowing the judiciary to resolve unforeseen issues fairly; federal common law shows no signs of diminishing in importance."[10]

As legal historian Morton Horwitz wrote, the greatest issue, to the mind of eighteenth-century American jurists, was that the common law was simply too unpredictable.[11] Given the tremendous uncertainties of the American War for Independence, the last thing American leaders needed was more uncertainty. America, like an offspring born in the wild, needed to be able to run with the business of government immediately after independence was achieved. The Founders did not have the luxury of adapting centuries of legal maturation into a system of law. America needed a system based on a verifiable document, a manuscript which, allowing for changes, would form the foundation of a government, a society, and a civilization.

The paradigm altering shift from common law would include its nearest cousin, natural law. As legal scholar Morton Horwitz wrote, "In short, common law doctrines were derived from natural principles of justice, statutes were acts of will; common law rules were discerned, statutes were made."[12] As the Declaration of Independence founded its grounding in natural law, the Constitution did not. As the Founders, "sought to redefine the basis of legal obligation in terms of popular sovereignty, they tended to assert the ultimate primacy of the legislative and of statute law."[13]

The 1790s

Throughout the decade of the 1790s, the Justices grappled with many issues in forming the new Supreme Court, and by extension American law. The notion of what to do with acts not specifically called for in the Constitution or involving statute law was ever present. Actions believed to be criminal but not specified, needed, if prosecuted, to be grounded in some legal framework. Chief Justice Ellsworth, writing in 1799, saw such instances as being liable to prosecution based on "the rules of a known law, matured by the reason of ages and which Americans have ever been tenacious of as a birthright."[14] Chief Justice Ellsworth's views were not taken by everyone, there was a considerable viewpoint contrary to him which held his comments "deeply abhorrent" and "who believed that the powers of the government were restricted to the express grants of the Constitution."[15] The attempt to parse the meaning of a possible American common law was approached by James Madison in *Federalist* 42. According to Madison:

> Neither the common, nor the statute law of that [Britain] or any other nation ought to be a standard for the proceedings of this, unless previously made its own by legislative adoption. The meaning of the term as defined in the codes of the several states, would be as impracticable as the former would be a dishonorable and illegitimate guide. It is not precisely the same in any two of the states; and varies in each with every revision of its criminal law.[16]

Madison seemed unsure about how much credibility to lend to common law in the proposed Constitution when he wrote the essay. This passage serves to highlight how fluid the forms and applications of law were during the late 1780s and early 1790s. Indeed, during the decades leading to the Revolution, there was great "uncertainty as to whether they [judges] were entitled at all to use and apply common law rules in the newly settled land. It seems therefore that, at most, the judges were looking to the legislature for authority to impose common law standards in criminal cases."[17]

The anonymous writer known as "The Impartial Examiner" wrote an essay in the *Virginia Independent Chronicle* on February 27, 1788, wherein he saw the absolute need for a common law, especially when in connection with trial by jury. In some instances, the anonymous writer stated, "The much admired common law process will give way to some quick and summary mode, by which the unhappy defendant will find himself reduced, perhaps to ruin, in less time than a change could be exhibited against him in the usual course."[18] The writer clearly saw common law as a benefit for the accused in a trial.

In Hamilton's review of the Supreme Court in *The Federalist* papers, he looked at the role of the common law with the Court in essay 81. Published in newspaper form on May 28, 1788, Hamilton argued that:

> The appellate jurisdiction of the Supreme Court ... will extend to causes determinable in different modes, some in the course of the COMMON LAW, and others in the course of the CIVIL LAW. In the former, the revision of the law only, will be, generally speaking, the proper province of the Supreme Court; in the latter, the reexamination of the fact is agreeable to usage, and in some cases, of which prize causes an example, might be essential to the preservation of the public peace [emphasis in original].[19]

During the state ratification process in 1788, most states went beyond a simple yes or no vote on the proposed Constitution. Many wrote resolutions on several topics related to the Constitution. The state of New York for example expressed their strong support for the common law concept and for the trial by jury: "That the trial by jury in the extent that it obtains by the common law of England is one of the greatest securities to the rights of a free people and ought to remain inviolate."[20]

The State of Massachusetts too had strong views of the trial by jury concept. Their resolutions stated: "In civil actions, between citizens of different states, every issue of fact arising in actions at common law shall be tried by a jury, if the parties, or either of them, request it."[21]

Similarly, neighboring New Hampshire expressed a desire that: "All common law causes between citizens of different states shall be commenced in the common law courts of the respective states—and no appeal shall be allowed to the federal court in such cases, unless the sum or value of the thing in controversy amount to 3,000 dollars."[22] Virginia delegates to the state's ratifying convention were among the most vocal critics for not adopting a common law through the Constitution as any of their colleagues in other states.[23]

It is abundantly clear that James Madison, later in his responses to the Alien and Sedition Acts in 1798, was much aware of the debate over common law, jury trial, and the application of both separately, or together, in criminal and/or civil cases. There was indeed a lot to unravel for the justices during the first decade of the United States under the new Constitution.

Appendix A: Article III
of the United States Constitution

Section 1

The judicial power of the United States, shall be vested in one supreme court, and in such inferior courts as the Congress may, from time to time, ordain and establish. The judges, both of the supreme and inferior courts, shall hold their offices during good behavior, and shall, at stated times, receive for their services a compensation, which shall not be diminished during their continuance in office.

Section 2

1. The judicial power shall extend to all cases, in law and equity, arising under this constitution, the laws of the United States, and treaties made, or which shall be made under their authority; to all cases affecting ambassadors, other public ministers and consuls; to all cases of admiralty and maritime jurisdiction; to controversies to which the United States shall be a party; to controversies between two or more states, between a state and Citizens of another state, between Citizens of different states, between Citizens of the same state, claiming lands under grants of different states, and between a state, or the Citizens thereof, and foreign states, Citizens or subjects. [*This section is modified by Amendment XI.*]

2. In all cases affecting ambassadors, other public ministers and consuls, and those in which a state shall be a party, the supreme court shall have original jurisdiction. In all the other cases before-mentioned, the supreme court shall have appellate jurisdiction, both as to law and fact, with such exceptions, and under such regulations as the Congress shall make.

3. The trial of all crimes, except in cases of impeachment, shall be by

jury; and such trial shall be held in the state where the said crimes shall have been committed; but when not committed within any state, the trial shall be at such place or places as the Congress may by law have directed.

Section 3

1. Treason against the United States shall consist only in levying war against them, or in adhering to their enemies, giving them aid and comfort. No person shall be convicted of treason unless on the testimony of two witnesses to the same overt act, or on confession in open court.

2. The Congress shall have power to declare the punishment of treason, but no attainder of treason shall work corruption of blood, or forfeiture, except during the life of the person attainted.

Appendix B: Selections from the Judiciary Act of 1789

The September 24, 1789, Judiciary Act, primarily the work of Senators Oliver Ellsworth and William Paterson (both future Supreme Court justices), is an enormous document. Below are some of the opening sections of the act which provide an instructive general overview of the law.[1]

Section 1. *Be it enacted,* That the supreme court of the United States shall consist of a chief justice and five associate justices, any four of whom shall be a quorum, and shall hold annually at the seat of government two sessions, the one commencing the first Monday of February, and the other the first Monday of August. That the associate justices shall have precedence according to the date of their commissions, or when the commissions of two or more of them bear date on the same day, according to their respective ages.

Section 2. That the United States shall be, and they hereby are, divided into thirteen districts....

Section 3. That there be a court called a District Court in each of the aforementioned districts, to consist of one judge, who shall reside in the district for which he is appointed....

Section 13. That the Supreme Court shall have exclusive jurisdiction of all controversies of a civil nature, where a state is a party, except between a state and its citizens; and except also between a state and citizens of other states, or aliens, in which latter case it shall have original but not exclusive jurisdiction. And shall have exclusively all such jurisdiction of suits or proceedings against ambassadors or other public ministers, or their domestics, or domestic servants, as a court of law can have or exercise consistently with the law of nations; and original, but not exclusive jurisdiction of all suits brought by ambassadors or other public ministers, or in which a consul or vice-consul shall be a party. And the trial of issues in fact in the Supreme Court in all actions at law against citizens of the United States shall be by jury. The Supreme Court shall also have appellate jurisdiction from the circuit courts and courts of the several States in the cases herein after specially provided for; and shall have power to issue writs of prohibition to the district courts, when proceeding as courts of admiralty and maritime jurisdiction, and writs of mandamus, in cases warranted by the principle and usages of law, to any courts appointed, or person holding office under the authority of the United States....

That a final judgment or decree in any suit, in the highest court of law or equity of a State in which a decision in the suit could be had, where is drawn in question the validity of a treaty or statute of, or an authority exercised under, the United States, and the decision is against their validity; or where is drawn in question the validity of a statute of, or an authority exercised under, any State, on the ground of their being repugnant to the constitution, treaties, or laws of the United States, and the decision is in favor of their validity, or where is drawn in question the construction of any clause of the constitution, treaty, statute, or commission, may be reexamined, and reversed or affirmed in the Supreme Court of the United States upon a writ of error, the citation being signed by the chief justice, or judge or chancellor of the court rendering or passing the judgment or decree complained of, or by a justice of the Supreme Court of the United States, in the same manner and under the same regulations, and the writ shall have the same effect as if the judgment or decree complained of had been rendered or passed in a circuit court, and the proceedings upon the reversal shall also be the same, except that the Supreme Court, instead of remanding the cause for a final decision as before provided, may, at their discretion, if the cause shall have been once remanded before, proceed to a final decision of the same, and award execution. But no other error shall be assigned or regarded as a ground of reversal in any such case as aforesaid, than such as appears on the face of the record, and immediately respects the before-mentioned questions of validity or construction of the said Constitution, treaties, statutes, commissions, or authorities in dispute....

Appendix C: Chief Justice John Jay's Instructions to a New York Grand Jury, April 4, 1790

Whether any people can long govern themselves in an equal, uniform, and orderly manner, is a question which the advocates for free government justly consider as being exceedingly important to the cause of liberty.[1] This question, like others whose solution depends on facts, can only be determined by experience. It is a question on which many think some room for doubt still remains. Men have had very few fair opportunities of making the experiment; and this is one reason why less progress has been made in the science of government than in almost any other. The far greater number of the constitutions and governments of which we are informed have originated in force or in fraud, having been either imposed by improper exertions of power, or introduced by the arts of designing individuals, whose apparent zeal for liberty and public good enabled them to take advantage of the credulity and misplaced confidence of their fellow-citizens....

Wise and virtuous men have thought and reasoned very differently respecting government, but in this they have at length very unanimously agreed, viz., that its powers should be divided into three distinct, independent departments—the executive, legislative, and judicial. But how to constitute and balance them in such a manner as best to guard against abuse and fluctuation, and preserve the Constitution from encroachments, are points on which there continues to be a great diversity of opinions, and on which we have all as yet much to learn. The Constitution of the United States has accordingly instituted these three departments, and much pains have been taken so to form and define them as that they may operate as checks one upon the other, and keep each within its proper limits; it being universally agreed to be of the last importance to a free people, that they who are vested with executive, legislative, and judicial powers should rest satisfied with their respective portions of power, and neither encroach on the provinces of each other, nor suffer themselves to intermeddle with the rights reserved by the Constitution to the people. If, then, so much depends on our rightly improving the beforementioned opportunities, if the most discerning and enlightened minds may be mistaken relative to theories unconfirmed by practice, if on such difficult questions men may differ in opinion and yet be patriots, and if the merits of our opinions can only be ascertained by experience, let us patiently abide the trial, and unite our endeavors to render it a fair and an impartial one....

We had become a nation. As such we were responsible to others for the observance of the *Laws of Nations;* and as our national concerns were to be regulated by *national laws*, national tribunals became necessary for the interpretation and execution of them both. No tribunals of the like kind and of extent had heretofore existed in this country. From such, therefore, no light of experience nor facilities of usage and habit were to be derived. Our jurisprudence varied in almost every state, and was accommodated to local, not general convenience; to partial, not national policy. This convenience and this policy were nevertheless to be regarded and tenderly treated. A judicial control, general and final, was indispensable; the manner of establishing it with powers neither too extensive nor too limited, rendering it properly independent, and yet properly amenable, involved questions of no little intricacy.

The expediency of carrying justice, as it were, to every man's door, was obvious; but how to do it in an expedient manner was far from being apparent. To provide against discord between national and state jurisdictions, to render them auxiliary instead of hostile to each other, and so to connect both as to leave each sufficiently independent, and yet sufficiently combined, was and will be arduous....

It cannot be too strongly impressed on the minds of us all how greatly our individual prosperity depends on our national prosperity, and how greatly our national prosperity depends on a well-organized, vigorous government, ruling by wise and equal laws, faithfully executed; nor is such a government unfriendly to liberty—to that liberty which is really inestimable; on the contrary, nothing but a strong government of laws irresistibly bearing down arbitrary power and licentiousness can defend it against those two formidable enemies. Let it be remembered that civil liberty consists not in a right to every man to do just what he please, but it consists in an equal right to all the citizens to have, enjoy, and to do, in peace, security, and without molestation, whatever the equal and constitutional laws of the country admit to be consistent with the public good. It is the duty and the interest, therefore, of all good citizens, in their several stations, to support the laws and the government which thus protect their rights and liberties.

Appendix D:
President John Adams
and John Jay

The famous story of President John Adams offering the chief justice position to John Marshall is a classic American tale, but the reason why Adams had to offer it to Marshall is somewhat less known. When Chief Justice Oliver Ellsworth resigned in December 1800, John Jay, former chief justice and soon to be former governor of New York, was looking forward to retirement at his home in Katonah, New York. President Adams nominated Jay without his approval and sent Jay a letter stating as much on December 19, 1800. The letter Jay wrote back to the president is something of a classic itself in that it highlights the major problems that were festering within the Supreme Court during the past decade.

There was the ever-present issue of circuit riding, something both Presidents Washington and Adams acknowledged was a problem and sought to have the Congress respond to. Naturally, retirement was a strong lure for someone like Jay who had spent his entire adult life in the service of the United States. From the very beginning in the early 1770s, Jay had placed himself at the service of his country. He was a revolutionary and sought American freedom and independence as a natural outgrowth of the colonial experience. Jay served both the United States and his home state of New York and genuinely felt the Supreme Court, as it operated in 1800, was a thankless branch of the government.

That is not to suggest he felt the administration of law under the Constitution to be valueless, quite the contrary. What Jay found reprehensible was the way the Court had failed to be seen as equal by the executive and legislative; how the Court was becoming a political playground where its members had no say whatsoever in how events played out. All of that could have changed with a strong leader, but Jay was not that man. The task called for a young man (Marshall was ten years younger than Jay) who was willing to go head-to-head with the other branches.

Jay wrote to President Adams:

> I have been honored with your letter of the 19th ult. informing me that I had been nominated to fill the office of Chief Justice of the United States, and yesterday I received the commission. This nomination so strongly manifests your esteem, that it affords me particular satisfaction....
>
> I left the bench perfectly convinced that under a system so defective it would not obtain the energy, weight, and dignity which are essential to its affording due support to the national government, nor acquire the public confidence and respect which, as the last resort of the justice of the nation, it should possess. Hence I am induced to doubt both the propriety and the expediency of my returning to the bench under the present system; especially as it would give some countenance to the neglect and indifference with which the opinions and remonstrances of the judges on this important subject have been treated....[1]

Appendix E:
A Place to Call Home

With the move of the federal government to Washington, D.C., in 1800, the Supreme Court found itself without a home. Thus, began a quixotic journey that would span decades until Chief Justice William Howard Taft, a former president, secured funding from Congress for the construction of a new permanent residence.

The United States Supreme Court did not always have the Greek temple–inspired design building it occupies today. While the earliest parts of the United States capitol building and the White House date to the late eighteenth century, the Supreme Court building, designed by Cass Gilbert, opened in 1935, nearly one hundred and forty-five years after the Court was formed. This led to the inevitable question of where the Court met prior to its "new" home in 1935 at 1 First Street NE in Washington, D.C.

From the start, the Court would not have its own fixed location until 1810, when a space was created in the Capitol building. The Court occupied this space from 1810 to 1860, when it moved into the old Senate chamber until 1935, when it acquired its own permanent building. Prior to 1810, the Court led a somewhat wandering existence within the Capitol in terms of a meeting place.

The First Court Room

The very first meeting place for the new Supreme Court in 1790 was the Royal Exchange Building in New York City. This structure, which had an open first floor to allow for business and market transactions, housed the Court for two terms, the February and August terms of 1790. "The Justices deliberated on the second floor of the gambrel-roofed hall. A brick arcade shades the ground floor, an open-air market where Broad and Water street intersect in what is now the financial district."[1]

Old City Hall, Philadelphia. Adjacent to the Pennsylvania State House (Indepen-dence Hall). Home of the Supreme Court from 1791 to 1800 (from the Historical Collection of Herman H. Diers, Collection of the Supreme Court of the United States).

When Philadelphia became the federal capital in 1791, the Supreme Court moved there with the president and national Congress. The Court was briefly housed in the Pennsylvania State House (less than a week), before moving to a space in the Old City Hall. Here, for the next ten years, the Court carried out its business before moving to the new federal city of Washington, D.C. For nearly ten years, the scenes of the evolving Supreme Court played out in this chamber at the corner of 5th and Chestnut Streets. With the Congress meeting in the same building, and the president's house two blocks away, the federal government during the 1790s occupied a tight section of Philadelphia.

Opposite, top: **One of two areas utilized by the Supreme Court in the U.S. Capitol Building, ca. 1810–1860 (Architect of the Capitol).** *Bottom:* **Rededication of the Supreme Court room at the Old City Hall, 1922. Chief Justice William Howard Taft presiding in the middle chair (Keystone View Co., Collection of the Supreme Court of the United States).**

As for the move to Washington, D.C., in 1800, no provision was made in the city for the Supreme Court. Congress, in the new capitol building, had the foresight to offer space to the Court. The new executive mansion for the president could not accommodate them and funding for a separate building was not available. The Court would occupy space in the capitol building for the next one hundred and thirty-five years. Occasionally, during the early years, while construction on the capitol building was taking place, the Court was forced to meet in boarding houses or taverns; this would also be the case after the British destroyed Washington during the War of 1812.

Once the turmoil of 1812 subsided, the Court found a measure of permanency in the Capitol, occupying two spaces and making themselves at home until the arrival of Chief Justice Taft in 1921, who finally fulfilled the dreams of every justice since John Jay for a separate, permanent location for the Court.

The peripatetic existence from their inception in 1789 did not alter the work of the Court which continued under, at times, less than ideal conditions. It is a testament to the spirit of the justices, and their commitment to American jurisprudence, that they functioned without a true home until 1935.

Chapter Notes

Preface

1. Historian Paul Samuel Reinsch suggested that the Americans would have had the best of the English lawyers; Reinsch wrote, "Blackstone was outdone by American lawyers in extravagant panegyrics." Paul Samuel Reinsch, *Select Essays in Anglo-American Legal History*, Vol. 1 (New York: The Lawbook Exchange, 1992), 367.

2. J.R. Pole, "Reflections on American Laws and the American Revolution," *The William and Mary Quarterly* 50, no. 1 (Jan. 1993), 123.

3. Michael Grossberg and Christopher Tomlins, eds., *The Cambridge History of Law in America; Early America (1580–1815)*, Vol. 1 (Cambridge: Cambridge University Press, 2008), 79.

4. *Ibid.*, 80.

5. *Ibid.*, 82.

6. *Ibid.*, 83.

7. *Ibid.*, 29.

8. *Ibid.*

9. *Ibid.*, 176.

10. George L. Haskins, "Law and Colonial Society," *American Quarterly* 9, no. 3 (Autumn 1957), 358.

11. Reinsch, *Select Essays in Anglo-American Legal History*, Vol. 1 (New York: The Lawbook Exchange, 1992), 368.

12. Charles Grove Haines, *The Role of the Supreme Court in American Government and Politics 1789–1835* (New Jersey: The Lawbook Exchange, 2002), 3.

13. Jack N. Rakove, ed., *James Madison, Writings* (New York: Literary Classics of the United States, 1999), 772–773.

Introduction

1. As Marshall wrote to Justice Story in July of 1827:

On the resignation of Chief Justice Ellsworth, I recommended Judge Paterson as his successor. The President objected to him, and assigned as his ground of objection that the feelings of Judge Cushing would be wounded by passing him and selecting a junior member of the bench. I never heard him assign any other objection to Judge Paterson, though it was afterwards suspected by many that he was believed to be connected with the party which opposed the second attempt at negotiation with France. The President himself mentioned Mr. Jay, and he was nominated to the Senate. When I waited on the President with Mr. Jay's letter declining the appointment he said thoughtfully "Who shall I nominate now?" I replied that I could not tell, as I supposed that his objection to Judge Paterson remained. He said in a decided tone "I shall not nominate him." After a moment's hesitation he said "I believe I must nominate you." I had never before heard myself named for the office and had not even thought of it. I was pleased as well as surprised, and bowed in silence. Next day I was nominated, and, although the nomination was suspended by the friends of Judge Paterson, it was I believe when taken up unanimously approved. I was unfeignedly gratified at the appointment, and have had much reason to be so. I soon received a very friendly letter from Judge Paterson congratulating me on the occasion and expressing [his?] hopes that I might long retain the office. I felt truly grateful for th[e] real cordiality towards me which uniformly marked his conduct.

The Papers of John Marshall Digital Edition, Charles Hobson, ed. (Charlottesville: University of Virginia Press, Rotunda, 2014). http://rotunda.upress.virginia.edu/founders/JNML-01-11-02-0017 (accessed October 9, 2016). Original source: Volume 11, Correspondence, Papers, and Selected Judicial Opinions, April 1827–December 1830.

2. Another reason the first decade of the Supreme Court is not as well known is that the collected papers of the Court were not compiled until a project, which ran nearly twenty years, began at the end of the twentieth century. *The Documentary History of the Supreme Court of the United States*, edited by Mavea Marcus, is the most comprehensive collection of 1790s Supreme Court material available.

3. Frederick C. Hicks, *Men and Books Famous in the Law* (Clark, NJ: The Lawbook Exchange, 2008), 17.

4. This book will not, except for occasional indirect references, study the ancient world of law.

5. Great Britain did not create a supreme court until 2009. The concept existed in theory and practice for centuries, but it was not until 2009 that a formal institution called a supreme court was established. From the website of the court:

The United Kingdom Supreme Court (UKSC) was established to achieve the complete separation of the United Kingdom's senior judges from the upper House of Parliament, emphasizing the independence of the then Law Lords (now UKSC Justices) and increasing transparency at the top of the judicial system.

In August 2009 the Law Lords moved out of the House of Lords (where they sat as the Appellate Committee of the House of Lords) into their own building on the opposite side of Parliament Square. They sat for the first time as Justices of the UKSC in October 2009 [https://www.supremecourt.uk/faqs.html#1a; accessed August 13, 2016].

6. Stanford Encyclopedia of Philosophy, "The Nature of Law," http://plato.stanford.edu/entries/lawphil-nature/ (accessed August 13, 2016).

7. In 1811, Bryant Barrett of Gray's Inn prepared a study of the Code Napoleon. In his introduction, he mused on the place of law in the overall understanding of a society's history and overall approach to life. Barrett wrote: "The civil laws of nations form the most instructive part of their domestic history, whilst, from the general interest in their preservation, they are the most authentic documents of the countries to which they relate." Bryant Barrett, ed., *The Code Napoleon, Verbally Translated from the French, to Which Is Prefixed an Introductory Discourse* (Rpt., Birmingham: The Legal Classics Library, 1983), i.

8. George L. Haskins, "Law and Colonial Society," *American Quarterly* 9, no. 3 (Autumn 1957), 357.

9. Pollock, *Select Essays in Anglo-American*

Legal History, Vol. 1 (New York: The Lawbook Exchange, 1992), 89.

10. Charles Warren, *Congress, the Constitution, and the Supreme Court* (Boston: Little, Brown, 1925), 4.

11. Roscoe Pound, *The Formative Era of American Law* (Boston: Little, Brown, 1938), 7.

12. Reinsch, *Select Essays in Anglo-American Legal History*, Vol. 1 (New York: The Lawbook Exchange, 1992), 367.

13. Pound, *The Formative Era of American Law*, 8.

Chapter 1

1. Roscoe Pound, *The Formative Era of American Law* (Boston: Little, Brown, 1938), 9.

2. Catholic Guy Fawkes had sought to blow up the House of Lords during a visit by Protestant King James I in November 1605. This, according to the plan, would signal a revolt to place James's Catholic daughter on the throne. The plot was discovered, and Fawkes and several others were executed.

3. Allen D. Boyer, ed., *Law, Liberty, and Parliament: Selected Essays on the Writings of Sir Edward Coke* (Indianapolis: The Liberty Fund, 2004), xi.

4. *Ibid.*, xi.

5. *Ibid.*, xii.

6. The four Institutes are: 1) Commentary on Littleton; 2) Exposition of Ancient Statutes; 3) High Treason and Pleas of the Crown; 4) Jurisdiction of Courts. No author. Review of "The First Part of the Institutes of the Laws of England, or a Commentary upon Littleton, &c. By Sir Edward Coke. First American from the Sixteenth European Edition," *The North American Review* 13, no. 33 (Oct. 1821), 281.

7. *Ibid.*, 281.

8. Frederick C. Hicks, *Men and Books Famous in the Law* (Clark, NJ: The Lawbook Exchange, 2008), 91.

9. Quoted in Boyer, ed., *Law, Liberty, and Parliament*, xiv.

10. Hicks, *Men and Books Famous in the Law*, 83.

11. Boyer, ed., *Law, Liberty, and Parliament*, 24.

12. *Ibid.*, 25.

13. Merrill D. Peterson, ed., *Thomas Jefferson: Writings* (New York: Literary Classics of the United States, 1984), 735.

14. *The Papers of Thomas Jefferson, Digital Edition*, ed. James P. McClure and J. Jefferson Looney (Charlottesville: University of Virginia Press, Rotunda, 2008–2017).

15. *The North American Review* is still in publication, over two centuries later.

16. *Ibid.* No author. Review of "The first part of the *Institutes of the Laws of England*, or a *Commentary upon Littleton*, &c. By Sir Edward Coke," 255.

17. *Ibid.*, 255.

18. Walter Scott, *The Antiquary* (Oxford: Oxford University Press, 2002), 332. Scott's father was an attorney, and Scott himself studied law for a while. No doubt he was quite familiar with Edward Coke.

19. *Ibid.*, 286.

20. Charles M. Hepburn, "The Inns of Court and Certain Conditions in American Legal Education," *Virginia Law Review* 8, No. 2 (Dec. 1921), 100.

21. Basil Brown, *Law Sports at Gray's Inn* (Rpt., Clark, NJ: The Lawbook Exchange, 2009), 1–2. Volumes have been written about Shakespeare and the law—specifically, how he used it to great advantage in his plays. It shows the significance of law in everyday life that Shakespeare felt comfortable enough with his audiences' awareness and knowledge of law to include it in many of his plays.

22. Wilfrid Prest, "Legal Education of the Gentry at the Inns of Court, 1560–1640," *Past & Present*, No. 38 (Dec. 1967), 23.

23. Pound, *The Formative Era of American Law*, 8.

24. Quoted in Charles Warren, *History of the Harvard Law School and of Early Legal Conditions in America*, Vol. 1. (Clark, NJ: The Lawbook Exchange, 1999), 120.

25. Thomas Jefferson would refer in later life to Blackstone's Commentaries as "the most lucid in arrangement, which had yet been written, correct in its matter, classical in style, and rightfully taking its place by the side of the Justinian Institutes." From a letter to Thomas Cooper, January 16, 1814. The Papers of Thomas Jefferson Digital Edition, ed. James P. McClure and J. Jefferson Looney. Charlottesville: University of Virginia Press, Rotunda, 2008–2017.

26. Blackstone held the post of Vinerian professor of English law. Charles Viner had left money to Oxford for the establishment of such a post and Blackstone was the first holder of the position.

27. William Blake Odgers, "Sir William Blackstone," *The Yale Law Journal* 27, No. 5 (Mar. 1918), 604.

28. Rene A. Wormser, *The Story of the Law and the Men Who Made it—From the Earliest Times to the Present* (New York: Simon & Schuster, 1962), 293.

29. Hicks, *Men and Books Famous in the Law*, 126.

30. From a letter to Thomas Cooper, January 1814. *The Papers of Thomas Jefferson Digital Edition*, ed. James P. McClure and J. Jefferson Looney. Charlottesville: University of Virginia Press, Rotunda, 2008–2017.

31. Daniel J. Boorstin, *The Americans: The Colonial Experience* (New York: Vintage Books, 1958), 303–304.

32. Hicks, *Men and Books Famous in the Law*, 127.

33. Lawbook Exchange, Catalog 84, pg. 8.

34. Lawbook Exchange, Catalog 84, pg. 8.

35. Hicks, *Men and Books Famous in the Law*, 129.

36. Warren, *History of the Harvard Law School*, 141.

37. Maeva Marcus, ed., *The Documentary History of the Supreme Court of the United States, 1789–1800*, Vol. 4 (New York: Columbia University Press, 1992), 430.

38. *North American Review*, No. 1, Boston, January 1829.

39. *Ibid.*, 419.

40. *Ibid.*, 419.

41. William E. Nelson, *The Common Law in Colonial America: The Chesapeake and New England, 1607–1660*, Vol. 1 (Oxford: Oxford University Press, 2008), 3.

42. *Ibid.*, 6.

43. Paul Samuel Reinsch, *Select Essays in Anglo-American Legal History*, Vol. 1 (New York: The Lawbook Exchange, 1992), 372.

44. Reinsch, *Select Essays in Anglo-American Legal History*, Vol. 1, 414.

45. Warren, *History of the Harvard Law School*, 27.

46. *Ibid.*, 28.

47. *Ibid.*, 40.

48. Nelson, *The Common Law in Colonial America*, 26.

49. *Ibid.*, 27.

50. G. Edward White, *Law in American History*, Vol. 1: *From the Colonial Years Through the Civil War* (Oxford: Oxford University Press, 2012), 49.

51. Lawrence M. Friedman, *A History of American Law* (New York: Simon & Schuster, 1985), 56.

52. Reinsch, *Select Essays in Anglo-American Legal History*, Vol. 1, 372.

53. Nelson, *The Common Law in Colonial America*, 49.

54. Warren, *History of the Harvard Law School*, 4.

55. Reinsch, *Select Essays in Anglo-American Legal History*, Vol. 1, 412.

56. Quoted, *ibid.*, 368.

57. Warren, *History of the Harvard Law School*, 25.

58. Reinsch, *Select Essays in Anglo-American Legal History*, Vol. 1, 371. Lawyers played a role in this as well. Those trained in the law naturally

helped to facilitate its acceptance in the colonies. "Then there began to be trained lawyers practicing in the courts manned by trained lawyers, so that the reception of the common law and reshaping it into a law for America were well begun at the time of the Revolution." Pound, *The Formative Era of American Law*, 6–7.

59. Friedman, *A History of American Law*, 91.

60. Reinsch, *Select Essays in Anglo-American Legal History*, Vol. 1, 410.

61. Friedman, *A History of American Law*, 33.

62. Reinsch, *Select Essays in Anglo-American Legal History*, Vol. 1, 413.

63. Litchfield Law School was founded as an institution strictly devoted to the study of law. It was founded in 1784 and continued until 1833.

64. Charles Warren, *A History of The American Bar* (Boston: Little, Brown, 1911), 67.

65. Warren, *History of the Harvard Law School*, 13.

66. *Ibid.*, 18.

67. *Ibid.*, 1.

68. *Ibid.*, 1.

69. James Kent, *Select Essays in Anglo-American Legal History*, Vol. 1 (New York: The Lawbook Exchange, 1992), 837.

70. *Ibid.*, 838.

71. *Ibid.*, 838.

72. *Ibid.*, 838.

73. *Ibid.*, 838–839.

74. In 1826, Kent published *Commentaries on American Law* which he modeled on Blackstone's *Commentaries on English Law*.

75. Frank L. Dewey, *Thomas Jefferson, Lawyer* (Charlottesville: University Press of Virginia, 1987), 13.

76. Kinvin L. Wroth, and Hiller B. Zobel, eds. *Legal Papers of John Adams* (New York: Atheneum, 1968), lxxiv.

77. Quoted in Warren, *History of the Harvard Law School*, 137.

78. Quoted, *ibid.*, 137.

79. Quoted, *ibid.*, 138.

80. Quoted, *ibid.*, 141.

81. Quoted, *ibid.*, 132.

82. Quoted, *ibid.*, 135.

83. Charles M. Hepburn, "The Inns of Court and Certain Conditions in American Legal Education," *Virginia Law Review* 8, no. 2 (Dec. 1921), 93.

Chapter 2

1. Michael Grossberg and Christopher Tomlins, eds. *The Cambridge History of Law in*

America; *Early America (1580–1815)*, Vol. 1 (Cambridge: Cambridge University Press, 2008), 450.

2. Jack N. Rakove, ed., *James Madison, Writings* (New York: Literary Classics of the United States, 1999), 807.

3. *Ibid.*, 807.

4. *Ibid.*, 807.

5. *Ibid.*, 808.

6. *Ibid.*, 808.

7. *Ibid.*, 90–91.

8. *Ibid.*, 42.

9. *Ibid.*, 42.

10. *Ibid.*, 43.

11. *Ibid.*, 82.

12. Adrienne Koch, ed., *Notes of Debates in the Federal Convention of 1787 Reported by James Madison* (New York: W.W. Norton, 1987), 115.

13. *Ibid.*, 120.

14. *Ibid.*, 121.

15. *Ibid.*, 139.

16. *Ibid.*, 143.

17. *Ibid.*, 305–306.

18. *Ibid.*, 381, 383.

19. Rakove, ed., *James Madison, Writings*, 135.

20. *Ibid.*, 148.

21. *Ibid.*, 394.

22. *Ibid.*, 397.

23. Alexander Hamilton, James Madison and John Jay, *The Federalist Papers* (Norwalk: The Easton Press, 1979), 519.

24. *Ibid.*, 519.

25. *Ibid.*, 520.

26. *Ibid.*, 521.

27. *Ibid.*, 521.

28. *Ibid.*, 522.

29. *Ibid.*, 524.

30. *Ibid.*, 528.

31. While estimates vary, the average life expectancy in 1790 for a male was less than fifty years.

32. Hamilton, Madison, Jay, *The Federalist Papers,* 532.

33. *Ibid.*, 533.

34. *Ibid.*, 541.

35. *Ibid.*, 550.

36. *Ibid.*, 551.

37. *Ibid.*, 552.

38. *Ibid.*, 556.

39. *Ibid.*, 557.

40. Julius Goebel, Jr., *Antecedents and Beginnings to 1801* (New York: Macmillan, 1971), 87.

41. Max Farrand, *The Framing of the Constitution of the United States* (New Haven: Yale University Press, 1913), 185.

42. *Ibid.*, 185.

43. *Ibid.*, 58.

44. *Ibid.*, 58.

45. *Ibid.*, 71.

46. Bernard Bailyn, ed., *The Debate on the*

Constitution: Federalist and Antifederalist Speeches, Articles, and Letters During the Struggle over Ratification, Vol. 1 (New York: Literary Classics of the United States, 1993), 706.

47. Ibid., 540.

48. Ibid., 358.

49. Ibid., 347.

50. Ibid., 371.

51. J.R. Pole, "Reflections on American Laws and the American Revolution," The William and Mary Quarterly 50, no. 1 (Jan. 1993), 141.

52. Ibid., 142.

53. Bailyn, ed., The Debate on the Constitution, Vol. 1, 65.

54. Ibid., 71.

55. Ibid., 95. The Zinger case was decided in 1735 and was a landmark case for freedom of the press.

56. Ibid., 151.

57. Koch, ed., Notes of Debates in the Federal Convention of 1787, 393.

58. Ibid., 229.

59. Ibid., 229.

60. Ibid., 230.

61. Bailyn, ed., The Debate on the Constitution, Vol. 2, 129.

62. Ibid., 129.

63. Ibid., 130.

64. Ibid., 130.

65. Ibid., 171.

66. Ibid., 174.

67. Ibid., 177.

68. Ibid., 179.

69. Ibid., 224.

70. Ibid. 159.

71. Ibid., 254.

72. Ibid., 254.

73. Ibid., 258.

74. Ibid., 259.

75. Ibid., 260.

76. Ibid., 260.

77. Ibid., 265.

78. Ibid., 290.

79. Ibid., 290–291.

80. Ibid., 376–377.

81. Ibid., 609.

82. Ibid., 720.

83. Ibid., 725.

84. Ibid., 726.

85. Ibid., 730.

86. Ibid., 890.

87. Ibid., 893.

88. Bailyn, ed., The Debate on the Constitution, Vol. 1, 895.

Chapter 3

1. Wilfred J. Ritz, Rewriting the History of the Judiciary Act of 1789: Exposing Myths, Challenging Premises, and Using New Evidence (Norman: University of Oklahoma Press, 1990), 17.

2. Ibid., 17.

3. As quoted in Irving Brant, The Fourth President; A Life of James Madison (Norwalk, CT: Easton Press, 1985), 223.

4. George B. Galloway, "Precedents Established in the First Congress," The Western Political Quarterly 11, no. 3 (Sept. 1958), 463.

5. Wythe Holt, The United States Supreme Court; The Pursuit of Justice, ed. Christopher Tomlins (Boston: Houghton Mifflin, 2005), 18.

6. Ibid., 19.

7. The Papers of James Madison Digital Edition. J.C.A. Stagg, ed. Charlottesville: University of Virginia Press, Rotunda, 2010. Congressional Series, Volume 12.

8. Holt, The United States Supreme Court; The Pursuit of Justice, ed. Christopher Tomlins, 19.

9. Ibid., 20.

10. Ritz, Rewriting the History of the Judiciary Act of 1789, 6.

11. This overview is adapted from Jude M. Pfister, "Constitutional Development in the United States Supreme Court During the 1790s," (D.Litt. diss., Drew University, 2007), 26–50.

12. Bernard Bailyn, ed., The Debate on the Constitution: Federalist and Antifederalist Speeches, Articles, and Letters During the Struggle over Ratification, Vol. 2 (New York: Literary Classics of the United States, 1993), 883.

13. Ibid., 883. See also William R. Casto, The Supreme Court in the Early Republic: The Chief Justiceships of John Jay and Oliver Ellsworth (Columbia: University of South Carolina Press, 1995), 32. As Casto wrote, expanding "the judicial power to the limits of the Constitution would have played directly into the theoretical and practical fears of those who opposed the federal courts."

14. Ibid., 19.

15. Ibid., 20.

16. See Hamilton Federalist 80 for his discussion of the "Hydra" factor which would be created by thirteen separate systems without a central system. Hamilton, Alexander, James Madison, John Jay, The Federalist Papers (Norwalk: The Easton Press, 1979), 532–539. See also Hamilton No. 22, where he discussed the need to "establish one court permanent to the rest." Ibid., 134–144.

17. Holt, The United States Supreme Court: The Pursuit of Justice, ed. Christopher Tomlins, 21.

18. Ibid., 22.

19. Ibid., 20.

20. Maeva Marcus, ed., The Documentary

History of the Supreme Court of the United States, 1789-1800, Vol. 4 (New York: Columbia University Press, 1992), 369.

21. Julius Goebel, Jr., *Antecedents and Beginnings to 1801* (New York: Macmillan, 1971), 472.

22. Marcus, ed., *The Documentary History of the Supreme Court of the United States,* Vol. 4, 28.

23. *Ibid.,* 28.

24. *Ibid.,* 28.

25. *Ibid.,* 29.

26. Charles Grove Haines, *The Role of the Supreme Court in American Government and Politics 1789-1835* (Union, NJ: The Lawbook Exchange, 2002), 124.

27. Goebel, *Antecedents and Beginnings to 1801,* 363.

28. Marcus, ed., *The Documentary History of the Supreme Court of the United States,* Vol. 4, 30.

29. Casto, *The Supreme Court in the Early Republic,* 36.

30. *Ibid.,* 36.

31. Marcus, ed., *The Documentary History of the Supreme Court of the United States,* Vol. 4, 86.

32. Casto, *The Supreme Court in the Early Republic,* 37.

33. *Ibid.,* 38.

34. *Ibid.,* 38.

35. Goebel, *Antecedents and Beginnings to 1801,* 457.

36. *Ibid.,* 491.

37. *Ibid.,* 491.

38. *Ibid.,* 492.

39. *The Papers of James Madison Digital Edition,* J. C. A. Stagg, editor. Congressional Series, Volume 12.

40. *Ibid.*

41. *Ibid.*

42. *Ibid.*

43. *Ibid.*

44. *Ibid.*

45. *Ibid.*

46. *Ibid.*

47. *Ibid.*

48. *Ibid.*

49. *Gazette of the United States,* Library of Congress, June 10, 1789 chroniclingamerica. loc.gov/iccn/sn83030483/1789-06-10/ed-1/seq-1/ (accessed November 30, 2016).

50. *Ibid.*

51. *The Papers of Thomas Jefferson Digital Edition,* ed. James P. McClure and J. Jefferson Looney. Charlottesville: University of Virginia Press, Rotunda, 2008–2016. Main Series, Volume 18.

52. Goebel, *Antecedents and Beginnings to 1801,* 458.

53. *Ibid.,* 472.

54. *Ibid.,* 475.

55. As quoted in Charles Warren, *The Supreme Court in United States History,* Vol. 1 (Boston: Little, Brown, 1926), 31.

56. Marcus, ed., *The Documentary History of the Supreme Court of the United States,* Vol. 1, part 2, 603.

57. Charles Grove Haines, *The Role of the Supreme Court in American Government and Politics 1789-1835* (Union, NJ: The Lawbook Exchange, 2002), 120.

58. *Ibid.,* 363.

59. *Ibid.,* 363.

60. *Ibid.,* 365.

61. *Ibid.,* 420.

62. *Ibid.,* 369.

63. *Ibid.,* 372.

64. *Ibid.,* 380.

65. *Ibid.,* 380.

66. *Ibid.,* 401.

67. *Ibid.,* 402.

68. *Ibid.,* 402.

69. *Ibid.,* 418.

70. *Ibid.,* 418.

71. *Ibid.,* 418.

72. *Ibid.,* 430.

73. *Ibid.,* 427.

74. *Ibid.,* 435.

75. *Ibid.,* 440.

76. *Ibid.,* 464.

77. *Ibid.,* 449.

78. *Ibid.,* 451.

79. *Ibid.,* 500.

80. *Ibid.,* 503.

81. *Ibid.,* 511.

82. *Ibid.,* 512.

83. *Ibid.,* 513.

84. *Ibid.,* 513.

85. *Ibid.,* 522.

86. *Ibid.,* 523.

87. *Ibid.,* 537.

88. As quoted in Warren, *The Supreme Court in United States History,* Vol. 1, 39.

Chapter 4

1. James R. Perry, "Supreme Court Appointments, 1789–1801: Criteria, Presidential Style, and the Press of Events," *Journal of the Early Republic* 6, no. 4 (Winter, 1986), 379.

2. George J. Lankevich, *The Federal Court 1787–1801* (Danbury, CT: Grolier Educational Corporation, 1995), viii.

3. *The Papers of George Washington Digital Edition,* ed. Theodore J. Crackel. Charlottesville: University of Virginia Press, Rotunda, 2008. Presidential Series, Volume 4.

4. *Ibid.*

5. *Ibid.*, Volume 3.
6. *Ibid.*
7. *Ibid.*
8. *Ibid.*, Volume 4.
9. *Ibid.*
10. *The Adams Papers Digital Edition*, ed. C. James Taylor. Charlottesville: University of Virginia Press, Rotunda, 2008–2016. Adams Family Correspondence, Volume 8.
11. Maeva Marcus, ed., *The Documentary History of the Supreme Court of the United States, 1789–1800*, Vol. 1, Part 1 (New York: Columbia University Press, 1986), 11.
12. *Ibid.*, 11.
13. Marcus, ed., *The Documentary History of the Supreme Court of the United States*, Vol. 1, Part 2, 674.
14. *Ibid.*, 675.
15. *Ibid.*, 677.
16. William Jay, ed., *The Life of John Jay*, Vol. 1, Reprint (Elibron Classics, 2005), 3.
17. Jay, ed., *The Life of John Jay*, Vol. 1, 11.
18. *Ibid.*, 107.
19. Marcus, ed., *The Documentary History of the Supreme Court of the United States*, Vol. 4, 709.
20. Jay, ed., *The Life of John Jay*, Vol. 1, 275.
21. Henry Flanders, "Chief Justice Rutledge. An Address Before the Law Department of the University of Pennsylvania," *The American Law Register (1898–1907)* 54, no. 4, Volume 45 New Series (Apr. 1906), 204.
22. Morristown National Historical Park, Lloyd W. Smith Rare Book and Manuscript Collection, number 3420.
23. *Ibid.*
24. Robert W. Barnwell, Jr., "The Dictator," *The Journal of Southern History* 7, no. 2 (May 1941), 216.
25. *Ibid.*, 221.
26. Adrienne Koch, ed., *Notes of Debates in the Federal Convention of 1787 Reported by James Madison* (New York: W.W. Norton, 1987), 610.
27. *Ibid.*, 502.
28. *Ibid.*, 507.
29. *Ibid.*, 517.
30. *Ibid.*, 405.
31. *Ibid.*, 642.
32. *The Papers of George Washington Digital Edition*. Charlottesville: University of Virginia Press, Rotunda, 2008, Presidential Series, Volume 4.
33. *Ibid.*
34. *Ibid.*
35. Marcus, ed., *The Documentary History of the Supreme Court of the United States*, Vol. 1, Part 2, 830.
36. Leon Friedman and Fred L. Israel, *The Justices of the United States Supreme Court*

1789–1978; Their Lives and Major Opinions, Vol. 1 (New York: Chelsea House, 1980), 49.
37. *Ibid.*, 57.
38. Arthur P. Rugg, "William Cushing," *The Yale Law Journal* 30, no. 2 (Dec. 1920), 130.
39. Under Chief Justice Cushing, the Massachusetts Superior Court had many trappings of the British courts: big wigs, elaborate robes, unique rituals. It was not until well after the Revolution that many of these quirks receded into a more American standard of dress and practice.
40. *The Papers of George Washington Digital Edition*, Presidential Series, Volume 4.
41. *The Papers of George Washington Digital Edition*, Presidential Series, Volume 9.
42. Rugg, "William Cushing," 128.
43. *Ibid.*, 128.
44. *The Papers of Thomas Jefferson Digital Edition*, ed. James P. McClure and J. Jefferson Looney. Charlottesville: University of Virginia Press, Rotunda, 2008–2017. Retirement Series, Volume 3.
45. *Ibid.*
46. Marcus, ed., *The Documentary History of the Supreme Court of the United States*, Vol. 1, Part 1, 58.
47. The six men were: George Clymer (Pennsylvania), Benjamin Franklin (Pennsylvania), Robert Morris (Pennsylvania), George Read (Delaware), Roger Sherman (Connecticut), and James Wilson (Pennsylvania).
48. In 1906 James Wilson was reinterred in Christ Churchyard, Philadelphia.
49. Morristown National Historical Park. Lloyd W. Smith Rare Book and Manuscript Collection number 1248.
50. *Ibid.*, number 1258.
51. James Wilson, *Collected Works of James Wilson*, eds. Kermit L. Hall and Mark David Hall, Vol. 1 (Indianapolis, IN: Liberty Fund, 2007), xi.
52. *Ibid.*, xiv.
53. *Ibid.*, xiv.
54. *Ibid.*, xv.
55. *Ibid.*, 92.
56. Adrienne Koch, ed., *Notes of Debates in the Federal Convention*, 71.
57. *Ibid.*, 72–73.
58. Wilson, *Collected Works of James Wilson*, eds. Kermit L. Hall and Mark David Hall, Vol. 1, 90–91.
59. *Ibid.*, 117.
60. *Ibid.*, 121.
61. Edmund Randolph made the first draft— "He considered the constitution to be a legal, rather than a philosophical, document." Richard Beeman, *Plain, Honest Men: The Making of the American Constitution* (New York: Random House, 2010), 271.

62. *Ibid.*, 273.
63. David O. Stewart, *The Summer of 1787, The Men Who Invented the Constitution* (New York: Simon & Schuster, 2007), 172–173.
64. *Ibid.*, 276.
65. Kermit L. Hall and Mark David Hall, eds., *Collected Works of James Wilson*, Vol. 1, 177.
66. *Ibid.*, 171.
67. *The Papers of George Washington Digital Edition.* Charlottesville: University of Virginia Press, Rotunda, 2008.
68. As quoted in Charles Warren, *The Supreme Court in United States History,* Vol. 1 (Boston: Little, Brown, 1926), 43.
69. Marcus, ed., *The Documentary History of the Supreme Court of the United States,* Vol. 1, Part 1, 35.
70. *Ibid.*, 36.
71. *Ibid.*, 36.
72. *Ibid.*, 37.
73. The John Marshall Foundation: http://www.johnmarshallfoundation.org/.
74. Marcus, ed., *The Documentary History of the Supreme Court of the United States,* Vol. 1, Part 1, 39.
75. *Ibid.*, 40. Hamilton too wrote to Harrison with a similar argument. *Ibid.*, 41.
76. *Ibid.*, 40.
77. *Ibid.*, 42.
78. Joanne B. Freeman, ed., *Alexander Hamilton: Writings* (New York: Literary Classics of the United States, 2001), 121.
79. Friedman and Israel, *The Justices of the United States Supreme Court 1789–1978,* Vol. 1, 126.
80. *Ibid.*, 151.
81. As quoted in Perry, "Supreme Court Appointments, 1789–1801: Criteria, Presidential Style, and the Press of Events," 384.
82. This section is adapted from Jude M. Pfister, "William Paterson's Notebook," *Supreme Court Historical Society Quarterly,* XXXIII, no. 1 (2011), 4–6.
83. Friedman and Israel, *The Justices of the United States Supreme Court 1789–1978,* Vol. 1, 186.
84. *Ibid.*, 197.
85. This section is adapted from Jude M. Pfister, *America Writes Its History, 1650–1850: The Formation of a National Narrative* (Jefferson, NC: McFarland, 2014), 118–121.
86. David Leslie Annis, "Mr. Bushrod Washington, Supreme Court Justice on the Marshall Court," (PhD diss., University of Notre Dame, 1974), 105.
87. *Ibid.*, 19.
88. *Ibid.*, 20.
89. *Ibid.*, 22.
90. *Ibid.*, 23.
91. Horace Binney, *Bushrod Washington* (Philadelphia: Privately Published, 1858), 6.
92. *Ibid.*, 7.
93. Clare Cushman, ed., *The Supreme Court Justices Illustrated Biographies, 1789–1995* (Washington, D.C.: Congressional Quarterly, 1995), 51.
94. Annis, "Mr. Bushrod Washington, Supreme Court Justice on the Marshall Court," 28.
95. *Ibid.*, 33.
96. *Ibid.*, 33.
97. *Ibid.*, 36.
98. *Ibid.*, 37.
99. *Ibid.*, 38.
100. *Ibid.*, 38.
101. *Ibid.*, 55.
102. *The Papers of George Washington Digital Edition,* ed. Theodore J. Crackel. Charlottesville: University of Virginia Press, Rotunda, 2008.
103. Michael C. Toth, *Founding Federalist: The Life of Oliver Ellsworth* (Wilmington, DE: ISI Books, 2011), 21.
104. Quoted in Friedman and Israel, *The Justices of the United States Supreme Court 1789–1978,* Vol. 1, 226.

Chapter 5

1. As quoted in a footnote in Charles Warren, *The Supreme Court in United States History,* Vol. 1 (Boston: Little, Brown, 1926), 48.
2. *Ibid.*, 51.
3. As quoted in Warren, *The Supreme Court in United States History,* Vol. 1, 50.
4. Charles Grove Haines, *The Role of the Supreme Court in American Government and Politics 1789–1835* (Union, NJ: The Lawbook Exchange, 2002), 123.
5. Julius Goebel, Jr., *Antecedents and Beginnings to 1801* (New York: Macmillan, 1971), 665.
6. These designations have no meaning for the general purpose of this book. For the legal practioner, the citations do have meaning. The list relied upon in this book was compiled in 2006 by Anne Ashmore from the library of the Supreme Court of the United States. As Ms. Ashmore wrote: "The primary source for dates are the handwritten engrossed minutes. The originals are at the National Archives and a microfilm copy is available." The most recent compilation of 1790s Supreme Court material is by Maeva Marcus, *The Documentary History of the United States Supreme Court.* The Marcus edition does not however include every case that the Court dealt with. Indeed, there are some in Marcus which are not from the list compiled by Ms. Ashmore from *U.S. Reports.*

7. Maeva Marcus, ed., *The Documentary History of the Supreme Court of the United States, 1789–1800,* Vol. 6 (New York: Columbia University Press, 1998), 10.

8. *Ibid.,* 10.

9. *Ibid.,* 18.

10. *Ibid.,* 18.

11. *Ibid.,* 22.

12. *Ibid.,* 23.

13. *Ibid.,* 23.

14. *Ibid.,* 25.

15. *Ibid.,* 26.

16. *Ibid.,* 26.

17. See the opinion of Justice Frankfurter in *Joint Anti-Fascist Refugee Committee v. Mc-Grath.* Frankfurter, citing *Hayburn,* stated that it was an example of the failure to constitute a "case or controversy" and *Hayburn* should never have occurred as it did. Frankfurter's comments can clearly be seen as an example of the difficulty, even for justices, to project contemporary understandings into the past. The abstract is contained in Maeva Marcus and Robert Teir, "Hayburn's Case: A Misinterpretation of Precedent," *Wisconsin Law Review* 12, no.2 (1988), 543.

18. For an opposing view, see Mary Bilder, *The Transatlantic Constitution-Colonial Legal Culture and the Empire.* (Cambridge, 2004), 196. Bilder believes the concept of judicial review was "not completely planned." Whereas this book, argues just the opposite. See also Charles Warren, *Congress, the Constitution, and the Supreme Court* (Boston: Little, Brown, 1925), 50–51. Warren gave ample evidence that the Federal Convention was quite aware of the implications of granting judicial review power to the Supreme Court and indeed intended to. Elbridge Gerry, Luther Martin, James Madison, and James Wilson are just some of the framers who spoke in favor of the concept.

19. Most recent studies of the Federalist period do not approach the topic in any depth. See *Federalists Reconsidered* and *The Age of Federalism.* It would seem that as a conceptual branch of the government the Supreme Court would generate some discussion in works focusing on the decade of the 1790s. Perhaps by omission these writers are implying the Court did not function as a separate, equal branch within the government—something this book argues against. Naturally, it could also mean that the authors found the Court an insignificant player in the government—something this book argues against as well.

20. Edward Jenks, *Select Essays in Anglo-American Legal History,* Vol. 1 (New York: The Lawbook Exchange, 1992), 58.

21. *Ibid.,* 61.

22. *Ibid.,* 63.

23. See introduction by Allen T. Boyer in Allen T. Boyer, *Law, Liberty, and Parliament—Selected Essays on the Writings of Sir Edward Coke.* (Indianapolis, Liberty Fund, 2004), xi. See also the essay by Theodore F.T. Plucknett, *Bonham's Case and Judicial Review, ibid.,* 150. For an opposing view of the power of the judiciary by another distinguished British jurist, see William Blackstone, *Commentaries on the Laws of England.* (London, 1966), reprint of first 1765 edition, Vol. 1, 91. Blackstone knows of "no power that can control" parliament if it passes an act void of reason.

24. See *Seminole Tribe of Florida v. Florida,* 517 U.S. 44, 162 (1996). Justice Souter references Bonham's case as a foundation of the American Constitutional approach to judicial review. See also *Mistretta v. United States* (109 S. Ct. 647 (1989)) where Justice Blackmum cites *Hayburn* as a case which impacts dual holding, cited in Mark Tushnet, *Dual Office Holding and the Constitution: A view from Hayburn's case.* Supreme Court Historical Society 1990 Yearbook, 1, http://supremecourthistory. org/pub_journal_archive.html. In all, *Hayburn,* since 1794, has been cited forty-four times. See Marcus and Teir, "Hayburn's Case: A Misinterpretation of Precedent," 528. See also page 541 of the same work for a further discussion about why future Courts saw *Hayburn* as an example of judicial restraint. It has mostly been seen as either a case impacting "separation of powers" or a "case or controversy" case.

25. Charles S. Hyneman, ed., *American Political Writing during the Founding Era 1760–1805* (Indianapolis: Liberty Fund, 1983), 941.

26. *Ibid.,* 941.

27. *Ibid.,* 943.

28. For a discussion of the temperament concerning judicial review in the early nineteenth century, see Warren, *Congress, The Constitution, and The Supreme Court,* 95. Warren includes quotes from jurists reflecting on the concept of judicial review who clearly state that it had its beginnings in the 1780s and the fallout of the American Revolution.

29. See William M. Meigs, "Some recent attacks on the American doctrine of Judicial Power," *The American Law Review* (Sept.–Oct. 1906), 640–670. Meigs argues with dismay over the recent (early twentieth century) events in the theory of judicial review which had occurred since 1900, namely the trend to reject the concept of judicial review in exchange for a more powerful Congress and especially a more powerful president. His discussion is still quite relevant one hundred years later.

30. Based on a review of Max Farrand, *The Records of the Federal Convention of 1787* Vol.

4 (New Haven: Yale University Press, 1966), 166–167.

31. Marcus, ed., *The Documentary History of the Supreme Court of the United States,* Vol. 6, 370.

32. *The Papers of Thomas Jefferson Digital Edition,* ed. James P. McClure and J. Jefferson Looney. Charlottesville: University of Virginia Press, Rotunda, 2008–2017. Main Series, Volume, 27.

33. See Marcus, ed., *The Documentary History of the Supreme Court of the United States,* Vol. 6, 53, for the text of what could be described as a Constitutional primer which Justice Wilson wrote to President Washington and was signed by the other members of the circuit, in which Wilson outline why the act was incompatible with the Constitution.

34. See James Madison's letter to Henry Lee in Marcus, ed., *The Documentary History of the Supreme Court of the United States,* Vol. 6, 50. Admittedly, it is never stated by the justices which article of the Constitution they base their arguments on. Article III, Section II, would seem the likeliest one. It stipulates that "the Judicial Power shall extend to all Cases, in Law and Equity, arising under this Constitution...." *Hayburn* clearly was not a case and therefore asking the justices to exercise judicial power was void because it was outside the parameters established by the Constitution. This is made clearer from reading the opinions of the justices. Chief Justice Jay and Justice Cushing wrote, "That neither the Legislative nor the Executive branches, can constitutionally assign to the judiciary any duties, but such as are properly judicial." Justices Wilson and Blair wrote that they would not perform as prescribed by the act "because the business directed by this act is not of a judicial nature." See George J. Lankevich, ed., *The United States Supreme Court—The Federal Court 1787–1801* (Danbury, CT: Grolier Educational Corporation, 1995), 147–148. Justice Iredell followed the same line of reasoning when he wrote of "some doubts as to the propriety of giving an opinion in a case which has not yet come regularly and judicially before us." See Marcus, ed., *The Documentary History of the Supreme Court of the United States,* Vol. 6, 284.

35. *Ibid.,* 284.

36. See *ibid.,* 50, for a letter by Congressman William Vans Murray of Maryland who decries the justices approach to the "very humane act of Congress." Murray was also aghast over the finding that the act was unconstitutional. He found the prospect of judicial review by the Court of Congress to be "extraordinary controul." See also pg. 58 for reference to the humane actions of the Congress via the act. See

also pg. 293 for reference from *Ex parte Chandler* and the humanitarian desires associated with that case (a spin-off of *Hayburn*).

37. See Max Farrand, "The First Hayburn Case, 1792," *The American Historical Review,* Vol. 13, no. 2 (Jan. 1908), 282, for a brief discussion of how Congress first reacted to *Hayburn* and asked Attorney General Edmund Randolph to "obtain an adjudication of the Supreme Court of the United States, on the validity of any such rights claimed under the Act aforesaid." Presumably, a test case would have been one approach to this.

38. Maeva Marcus, in her introduction to the manuscripts relating to *Hayburn,* argues that the Court was acting from purely political motives. See Marcus, ed., *The Documentary History of the Supreme Court of the United States,* Vol. 6, 38. Conversely, Wythe Holt argues that the Court was under no such political pressure and in fact decided on the course of action relatively quickly—implying not much time would have been spent on political worries. In Scott Douglas Gerber, *Seriatim, The Supreme Court Before John Marshall* (New York: New York University Press, 1998), 173. Holt further feels that the Supreme Court was agitated over Congress' refusal to halt circuit riding and therefore was in the mood for a showdown over a constitutional issue. *Ibid.,* 173.

39. Wythe Holt writes that it sent "shock waves through Philadelphia." Gerber, *Seriatim, The Supreme Court before John Marshall,* 174.

40. See Marcus, ed., *The Documentary History of the Supreme Court of the United States,* Vol. 6, 48, for proceeding of the House of Representatives which states, "This being the first instance, in which a court of justice had declared a law of Congress to be unconstitutional." This is the first instance of the word unconstitutional in an official capacity.

41. Mark Tushnet argues that the Constitution itself was "too facile to identify policy with the legislative, law with the judiciary, and administration with the executive branch. Rather, the allocation of those functions to different branches was worked out in the early decades of the Republic." In the Supreme Court Historical Society *Yearbook 1990,* 16. http://supremecourthistory.org/pub_journal_archive.html. By Tushnet's interpretation, the issue was not the concept of "unconstitutional," it was not enough Constitution. The Constitution itself did not provide enough explicit information to even declare *Hayburn* unconstitutional. The opposite side of that argument is whether the Constitution could declare *Hayburn* Constitutional. For Tushnet, and those of his opinion, *Hayburn* represents the first in many

episodes wherein the branches of government test the boundaries in a semi-official capacity as to which branch will have what power when the Constitution is ambivalent. Article I, Section VI, Clause II, does prohibit representatives and Senators from holding dual positions, but does not stipulate as to justices, or the executive.

42. Contrast Mary Bilder's approach to the repugnancy clause (her words) in section twenty-five of the Judiciary Act. As a matter of semantics, "unconstitutional" would seem to be a stronger and less ambiguous term than "repugnant." *Hayburn's* case only accentuates the power of the term. Mary Bilder, *The Transatlantic Constitution—Colonial Legal Culture and the Empire* (Cambridge: Harvard University Press, 2004), 193. See also Maeva Marcus and Robert Teir, "Hayburn's Case: A Misrepresentation of Precedent," 530. They point out that because the Court (although Congress, James Madison, and the press did) did not use the term "unconstitutional," that the concept was thus somehow preserved for Marshall in *Marbury v. Madison*. Oddly, Marshall never used the term either.

43. See Marcus, ed., *The Documentary History of the Supreme Court of the United States*, Vol. 6, 46, for the brief full text version of the decision reached on April 11, 1792, by the circuit court in Pennsylvania relating to the appearance of William Hayburn before that court. The House of Representatives two days later on April 13, 1792, commented on receipt of the circuit court decision and noted that Hayburn, having been rejected by the circuit court, thereupon petitioned Congress directly. Congress acknowledged that the justices found the act to be unconstitutional and further that the justices felt the act placed a burden on them that was "extraordinary."

44. From the very beginning of the entire episode, Attorney General Edmund Randolph argued the Justices were overstepping their bounds. Within a few days of passage of the act, Justice Wilson was already voicing his concerns. He and Randolph crossed paths on a street in Philadelphia and exchanged words over the constitutionality of the act and the potential course the justices were to take. See a letter from Randolph to President Washington in Marcus, ed., *The Documentary History of the Supreme Court of the United States*, Vol. 6, 45.

45. See *ibid.*, 63, for Justice Iredell's view of Attorney General Randolph's position on *ex officio*. See also pgs. 67–69 for further discussion on the mandamus and *ex officio* issues. See also pg. 295 for the Supreme Court opinion in *Ex Parte Chandler* of February 14, 1794, stating that a mandamus could not be enjoined. See

also Marcus and Teir, "Hayburn's Case: A Misrepresentation of Precedent," (535–38) for a further discussion on the mandamus issue raised by Randolph. When Randolph appeared before the Court, he was not representing a client, although he claimed to represent the United States. Justice Iredell is known to have likened Randolph's role of attorney general to that of his English counterpart. Thus, Iredell was inclined to allow Randolph to continue in pursuing the *mandamus*. The full Court however split evenly over whether to grant Randolph's request. A split meant the appellant (which in theory Randolph was) would not receive the relief sought of the Court. The Court seemed more inclined to receive Randolph *ex parte* but would not receive him as acting without the approval of President Washington.

46. See the report of the Supreme Court and the letter from Attorney General Bradford to Secretary of War Knox, in Marcus, ed., *The Documentary History of the Supreme Court of the United States*, Vol. 6, 381.

47. See *ibid.*, 295.

48. See Mary Bilder, *The Transatlantic Constitution-Colonial Legal Culture and the Empire.* (Cambridge, 2004), 194, who feels that federal judicial review of federal legislation first occurred in 1803 (Bilder inadvertently states 1801). Like many legal history scholars, Bilder almost blindly follows the misconceived notion that Marshall somehow pulled the concept of judicial review out of thin air and inaugurated it. See also Scott Gerber for the "Myth of Marbury v. Madison" in Scott Douglas Gerber, ed., *Seriatim: The Supreme Court Before John Marshall*, 9–11. Also see William Michael Treavor, "Judicial Review Before *Marbury*," 58 *Stanford Law Review* (2005), 518. One still unanswered question is why the 1790s Court has not been treated the way the Court has been studied commencing with the arrival of Marshall? Treavor feels the period in the Courts history has simply been ignored. The gravitational pull of Marshall has significantly weakened the serious study of the 1790s Court, much to the detriment of Federalist-era scholarship. See also Marcus, ed., *The Documentary History of the Supreme Court of the United States*, Vol. 1, Part 1, xli, for a similar lament on the lack of scholarship regarding this period of the Court's history.

49. Mark D. Hall, quotes St. George Tucker who edited Blackstone's *Commentaries* in 1803. Tucker "cites *Hayburn's* case as evidence that the judiciary has the duty to void an unconstitutional act of Congress." In Gerber, ed., *Seriatim: The Supreme Court Before John Marshall*, 137.

50. See William Casto, *The Supreme Court*

in the Early Republic (Columbia: New York University Press, 1995), 177. *Yale Todd*, decided in an actual Court sitting, did find that Justices "were not authorized to serve as commissioners." Although this case occurred after Congress had updated the act to comply with the justices' advice, the Court found that the attempt of Chief Justice Jay to find a compromise with the initial legislative directive was not valid either. Therefore, not only was the act unconstitutional, but the proposed compromise—under which *Yale Todd* was assisted— was invalid. Justices could not serve outside their Constitutional capacity. This of course left the Court with something of a dichotomy in that the Court could not gather information for Congress, or any other branch, but that is exactly how the *Hayburn* case played out. Although the initial concerns expressed by the justices should more appropriately be seen as warnings in an as yet untried system. The Court warned Congress that they would find the act unconstitutional if it would come before them. Essentially, the Court, and Congress, were trying to find their way.

51. See Justice Cushing's opinion in *Chisholm v. Georgia* where he draws a similar comparison. Julius Goebel, Jr., *Antecedents and Beginnings to 1801* (New York: Macmillan, 1971), 731.

52. The Founders' Constitution Volume 4, Article 3, Section 2, Clause 1, Document 37 http://press-pubs.uchicago.edu/founders/documents/a3_2_1s37.html. University of Chicago Press.

53. See Marcus, ed., *The Documentary History of the Supreme Court of the United States,* Vol. 6, 40.

54. See Wythe Holt in Gerber, ed., *Seriatim: The Supreme Court Before John Marshall*, 174.

55. Marcus and Teir, "Hayburn's Case: A Misrepresentation of Precedent," 540.

56. See Marcus, ed., *The Documentary History of the Supreme Court of the United States,* Vol. 6, 48–59.

57. See Marcus, ed., *The Documentary History of the Supreme Court of the United States,* Vol. 6, 48, for the proceedings of the House of Representatives for April 13, 1792, for the full text of the response of Congress to the action of the Justices.

58. The Founders' Constitution Volume 4, Article 3, Section 2, Clause 1, Document 37 http://press-pubs.uchicago.edu/founders/documents/a3_2_1s37.html. University of Chicago Press.

59. Bilder, *The Transatlantic Constitution- Colonial Legal Culture and the Empire,* 196, equates the American concept of judicial review as being inherited from the English Privy Council and its repugnancy approach to contrary laws. She sees the Revolutionary period as being an attempt to re-establish this concept which apparently had somehow been lost. See also Marcus and Teir, "Hayburn's Case: A Misrepresentation of Precedent," 532, who see the term "unconstitutional" as "taboo" in the 1790s.

60. See Bilder, *The Transatlantic Constitution- Colonial Legal Culture and the Empire,* 8. Bilder discusses the problems of studying the eighteenth-century legal issues with a twenty-first-century legal vocabulary: "Seemingly familiar entities often have unfamiliar dimensions." See also Wythe Holt in Gerber, ed., *Seriatim: The Supreme Court Before John Marshall,* 175, for a further discussion on why *Hayburn* does not fit into the language of twenty-first-century jurisprudential writing. See also Max Farrand, "The First Hayburn Case, 1792," *The American Historical Review*, Vol. 13, no. 2 (Jan. 1908), 285, for an early twentieth-century vocabulary viewpoint where Farrand writes: "In view of all these things there would seem to be no reasonable doubt that on April 11, James Wilson, John Blair, and Richard Peters declared the Invalid Pension Act of 1792 unconstitutional."

61. In all, Georgia was a party to three cases before the Court in the 1790s. See Doyle Mathis, "Georgia Before the Supreme Court," *The American Journal of Legal History* 12, no. 2 (1968), 112–121. Mathis offers a brief overview of the three cases.

62. See Sandra Frances VanBurkleo, in Gerber, ed., *Seriatim: The Supreme Court Before John Marshall,* 48. VanBurkleo writes that Georgia originally returned the summons to the circuit court "claiming immunity from federal process," not claiming the issue of suability.

63. Contrast with Leonard W. Levy, who sees *The Federalist* papers as a poor basis for an argument for the beliefs of the authors, particularly in regard to judicial review. Levy sees number 78 as one part of the puzzle of judicial review which leaves it uncompleted. This book however sees number 78, and others, as part of the puzzle which lends to completing it. Levy further criticizes Charles Beard for relying too much on number 78 in his writings, while Beard, if he were alive, could just as easily criticize Levy for not placing enough reliance on number 78. See Leonard W. Levy, "Judicial Review, History, and Democracy: An Introduction," in Leonard W. Levy, ed., *Judicial Review and the Supreme Court* (New York: Harper Torchbooks, 1967), 6. See also Charles A. Beard, *The Supreme Court and the Constitution* (Englewood Cliffs, NJ: Prentice-Hall, 1962).

64. Clinton Rossiter, ed., *The Federalist Papers* (New York: Penguin Group, 1999), 71.

65. *Ibid.*, 194. Hamilton makes a similar argument in number 82 as well, *ibid.*, 491. Also, in number 82, he draws the comparison of the states coming together in a new arrangement: "The establishment of a constitution founded upon the total or partial incorporation of a number of distinct sovereignties." *Ibid.*, 490. See also Kemp Plummer Yarborough, "*Chisholm v. Georgia*: A study of the Minority Opinion" (Ph.D. diss., Columbia University, 1963). Yarborough discusses at length the not always consistent contributions of Hamilton to the concept of state sovereignty in *The Federalist* papers.

66. David P. Currie, *The Constitution in the Supreme Court—The First Hundred Years 1789–1888* (Chicago: University of Chicago Press, 1985), 18.

67. Papers of John Jay at http://www.columbia.edu/cu/lweb/digital/jay/. Contained at the link http://www.columbia.edu/cu/lweb/digital/exhibitions/constitution/essay.html. (accessed March 1, 2004).

68. Chief Justice Jay phrased his reading of Article III, Section II, in his opinion to say: "If we attend to the words we find them to be express, positive, free from ambiguity, and without room for such implied expressions" as Georgia was insinuating. George Lankevich, ed., *The Federal Court 1787-1801* (Danbury, CT: The Grolier Educational Corporation, 1995), 160. See also *ibid.*, 162, for the opinion of Justice Wilson, who wrote concerning the pre–Eleventh Amendment text of Article III, Section II, in relation to citizens and states in legal suits, "Could this strict and appropriated language, describe, with more precise accuracy, the cause now depending before the tribunal?"

69. See William F. Swindler, "Mr. Chisholm and the Eleventh Amendment." Supreme Court Historical Society *1981 Yearbook*, 2. http://supremecourthistory.org/pub_journal_archive.html. He sees the Eleventh Amendment as "the first substantial alteration in the original language of the Constitution of 1787." However, for an alternate view see Yarborough, "*Chisholm v. Georgia*: A study of the Minority Opinion," 342. Yarborough sees the eleventh as not changing the Constitution but rather as a substitute decision for the Court, although not by the Court. He writes, "it simply overrules the Court's construction of the Judicial Article of the Constitution and imposes another and a different construction."

70. In the introduction to volume five of *The Documentary History of the Supreme Court*, editor Mavea Marcus comments that "the issue of state suability … had long been a matter of controversy and debate." She and her staff found records of seven cases reaching the Court in the early 1790s. The cases are: (1) *Van Staphorst v. Maryland*; (2) *Oswald v. New York*; (3) *Chisholm v. Georgia*; (4) *Hollingsworth v. Virginia*; (5) *Vassall v. Massachusetts*; (6) *Cutting v. South Carolina*; and (7) *Moultrie v. Georgia*. The issue of state sovereignty has roots in the ancient world and progressing up through the centuries when the English monarchs claimed the prerogative not to be sued without their permission. This thinking transferred to the states and they maintained this position even after the passage of the Constitution. Marcus, ed., *The Documentary History of the Supreme Court of the United States 1789–1801*, Vol. 5, 1–3. Julius Goebel, attributes the rash of cases to "state impeditive legislation or the shortcomings of extant judicial machinery." Julius Goebel, Jr., *Antecedents and Beginnings to 1801* (New York: Macmillan, 1971), 722. This reference serves to highlight the uniqueness, or the wholly new separate arrangement that existed under the Constitution. State legislation and antiquated judicial systems could not, and would not, be relied upon to solve the problems engendered by the growing commercial nation. Goebel further states that the Court "having decided upon the construction of Article III, Section 2, considered itself bound by precedent is evident from the proceedings in *Hollingsworth, Cutting, and Moultrie*." *Ibid.*, 738. Although these latter three cases were filed after *Chisholm*, but before the Eleventh Amendment was proclaimed by the president (February 10, 1798), the Court quite rightly followed it first precedent in cases of similar nature. However, on February 14, 1798, "the Court decided unanimously that the amendment being constitutionally adopted, no jurisdiction in any case past or future could be exercised in any case in which a state was sued by citizens of another state or by citizens and subjects of any foreign state." *Ibid.*, 741.

71. Marcus, ed., *The Documentary History of the Supreme Court of the United States 1789–1801*, Vol. 5, 142.

72. Julius Goebel sees Georgia's overall stance to the case as "intemperate, reflecting not only wounded pride, but also … hotheadedness." See Goebel, Jr., *Antecedents and Beginnings to 1801*, 734.

73. Marcus, ed., *The Documentary History of the Supreme Court of the United States 1789–1801*, Vol. 5, 143.

74. William Casto views Justice Iredell's opinion as virtually ignoring the Constitution in favor of the notion of state sovereignty. Casto, *The Supreme Court in the Early Republic: The Chief Justiceships of John Jay and Oliver*

Ellsworth, 190. Casto goes on to state that Iredell's reasoning was "deeply flawed." *Ibid.*, 197.

75. George Lankevich, ed., *The Federal Court 1787–1801* (Danbury, CT: The Grolier Educational Corporation, 1995), 162. Justice Wilson's colleague Justice Iredell clearly saw the issue of sovereignty as a debatable point. See his notes on the Court case in Marcus, ed., *The Documentary History of the Supreme Court of the United States*, Vol. 5, 215.

76. See Doyle Mathis, "Georgia Before the Supreme Court," *The American Journal of Legal History* 12, no. 2 (1968), 22. See also Justice Wilson's opening comments in his decision in the *Chisholm* case. He states the case is "of uncommon magnitude," and that Georgia, "whose claim soars so high," is questioning whether it "is amenable to the jurisdiction of the supreme court of the United States?" Lankevich, ed., *The Federal Court 1787–1801*, 162.

77. Doyle Mathis, "Georgia Before the Supreme Court," *The American Journal of Legal History* 12, no. 2 (1968), 23.

78. Marcus, ed., *The Documentary History of the Supreme Court of the United States*, Vol. 5, 131.

79. Yarborough, "*Chisholm v. Georgia*: A study of the Minority Opinion," 2.

80. While Yarborough spends an entire dissertation arguing why Iredell's opinion should not be seen as a precursor to the later states' rights arguments of someone like John C. Calhoun, it is difficult to see how Iredell does not in some incipient way fit into the pedigree of someone like Calhoun. For a contrast, see Richard B. Morris, *John Jay, the Nation, and the Court* (Boston: Boston University, 1967), 60–61. Morris writes that "so intense was the hostility to federal jurisdiction in North Carolina that in 1790 the members of the lower house refused to take an oath to support the Constitution. The intensity of states' rights feeling could not have been lost on Iredell and indubitably was reflected in his carefully reasoned dissenting opinion." See also Morris's discussion, *ibid.*, 66, concerning Iredell's influence on later states' rights ideology.

81. However lonely Justice Iredell was within the Court concerning his opinion, in his home state of North Carolina, it was "universally applauded." Marcus, ed., *The Documentary History of the Supreme Court of the United States*, Vol. 5, 229.

82. *Ibid.*, 150. Further, Iredell, in his opinion at the Court, considers the *Chisholm* case to involve a "great Constitutional Question." *Ibid.*, 186.

83. See the website at http://www.constitution.org/uslaw/judiciary_1789.htm.

84. *Ibid.*

85. Marcus, ed., *The Documentary History of the Supreme Court of the United States*, Vol. 5, 152.

86. George Lankevich, ed., *The Federal Court 1787–1801* (Danbury, CT: The Grolier Educational Corporation, 1995), 165.

87. Contrast Charles Warren's reasoning on the stability of the Supreme Court as created, just as Congress was created, under the Constitution. Further, Warren denotes a much broader scale application of power to the Supreme Court as opposed to Congress due to the wording of the delegation of that power in the Constitution. The Congress has that power which was *granted* by the Constitution, whereas the Supreme Court has *the* judicial power. In other words, Congress has all of its power created and controlled by the Constitution. The Supreme Court has a pre-existing judicial power which is beyond the power of the Constitution. The Congress can however delimit how power within the broad general grant of power is allocated. Charles Warren, *Congress, the Constitution, and the Supreme Court.* (Boston: Little, Brown, 1925), 56.

88. Yarborough, "*Chisholm v. Georgia*: A study of the Minority Opinion," 24.

89. Only five justices are listed due to Justice Johnson's continuing illness. He would shortly leave the Court.

90. William F. Swindler, "Mr. Chisholm and the Eleventh Amendment," Supreme Court Historical Society *Yearbook 1981*, 3. http://supremecourthistory.org/pub_journal_archive.html. Swindler sees Georgia as having expropriated the supplies that Farquhar had sold to Stone and Davies (as Georgia's representatives) and therefore that issue was a moot point and all that remained was to exert state sovereignty.

91. Naturally, both of these cases produced enormous concern among the other states. The idea that states would so jealously put forth the notion of state sovereignty as to create a constitutional amendment is today difficult to grasp. William Swindler, *ibid.*, 2. He categorizes the reaction as "outraged screams rent the air" over the decisions concerning the right of individuals to sue a state without its permission. On the other side of the argument, Attorney General Edmund Randolph can be said to represent the opinion of those who, like himself and Chief Justice Jay, felt that states should not be exempt from federal judicial power. He commented, "Shall the tranquility of our country be at the mercy of every state?" Sandra VanBurkleo writes that the Supreme Court found (with the exception of Justice Iredell) "sovereign immunity inappropriate in a republic." Both the Randolph and VanBurkleo quotes are

found in Sandra Frances VanBurkleo, "Honour, Justice, and Interest" in Gerber, ed., *Seriatim, The Supreme Court Before John Marshall*, 48.

92. Lankevich, ed., *The Federal Court 1787–1801*, 159.

93. See also Justice Wilson's opinion, where he states that only the people are sovereign. *Ibid.*, 162.

94. *Ibid.*, 160.

95. A century later, the Court would rule in *Hans v. Louisiana* (1890), that states had immunity not only from citizens of another state as provided by the Eleventh Amendment, it also had immunity from its own citizens. See David P. Currie, *The Constitution in the Supreme Court—The First Hundred Years 1789–1888* (Chicago: University of Chicago Press, 1985), 19.

96. Lankevich, ed., *The Federal Court 1787–1801*, 161. Jay ends his opinion by enjoining Americans that "nothing but the free course of constitutional law and government can insure the continuance and enjoyment" of the privileges secured through a federal system of governance.

97. Marcus, ed., *The Documentary History of the Supreme Court of the United States*, Vol. 5, 158.

98. No genuine debate occurred mainly because there was near unanimity among Georgia legislatures that the ruling, and indeed the filing, was bogus. By late 1793, legislation was pending which threatened any "Federal Marshal," or anyone associated with Chisholm or with any federal court with hanging without trail by the imposition of a felony conviction simply by fiat. See Marcus, ed., *The Documentary History of the Supreme Court of the United States*, Vol. 5, 236, for this unique approach to law.

99. *Ibid.*, 163.

100. *Ibid.*, 223.

101. While little evidence can be found, it begs the question as to how the phrase got into the Constitution in the first place given the huge negative response to the ruling. It is also interesting how many of the negative responses dealt with the fact that although the Constitution may indeed say a certain thing (as Justice Iredell pointed out in his opinion), that should not necessarily force the Court to rule that way. On one hand this would almost seem as though those who opposed the ruling (virtually everyone it seemed) reverted to the notion of common law adjudication rather than constitutional adjudication. Furthermore, it was the Supreme Court which truly embodied the language and the spirit of the Constitution. In other words, the Court was centuries ahead of the opposition from the standpoint of federal supremacy. While the concept of Federalism is still played out in the Court today, the Jay Court has offered the only opinion free of transitory interpretation of the Constitution concerning this issue.

102. One later case, filed after *Chisholm* but prior to the actual approval of the Eleventh Amendment, dealt with the estate of the Prince of Luxembourg (*Cutting v. South Carolina* a.k.a. *Catlin v. South Carolina*). See Goebel, Jr., *Antecedents and Beginnings to 1801*, 737.

103. This case was reenacted on September 19, 2016, in the original courtroom in Philadelphia. When one thinks of reenactment of historical events, battles generally come to mind. However, in this instance, a famous Supreme Court case was the topic. Chief Justice John Roberts, with Justices Stephen Breyer and Samuel Alito, "heard" the case.

104. Wythe W. Holt, "The Establishment of the Federal Court System," 5. "A real government [which the United States seemed only to aspire to] had respect for foreign dignitaries, providing them with a national court to which they could take disputes."

105. Maeva Marcus, *The Documentary History*, Vol. 6, 74.

106. *Ibid.*, 156. See Edmund Pendleton to Nathaniel Pendleton. Edmund wrote, "It seems to me that the treaty comes before the Court as a law of mutual Obligations." Pendleton is referring to the exchange of mutual obligation between nations.

107. *Ibid.*, 75. The *Georgia Gazette* on May 3, 1792, referred to Brailsford as "a real British subject." *Ibid.*, 115. In the same report, the paper matter-of-factly reported the outcome of the case without offering an opinion.

108. *Ibid.*, 76.

109. *Ibid.*, 95. As District Judge Pendleton stated in his opinion of May 2, 1792, "The question now to be decided would still remain, whether it is not repealed [the Georgia law], or at least removed out of the way of British Creditors, by the Treaty of Peace." Judge Pendleton continues that the Treaty was in effect when the Constitution was adopted "and as such it was admitted and declared to be the supreme law of the land by the consent of all the states."

110. *Ibid.*, 95. Judge Pendleton considered this argument of the state of Georgia, and found it wanting. He felt Georgia's reasoning that it can "invalidate the Treaty" due to the "inefficacy of Congress ... to enforce obedience" to be "strange reasoning."

111. Julius Goebel, Jr., *Antecedents and Beginnings to 1801*. (New York: Macmillan, 1971), 744. Chief Justice Jay commented on the two

cases by noting that in *Chisholm,* Georgians do not want non-citizens suing them; whereas in *Brailsford,* Georgians wanted to be able to sue non-citizens.

112. Bernard Bailyn, *The Debate on the Constitution,* Vol. 2, 530. "Phocion," writing in the *United States Chronicle* from Providence, Rhode Island, on July 17, 1788, believed the small states, including Georgia, "clearly saw that if the Constitution was rejected, in the hurly-burly of confusions and anarchy which would arise, they should be swallowed up by their more powerful neighbors."

113. Julius Goebel, *Antecedents and Beginnings,* 746—as James Madison observed when he wrote to Thomas Jefferson, "That State is threatened with a dangerous war with the Creek Indians." However, Madison also wrote to Edmund Randolph, before he had learned of Georgia's ratification, "I consider every thing as problematic from Maryland Southward."

114. Maeva Marcus, *The Documentary History,* Vol. 6, 96. Judge Pendleton in his opinion addressed the pertinent articles of the Georgia Act of Confiscation which declared "all debts due to merchants and others residing in Great Britain should be sequestered." Judge Pendleton contrasts the Act of Confiscation with the holding "that debts contracted on the faith of commercial intercourse ought to be deemed a sacred and inviolable nature."

115. See Article VI of the Constitution.

116. Maeva Marcus, *The Documentary History,* Vol. 6, 102.

117. *Ibid.,* 102. This question "will depend on the construction of certain Acts of Assembly of this State, and the operation of the Treaty of Peace upon them."

118. *Ibid.,* 114. In the end, he concluded, "Nothing is objected in this case but the legal Impediment in the State law."

119. William Casto, *The Supreme Court in the Early Republic,* 30.

120. Maeva Marcus, *The Documentary History,* Vol. 6, 113. Justice Iredell in his circuit court opinion pursued a straight-line definition of Article VI, Section II that treaties made under the authority of the United States "shall be the Supreme Law of the Land" and any state law to the contrary is void. The section, coupled with the preceding section I, clearly gives the United States through the Constitution the authority to bind obligations assumed through the Treaty of Paris and subsequently through the Constitution. Justice Iredell also commented on the international implications of a case such as *Chisholm,* where the "national faith" is placed in peril relative to the conduct of nations.

121. Maeva Marcus, *The Documentary History,* Vol. 6, 115. Even though the Treaty of Paris was concluded and ratified prior to the adoption of the Constitution, it remained in effect in part due to Article VI, Section I, of the Constitution. The day after the decisions were made known on May 22, 1792, the *Georgia Gazette* in Savannah, Georgia, reported on the case by stating, "The Treaty of Peace, as confirmed by the Constitution of the United States, must have the effect of an express repeal of that part of the act of Assembly which had created an impediment to his [Brailsford] recovery."

122. *Ibid.,* 81.

123. Goebel, Jr., *Antecedents and Beginnings to 1801,* 744.

124. *Ibid.,* 744. Justices Cushing and Johnson "dissented because they believed that Georgia had an adequate remedy at law." For Chief Justice Jay, see Maeva Marcus, *The Documentary History,* Vol. 6, 170. Chief Justice Jay, in his charge to the jury, stated "the Debts were not confiscated by the statute of Georgia" but only sequestered. Jay continued "his [Brailsford] right to recover them revived at the peace [by] the law of Nations and by the Treaty of Peace."

125. Maeva Marcus, *The Documentary History,* 171.

126. Charles Warren, *The Supreme Court in United States History.* (Boston: Little, Brown, 1926), Vol. I, 144.

127. William Casto, *The Supreme Court in the Early Republic,* 36. The Justices seemed intent on addressing every conceivable system of law to ensure a balanced decision was reached in *Brailsford.* William Casto writes: "The Supreme Court appellate power over the state courts' administration of the common law would have arisen in any state court litigation involving citizens of different states [some of Brailsford's associates were from South Carolina] or aliens [Brailsford]. But the power was also inherent in the Court's appellate jurisdiction over cases arising under federal law."

128. Stanley Elkins and Eric McKitrick, *The Age of Federalism* (New York: Oxford University Press, 1993), 330.

129. *Ibid.,* 354.

130. *Ibid.,* 142.

131. *The Papers of Thomas Jefferson Digital Edition,* ed. James P. McClure and J. Jefferson Looney. Charlottesville: University of Virginia Press, Rotunda, 2008–2017. Main Series, Volume 26.

132. *Ibid.*

133. *Ibid.*

134. Gordon Wood, *Empire of Liberty: A History of the Early Republic, 1789–1815* (Oxford: Oxford University Press, 2009), 185.

135. Adrienne Koch, *Jefferson and Madison: The Great Collaboration* (New York: Alfred A. Knopf, 1950), 142–143.

136. Merrill D. Peterson, ed., *Thomas Jefferson: Writings* (New York: Literary Classics of the United States, 1984), 1008–1009.

137. Joanne B. Freeman, ed., *Alexander Hamilton: Writings* (New York: Literary Classics of the United States, 2001), 952.

138. John Rhodehamel, ed., *George Washington, Writings* (New York: Literary Classics of the United States, 1997), 876.

139. *Ibid.*, 876.

140. *Ibid.*, 885.

141. *Ibid.*, 884.

142. *Ibid.*, 884–885.

143. Wood, *Empire of Liberty: A History of the Early Republic*, 136.

144. *Ibid.*, 134.

145. Leonard D. White, *The Federalists: A Study in Administrative History 1789-1801* (New York: The Free Press, 1965), 419.

146. Merrill D. Peterson, ed., *Thomas Jefferson: Writings* (New York: Literary Classics of the United States, 1984), 1015.

147. *Ibid.*, 1016.

148. Joanne B. Freeman, ed., *Alexander Hamilton: Writings* (New York: Literary Classics of the United States, 2001), 823.

149. *Ibid.*, 824.

150. *Ibid.*, 825.

151. Rhodehamel, ed., *George Washington, Writings*, 882.

152. *Ibid.*, 883.

153. *The Papers of James Madison Digital Edition*, J. C. A. Stagg, editor. Charlottesville: University of Virginia Press, Rotunda, 2010. Congressional Series, Volume 16.

154. *Ibid.*

155. Kinvin L. Wroth, and Hiller B. Zobel, eds., *Legal Papers of John Adams*, Vol. II (New York: Atheneum, 1968), 356.

156. *The Adams Papers Digital Edition*, ed. Sara Martin. Charlottesville: University of Virginia Press, Rotunda, 2008-2017. Adams Family Correspondence, Volume 2.

157. Wroth, and Zobel, eds., *Legal Papers of John Adams*, Vol. II, 389.

158. *Ibid.*, 365.

159. *Ibid.*, 368.

160. Marcus, ed., *The Documentary History of the Supreme Court of the United States*, Vol. 6, 399.

161. As quoted in Wroth, and Zobel, eds., *Legal Papers of John Adams*, Vol. II, 374.

162. As quoted, *ibid.*, 376.

163. Marcus, ed., *The Documentary History of the Supreme Court of the United States*, Vol. 6, 415.

164. Charles Warren, *The Supreme Court in United States History*, Vol. 1 (Boston: Little, Brown, 1926), 58.

165. Marcus, ed., *The Documentary History of the Supreme Court of the United States*, Vol. 4, 547.

166. *Ibid.*, 555.

167. *Ibid.*, 556.

168. *Ibid.*, 561.

169. *Ibid.*, 563.

170. *Ibid.*, 563.

171. *Ibid.*, 567.

172. *Ibid.*, 567.

173. *Ibid.*, 569.

174. *Ibid.*, 574.

175. *Ibid.*, 584.

176. *Ibid.*, 587.

177. *Ibid.*, 587.

178. *Ibid.*, 594.

179. *Ibid.*, 594. An understanding from August 1792, according to the editors of the *Documentary History of the Supreme Court of the United States*, did exist from that date.

180. *Ibid.*, 594.

181. *Ibid.*, 597.

182. *Ibid.*, 604.

183. *Ibid.*, 608.

184. *The Adams Papers Digital Edition*, ed. C. James Taylor. Charlottesville: University of Virginia Press, Rotunda, 2008–2016. Adams Family Correspondence, Volume 9.

185. See Marcus and Teir, "Hayburn's Case: A Misrepresentation of Precedent," 539, for a discussion on the Court's reluctance to declare an Act unconstitutional.

186. Establishing a foundation of American jurisprudence was one thing, establishing an American reputation for jurisprudence was quite another. The actions of the 1790s Supreme Court were analogous to creating a two-tiered wall of acknowledgment so vital for international relations. The English, as America's "parent," had over a thousand years of law which they saw as the foundation of civil society and a vital component of civilization. The Supreme Court could never match that long term development as with the English legal system. The Supreme Court could however establish a solid foundation of American law and practice, and within ten years they had succeeded.

Chapter 6

1. Maeva Marcus, ed., *The Documentary History of the Supreme Court of the United States, 1789-1800*, Vol. 6 (New York: Columbia University Press, 1998), 699–700.

2. *Ibid.*, 651. The Treaty in question was signed by the desperate American's who were

facing imminent defeat if France did not sign onto the cause. The Treaty, allowing privateering, ensured the French would have some means to recoup the money they were investing in the American effort. Privateering could be a lucrative profession and the French felt it a worthwhile trade for offering America assistance.

   3. *Ibid.*, 651.

   4. *Ibid.*, 653.

   5. *Ibid.*, 657.

   6. *Ibid.*, 658.

   7. Writing nearly forty years after the debt cases when the issue was firmly established, Justice Joseph Story commented on the topic in his *Commentaries on the Constitution* (1833). Story wrote: "This can be considered in no other light, than as a declaratory proposition, resulting from the law of nations, and the moral obligations of society. Nothing is more clear upon reason or general law, than the doctrine, that revolutions in government have, or rather ought to have, no effect whatsoever upon private rights, and contracts, or upon the public obligations of nations. It results from the first principles of moral duty, and responsibility, deducible from the law of nature, and applied to the intercourse and social relations of nations. A change in the political form of a society ought to have no power to produce a dissolution of any of its moral obligations." Story's commentary illustrates, in unfamiliar language, how the issue was viewed in the aftermath of the cases two generations removed. Further, Story was writing in a country which viewed itself, and was viewed by others, in a much different perspective in 1833 than in the late 1790s. http://www.constitution.org/js/js_342.htm

   8. Walter Stahr, *John Jay: Founding Father* (New York: Hambeldon & London, 2005), 276. Stahr, in discussing a grand jury charge which Jay gave in 1790, writes that "the United States could not expect Britain to observe the treaty of peace unless it also observed the treaty, and in particular the debt provisions." Stahr quotes Jay in comparing an international treaty to a "fair and legal contract between two men." The United States therefore has duties to fulfill under international treaties which are through the Constitution part of American law. See also Marcus, ed., *The Documentary History of the Supreme Court of the United States*, Vol. 7, 240. Justice Iredell in his notes on *Ware v. Hylton* seemed to indicate a similar notion when he writes, "National debt depend on the faith of government."

   9. As mentioned in the previous chapter, Justice Iredell is quoted as having felt *Ware* to be "the greatest Cause which ever came before

a Judicial court *in the world* [emphasis in original]." See Marcus, ed., *The Documentary History of the Supreme Court of the United States*, Vol. 6, 319–320. The Constitution was getting a tremendous workout in terms of judicial scrutiny and the terms of the document were upheld.

   10. Hylton's lead attorney, John Marshall, was certainly in favor of the viewpoint. In the opinion of some historians, Marshall is believed to have been behind efforts to organize opposition to British debt cases and against a national view of repayment. See Marcus, ed., *The Documentary History of the Supreme Court of the United States*, Vol. 6, 215.

   11. Philip B. Kurland, ed., *The Founders' Constitution*, Vol. IV (Chicago: University of Chicago Press, 1987), 585. Not only did the Treaty of Paris recognize this but the same line of argument was present at the Constitutional Convention in 1787. On August 21, 1787, James Madison recorded that Governor Livingston made the following statement: "The Legislature of the U.S. shall have power to fulfill the engagement which have been entered into by Congress, and to discharge as well the debts of the U[nited] S[tates]: as the debts incurred by the several States during the late war, for the common defense and general welfare." Livingston was reporting the findings of the Committee of the Eleven "to whom was referred the propositions respecting the debts of the several states." Livingston's committee saw beyond the issues of state law respecting British debt and recognized the Articles of Confederation and the Treaty of Paris. Both documents stipulated that British debt be repaid not just as a matter of policy respecting contracts, but also as a means to establish the credibility of the United States within the community of nations.

   12. Kurland, ed., *The Founders' Constitution*, Vol. IV, 239. See Justice Iredell's note for *Ware v. Hylton* where he writes, "Who shall judge? Must not the nation?" Iredell seemed to indicate that expediency would perhaps dictate.

   13. *Ibid.*, 585.

   14. *Ibid.*, 587. Elbridge Gerry, in a debate in the House on public credit on February 25, 1790, stated "that the assumption of the state debts was in contemplation from the very commencement of the new Government."

   15. *Ibid.*, 589. Nearly a decade earlier, Jay, then the secretary of foreign affairs under the Articles of Confederation, wrote, "In some of the states too little attention appears to have been paid to the public faith pledged by that [Paris] treaty." Jay clearly saw the implications of national credibility and maintained his commitment through his tenure as chief.

16. Justice Samuel Chase would write an opinion in *Ware* that contained the strongest language on the subject of federal law versus state law. Justice Chase wrote, "A treaty cannot be the supreme law of the land ... if any act of a state legislature can stand in its way ... [L]aws of any of the states, contrary to a treaty, shall be disregarded.... [I]t is the declared duty of the state judges to determine any constitution or laws of any state, contrary to that treaty..., null and void." As quoted by David Currie, in David P. Currie, *The Constitution in the Supreme Court—The First Hundred Years 1789–1888* (Chicago: University of Chicago Press, 1985), 39–40.

17. Marcus, ed., *The Documentary History of the Supreme Court of the United States,* Vol. 7, 223. "Judex" believed that certain cases impacting British debts will soon come before the Court and the British creditors should find a "favorable decision" from Jay and his followers on the Court. Essentially, Judex was concerned whether or not Jay, as a negotiator of the Treaty in 1783, should sit in judgment on cases impacting the treaty.

18. Akil Amar writes that Article VI "sought to boost the Constitution *economically* and *internationally...*" (italics from the original). Akhil Reed Amar, *America's Constitution, a Biography* (New York: Random House, 2005), 302.

19. Akhil Amar sees Article VI as "the Constitution's most sustained meditation upon itself." *Ibid.*, 299. Amar's comment seems loaded with both symbolism and reality. It is as though the Constitution is a living document contemplating itself and acknowledging the power it has as the real manifestation of federal power. Amar continues: "Article VI echoed that phrase [this Constitution] four times in three short paragraphs, clarifying the precise status of the document vis-à-vis the old Confederation, the new federal government, and state governments."

20. *Ibid.*, 228–229. See also *ibid.*, 237 in a letter from Justice Iredell to Samuel Johnson, May 29, 1793. Justice Iredell felt that the defense of the British not upholding their portion of the Treaty was a non-argument. Justice Iredell wrote, "I am astonished to find that the defendant's [Hylton] lawyers here ... think the defense as to the breach of the Treaty by G[reat] B[ritain] seriously tenable."

21. *Ibid.*, 230. In a footnote Marcus includes a letter which the British minister to America, George Hammond, wrote to Lord Grenville, the foreign secretary, concerning the apparent sectional problems with the Paris Treaty of 1783. Hammond wrote: "I learn that in the New England and other states, which are attached to the present form of government, there exists the strongest disposition to observe implicitly the terms of the treaty. In the few causes for debt that have been brought before the federal Courts of these states ... have been uniformly consonant with the spirit of the Treaty and consequently favorable to the claims of the British Creditors. Unfortunately however, in many of the Southern States, a secret disinclination to the present constitution seems to retard the operation of its principles."

22. See Scott Douglas Gerber, "Deconstructing William Cushing," in Scott Douglas Gerber, ed., *Seriatim, The Supreme Court Before John Marshall* (New York: New York University Press, 1998), 111. Gerber writes that "as in *Chisholm*, James Iredell appeared to forget in *Ware* the difference between a politician and a judge."

23. Amar, *America's Constitution, a Biography,* 292. See pages 262–263 for the individual pleas which Justice Iredell referred to.

24. *Ibid.*, 263. Debt is sacred. And it is one of the most valuable ways in which a country can establish itself as a respected participant on the international scene.

25. *Ibid.*, 293. Jay continued: "By the dissolution of the government, the creditor necessarily lost the judicial means of compelling payment in this country, but the mere dissolution of the government could not destroy his right to compel it whenever and wherever he should find such means."

26. *Ibid.*, 309. Jay continued: "And so far as they affected the creditors, were, by the article, extinguished with it [the War]."

27. Contrast with David Currie, who sees "the most important constitutional holding of *Ware v. Hylton* was that the federal courts had the power to determine the constitutionality of state laws." In David P. Currie, *The Constitution in the Supreme Court—The First Hundred Years 1789–1888* (Chicago: University of Chicago Press, 1985), 39.

28. *Ibid.*, 339. See a letter from Jeremiah Smith to William Plumer on February 17, 1796. Smith outlined the arguments in the case and gave John Marshall, Hylton's lead attorney, high praise. Smith also speculated that "Cushing, Wilson & Patterson will be in favor of the British Creditor Iredel [sic] & Chace are contra but this is mere conjecture." Smith was obviously unaware that Justice Iredell had removed himself from consideration due to his involvement at the circuit court level. One observer compared Marshall's performance to that of the ancients: he "...spoke with the Judgment of a Demostenes, joined with the animation of a Cicero." *Ibid.* 340. John Milledge to Sheftall Sheftall, February 26, 1796.

29. The practice of not registering a Court opinion is probably one reason why the early Court is so often neglected. Scholars and lawyers tend to prefer the neat package of a unified opinion which they can point to. Individual opinions seem to create a sense of confusion about where the law actually lies. It is simple enough to take a tally of what side an individual justices vote for, and the one with the most votes wins the case. However, in attempting to establish law and precedent, individual opinions cast by the 1790s Court have tended to dissuade researchers from approaching their work.

30. David Currie's comment is a good example of the view of the opinions of justices: "Paterson, Wilson, and Cushing issued forgettable opinions confined almost entirely to the interpretation of the treaty." Currie, *The Constitution in the Supreme Court*, 37.

31. George J. Lankevich, *The Federal Court 1787–1801* (Danbury, CT: Grolier Educational Corporation, 1995), 181. While these comments seem textual in their approach, scholars have found them inspirational.

32. *Ibid.*, 181.

33. In support of this contention of the Court impacting national development through the establishment of constitutional interpretation, see Amar, *America's Constitution, a Biography*, 299. Amar sees Article VI as the one article designed to instill confidence abroad and a sense of commitment at home. Through upholding such concepts, the Court established precedent concerning the constitutional development of the Court and of American national government. Amar writes: "Article VI began by smoothing over the juridical rupture between the old 'Confederation' and the new 'Constitution,' reassuring America's creditors and treaty partners that the new United States would stand behind all the 'Debts' and 'Engagements' of its predecessor, even if the new union ultimately failed to encompass all thirteen of the original states."

34. There are very few surviving newspaper accounts of the case and those which do are confined to straight reporting without editorial. The best description of what occurred in *Ware v. Hylton* from a constitutional standpoint is contained in a letter from Phineas Bond (counsel general) to Lord Grenville (foreign secretary) on March 8, 1796. Bond wrote, "The Judges of the Supreme Court of the United States, four against one, have given Judgment upon the great Question which involved the Payment of Paper Money into the Loan Office of Virginia, in Discharge of British Debts: these Payments are declared to be absolute Nullities, and by this Judgment all Regulations under the

Laws or Constitutions of the individual States, incompatible with the Stipulations of the Treaty of Peace, are rendered of no Avail...." Amar, *America's Constitution, a Biography,* 348. Further, see William Casto, *The Supreme Court in the Early Republic: The Chief Justiceships of John Jay and Oliver Ellsworth* (Columbia: University of South Carolina Press, 1995), 100. Casto writes on the importance of *Ware* and the debt cases in general: "In *Ware* the Court gave its uncompromising support to the enforcement of the national government's treaty obligations and established the important precedent that the Constitution's Supremacy Clause would be enforced even in highly charged political controversies like the British debt problem."

35. Marcus, ed., *The Documentary History of the Supreme Court of the United States,* Vol. 7, 227. From a letter by James Madison to Edmund Pendleton, January 2, 1791. There is no record other than this reference as to whether Iredell actually stated this. It would not be an unusual statement though, given that Daniel Hylton was a perceptive observer of the political scene and was a close confidant of Thomas Jefferson. Further, Hylton came from, and represented, the most recalcitrant state in terms of repayment of British debt, Virginia. See also Marcus, ed., *The Documentary History of the Supreme Court of the United States,* Vol. 7, 262, where Justice Iredell does say in the opening to his circuit court opinion that the case is one of "uncommon magnitude." For a view of British impressions concerning the significance of the case in terms of their reasons why it is important, see Marcus, ed., *The Documentary History of the Supreme Court of the United States,* Vol. 7, 234. In a letter from British Minister George Hammond to Lord Grenville, the foreign secretary, where Hammond comments that Virginia is the only state "in which no adjudication by the Courts of the United States relative to the British debts has hitherto taken place."

Chapter 7

1. George J. Lankevich, *The Federal Court 1787–1801,* Vol. 1 (Danbury, CT: Grolier Educational Corporation, 1995), 199.

2. *Ibid.*, 199.

3. Maeva Marcus, ed., *The Documentary History of the Supreme Court of the United States, 1789–1800,* Vol. 7 (New York: Columbia University Press, 2004), 734.

4. *Ibid.*, 737.

5. *Ibid.*, 738.

6. Lankevich, *The Federal Court 1787–1801,* Vol. 1, 199.

7. *Ibid.*, 200.

8. *Ibid.*, 202.

9. *Ibid.*, 197–198.

10. Marcus, ed., *The Documentary History of the Supreme Court of the United States,* Vol. 8, 91.

11. Lankevich, *The Federal Court 1787–1801,* Vol. 1, 208.

12. *Ibid.*, 209.

13. *Ibid.*, 209.

14. Marcus, ed., *The Documentary History of the Supreme Court of the United States,* Vol. 8, 94.

15. Lankevich, *The Federal Court 1787–1801,* Vol. 1, 206.

16. *Ibid.*, 207.

17. *Ibid.*, 207.

18. *Ibid.*, 208.

19. Marcus, ed., *The Documentary History of the Supreme Court of the United States,* Vol. 8, 393.

20. *Ibid.*, 397.

21. Lankevich, *The Federal Court 1787–1801,* Vol. 1, 226.

22. *Ibid.*, 226.

23. *Ibid.*, 226.

24. *Ibid.*, 228.

25. *Ibid.*, 228.

26. Michael C. Toth, *Founding Federalist: The Life of Oliver Ellsworth* (Wilmington, DE: ISI Books, 2011), 196.

27. *Ibid.*, 202.

28. *Ibid.*, 203.

29. *Ibid.*, 203.

Chapter 8

1. Jeffrey Schenker, "James Madison: Consistent Defender of Republican Values" (Ph.D., Drew University, 2004), 113.

2. According to Stanley Elkins and Eric McKitrick, his term was dominated by foreign relations to an extent "unequaled in any other American Presidency." Stanley Elkins and Eric McKitrick, *The Age of Federalism, The Early American Republic, 1788–1800* (Oxford: Oxford University Press, 1993), 529. See also Schenker, "James Madison: Consistent Defender of Republican Values," 114.

3. The failure of the mission to secure an agreement, and the ignoble treatment received by the American delegation by Messrs. XYZ, "'electrified all classes' and the nation began immediate preparations for war." James Morton Smith, *Freedom's Fetters—The Alien and Sedition Laws and American Civil Liberties* (Ithaca: Cornell University Press, 1966), 7.

4. Ironically, it was the three American ministers, Marshall, Pickney, and Gerry, who would rather self-righteously remonstrate against the French Directorate by comparing their commitment to liberty to the value placed by the United States Constitution on the issues of free speech and free press: "The opinion of the people of the United States, cannot be over-ruled by those who administer the Government. Among those principles deemed sacred in America, ... which the Government contemplates with awful reverence ... there is no one which the importance is more deeply impressed on the public mind than the liberty of the press." Smith, *Freedom's Fetters—The Alien and Sedition Laws and American Civil Liberties,* 509. These same three ministers, with the exception of Marshall for the most part, would soon disavow their words by their deeds in supporting the Alien and Sedition Acts. If it is argued that the Federalists lost the election in 1800 in part due to the Acts, then this statement of the public importance of a free press was certainly a prophetic utterance. Perhaps though, the ministers were simply more in tune with public perception than their Federalist colleagues back home.

5. Albert J. Beveridge, *The Life of John Marshall,* Vol. 2 (Boston: Houghton Mifflin, 1919), 577.

6. Alfred Kelly perhaps terms it better, "the crisis." Alfred H. Kelly and Winfred A. Harbison. *The American Constitution, Its Origins and Development* (New York: W. W. Norton, 1976), 429. James Morton Smith, writing in *The William and Mary Quarterly,* commented that, "the years between 1798 and 1801 afford the first instance under the Constitution in which American political leaders faced the problem of defining the role of public criticism in a representative government." James Morton Smith, "The Sedition Law, Free Speech, and the American Political Process," *The William and Mary Quarterly* 9, no. 4, 3rd ser (1952), 497.

7. "Intense excitement generated by the [European] war," Kelly and Harbison, *The American Constitution, Its Origins and Development,* 186. While Adams "rode the crest of popular enthusiasm stirred up by the XYZ affair," he allowed Congress to carry "the United States into a virtual state of undeclared war with France." Smith, *Freedom's Fetters—The Alien and Sedition Laws and American Civil Liberties,* 8.

8. "The Sedition Law, aimed directly at the Democratic-Republicans, was the capstone of the internal security program of the Federalist Party." Smith, *Freedom's Fetters—The Alien and Sedition Laws and American Civil Liberties,* 498.

9. "Were deliberately designed to suppress the partisan activities of the Republican political

opposition." Kelly and Harbison, *The American Constitution, Its Origins and Development*, 186. John Miller writes, "Under the name of liberty, the Federalists complained, these [Republicans] opposed the war effort and heaped obloquy and contempt on the highest officers of the government." John Miller, *The Federalist Era, 1789-1801* (New York: Harper and Row, 1963), 228.

10. For the various totals of indictments and convictions, see: Miller, *The Federalist Era, 1789-1801*, 235; Peter Shaw, *The Character of John Adams* (Chapel Hill: University of North Carolina Press, 1976), 257; Maeva Marcus, *The Documentary History of the Supreme Court of the United States*, Vol. 3 (New York: Columbia University Press, 1990), 233; and Smith, *Freedom's Fetters—The Alien and Sedition Laws and American Civil Liberties*, 185.

11. Marcus, ed., *The Documentary History of the Supreme Court of the United States*, Vol. 3, 234. See also John Miller, "The Acts in total sought to curb freedom of speech and press, and limited the freedom of foreigners in the United States." See Miller, *The Federalist Era, 1789-1801*, 229

12. Marcus, ed., *The Documentary History of the Supreme Court of the United States*, Vol. 3, 235. See also John Miller, "No Federalist leader questioned the constitutionality of the act," which included members of the Supreme Court and several reasons for this can be proposed. Miller, *The Federalist Era, 1789-1801*, 232.

13. Philip B. Kurland and Ralph Lerner, eds., *The Founders' Constitution*, Vol. 5 (Indianapolis: The Liberty Fund, 2000), 118.

14. Clinton Rossiter, ed., *The Federalist Papers* (New York: Signet Classic, 1999), 280-282.

15. Kurland and Lerner, eds., *The Founders' Constitution*, Vol. 5, 118.

16. *Ibid.*, 119.

17. *Ibid.*, 119.

18. Roscoe Pound, *The Spirit of the Common Law and Other Writings* (Birmingham, AL: The Legal Classics Library, 1985), 71.

19. Miller, *The Federalist Era*, 229. See also, Peter Shaw, "Adams attracted responsibility not by any complicity in framing the acts, but by his failure to take up against them the moderate position that his administration stood for." Shaw, *The Character of John Adams*, 257. Also, James Morton Smith, Adams did however endorse the Sedition Law "as a necessary curb on the dishonest and impious who took advantage of the feeble restraints of a mild government." Smith, *Freedom's Fetters—The Alien and Sedition Laws*, 240.

20. Scott Douglas Gerber, "Deconstructing William Cushing," in Scott Douglas Gerber, *Se-*

riatim: The Supreme Court Before John Marshall (New York: New York University Press, 1998), 106.

21. In the Federalist universe, "it was a greater offense to criticize one of the rulers than it was to criticize one of the people [public]." James Morton Smith, "The Sedition Law, Free Speech, and the American Political Process," *The William and Mary Quarterly* 9, no. 4, 3rd ser (1952), 500.

22. W. R. Waterman states, "In the end the Acts undoubtedly played no small part in the downfall of the Federalist party in the election of 1800." W. R. Waterman, review of *Crisis in Freedom: The Alien and Sedition Acts*, by John C. Miller, *Political Science Quarterly* 67, no. 4 (December 1952): 627. Leonard Baker comments on this when he writes: the passage of the Alien and Sedition Acts "caused them [Federalists] a great deal of trouble and ultimately destroyed their party." Leonard Baker, *John Marshall, A Life in Law* (New York: Macmillan, 1974), 298.

23. Kermit L. Hall, ed., *The Oxford Companion to the Supreme Court of the United States* (Oxford: Oxford University Press, 1992), 764.

24. *Ibid.*, 764.

25. See *ibid.*, 764. The American Alien and Sedition Acts, however, allowed truth as a defense from the start, although, no one prosecuted ever went free by telling the truth. In his review, Mark DeWolfe Howe asserts that, "Congress had carefully sought to eliminate from its enactment those elements in English law to which objections had been persistently made on both sides of the Atlantic during the eighteenth century." Mark DeWolfe Howe, review of *Freedom's Fetters: The Alien and Sedition Laws and American Civil Liberties*, by James Morton Smith, *The William and Mary Quarterly* 14, no. 4 (October 1956), 575. Kelly comments that truth "before hostile judges demonstrated for the first time in America how dubious a defense of truth might be." Alfred H. Kelly and Winfred A. Harbison, *The American Constitution, Its Origins and Development* (New York: W. W. Norton, 1976), 432.

26. Juries could only find "that the utterance [or writing] had in fact occurred. It was up to the judge to decide upon its seditious character." Kelly and Harbison, *The American Constitution*, 431. The acts did amend this to allow the jury, not the judge, to determine whether "the words used violated the law." James Morton Smith, "The Sedition Law, Free Speech, and the American Political Process," *The William and Mary Quarterly* 9, no. 4, 3rd ser (1952), 498. Even with this adjustment, due to the overwhelming strength of the Federalists

to control even down to jury selection, "trial by jury in any real sense was not to be had" if charged under the Acts. Beveridge, *The Life of John Marshall*, Vol. 3, 43. Additionally, "the instruction of the judges made verdicts of guilty virtually inevitable" James Morton Smith, "The Sedition Law, Free Speech, and the American Political Process," *The William and Mary Quarterly* 9, no. 4, 3rd ser (1952), 503.

27. Marcus, *The Documentary History of the Supreme Court of the United States*, Vol. 3, 235.

28. Ellsworth "began 1799 by writing private and public advisory opinions calculated to establish the act's constitutionality." William R. Casto, "Oliver Ellsworth," in Gerber, *Seriatim: The Supreme Court Before John Marshall*, 308.

29. Smith, *Freedom's Fetters—The Alien and Sedition Laws*, 385.

30. In fact, in the cursory debates which did occur, "the Republicans flatly denied that there was a Common Law of the United States." Smith, *Freedom's Fetters—The Alien and Sedition Laws*, 133. As Leonard Levy writes, the Republican rejection of the Blackstone argument would result in "a new promontory of libertarian thought jutting out of a stagnant Blackstonian sea." Leonard W. Levy, "Liberty and the First Amendment," *The American Historical Review* 68, no. 1 (October 1962), 22. The Federalists argued however, that, "the constitution granted the federal courts Common Law jurisdiction over criminal cases, including sedition." Smith, *Freedom's Fetters—The Alien and Sedition Laws*, 132. Over a century later, Oliver Wendell Holmes would write in his opinion in *Abrams v. U.S.*, "I wholly disagree with the argument of the government that the First Amendment left the common law as to seditious libel in force." Leonard W. Levy, "Liberty and the First Amendment," *The American Historical Review* 68, no. 1 (October 1962), 22. In contrast, Charles Warren felt convinced that "the framers of the constitution and the members of the first Congress assumed that the Federal courts had jurisdiction over common-law crimes." Mark DeWolfe Howe, review of *Freedom's Fetters: The Alien and Sedition Laws and American Civil Liberties*, by James Morton Smith, *The William and Mary Quarterly* 14, no. 4 (October 1956), 574. W. R. Brock commented on the contemporary views regarding the First Amendment in 1962 by pairing Zechariah Chafee and Leonard Levy. Chafee felt the First Amendment "sought to wipe out the common law of sedition, and make further prosecutions for criticism of the government, without any incitement to law-breaking, forever impossible" in America. W.R. Brock, review of "Legacy of Suppression," *The English Historical Review* 77, no. 304 (July 1962), 567. Levy, on the other

hand, saw the First Amendment as the acceptance of "Blackstone's definition of the freedom of the press as the absence of previous restraints upon publication 'and not in freedom from censure for criminal matter when published'" Leonard W. Levy, "Liberty and the First Amendment," *The American Historical Review* 68, no. 1 (October 1962), 567. Further, the Federalists believed "the act would be a proper use of the Constitution's 'necessary and proper' clause to protect the government." William R. Casto, "Oliver Ellsworth," in Gerber, *Seriatim: The Supreme Court Before John Marshall*, 308.

31. The theory being that the officials "partook of the majesty of the whole people." Smith, *Freedom's Fetters—The Alien and Sedition Laws*, 420.

32. Kurland and Lerner, eds., *The Founders' Constitution*, Vol. 3, 239.

33. *Ibid.*, 239.

34. *Ibid.*, 239.

35. Clinton Rossiter, ed., *The Federalist Papers* (New York: Signet Classic, 1999), 197.

36. *Ibid.*, 281.

37. Kurland and Lerner, eds., *The Founders' Constitution*, Vol. 3, 251.

38. As James Morton Smith references Sir James Fitzjames Stephen, "…seditious libel depends ultimately on the nature of the government and the relationship of the rulers to the people." Smith, *Freedom's Fetters—The Alien and Sedition Laws*, ix.

39. Kurland and Lerner, eds., *The Founders' Constitution*, Vol. 2, 24.

40. "Indeed, the chief enforcement effort was tied directly to the campaign of 1800." James Morton Smith, "The Sedition Law, Free Speech, and the American Political Process," *The William and Mary Quarterly* 9, no. 4, 3rd ser (1952), 504.

41. *Ibid.*, 504.

42. Marshall Smelser has written, "These statutes represent the fiercest convulsion of the most ferocious political battle between the American Revolution and the Jacksonian age." Marshall Smelser, "George Washington and the Alien and Sedition Acts," *The American Historical Review* 59, no. 2 (January 1954): 322.

43. Smith, "The Sedition Law, Free Speech, and the American Political Process," 510. It further held that all "crimes against the United States must be established by statutes." Smith, "The Sedition Law, Free Speech, and the American Political Process," 510.

44. Adams ultimately pardoned Fries fully. Smith, *Freedom's Fetters—The Alien and Sedition Laws*, 335, and Shaw, *The Character of John Adams*, 266.

45. Marcus, *The Documentary History of the Supreme Court of the United States*, Vol. 3, 235.

46. Smith, *Freedom's Fetters—The Alien and Sedition Laws*, 230.

47. *Ibid.*, 241.

48. Marcus, ed., *The Documentary History of the Supreme Court of the United States,* Vol. 3, 293.

49. *Ibid.*, 293.

50. *Ibid.*, 293.

51. *Ibid.*, 294.

52. *Ibid.*, 294.

53. As quoted by Charles Warren, Bayard stated the judges simply sought to "explain the principles of the Constitution," and as Bayard continued, "when some of the laws have been denounced by the enemies of the Administration as unconstitutional the Judges have felt themselves called upon to express their judgements upon that point and the reasons of their opinion." Charles Warren, *The Supreme Court in United States History*, Vol. 1 (Boston: Little, Brown, 1926), 167.

54. *Ibid.*, 165.

55. Marcus, ed., *The Documentary History of the Supreme Court of the United States,* Vol. 4, 608.

56. "The law of seditious libel was thus the product of the view that the government was master." Smith, "The Sedition Law, Free Speech, and the American Political Process," 499. The Federalists envisioned a pre-revolutionary conception of leader and follower—"the evidence is conclusive that the Sedition Law, as enforced, reduced the limits of speech and press in the United States to those set by the English common law in the days before the American Revolution." *Ibid.*, 505.

57. *Ibid.*, 508. Italic added.

58. Merrill D. Peterson, *Thomas Jefferson and the New Nation* (Norwalk: The Easton Press, 1987), 607.

59. *Ibid.*, 607.

60. Joanne B. Freeman, ed., *Alexander Hamilton: Writings* (New York: Literary Classics of the United States, 2001), 632.

61. *Ibid.*, 633.

62. *Ibid.*, 633.

63. *Ibid.*, 633.

64. *Ibid.*, 635.

65. *Ibid.*, 641.

66. *Ibid.*, 641.

67. Julius Goebel, Jr., *Antecedents and Beginnings to 1801* (New York: Macmillan, 1971), 653.

68. *Ibid.*, 654.

69. *Ibid.*, 655.

70. *Ibid.*, 655.

71. *Ibid.*, 655.

72. *Ibid.*, 629.

73. *Ibid.*, 641.

74. *Ibid.*, 642.

75. *Ibid.*, 646.

76. *Ibid.*, 645.

77. *Ibid.*, 709.

78. *Ibid.*, 715–716.

79. *Ibid.*, 707.

Chapter 9

1. Charles Grove Haines, *The Role of the Supreme Court in American Government and Politics 1789–1835* (Union, NJ: The Lawbook Exchange, 2002), 116.

2. *Ibid.*, 122–123.

3. James R. Perry, "Supreme Court Appointments, 1789–1801: Criteria, Presidential Style, and the press of Events," *Journal of the Early Republic* 6, no. 4 (Winter, 1986), 398.

4. *Ibid.*, 400.

5. *Ibid.*, 372.

6. *Ibid.*, 373.

7. Morton J. Horwitz, *The Transformation of American Law, 1780–1860* (Cambridge: Harvard University Press, 1977), 11.

8. Kermit L. Hall, ed., *The Oxford Companion to the Supreme Court of the United States* (Oxford: Oxford University Press, 1992), 198.

9. Quoted, *ibid.*, 321.

10. *Ibid.*, 321.

11. Horowitz, *The Transformation of American Law*, 14.

12. *Ibid.*, 7.

13. *Ibid.*, 17.

14. Quoted in Charles Warren, *The Supreme Court in United States History*, Vol. 1 (Boston: Little, Brown, 1926), 162.

15. *Ibid.*, 163.

16. Bernard Bailyn, ed., *The Debate on the Constitution: Federalist and Antifederalist Speeches, Articles, and Letters During the Struggle over Ratification,* Vol. 2 (New York: Literary Classics of the United States, 1993), 64.

17. Horowitz, *The Transformation of American Law*, 13.

18. Bailyn, ed., *The Debate on the Constitution*, Vol. 2, 253.

19. *Ibid.*, 491.

20. *Ibid.*, 538.

21. *Ibid.*, 549.

22. *Ibid.*, 551.

23. Julius Goebel, Jr., *Antecedents and Beginnings to 1801* (New York: Macmillan, 1971), 652.

Appendix B

1. Abridged from George Lankevich, ed., *The Federal Court 1787–1801* (Danbury, CT: The Grolier Educational Corporation, 1995), 133–136.

Appendix C

1. Abridged from George Lankevich, ed., *The Federal Court 1787–1801* (Danbury, CT: The Grolier Educational Corporation, 1995), 140–143.

Appendix D

1. Abridged from George Lankevich, ed., *The Federal Court 1787–1801* (Danbury, CT: The Grolier Educational Corporation, 1995), 229–230.

Appendix E

1. Supreme Court Historical Society website, http://supremecourthistory.org/history-of-the-court/home-of-the-court/ [accessed 3-13-2017].

Bibliography

Aiken, P. F. *A Comparative View of the Constitutions of Great Britain and the United States of America.* London: Longman, 1842.

Amar, Akhil Reed. *America's Constitution, a Biography.* New York: Random House, 2005.

Annis, David Leslie. "Mr. Bushrod Washington, Supreme Court Justice on the Marshall Court." PhD diss., University of Notre Dame, 1974.

Atkinson, David N. *Leaving The Bench: Supreme Court Justices at the End.* Lawrence: University Press of Kansas, 1999.

Bailyn, Bernard, ed. *The Debate on the Constitution: Federalist and Antifederalist Speeches, Articles, and Letters During the Struggle Over Ratification.* New York: Literary Classics of the United States, 1993.

Barrett, Bryant, ed. *The Code Napoleon, Verbally Translated from the French, to Which Is Prefixed an Introductory Discourse.* Reprint. Birmingham, AL: The Legal Classics Library, 1983.

Barton, D. Plunket. *The Story of Our Inns of Court.* Boston: Houghton Mifflin, 1928.

Beard, Charles A. *The Supreme Court and the Constitution.* Englewood Cliffs, NJ: Prentice-Hall, 1962.

Beeman, Richard. *Plain, Honest Men: The Making of the American Constitution.* New York: Random House, 2010.

Berolzheimer, Fritz. *The World's Legal Philosophers.* Clark, NJ: The Lawbook Exchange, 2010.

Berring, Robert C., ed. *Great American Law Reviews.* Vol. 1. Birmingham, AL: The Legal Classics Library, 1984.

Beveridge, Albert J., *The Life of John Marshall,* Boston: Houghton Mifflin, 1919.

Bilder, Mary Sarah. *Madison's Hand: Revising the Constitutional Convention.* Cambridge: Harvard University Press, 2015.

_____. *The Transatlantic Constitution—Colonial Legal Culture and the Empire.* Cambridge: Harvard University Press, 2004.

Boorstin, Daniel J. *The Mysterious Science of the Law.* Chicago: University of Chicago Press, 1996.

_____. *The Americans: The Colonial Experience.* New York: Vintage Books, 1958.

_____. *The Lost World of Thomas Jefferson.* Chicago: University of Chicago Press, 1981.

Boyer, Allen D., ed. *Law, Liberty, and Parliament: Selected Essays on the Writings of Sir Edward Coke.* Indianapolis: The Liberty Fund, 2004.

Brant, Irving. *The Fourth President: A Life of James Madison.* Norwalk, CT: The Easton Press, 1985.

Brown, Basil. *Law Sports at Gray's Inn.* Reprint. Clark, NJ: The Lawbook Exchange, 2009.

Casto, William R. *The Supreme Court in the Early Republic: The Chief Justiceships of John Jay and Oliver Ellsworth.* Columbia: University of South Carolina Press, 1995.

Colby, James F., ed. *A Sketch of English Legal History.* New York: G. P. Putnam's Sons, 1915.

Corwin, Edward S. *The Doctrine of Judicial Review: Its Legal and Historical Basis and Other Essays*. Princeton: Princeton University Press, 1914.

Currie, David P. *The Constitution in the Supreme Court—The First Hundred Years 1789–1888*. Chicago: University of Chicago Press, 1985.

Cushman, Clare, ed. *The Supreme Court Justices Illustrated Biographies, 1789–1995*. Washington, D.C.: Congressional Quarterly, 1995.

Dewey, Frank L. *Thomas Jefferson, Lawyer*. Charlottesville: University Press of Virginia, 1987.

Ehrlich, J. W. *Ehrlich's Blackstone*. San Carlos, CA: Nourse Publishing, 1950.

Elkins, Stanley, and Eric McKitrick. *The Age of Federalism*. New York: Oxford University Press, 1993.

Farrand, Max. *The Fathers of the Constitution*. Birmingham, AL: The Classics of Liberty Library, 2002.

_____. *The Framing of the Constitution of the United States*. New Haven: Yale University Press, 1913.

Freeman, Joanne B., ed. *Alexander Hamilton: Writings*. New York: Literary Classics of the United States, 2001.

Friedman, Lawrence M. *A History of American Law*. New York: Simon & Schuster, 1985.

Friedman, Leon, and Fred L. Israel. *The Justices of the United States Supreme Court 1789–1978: Their Lives and Major Opinions*. Volume 1. New York: Chelsea House, 1980.

Gerber, Scott Douglas, ed. *Seriatim: The Supreme Court Before John Marshall*. New York: New York University Press, 1998.

Goebel, Julius, Jr. *Antecedents and Beginnings to 1801*. New York: Macmillan, 1971.

Gray, Charles M., ed. *Sir Matthew Hale: The History of the Common Law of England*. Chicago: University of Chicago Press, 1971.

Grossberg, Michael, and Christopher Tomlins, eds. *The Cambridge History of Law in America: Early America (1580–1815)*, Volume 1. Cambridge: Cambridge University Press, 2008.

Haines, Charles Grove. *The Role of the Supreme Court in American Government and Politics 1789–1835*. Union, NJ: The Lawbook Exchange, 2002.

Hall, Kermit L., ed. *The Oxford Guide to the Supreme Court*. New York: Oxford University Press, 2005.

_____. and Mark David Hall, eds. *Collected Works of James Wilson*. Indianapolis: Liberty Fund, 2007.

Hamilton, Alexander, James Madison, and John Jay. *The Federalist Papers*. Norwalk, CT: Easton Press, 1979.

Hart, H. L. A. *The Concept of Law*. New York: Oxford University Press, 1990.

Hicks, Frederick C. *Men and Books Famous in the Law*. Clark, NJ: The Lawbook Exchange, 2008.

Holdsworth, William Searle. *The Historians of Anglo-American Law*. Hamden, CT: Archon Books, 1966.

Horwitz, Morton J. *The Transformation of American Law, 1780–1860*. Cambridge: Harvard University Press, 1977.

Jay, William, ed. *The Life of John Jay*. Reprint. Chestnut Hill, MA: Elibron Classics, 2005.

Kaplan, Catherine O'Donnell. *Men of Letters in the Early Republic*. Chapel Hill: University of North Carolina Press, 2008.

Kelly, Alfred H., and Winfred A. Harbison. *The American Constitution, Its Origins and Development*. New York: W. W. Norton, 1976.

Kent, William, ed. *Memoirs and Letters of James Kent, Late Chancellor of the State of New York*. Boston: Little, Brown, 1898.

Koch, Adrienne. *Jefferson and Madison: The Great Collaboration*. New York: Alfred A. Knopf, 1950.

_____, ed. *Notes of Debates in the Federal Convention of 1787 Reported by James Madison*. New York: W.W. Norton, 1987.

Kurland, Philip B., and Ralph Lerner, eds. *The Founders' Constitution*. Indianapolis: Liberty Fund, 1987.

Lankevich, George J. *The Federal Court 1787–1801*. Danbury, CT: Grolier Educational Corporation, 1995.

Levy, Leonard W., ed. *Judicial Review and the Supreme Court*. New York: Harper Torchbooks, 1967.

Lloyd, Dennis. *The Idea of Law*. Baltimore: Penguin Books, 1964.

Marcus, Maeva, ed. *The Documentary History of the Supreme Court of the United States, 1789–1800*. New York: Columbia University Press, 1992.

Meister, Charles W. *The Founding Fathers*. Jefferson, NC: McFarland, 1987.

Miller, John. *The Federalist Era, 1789–1801*. New York: Harper and Row, 1963.

Moore, Blaine Free. *The Supreme Court and Unconstitutional Legislation*. New York: Columbia University Press, 1913.

Nelson, William E. *The Common Law in Colonial America: The Chesapeake and New England, 1607–1660*, Volume 1. New York: Oxford University Press, 2008.

Pallister, Anne. *Magna Carta: The Heritage of Liberty*. Norwalk, CT: Easton Press, 1994.

Peterson, Merrill D. *Thomas Jefferson and the New Nation*. Norwalk, CT: Easton Press, 1987.

_____, ed. *Thomas Jefferson: Writings*. New York: Literary Classics of the United States, 1984.

Pfister, Jude M. "Constitutional Development in the United States Supreme Court During the 1790s." D.Litt. diss., Drew University, 2007.

_____. *America Writes Its History, 1650–1850: The Formation of a National Narrative*. Jefferson, NC: McFarland, 2014.

Pound, Roscoe. *The Spirit of the Common Law and Other Writings*. Birmingham, AL: The Legal Classics Library, 1985.

_____. *The Formative Era of American Law*. Boston: Little, Brown, 1938.

Prest, Wilfrid. *William Blackstone; Law and Letters in the Eighteenth Century*. New York: Oxford University Press, 2008.

Rakove, Jack N., ed. *James Madison, Writings*. New York: Literary Classics of the United States, 1999.

Rhodehamel, John, ed. *The American Revolution; Writings from the War of Independence*. New York: Literary Classics of the United States, 2001.

_____. *George Washington, Writings*. New York: Literary Classics of the United States, 1997.

Ritz, Wilfred J. *Rewriting the History of the Judiciary Act of 1789: Exposing Myths, Challenging Premises, and Using New Evidence*. Norman, OK: University of Oklahoma Press, 1990.

Rossiter, Clinton, ed. *The Federalist Papers*. New York: Penguin Group, 1999.

Schwartz, Bernard. *A History of the Supreme Court*. New York: Oxford University Press, 1993.

Scott, Walter. *The Antiquary*. New York: Oxford University Press, 2002.

Shaw, Peter. *The Character of John Adams*. Chapel Hill: University of North Carolina Press, 1976.

Smith, James Morton. *Freedom's Fetters—The Alien and Sedition Laws and American Civil Liberties*. Ithaca, NY: Cornell University Press, 1966.

Stahr, Walter. *John Jay: Founding Father*. New York: Hambeldon & London, 2005.

Stewart, David O. *The Summer of 1787, The Men Who Invented the Constitution*. New York: Simon & Schuster, 2007.

Tomlins, Christopher, ed. *The United States Supreme Court: The Pursuit of Justice*. Boston: Houghton Mifflin, 2005.

Toth, Michael C. *Founding Federalist: The Life of Oliver Ellsworth*. Wilmington, DE: ISI Books, 2011.

Various. *Select Essays in Anglo-American Legal History*. New York: The Lawbook Exchange, 1992.

Warren, Charles. *The Supreme Court in United States History*. Boston: Little, Brown, 1926.

_____. *Congress, The Constitution, and The Supreme Court*. Boston: Little, Brown, 1925.

_____. *A History of the American Bar*. Boston: Little, Brown, 1911.

_____. *History of the Harvard Law School and of Early Legal Conditions in America*. Vol. 1. Union, NJ: The Lawbook Exchange, 1999.

Westin, Alan F., ed. *An Autobiography of the Supreme Court*. New York: Macmillan, 1963.
White, G. Edward. *Law in American History, Volume 1; From the Colonial Years Through the Civil War*. New York: Oxford University Press, 2012.
White, Leonard D. *The Federalists: A Study in Administrative History 1789–1801*. New York: The Free Press, 1965.
Wood, Gordon. *Empire of Liberty: A History of the Early Republic, 1789–1815*. New York: Oxford University Press, 2009.
Wormser, Rene A. *The Story of the Law and the Men Who Made it—From the Earliest Times to the Present*. New York: Simon & Schuster, 1962.
Wroth, L. Kinvin, and Hiller B. Zobel, eds. *Legal Papers of John Adams*. New York: Atheneum, 1968.
Yarborough, Kemp Plummer. "*Chisholm v. Georgia*: A study of the Minority Opinion." Ph.D. diss., Columbia University, 1963.
Zane, John Maxcy. *The Story of Law*. Indianapolis: Liberty Fund, 1998.

Articles

Adams, Norma. Review of "A Catalogue of the Library of Sir Edward Coke." *Speculum* 28, no. 1 (Jan. 1953), 164–166.
Adams, Randolph. "The Legal Theories of James Wilson." *University of Pennsylvania Law Review and American Law Register* 68, no. 4 (Jun. 1920), 337–355.
Alexander, Lucien Hugh. "James Wilson, Patriot, and the Wilson Doctrine." *The North American Review* 183, no. 603 (Nov. 16, 1906), 971–989.
Barnwell, Robert W. Jr. "The Dictator." *The Journal of Southern History* 7, no. 2 (May 1941), 215–224.
Billings, Warren M. "Law in the Colonial South." *The Journal of Southern History* 73, no. 3 (Aug. 2007), 603–616.
Brown, William Garrott. "The Early Life of Oliver Ellsworth." *The American Historical Review* 10, no. 3 (Apr. 1905), 534–564.
Carpenter, Frank G. "Our Chief Justices Off the Bench." *The North American Review* 147, no. 381 (Aug. 1888), 205–218.
Farrand, Max. "The First Hayburn Case 1792." *The American Historical Review* Vol. 13, no. 2 (Jan. 1908), 281–285.
Flanders, Henry. "Chief Justice Rutledge. An Address Before the Law Department of the University of Pennsylvania." *The American Law Register (1898–1907)* 54, no. 4, Volume 45 New Series (Apr. 1906), 203–213.
Galloway, George B. "Precedents Established in the First Congress." *The Western Political Quarterly* 11, no. 3 (Sept. 1958), 454–468.
Gest, John Marshall. "The Writings of Sir Edward Coke." *The Yale Law Journal* 18, no. 7 (May 1909), 504–532.
Haskins, George L. "Law and Colonial Society." *American Quarterly* 9, no. 3 (Autumn, 1957), 354–364.
Hepburn, Charles M. "The Inns of Court and Certain Conditions in American Legal Education." *Virginia Law Review* 8, no. 2 (Dec. 1921), 93–102.
Konkle, Burton Alva. "The James Wilson Memorial." *The American Law Register 9 (1898–1907)* 55, no. 1, Volume 46 New Series (Jan. 1907), 1–11.
Marcus, Maeva. "John Marshall Was Not the First Chief Justice." *Proceedings of the American Philosophical Society* 153, no. 1 (Mar. 2009), 48–55.
_____, and Robert Teir. "Hayburn's Case: A Misrepresentation of Precedent" 12, no. 2 *Wisconsin Law Review*, 1988.
Mathis, Doyle. "Georgia Before the Supreme Court." *The American Journal of Legal History* 12, no. 2 (1968), 112–121.
Odgers, William Blake. "Sir William Blackstone." *The Yale Law Journal* 27, no. 5 (Mar. 1918), 599–618.

_____. "Sir William Blackstone." *The Yale Law Journal* 28, no. 6 (Apr. 1919), 542–566.

Perry, James R. "Supreme Court Appointments, 1789–1801: Criteria, Presidential Style, and the Press of Events." *Journal of the Early Republic* 6, no. 4 (Winter, 1986), 371–410.

Pfister, Jude M. "William Paterson's Notebook." *Supreme Court Historical Society Quarterly*, XXXIII, no. 1 (2011), 4–6.

Pole, J.R. "Reflections on American Laws and the American Revolution." *The William and Mary Quarterly* 50, no. 1 (Jan. 1993), 123–159.

Prest, Wilfrid. "Legal Education of the Gentry at the Inns of Court, 1560–1640." *Past & Present* No. 38 (Dec. 1967), 20–39.

Review of "The First Part of the Institutes of the Laws of England, or a Commentary Upon Littleton, &c. By Sir Edward Coke. First American from the Sixteenth European Edition." *The North American Review* 13, no. 33 (Oct. 1821), 255–286.

Rugg, Arthur P. "William Cushing." *The Yale Law Journal* 30, no. 2 (Dec. 1920), 128–144.

Schmidhauser, John R. "Legal Imperialism: Its Enduring Impact on Colonial and Post-Colonial Judicial Systems." *International Political Science Review/Revue Internationale de Science Politique* 13, no. 3 (Jul. 1992), 321–334.

Smith, James Morton. "The Sedition Law, Free Speech, and the American Political Process," *The William and Mary Quarterly* 9, no. 4, 3rd ser (1952), 497–511.

Swindler, William F. "Mr. Chisholm and the Eleventh Amendment," *Supreme Court Historical Society Yearbook 1981*.

Treanor, William Michael. "Judicial Review Before *Marbury.*" *Stanford Law Review* 58 (2005). 455–56.

Velasquez, Eduardo A. "Rethinking America's Modernity: Natural Law, Natural Rights and the Character of James Wilson's Liberal Republicanism." *Polity* 29, no. 2 (Winter, 1996), 193–220.

Woolsey, L. H. "Charles Warren." *The American Journal of International Law* 49, no. 1 (Jan. 1955), 50–54.

Zink, James R. "The Language of Liberty and Law: James Wilson on America's Written Constitution." *The American Political Science Review* 103, no. 3 (August 2009), 442–455.

_____. "James Wilson versus the Bill of Rights: Progress, Popular Sovereignty, and the Idea of the U.S. Constitution." *Political Research Quarterly* 67, no. 2 (June 2014), 253–265.

Websites

The Adams Papers Digital Edition, ed. Sarah Martin. Charlottesville: University of Virginia Press, Rotunda, 2008: http://rotunda.upress.virginia.edu/founders/default.xqy?keys=ADMS=print=ob&mode=TOC.

The Avalon Project at Yale Law School. http://avalon.law.yale.edu/ [accessed various times 2016–2017].

Federal Judicial Center, www.fjc.gov [accessed 07/20/2016].

http://www.constitution.org/js/js_342.htm [accessed 07/20/2016].

http://www.constitution.org/uslaw/judiciary_1789.htm [accessed 07/20/2016].

http://press-pubs.uchicago.edu/founders/documents/a3_2_1s37.html [accessed 07/20/2016]

http://supremecourthistory.org/pub_journal_archive.html [accessed 07/12/2016].

The Papers of Alexander Hamilton Digital Edition, ed. Harold C. Syrett. Charlottesville: University of Virginia Press, Rotunda, 2011: http://rotunda.upress.virginia.edu/founders/ARHN-01-17-02-0009 [accessed 14 Dec 2016]; ARHN-01-19-02-0039 [accessed 14 Dec 2016]; ARHN-01-25-02-0127 [accessed 14 Dec 2016].

The Papers of George Washington Digital Edition, ed. Theodore J. Crackel. Charlottesville: University of Virginia Press, Rotunda, 2008: http://rotunda.upress.virginia.edu/founders/GEWN-05-04-02-0177 [accessed 25 Nov 2016]; GEWN-05-07-02-0024 [accessed 25 Nov 2016]; GEWN-05-04-02-0046 [accessed 25 Nov 2016]; GEWN-05-04-02-0053 [accessed 22 Jun 2016]; GEWN-05-12-02-0053 [accessed 01Jul 2016]; GEWN-05-04-02-0067 [accessed 25 Nov 2016]; GEWN-05-04-02-*0077* [accessed 22 Jun 2016]; GEWN-05-03-02-*0075* [accessed 25 Nov 2016]; GEWN-05-04-02-*0118* [accessed 03 Mar 2017]; GEWN-05-03-02-*0147* [accessed 25 Nov 2016]; GEWN-05-13-02-*0173* [accessed 03 Mar 2017].

The Papers of James Madison Digital Edition, ed. J. C. A. Stagg. Charlottesville: University of Virginia Press, Rotunda, 2010: http://rotunda.upress.virginia.edu/founders/JSMN-01-12-02-0050 [accessed 25 Nov 2016]; JSMN-01-16-02-0041 [accessed 06 Mar 2017]; JSMN-01-12-02-0092 [accessed 25 Nov 2016]; JSMN-01-12-02-0113 [accessed 25 Nov 2016]; JSMN-01-12-02-0120 [accessed 25 Nov 2016]; JSMN-01-12-02-0141 [accessed 25 Nov 2016]; JSMN-01-12-02-0152 [accessed 14 Dec 2016]; JSMN-01-12-02-0168 [accessed 25 Nov 2016]; JSMN-01-17-02-0175 [accessed 14 Dec 2016].

Papers of John Jay at http://www.columbia.edu/cu/lweb/digital/jay/. Contained at the link http://www.columbia.edu/cu/lweb/digital/exhibitions/constitution/essay.html. [accessed March 1, 2004].

The Papers of John Marshall Digital Edition, ed. Charles Hobson. Charlottesville: University of Virginia Press, Rotunda, 2014: http://rotunda.upress.virginia.edu/founders/JNML=01=11=02=0017 [accessed 09 Oct 2018].

The Papers of Thomas Jefferson Digital Edition, ed. James P. McClure and J. Jefferson Looney. Charlottesville: University of Virginia Press, Rotunda, 2008–2016: http://rotunda.upress.virginia.edu/founders/TSJN-01-18-02-0070 [accessed 25 Nov 2016]; TSJN-03-03-02-0073 [accessed 08 Mar 2017]; TSJN-01-26-02-0239 [accessed 03 Apr 2017]; TSJN-03-07-02-0071 [accessed 28 Sep 2017].

Stanford Encyclopedia of Philosophy. https://plato.stanford.edu/ [accessed various times 2016–2017].

Supreme Court of the United Kingdom. https://www.supremecourt.uk/faqs.html#1a [August 13, 2016].

Index

www.ingramcontent.com/pod-product-compliance
Lightning Source LLC
Chambersburg PA
CBHW031414270326
41929CB00010BA/1456